on loss
and absence

textiles of
mourning
and survival

on loss
and absence
textiles of mourning and survival

Edited by
Isaac Facio
Nneka Kai
L Vinebaum
Anne Wilson

Contributions by
Jerry Bleem
Valerie Cassel Oliver
Gustavo Da Silva
Isaac Facio
Wafa Ghnaim
Jen Chen-su Huang
Nneka Kai
Cristian Koepfli
Alipio Melo
Sarah Molina
María José Murillo
Lucinda Pelton
Sharbreon Plummer
Jenni Sorkin
Barbara Teller Ornelas
Lynda Teller Pete
Cybele Tom
L Vinebaum
Melinda Watt
Danitza Willka
Anne Wilson
Folayemi Wilson

The Art Institute of Chicago
Distributed by Yale University Press, New Haven and London

Foreword

On Loss and Absence: Textiles of Mourning and Survival is the first major publication to explore how artists across time have used textiles and fiber to mediate and express the universal human experiences of death and grief. Through the Art Institute of Chicago's rich holdings—spanning three thousand years and five continents—this groundbreaking exhibition and book explore textiles' essential role in many of life's most important rites of passage.

This volume presents new curatorial and conservation research on dozens of objects from antiquity to today, representing regions around the world. The varied objects include burial shrouds and wrappings, ceremonial garments, fragments, funeral hangings, and mourning samplers, among many others. Throughout human history, textiles have brought people together—often as part of organized rituals—to mourn and mark the occasion of death and transition; to remember and memorialize lost loved ones; to resist oppressive systems; to heal from personal and collective traumas; to care for family and community; and to maintain ancestral, communal, and cultural connections.

The project emerged from the museum's unique connection to the School of the Art Institute of Chicago (SAIC), to which it has been inextricably linked for nearly one hundred fifty years. This relationship has taken many forms, one of the most important being the museum's role as a nexus of educational opportunities for the school's students. In 2021 artist and SAIC professor emerita Anne Wilson approached Melinda Watt, Chair and Christa C. Mayer Thurman Curator in Textiles, with an idea for a show drawn primarily from the department's global collection. One of the key components of her proposal was the exhibition's cocuration by artists and educators from SAIC, who could place our holdings in dialogue with work by contemporary practitioners. Wilson and her collaborators—associate conservator at the museum and educator in the school Isaac Facio; artist and SAIC alumna Nneka Kai; and SAIC associate professor L Vinebaum—represent decades of engagement with the SAIC community. Their roots in the Chicago art world run deep, and their professional experiences and knowledge extend far beyond the city. Crucially, all four curators are artists. Their hands-on knowledge of textile techniques informed the project's object-focused approach, while collaboration with conservators has led to new insights about several artworks. The COVID-19 pandemic and subsequent social upheaval further sharpened the curators' focus, leading them to explore more contemporary expressions of loss within the context of historic examples from the museum's permanent collection.

The exhibition's themes inspired artists to make new work for the show, and several were also invited to offer their reflections on objects in the museum's collection. When she was introduced to the project's themes, Diné (Navajo) artist Barbara Teller Ornelas was inspired to complete a decades-long series of weavings, which has become the museum's first acquisition of a living Diné weaver's work in almost thirty years. Longstanding relationships with Chicago-based artists led to key loans, including from multidisciplinary artists Nick Cave and Michael Olszewski, activist and quilter Dorothy Burge, and SAIC graduates Carina Yepez and Rivers (Qinnan Zhu), to name a few. The curatorial team also selected objects from across museum departments to help amplify the exhibition's themes, bringing a fresh perspective to works like the monumental Japanese scroll *Nehan: Death of the Buddha* (p. 109, fig. 2), which has not been on public view for more than twenty years. The new research and interpretive approaches brought to the Art Institute's textiles collection will continue to resonate long after the exhibition has ended, and we are proud to present this publication as a permanent record of these accomplishments. An invaluable endowment from the Mellon Foundation, which helps disseminate research on Art Institute collections, has made this publication possible.

On Loss and Absence interrogates the importance of fiber and textiles in global traditions and rituals relating to dying, death, and the possibilities of afterlives while also highlighting how textile arts can embody both individual and communal resistance and survival in the face of attempts at cultural erasure. We hope that this groundbreaking publication will serve as a foundational text in the relatively new discipline of textile scholarship, continuing the museum's longstanding role as a place of learning and as a resource for all.

James Rondeau
President and Eloise W. Martin Director
The Art Institute of Chicago

Acknowledgments

It is a rare privilege to be invited and entrusted to work with a museum's collection, especially as a team of outside curators. *On Loss and Absence: Textiles of Mourning and Survival* is the result of an extraordinary collaboration between the Textiles department at the Art Institute of Chicago and the Fiber and Material Studies department at the School of the Art Institute of Chicago (SAIC). This special partnership has been a source of growth, inspiration, and immense pride, and the project is a testament to the power of collaboration and mutual respect.

On Loss and Absence has benefited from the extraordinary support of James Rondeau, President and Eloise W. Martin Director of the Art Institute, along with the enthusiastic guidance of Sarah Guernsey, Deputy Director and Senior Vice President for Curatorial Affairs; Sarah Kelly Oehler, Vice President of Curatorial Strategy and Field-McCormick Chair and Curator, Arts of the Americas; David Nacol, Senior Vice President, Philanthropy; Katie Rahn, Senior Vice President, Marketing and Communications; Amy Allen, Vice President, Engagement; Emily Benedict, Vice President, Campus Operations; Francesca Casadio, Vice President and Grainger Executive Director, Conservation and Science; Thomas Ryan, Vice President, Facilities and Logistics; Aaron Andersen, Associate Vice President, Financial Planning and Analysis; and Ann Goldstein, Deputy Director and Senior Curator at Large.

Our team received invaluable mentorship and guidance from Art Institute colleagues Melinda Watt, Chair and Christa C. Mayer Thurman Curator of Textiles and senior museum advisor to the project; Janet Purdy, Associate Curator of Textiles; and Stephanie Caruso, Assistant Curator, Textiles and Arts of Greece, Rome, and Byzantium; and, at SAIC, Christine Tarkowski, Professor and Chair of Fiber and Material Studies. Katherine Andereck, Esther Espino, Elizabeth Pope, and Tess Smith in Textiles provided essential research and logistical support.

This book would not have been possible without our generous and thoughtful contributors, Jerry Bleem, Valerie

Cassel Oliver, Gustavo Da Silva, Wafa Ghnaim, Jen Chen-su Huang, Cristian Koepfli, Sarah Molina, Lucinda Pelton, Sharbreon Plummer, Jenni Sorkin, Barbara Teller Ornelas, Lynda Teller Pete, Cybele Tom, Melinda Watt, Folayemi Wilson, and the Noqanchis collective of Alipio Melo, María José Murillo, and Danitza Willka. This interdisciplinary group of authors—many of them also artists—contributed their knowledge and experiences to the unique record of this exhibition and our moment in time. We are grateful to the contemporary artists who lent work to the exhibition: Dorothy Burge, Nick Cave, Yanira Collado, Karen Hampton, Angela Hennessy, Noqanchis, and Carina Yepez. Barbara Teller Ornelas and Lynda Teller Pete generously advised us in the selection and presentation of Diné (Navajo) works in the exhibition and book, and Barbara Teller Ornelas's recent *Contemporary Chief Set (Three Miniatures)* (pp. 196–97, fig. 10) was acquired by the Art Institute and included in the exhibition. Alipio Melo, María José Murillo, and Danitza Willka of Noqanchis provided invaluable insights into histories of Indigenous Andean weaving that informed our selections and their display. In addition to lending a collective artwork to the exhibition, each member of Noqanchis created a new artwork in response to a Peruvian fragment from the Art Institute's collection. Michelle Scruggs agreed to be featured in a performative work conceived by her daughter, artist Nneka Kai, for the exhibition.

Our networks of artists, educators, researchers, and scholars, stemming from Fiber and Material Studies at SAIC and extending across the world, contributed their support and wisdom throughout this endeavor. They include Seyram Agbleze, Brock Brake and pt.2 Gallery, Dorothy Burge, Nick Cave, Yanira Collado, Douglas Dawson, Bob Faust, Surabhi Ghosh, Angela Hennessy, Gerhardt Knodel, Katarina Weslien, and Carina Yepez. Additional research assistance was provided by Lily Lloyd Burkhalter, Delaina Doshi, Atlas Erkan, Sofía Fernández Díaz, and Renée Thompson, SAIC; Cristian Koepfli and Gustavo Da Silva, University of Notre Dame, Indiana; Kathleen Bickford Berzock, Block Museum of Art, Northwestern University, Evanston, Illinois; Suzanne Karr Schmidt, Newberry Library, Chicago; and Lee Talbot, The Textile Museum, George Washington University, Washington, DC.

The exhibition featured objects from across the Art Institute's curatorial departments. We are especially grateful to Janice Katz, Roger L. Weston Associate Curator of Japanese Art, whose partnership enabled us to extend the exhibition into the museum's Ando Gallery with a presentation of Japanese screens and mourning garments. Other colleagues generously shared their expertise, including Ellenor Alcorn, Madeleine Hazelwood, Kate Heller (formerly), and Jonathan Worcester in Applied Arts of Europe; Constantine Petridis, Ashley Arico, Acassia Ferreira da Cunha, and Raymond Ramirez in Arts of Africa; Lois Taylor Biggs, Andrew James Hamilton, Elizabeth McGoey, Tim Roby, and Christopher Shepherd in Arts of the Americas; Tao Wang, Matthew Alicea, Madhuvanti Ghose, Seung Hee Oh, and Michael Solone in Arts of Asia; Lisa Ayla Çakmak, Elizabeth Benge, Katharine A. Raff, and Eric Warner in Arts of Greece, Rome, and Byzantium; Nick Barron, Mary Coyne (formerly), and Ann Goldstein in Modern and Contemporary Art; Gloria Groom in Painting and Sculpture of Europe; Matthew S. Witkovsky, Barbara Diener (formerly), Elizabeth Siegel (formerly), and Jamie Vaught in Photography and Media; and Kevin Salatino, Jay Clarke, Jamie Gabbarelli, and Mark Pascale in Prints and Drawings. Their expertise, generosity, and dedication to preserving cultural heritage have been pivotal to this project.

This collaboration has deepened our understanding of the profound responsibility of preserving and caring for works of art. Colleagues in Conservation and Science—Francesca Casadio, Lisa Ackerman, Mary Broadway, Christopher H. Brooks, Megan Creamer, Haddon Dine, Annette Gaspers, Clara Granzotto, Taylor Healy, Jim Iska, Kelly Keegan, Paulina Miąsik, Kimberley Muir, Lucinda Pelton (former Mellon fellow), Sylvie Penichon, Charles Pietraszewski, María Cristina Rivera Ramos,

Ruth Rolfsmeyer, Rachel Sabino, Mardy Sears, Katharine Shulman, Ken Sutherland, Andy Talley, Jann Trujillo, Giovanni Verri, and Daisy Wong—showed us the importance of continuous learning and reflection in stewardship.

The Art Institute's Publishing department, led by Katie Reilly, shepherded us through making this book. Kit Shields, with the support and guidance of Lisa Meyerowitz and assistance from Kati Woock, expertly edited the many contributions and tied up loose ends. David Khan-Giordano and Lauren Makholm managed the production with grace and good humor, with support from Isella Sandoval. Noah Lopez and Kristie Kahns sourced and licensed the images. Juliet Clark proofread and Mary Mortensen created the index. Under the leadership of Bonnie Rosenberg in Imaging, Nathan Keay, Robert Lifson, Jonathan Mathias, Juan Molina Hernández, Joe Tallarico, and Katherine Zuis created beautiful new photography of Art Institute works, while Hayley Hinsberger and Kaitlyn Fultz-Campion took on postproduction. Adam Michaels and V. E. Chen at IN-FO.CO devised a warm and inviting design that balances the publication's dark themes with a sense of lightness and hope.

Staff throughout the museum worked to realize this exhibition. Michael Hall, Julia Loughlin, Jessy Williams, and the crew in Collections and Loans managed the intricate movement and installation of artwork. Becca Schlossberg, Megan Hurlbert, and CJ Lamborn in Exhibitions planned every detail and helped keep us on track. Samantha Grassi in Exhibition Design; Logan Chappe, Devin Davis, Madeleine Giaconia, Gina Giambalvo, Kirill Mazor, Alex Quintanilla, Jesus Reyes, Layne Thue-Bludworth, and Christine Zavesky in Experience Design; Robert Ceisla in Facilities; Emily Fry and Loren Wright in Interpretation; and Kit Shields in Publishing shaped the physical, visual, and multimedia experience that helped visitors connect with and understand these artworks. We are grateful to Paul Jones in Communications; Joe Iverson in Engagement Programs; T. J. Kennedy and Thomas Ryan in Facilities and Logistics; Hilary Branch in the Office of the President and Director (formerly); Mary DeYoe in Institutional Advancement; Norissa Bailey (formerly), Ian Damont Martin, and Travonda Bennett in People and Culture; Erika Lowe Mullins, Anna Maria Carvallo VanMeter, Ian Gordon, Miriam McCue, Chelsea Southwood, and Teresa Sutter in Philanthropy; and Leslie Wilson and Rachel Joy Echiverri Rowland in the Research Center for their efforts to make this exhibition and book a reality.

The above text can hardly capture all the ways our colleagues have enriched our approach to conservation, curation, and storytelling. We began this project with enthusiasm and the knowledge of our own experiences, and in the end we were moved and gratified by the depth of beauty, history, and meaning to be found in the collections at the Art Institute. We are thrilled to now share these findings with readers. It has been a humbling experience, and a constant process of caring, healing, learning, listening, and sharing.

Isaac Facio, Nneka Kai, L Vinebaum, and Anne Wilson

     ACKNOWLEDGMENTS

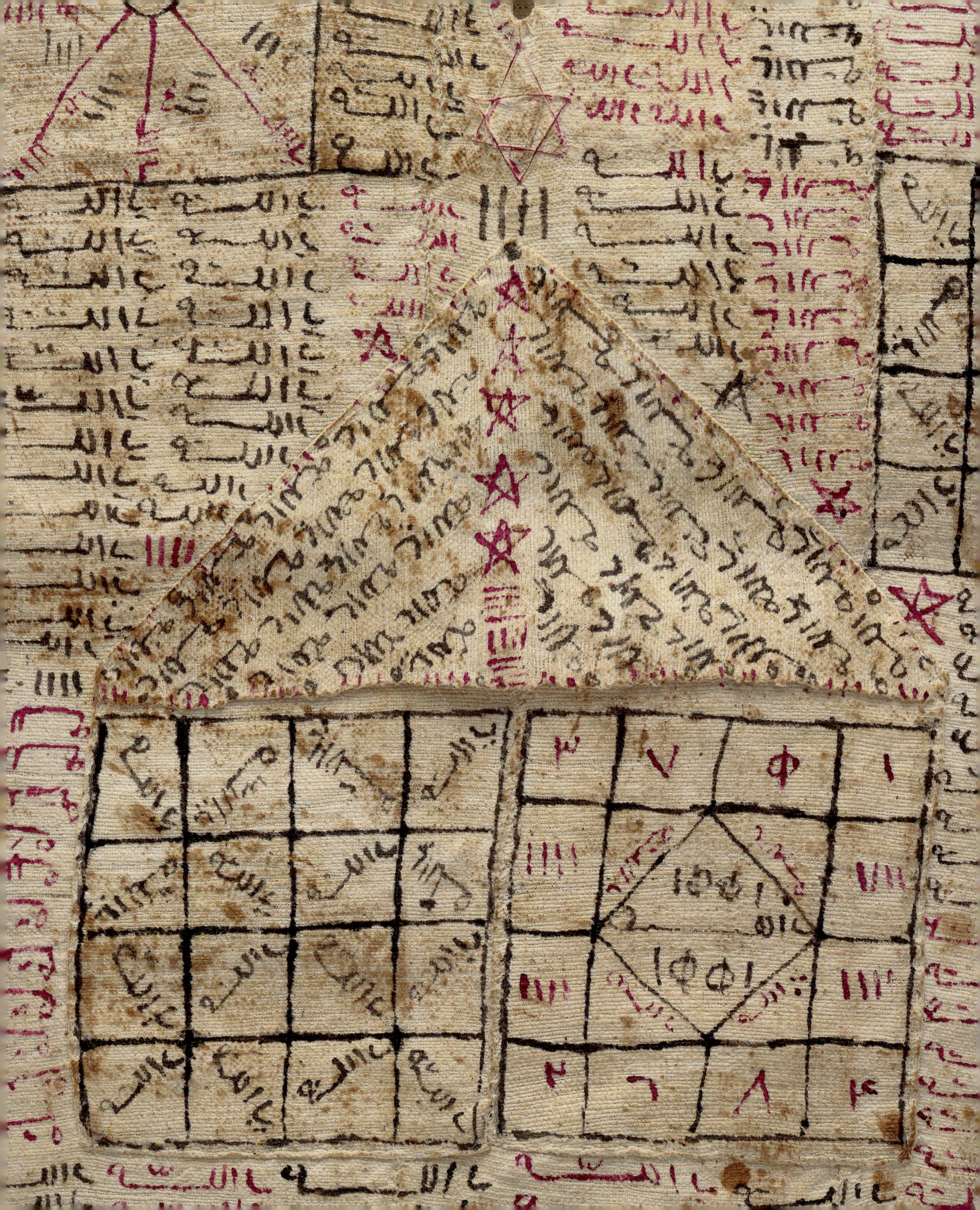

Introduction

Textiles of Mourning and Survival

Isaac Facio
Artist, conservator, and educator

Nneka Kai
Artist, educator, and writer

L Vinebaum
Artist, educator, and scholar

Anne Wilson
Artist and educator

This book seeks to understand experiences of loss and absence, life and death, and healing and survival through the medium of textiles. Like the exhibition of the same name that it accompanies, the book highlights extraordinary objects from the Art Institute of Chicago, whose holdings include one of the most significant textile collections in the United States.

On Loss and Absence features textiles from many different cultures and time periods, from ancient fragments to contemporary artworks, some of which were created for the exhibition. These varied, compelling works have histories, meanings, and uses that can be told in multiple ways and through multiple registers. They include burial masks, ceremonial garments, funerary hangings, mourning and mending samplers, quilts, shrouds, tapestries, and vestments.

Throughout human history, textiles have been used in funerary ceremonies to cover the deceased, accompany them to the afterlife, and comfort mourners. Textiles associated with lost loved ones and ancestors can preserve their memories and keep us connected to them even as we endure their absence. Textiles can also help individuals and communities heal and recover from trauma and loss. They can attest to survival by preserving and transmitting cultural knowledge, and in so doing can be a form of resistance to oppression and erasure.

The essays that follow explore some of the myriad ways that textiles mediate and shape aspects of life and death. Their authors come from a variety of disciplines, including art history, conservation, material culture, and the sciences, and they include curators, conservators, educators, historians, poets, scientists, and scholars. Several contributors are alumni of Fiber and Material Studies at the School of the Art Institute of Chicago. Importantly, many of the authors are artists. The book seeks to model creative forms of research and writing and to affirm artists as producers of scholarship.

We understand loss and absence as multidimensional human experiences: affective and embodied, with

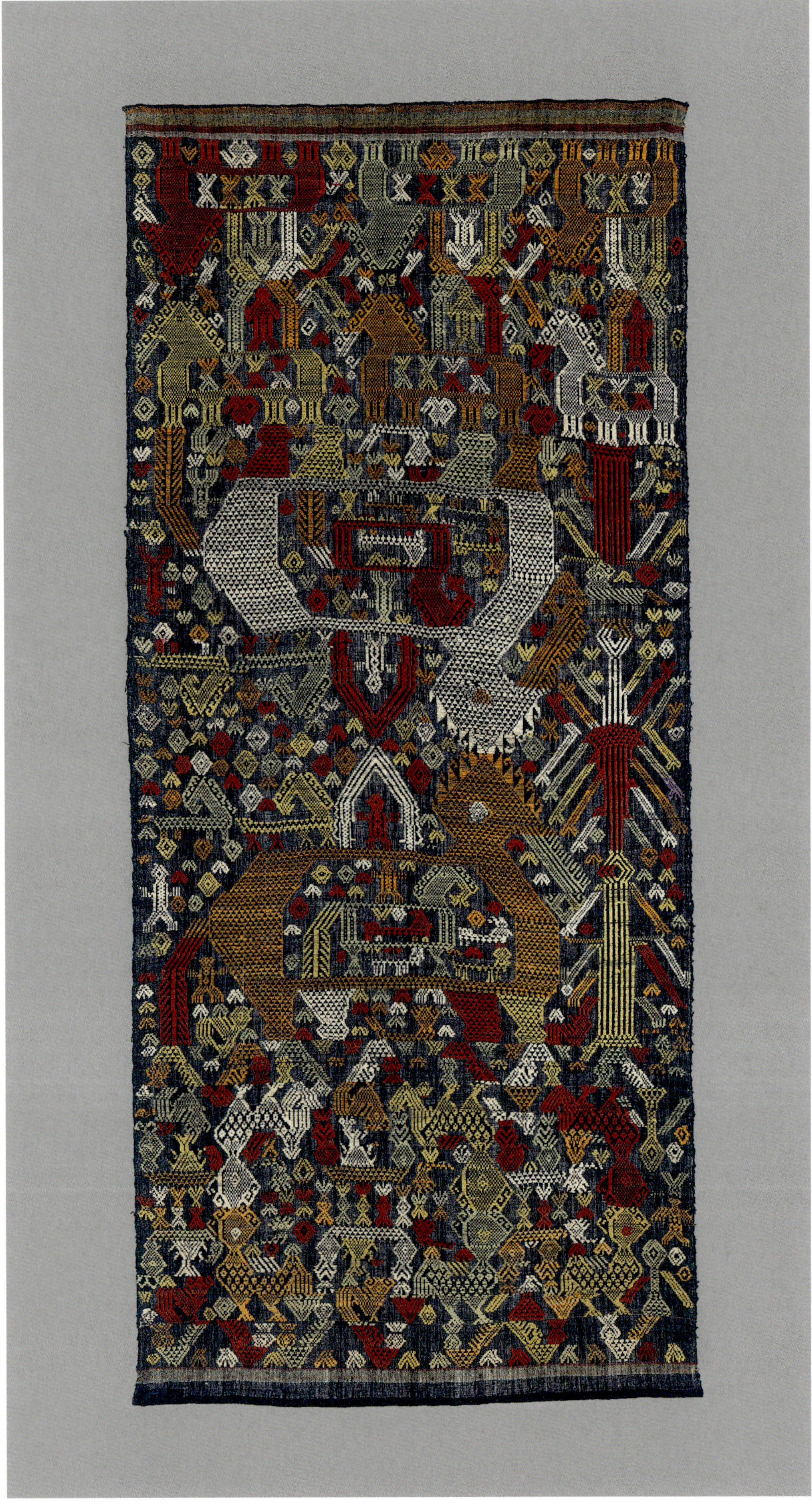

   FACIO, KAI, VINEBAUM, AND WILSON

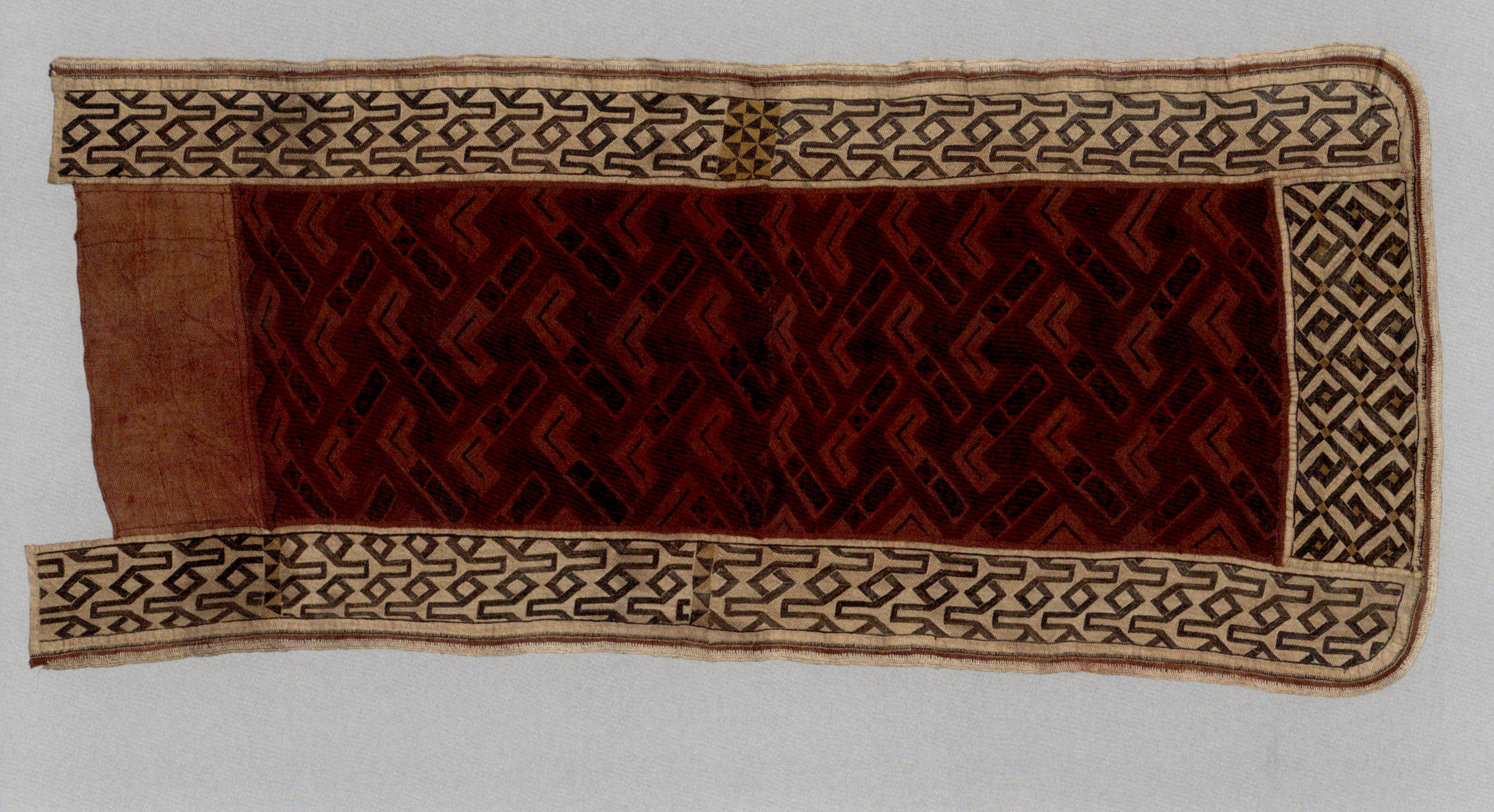

profound emotional, physical, psychic, and spiritual effects, navigated both individually and collectively. As curators, we were guided by several key questions: What can textiles teach us about how humans cope with various kinds of losses, historically and today? How do textiles contribute to healing and cultural survival? What can they tell us about their makers and cultures? What kinds of losses have the objects themselves endured, and what is the role of a museum in their care and display? This introduction highlights objects and their stories while illuminating our curatorial inspirations, motivations, and objectives.

Organizing Themes

The book, like the exhibition, is structured around four central themes:

Death and mourning: Textiles play pivotal roles in rituals of death and processes of grief. They bring comfort and protection to the dying, deceased, and living alike and help us mourn and remember lost loved ones. Objects like burial shrouds, funerary hangings, and wrappings (see fig. 1) are used in rituals and ceremonies of death and mourning to envelop and accompany the deceased as they are laid to rest. Textiles created by the Kuba people from the heart of what is now the Democratic Republic of the Congo (see fig. 2) wrap

Fig. 2 **Woman's Overskirt, 19th century. Bushong, Kuba; Mushenge, Democratic Republic of the Congo. Raffia, plain weave; pieced; embroidered in lateral looping, and stem and running stitches cut to form pile; couching; joined by buttonhole, pearl, and trammed twisted buttonhole stitches; edged in lateral looping stitches; 72.2 × 162.1 cm (28⅜ × 63¾ in.). The Art Institute of Chicago, Tillie C. Cohn Fund and Tillie C. Cohn Fund in memory of her parents, Max and Rose N. Cohn, 1987.163.**

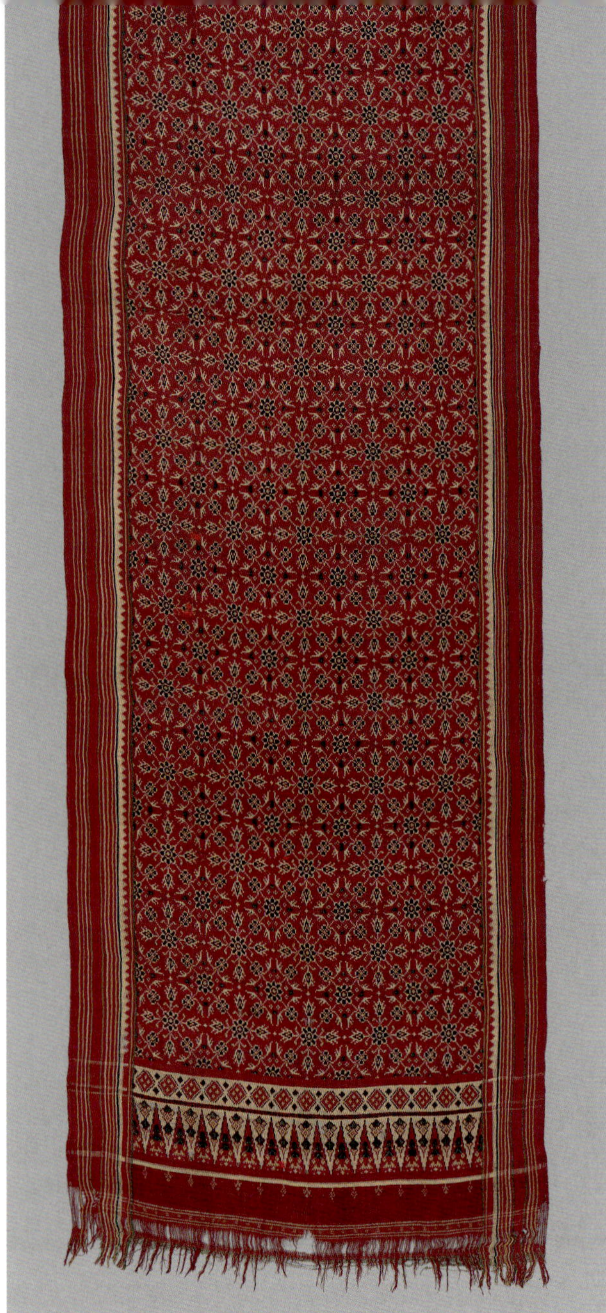

Fig. 3 **Patolu (detail), 18th–19th century. Gujarat, India. Silk and silver-metal-strip-wrapped silk, stripes of warp and weft resist dyed (double ikat), plain weave, stripes of weft resist dyed (weft ikat), plain weave, bands of plain weave and bands of open warps; plied and knotted main warp fringe; 510.5 × 121.9 cm (201 × 48 in.). The Art Institute of Chicago, gift of E. M. Bakwin Indonesian Textile Collection, 2002.916.**

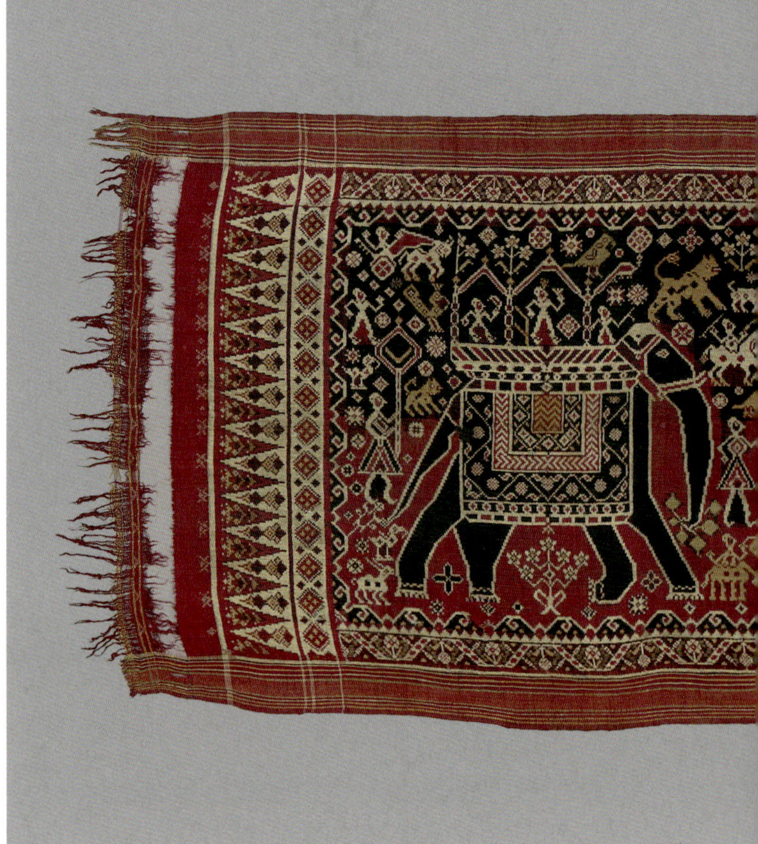

the bodies of the deceased to escort them on their journeys to the next realm and are also worn by the living to maintain their connection to the dead. Patola (see figs. 3–4) woven in Gujarat, India, were given to rulers in eastern Indonesia to curry favor for trade; some were placed atop the burial mounds of high-ranking community members to designate their wealth and status.[1] Textiles like these not only honor and protect the dead but also bring people together to acknowledge loss and grieve in community.

Grief has produced distinct types of objects, like mourning jewelry and samplers. As Jenni Sorkin observes in her essay in this volume, these objects emerged in the eighteenth and nineteenth centuries to serve as highly personal, bodily modes of connection between the living and the dead. Today, artists continue to use textiles to express their personal experiences of grief. Artist Michael Olszewski, for example, creates fabric collages (see fig. 5) to mark losses like the declining health and subsequent death of his father and the deaths of friends to AIDS.

When considering these themes, we could not help but reflect on losses inflicted by forms of targeted violence. Legacies of colonialism, genocide, slavery, and other structural forms of violence continually generate loss and create the need for comfort, giving rise to new forms of activism and protest, as several of the authors in this volume discuss. Valerie Cassel Oliver, for instance, observes that contemporary artists, incuding Nick Cave, frequently use textiles in their work to process and protest widely broadcast

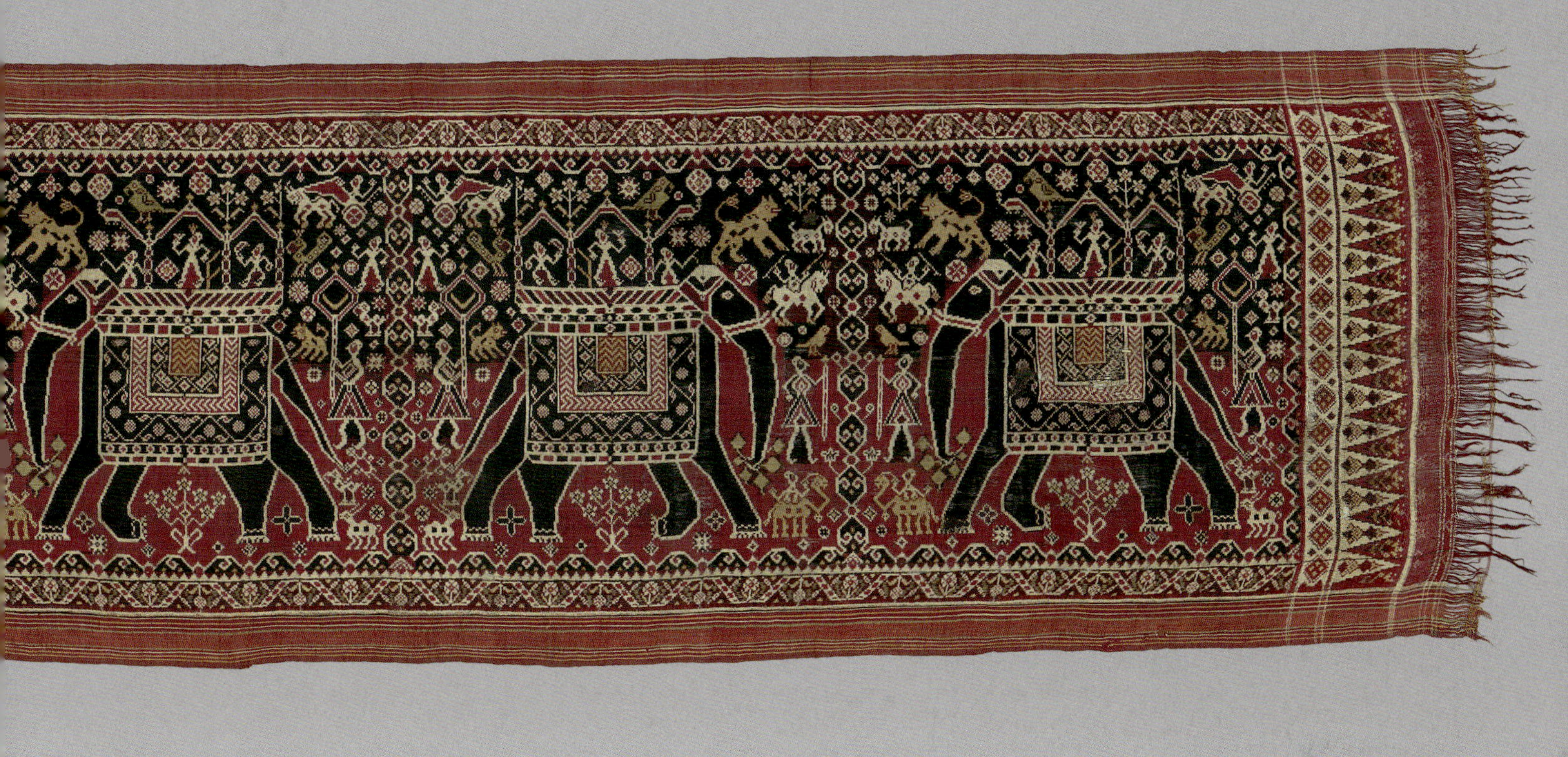

episodes of violence against Black Americans—as well as to promise a release from threats and violence.

Transition of realms: In cultures around the world, textiles mediate physical, spatial, and spiritual transitions to pluriversal realms like the heavens and the afterlife. Textiles like shrouds and garments buried with the deceased offer protection as they journey and transition to other worlds. Textiles are also used in rituals and ceremonies that join the worlds of the living and the dead. In her essay for this volume, Folayemi Wilson explores ceremonial textiles that facilitate the crossing of thresholds between the earthly and spiritual realms, strengthening the connections between them and allowing communities to maintain relationships with departed ancestors.

Objects like screens, robes, and vestments illustrate the cosmologies that organize these different worlds and can also facilitate passage between them. A pair of eighteenth-century Japanese screens (fig. 6), for instance, depicts the historical Buddha Shakyamuni's death in about 483 BCE and his subsequent entry into Nirvana (*nehan* in Japanese). In her poetic reflection on an elaborate Taoist vestment, Jen Chen-su Huang describes how the garment brings the realms of heaven and earth closer together and how contemplating it connects her to her ancestors.

Care and repair: Textiles envelop our bodies, providing comfort, protection, and warmth. In times of grief they can be transformed into quilts and other objects to serve as mementos of lost loved ones. Textiles can bring people

Fig. 4 **Patolu, 18th–19th century. Gujarat, India. Silk, gilt-metal-strip-wrapped thread, strips of plain weave and stripes of warp and weft resist dyed (double ikat), plain weave with gilt-metal-strip-wrapped silk or bast fiber brocading wefts; extended warp fringe; 102.9 × 407.6 cm (40½ × 160¼ in.). The Art Institute of Chicago, gift of E. M. Bakwin Indonesian Textile Collection, 2002.905.**

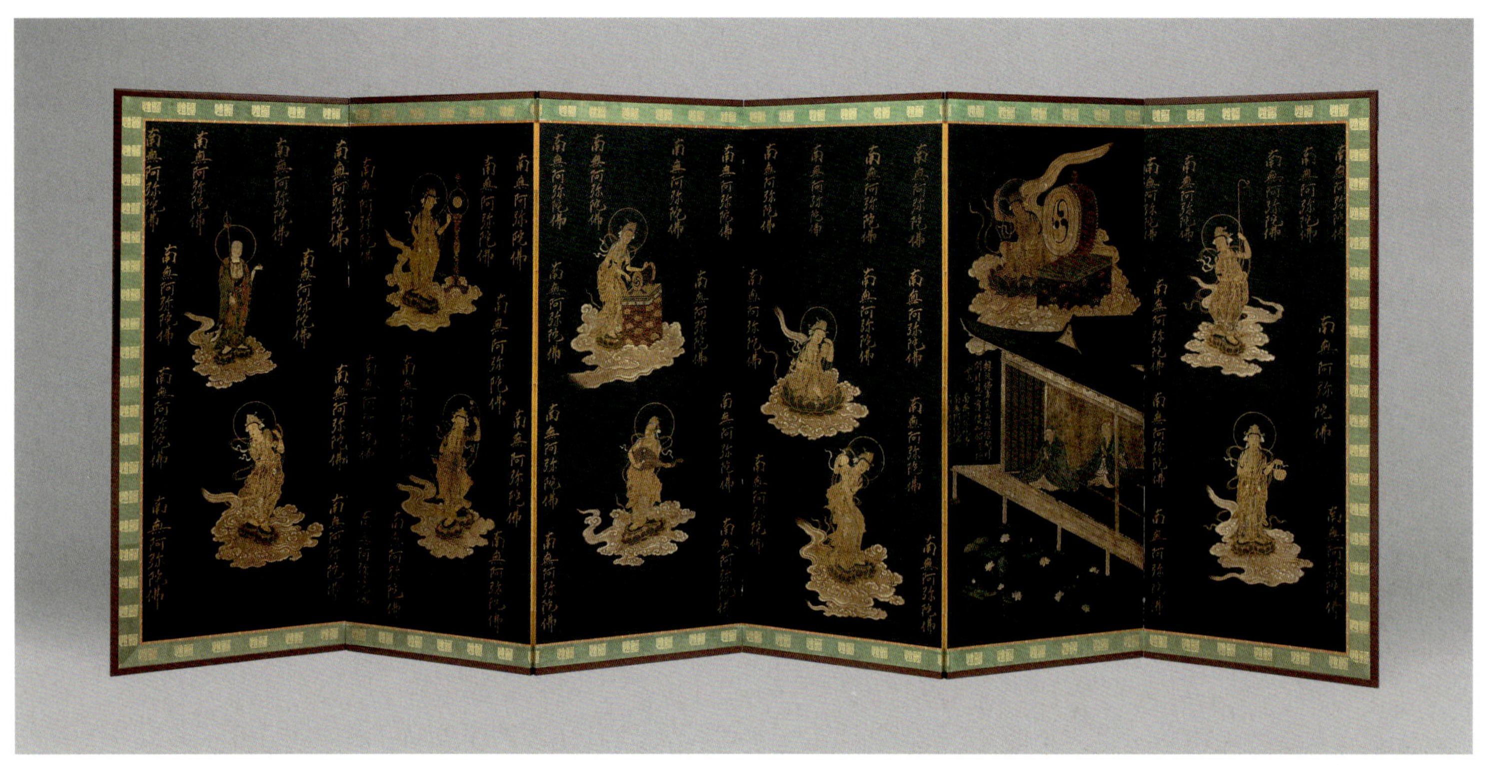

Fig. 5 Michael Olszewski (American, born 1950). *Mourning*, 1989. Silk, plain weave, pleated; appliquéd with layers of silk, plain weaves, some resist dyed, some printed, some dyed; embroidered with silk; 52.4 × 71.8 × 0.7 cm (20 ⅝ × 28 ¼ × ¼ in.). The Art Institute of Chicago, purchased with funds provided by the Textile Society, 2013.61.

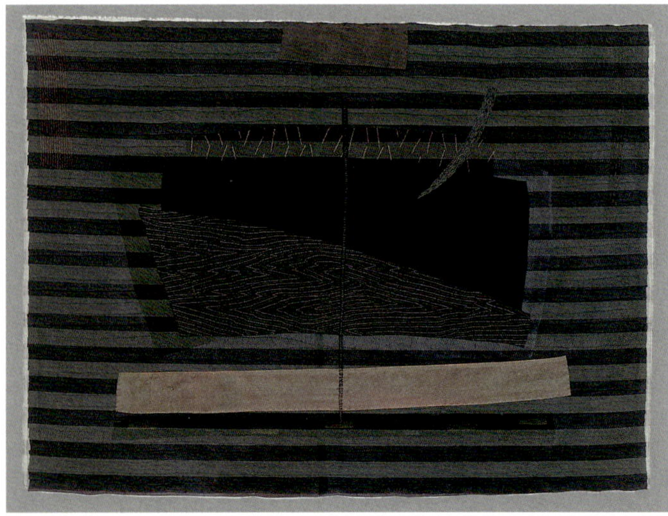

together to heal from absence, loss, and trauma. And they can help heal our spirits as we process grief and reckon with our own mortality. As Jerry Bleem writes in his essay for this volume, devotional textiles depicting sorrowful mourners tending to deities at the moment of their passing signal death as an end and a beginning, suggesting paths forward from grief. And textiles can also offer spiritual forms of protection, as in the case of a tunic from Mali (fig. 7); worn underneath regular clothing, it is inscribed with the name of God (Allah), symbolic references to Islamic beliefs and cosmologies, and numeric arrangements, or magic squares, that function as powerful amulets to shield the wearer.[2] Artist Karen Hampton's work *Ancestor's Cry* (fig. 8), inspired by large petroglyphs in Nevada, asks how our ancestors might respond to human grief and the global destruction of land, using cloth as a site of reflection and conduit for ancestral communication. Motifs such as circles, fauna, and celestial maps symbolic the relationship between spiritual and phsyical worlds.

Textile objects are subject to various kinds of losses, being vulnerable to physical and material degradation from daily wear and use. Textiles suffer losses like abrasion, decay, deterioration, stains, and tears caused by biological and environmental factors. Historical textile objects often arrive at museums with existing losses, and even under optimal museum conditions they remain vulnerable to light damage and physical stresses (see fig. 9). Textiles may enter museum collections in the form of fragments, some-times having been purposefully separated from a larger

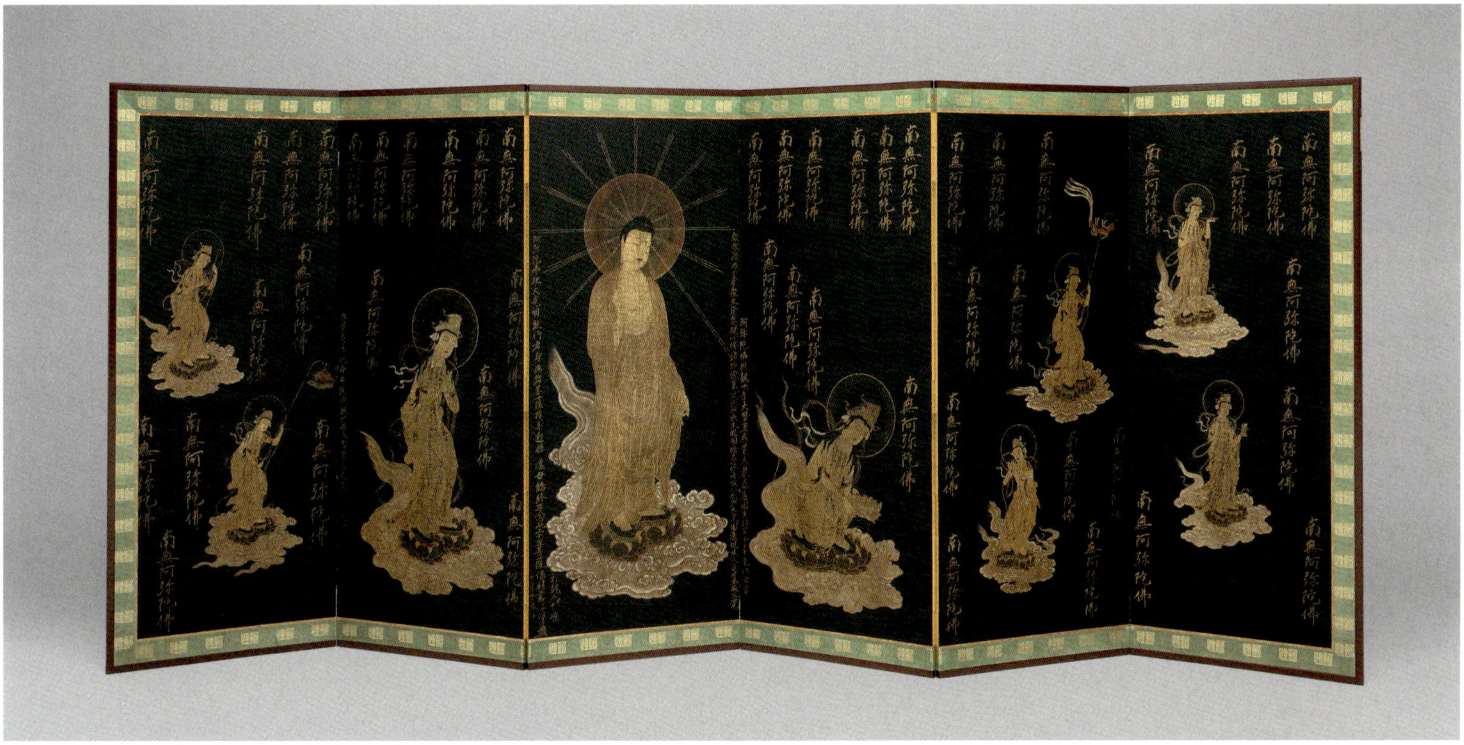

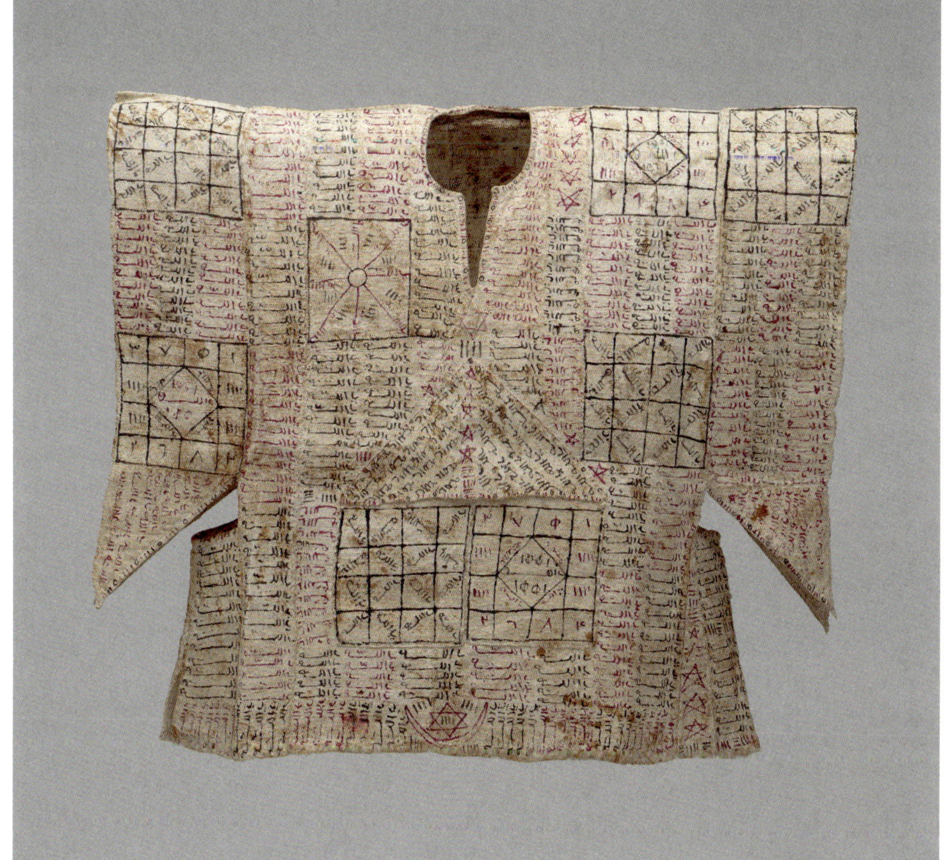

Fig. 6 (above and opposite) *Rebirth of the Nun Anyō* (安養尼往生), early 18th century. Japan. Pair of six-panel screens; ink, colors, and gold on paper; each: 151.5 × 373 cm (59⅝ × 147 in.). The Art Institute of Chicago, purchased with funds provided by the Joseph and Helen Regenstein Foundation, 1963.268–69.

Fig. 7 Talismanic Tunic, mid–late 20th century. Djenné or Tombouctou, Mali. Strips of cotton, plain weave; pieced; embroidered and painted; 94 × 81.3 cm (37 × 32 in.). The Art Institute of Chicago, Elizabeth M. Schultz Endowment Fund, 2023.3242.

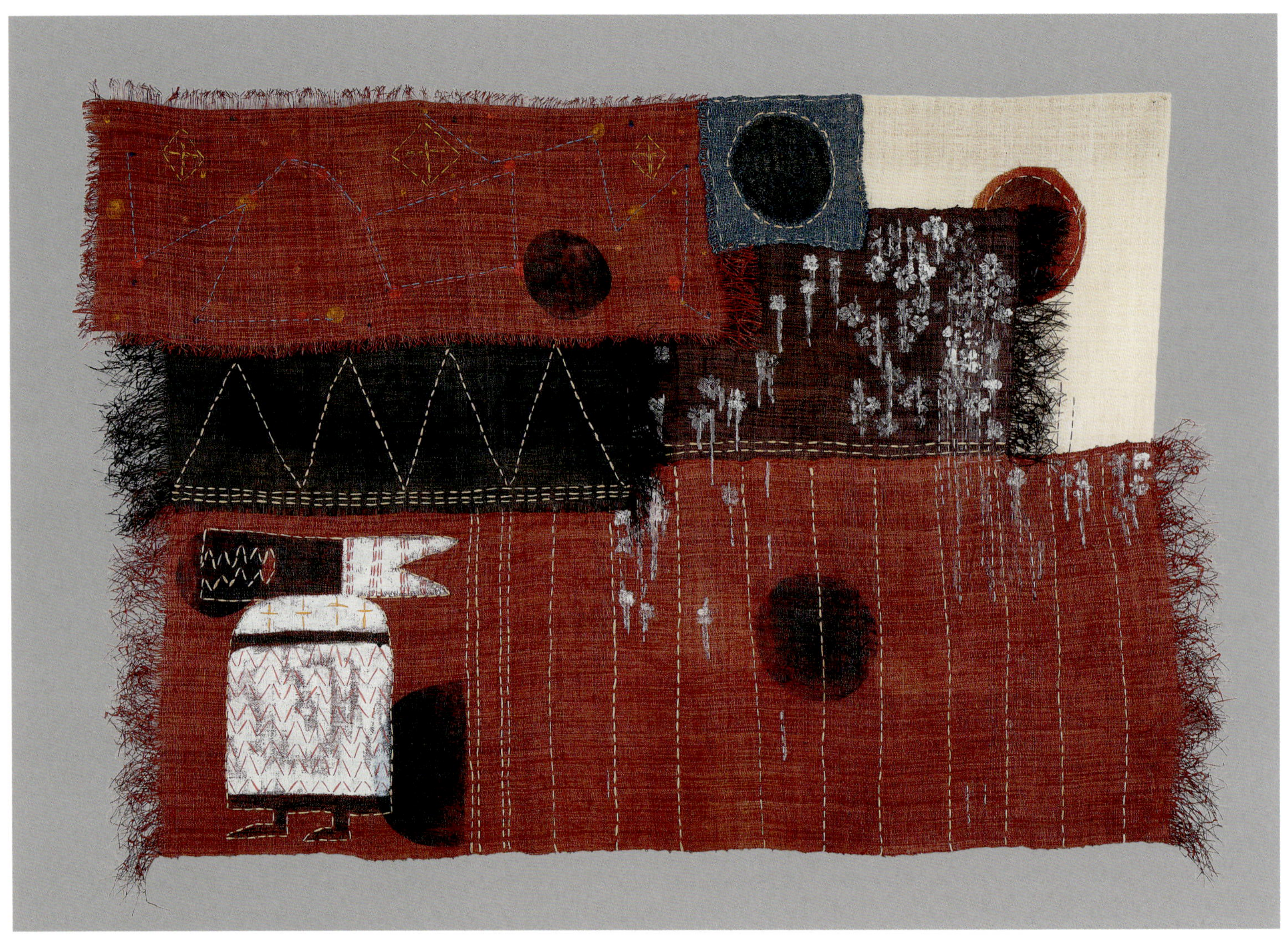

Fig. 8 **Karen Hampton (American, born 1959).** *Ancestor's Cry*, 2017. Raffia cloth, hemp, dye, pigment, dye sublimation, indigo, and linen paper; 111.8 × 177.8 cm (44 × 70 in.). Collection of the artist.

   FACIO, KAI, VINEBAUM, AND WILSON

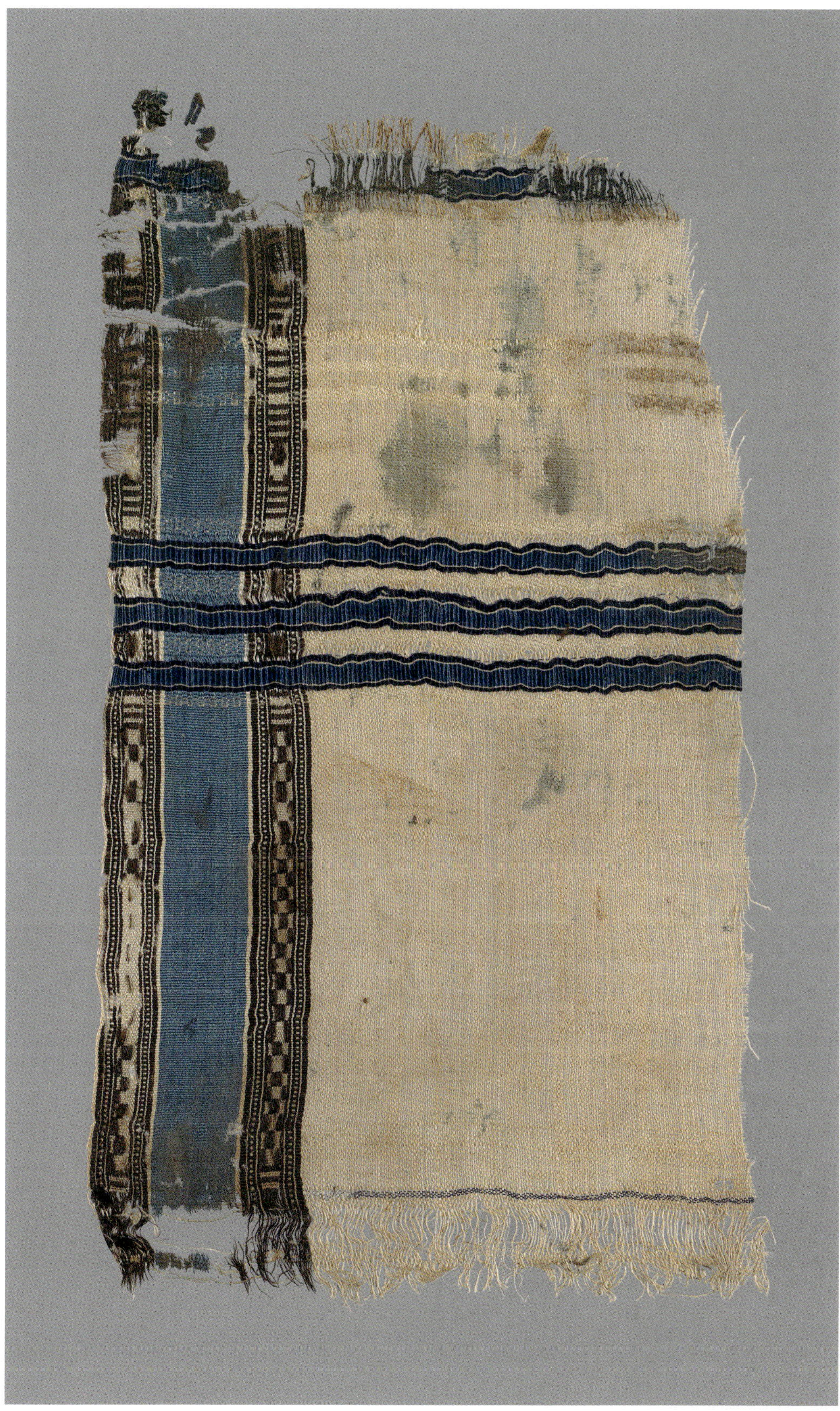

Fig. 9 Fragment of Striped Silk, 13th–15th century. Egypt. Linen and silk; plain weave, bands of weft-faced plain weave with paired warps, bands of twill weave; with stripes of warp-faced plain weave, and supplementary warp and weft float weaves; 24.2 × 14 cm (9½ × 5½ in.). The Art Institute of Chicago, gift of Martin A. Ryerson through the Antiquarian Society, 1900.421.

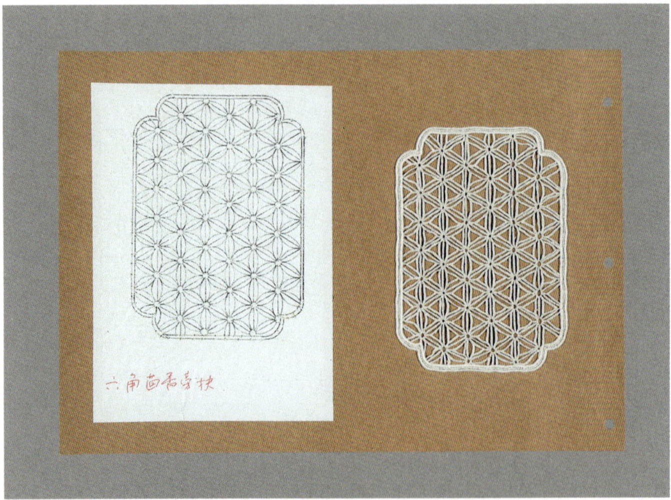

Fig. 10 Rivers (Qinnan Zhu; Chinese, born 1998). Page from *Xiaoshan Huabian* 萧山花边 (Xiaoshan Lace), with contributions from Fu Chunjiang (Chinese, born 1969) and Shen Lanying (Chinese, born 1955), 2021–22. Cotton Xiaoshan needle lace; printed paper illustration with ink; 26.7 × 39.4 cm (10 %16 × 15 %16 in.). Collection of the artist.

whole. Fragments have historically been a predominant form of textiles collected by museums in Europe and the United States. As Melinda Watt details in her essay in this volume, fragments have much to reveal about the histories, aesthetics, production, and politics of textiles, and they continue to inform scholarly discourse today, as researchers identify relationships among objects in various parts of the world. In the larger history of global textiles, losses are an important part of the story. Like fragments, small textile studies can also speak to larger histories. Inspired by Xiaoshan lace making, artist Rivers (Qinnan Zhu) creates such studies to examine historical intersections between Chinese and European hand-made lace (see fig. 10).

Textile conservation is a form of care and repair. Conservation efforts require profound knowledge of an object's composition, materials, and structure. The work of the conservator necessitates close, painstaking observation, often using magnification (see fig. 11), to develop an understanding of an object that can inform strategies for its preservation and display. Conservation efforts seek to sustain the object's integrity and extend its life; in so doing they can also honor and illuminate the textiles' makers, cultural contexts, and meanings.

Resistance and survival: While our project seeks to demonstrate loss and absence, as expressed through textiles, as defining and often beautiful aspects of human experience, it was also conceived with survival in mind. In the face of destructive forces—colonialism, imperialism, war—individuals, communities, and cultures find ways to survive and even thrive. So do textile skills and traditions. Traditions of plant cultivation, dyeing, and hair braiding, for instance, survived the Middle Passage and continued under a system of enslavement that explicitly sought the destruction of cultural and social ties among Black people. Indigenous textile practices have survived centuries of colonial efforts to subjugate and eliminate Native people and their ways of life. Textile skills and techniques continue to be passed down despite the violence of expulsion, exile, ethnic cleansing, and genocide in many parts of the world.

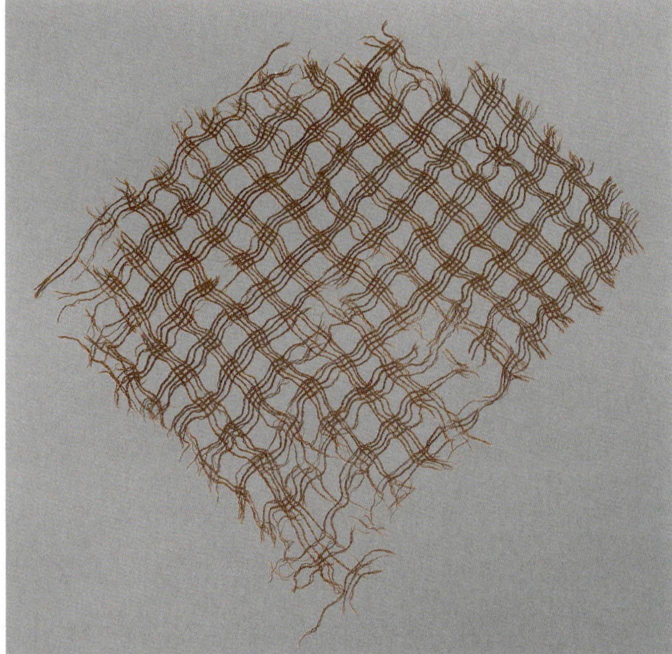

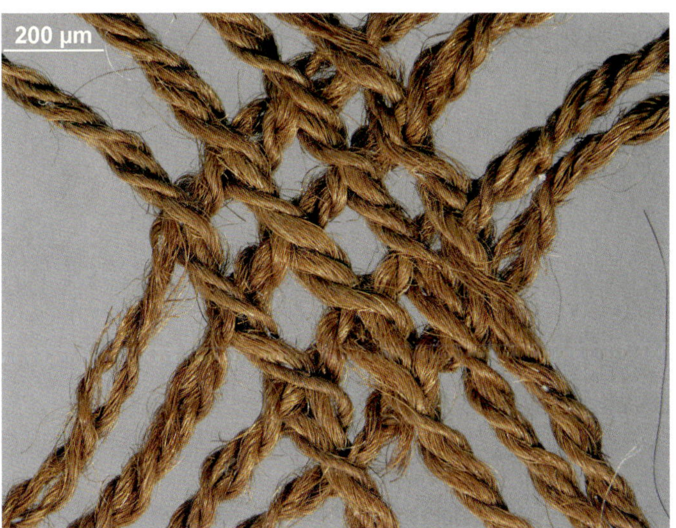

Fig. 11 Top: Fragment of Ply-Split Interlacement, possibly 800 BCE–600 CE. Nasca; Peru. Wool (camelid), oblique interlacing with plied elements; 36.9 × 36.9 cm (14½ × 14½ in.). The Art Institute of Chicago, Kate S. Buckingham Endowment, 1955.1734. While this object appears to the naked eye to have a woven structure (perpendicular interlacement of threads), magnification (bottom) reveals that it is composed of oblique interlacing and plied elements, with ply-split binding points.

Often such practices take on new significance as forms of resistance and expressions of freedom. Quilting has long been a vehicle for transforming trauma and grief into resilience and joy. As artists and educators based in Chicago, it was important for us to include local perspectives on textiles and resistance. Chicago artist, activist, and educator Dorothy Burge has used quilts to confront injustice in her community. Burge created two quilted works for the exhibition (p. 182, figs. 5–6) that celebrate the resilience of formerly incarcerated torture survivors La Tanya Jenifor-Sublett and Michelle Clopton. As Sharbreon Plummer observes in her essay in this volume, Burge's work inspires us "to turn mourning into hope."

Curatorial Methodologies

On Loss and Absence marks the first time that artists have worked with the Art Institute's textiles collection to curate a major exhibition. While the four of us have diverse professional identies—conservator, educator, scholar—we are all artists, and as such we bring unique forms of haptic and hands-on knowledge derived from rigorous material engagements in our individual practices and from years of study and training. Our experiences manipulating materials to give them form through processes like braiding, dyeing, mending, piecing, spinning, stitching, and weaving have provided us with deep understandings of textile objects and their processes of creation.

As makers ourselves, one of our key curatorial methodologies in studying this wide range of works was taking an object-centered approach that combined hands-on knowledge with slow, careful visual examination, or close looking.[3] Close looking begins with detailed observation to better understand the materials and techniques that give form to textile objects. These methodologies are rooted in the pedagogical philosophies of Fiber and Material Studies at the School of the Art Institute, where all four project curators studied or currently teach.

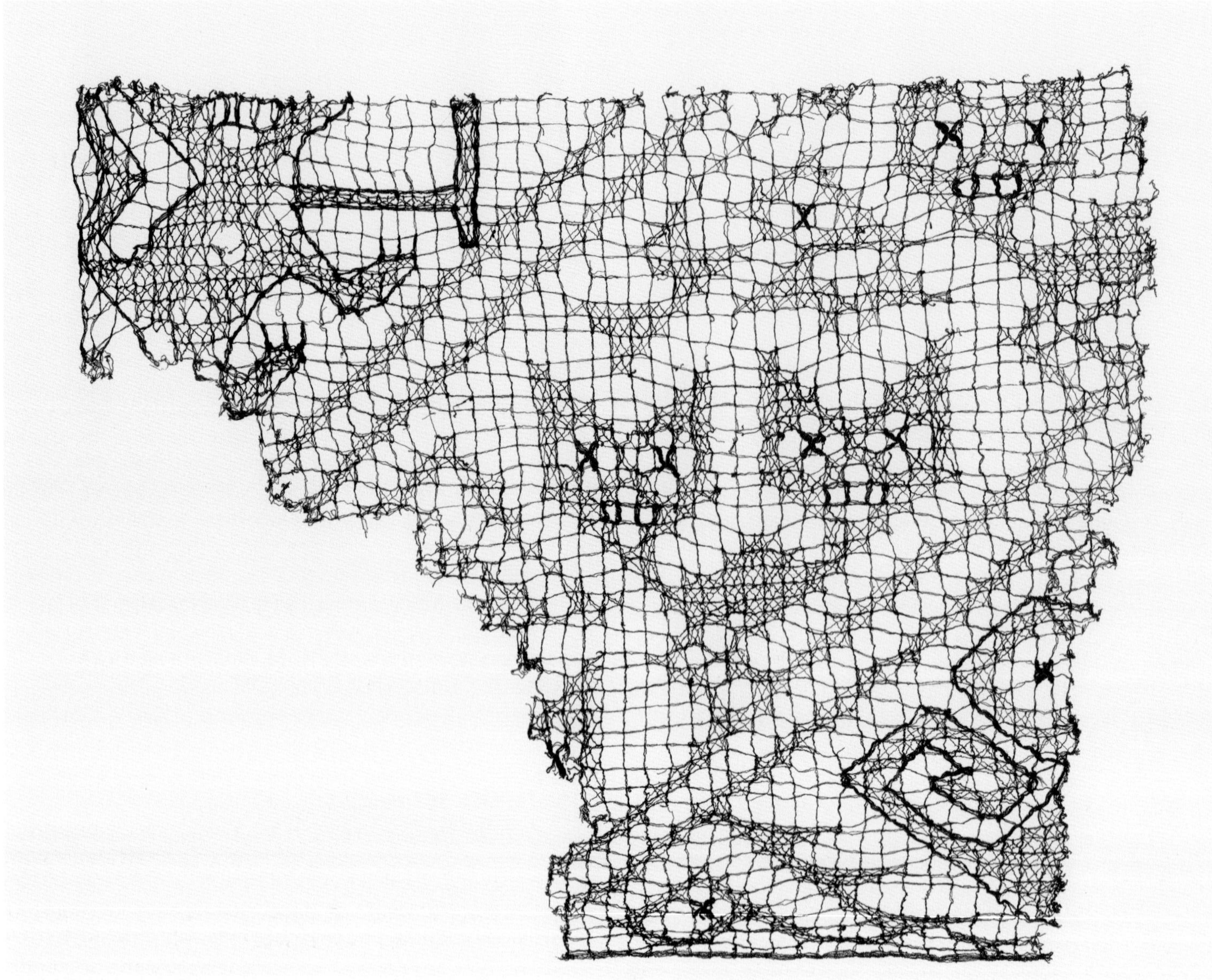

Fig. 12 Headcloth Fragment, 11th–15th
century. Chancay; central coast, Peru. Over
twist cotton; gauze weave, simple looping
stitch, and embroidery; 32.4 × 39.4 cm (12¾ ×
15½ in.). The Art Institute of Chicago, Kate S.
Buckingham Endowment, 1954.219.

Working with textiles in the Art Institute's Conservation and Science labs, we used a variety of analytical and technical tools, including magnification, to study materials, structures, and techniques not visible to the naked eye. High magnification reveals the object's microstructure: The physical characteristics of threads—interlacements, spin direction, and texture—become visible. The geometric patterns of interlacing, looping, and twining threads come into view. The back or interior of a textile often tells us more about the process of its making than the front or outside; we closely examined the objects from all sides to understand their full structures. Under magnification, we could see details that differentiate one technique from another. For example, a headcloth fragment (fig. 12) from Chancay, Peru, has a lacelike appearance, but magnification reveals it to be a woven gauze with cross-looping embroidery motifs.

Some information about textile objects may not be readily accessible, even under magnification. Thanks to our collaboration with the Koepfli Lab at the University of Notre Dame, we are fortunate to have had access to microbiological analysis for select objects, which can reveal additional evidence of a textile's use and wear. Textiles are like sponges that absorb not only the blood, sweat, and tears of those who interact with them at any point in their history but also any chemicals, organisms, or particles present in the environment—as Sarah Molina and Cybele Tom note in their essay in this volume, textiles "physically index their own histories" to a unique degree. For instance, a child's tunic (see pp. 52–53, fig. 1) from seventh-century Egypt is worn, fragmented, and stained with burial residue. We originally encountered the tunic during our first ever in-person visit to view the collection in 2021, and the life of its young wearer has gripped the curatorial team ever since. Who was the child who wore it? How did they die at such a young age? As detailed in the essay by Gustavo Da Silva, Isaac Facio, Cristian Koepfli, and Lucinda Pelton in this volume, DNA can be captured from textiles in the Art Institute's collection; analyzing this evidence can help us further understand how textiles can act as historical archives, literally holding blood, sweat, and other details from the lives of those who interacted with them.

Key Objectives

We embarked on this project with a desire to highlight the objects' stories and meanings and to honor the makers and communities that created them to the best of our ability. We occasionally encountered absences and gaps in the collection records—for instance, missing names of makers that were apparently lost or never recorded. A project like this presents opportunities to augment, correct, and update object histories through new research. We also sought to approach objects expansively, including authors' personal experiences with and reflections on certain textiles as valuable parts of the story.

Critically, we collaborated with living artists and scholars with ancestral and generational knowledge related to particular objects and techniques. These conversations informed us as we installed objects, created in-gallery didactics, and conceived this publication; we aimed to make the most culturally respectful, ethical, and considered choices possible within our means and based on the knowledge and research available to us. We were especially mindful of how to respectfully and appropriately display and describe textile objects created by Indigenous makers known and once known. It was essential for us to work with Indigenous Andean and Diné artists, who helped us select objects from their cultures to include in *On Loss and Absence* and guided us in how to display them.

From the very outset, we collaborated with master weavers Danitza Willka and Alipio Melo and contemporary weaving artist Maria José Murillo, cofounders of the Noqanchis collective based in Pitumarca, Cusco, Peru. The Art Institute has an impressive collection of pre-Hispanic Andean textiles but very few examples of works by living Andean weavers. This can give the erroneous impression that Andean weaving is a thing of the past. Noqanchis contributed four works to the exhibition (including pp. 172–73, fig. 11), created both collectively and individually. Andean weavings are conceived as living entities, as Noqanchis describe in their coauthored essay in this volume. They are meant to be viewed from all sides, not just from the "front," as is often the case in museum displays.[4] With Noqanchis' input, the Art Institute developed display cases that enable these textiles to be viewed in three dimensions.

Also from the very early stages of the project, we collaborated with sisters Barbara Teller Ornelas and Lynda Teller Pete, fifth-generation Diné weavers who have been weaving since they were young girls. They advised us on which Diné weaving to include in the exhibition, a work by Hosteen Klah (p. 191, fig. 5). It was especially important to the sisters that *On Loss and Absence* include a work by a named weaver. Their coauthored essay offers rare insight into the lives and works of legendary Diné weavers Klah and Daisy Taugelchee from the valuable perspectives and lived experiences of Diné weavers themselves and attests to the power of naming Indigenous makers. We are honored to include a new work by Teller Ornelas (pp. 196–97, fig. 10), acquired by the Art Institute's textiles department, in *On Loss and Absence*. Our collaborations with Noqanchis and the Teller sisters were among our most humbling and moving experiences as curators.

We also knew from the beginning that we wanted to include embroidery from Palestine, called *tatreez*. Little did we know as we were researching objects in other collections that the Art Institute itself was home to three exquisite Palestinian textiles, mistakenly labeled as having been made in Iran and Jordan.[5] Palestinian dress historian, scholar, author, and embroiderer Wafa Ghnaim began learning embroidery from her mother, award-winning artist Feryal Abbasi-Ghnaim, when she was two years old. Ghnaim has spent much of her life studying the motifs of Palestinian embroidery, and her essay in this volume details the motifs

and remarkably continuous tradition of tatreez, which has become a powerful symbol of cultural survival.

Hair emerged as a conceptual strand that weaves through the project themes and manifests in several objects—stitched and coiled in mourning samplers and jewelry (see p. 44, figs. 1–2, and p. 47, fig. 4), placed inside the braids on a ceremonial dance hat from the Bamiléké people in Cameroon (p. 155, fig. 3), represented abstractly with stamps on an adinkra cloth (p. 157–8, figs. 5–6) or in a sculptural work by contemporary artist Angela Hennessy (p. 45, fig. 3). Project cocurator Nneka Kai created a performance and video installation honoring the Black ancestral craft of hair braiding (see pp. 154, fig. 2), conceived in response to the underrepresentation of Black women in the Art Institute's textiles collection. Her essay for this volume describes her goal of activating both the objects in the gallery and the space itself through her performance, arguing that Black art requires the presence of Black bodies and inviting us to consider the museum as a place for community, care, and healing.

Conclusion

On Loss and Absence was conceived in 2020 during the COVID-19 pandemic and the protests in response to George Floyd's murder. In the five and a half years it has taken us to bring the project to fruition, we—like humanity at large—have all known grief, whether at the loss of loved ones or in response to geopolitical events. These experiences have profoundly affected this work. When we embarked on our curatorial journey, we often said that we wanted the textiles in *On Loss and Absence* to tell their own stories. One of the things we have since learned is that while objects have incredible tales to tell, they need many hands and many voices to bring them to life. The stories of textiles live in their cultures, communities, and makers. They often are not—and perhaps cannot be—contained solely in museum records, scholarship, or received histories. Stories can be forgotten, lost, or deliberately buried. The stories contained in textile objects will not be fully known until they include ancestral teachings, inherited and embodied knowledge, oral histories, memories, personal accounts and testimonies, and sensory information. Our task as curators was to do our best to learn about these objects in consultation and collaboration with authors, colleagues, and community members; to look and listen closely; to contextualize the objects and allow their multiple, intersecting, and beautiful stories to take shape, in the galleries and on these pages.

Notes

1   We are grateful to our friend and colleague Katerina Weslien for sharing her experience participating in one such funeral at the invitation of the community in the village of Melolo on the island of Sumba in 1984. A patolu similar to the one in fig. 3 was placed at the top of the burial mound of deceased ruler Raja Pau. See also Penelope Graham, "The 'Severed Shroud': Local and Imported Textiles in the Mortuary Rites of an Indonesian People," in *Contact, Crossover, Continuity: Proceedings of the Fourth Biennial Symposium of the Textile Society of America* (Textile Society of America, 1995): 159–66.

2   Thanks to Janet Purdy for providing contextual information about the talismanic textile.

3   See Shari Tishman, *Slow Looking: The Art and Practice of Learning Through Observation* (Routledge, 2018).

4   See María José Murillo, "On Diasporas and Returns," in *María José Murillo: Con otros ojos para ver/With Different Eyes to See*, exh. cat. (ICPNA and Artus, 2023). See also Denise Y. Arnold and Elvira Espejo Ayka, *The Andean Science of Weaving: Structures and Techniques of Warp-Faced Weaves* (Thames and Hudson, 2015).

5   Janet Purdy discovered the mislabeled Palestinian textiles in the Art Institute's collection. They are illustrated in the essay by Wafa Ghnaim in this volume.

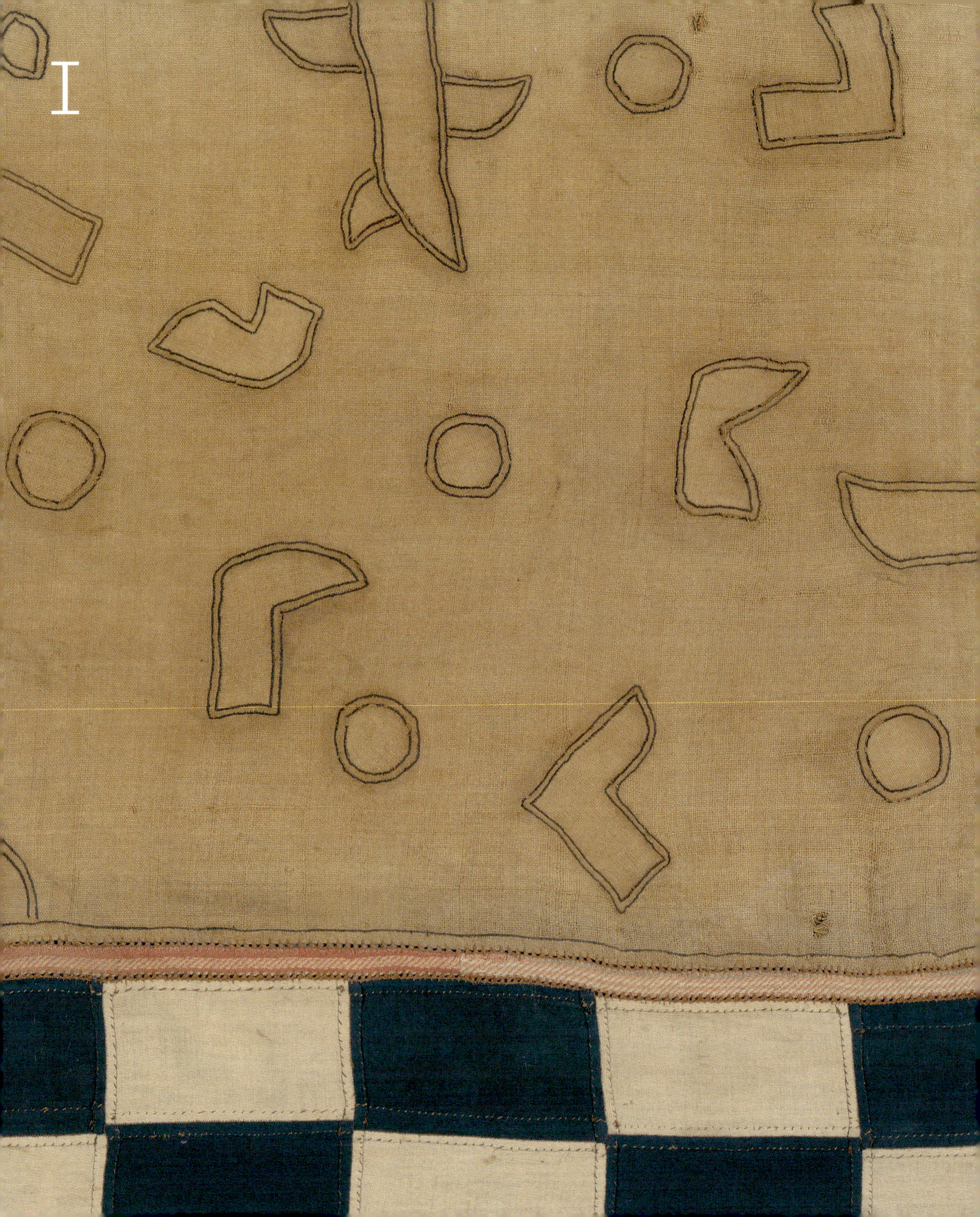

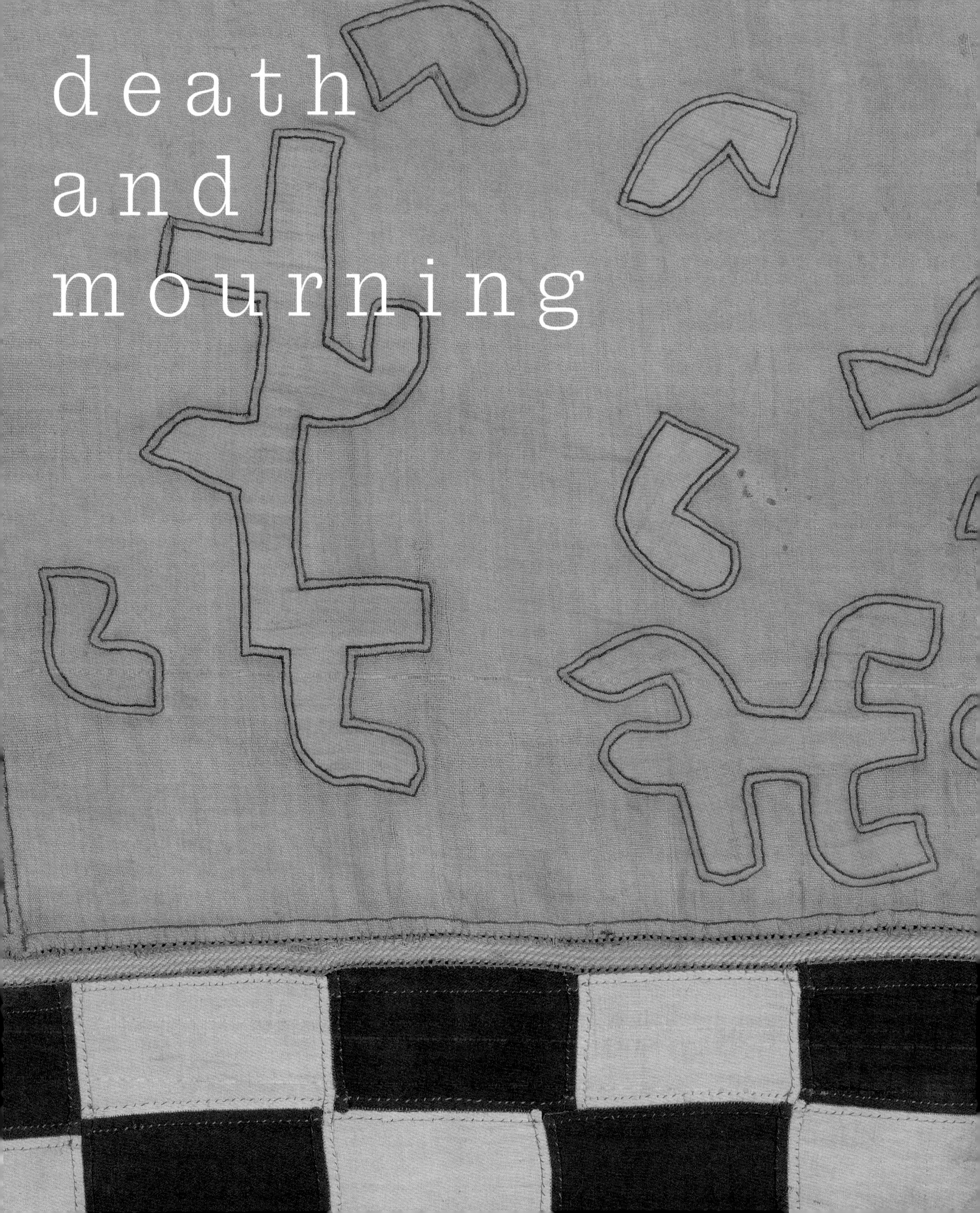

death and mourning

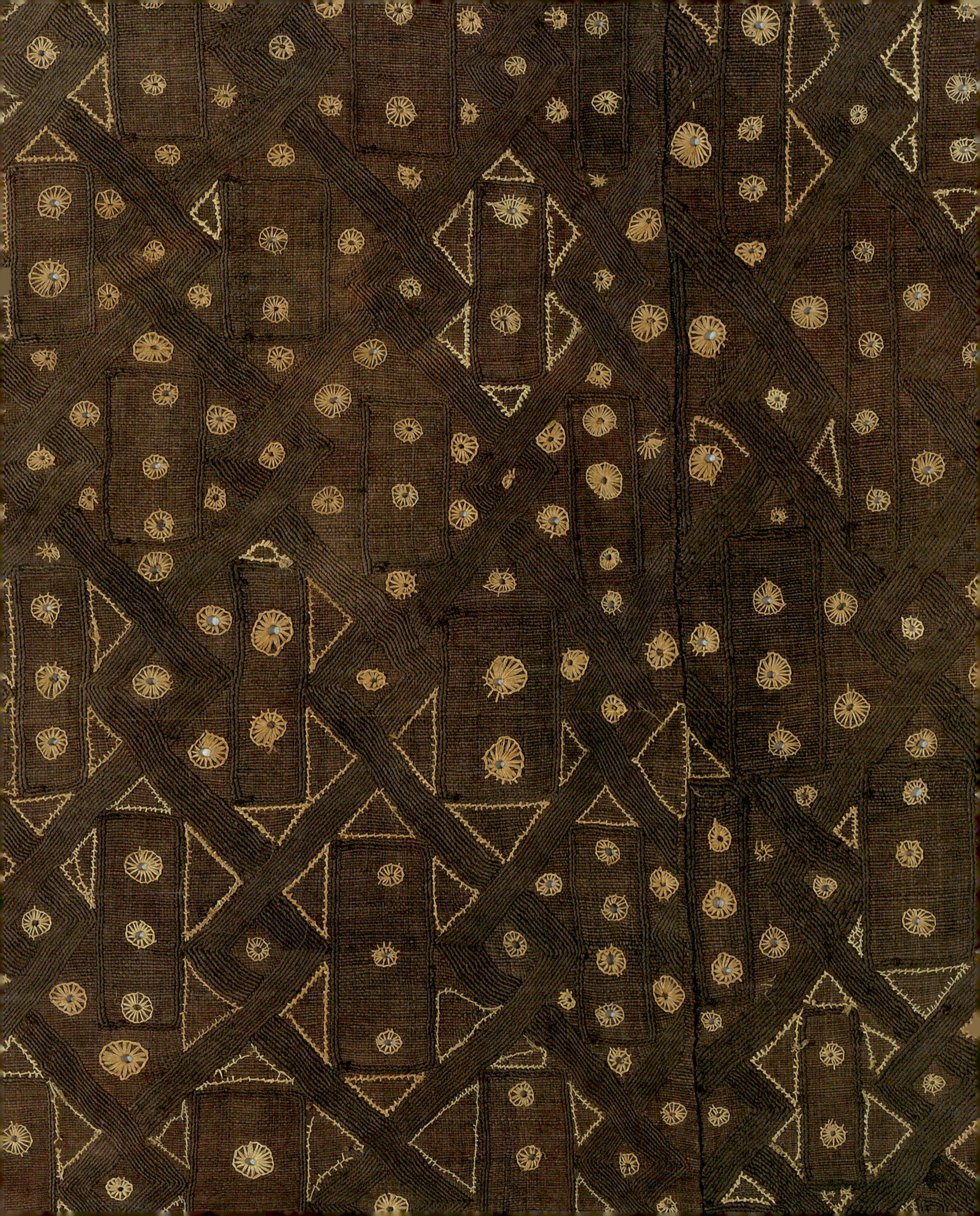

The Geometry of Loss

Valerie Cassel Oliver
Curator

There is an image seared into my mind's eye that comes into view when I think about the themes of absence, loss, and death. It is a photograph of Congressman John Lewis reclining in bed, propped up on his side, leaning on an elbow (fig. 1). He looks exhausted. The photo was taken just months before his death.[1]

Lewis's relaxed pose is countered by his expression: He gazes directly at the camera, his face as steely and serious as it looks in so many pictures. Still, he appears less like a stately icon in his simple white t-shirt, which seems to emphasize his vulnerability and humanity. On his bed are quilts he collected over the years, covering him, as quilts were designed to do, with the unshakable warmth of home, his native Alabama.

Whenever this image comes to me, I think of the comfort those quilts must have brought to the congressman in his final months, weeks, days, and hours of living. I consider his origins as an activist and statesman growing up in rural Alabama, African Americans' long and difficult path in this country, and the origins and evolution of African American quilts. While most Africans brought forcibly to the Americas came from West Africa, many also walked to the coast from neighboring interior lands like the vast Kuba Kingdom, which was located in the heart of what is now the Democratic Republic of the Congo. It is not a stretch to view Kuba cloth (see figs. 2–4), with its stitched, embroidered, and appliquéd geometric forms and patterns, as a visual influence on other African American expressive forms, especially quilting. Both traditions also have associations with comfort and memorialization: Kuba cloth is used in funerary rites; decorated with commemorative patterns, it is wrapped around the deceased. Living attendants wear corresponding patterns as they sit with the dead and offer songs and prayers for safe passage into the next realm. The Kuba cloth itself played a role in escorting the dying into the beyond while also keeping them connected to the living, acting like a kind of portal or vessel. The geometric patterns of the cloth relate to the Kuba understanding of

What do we do now, we asked. His posture answered for him as he stood wordlessly on the street, telling us that you grieve, you endure, you agitate, then you do more of the same.

—Jelani Cobb, "John Lewis: The Last Interview"[1]

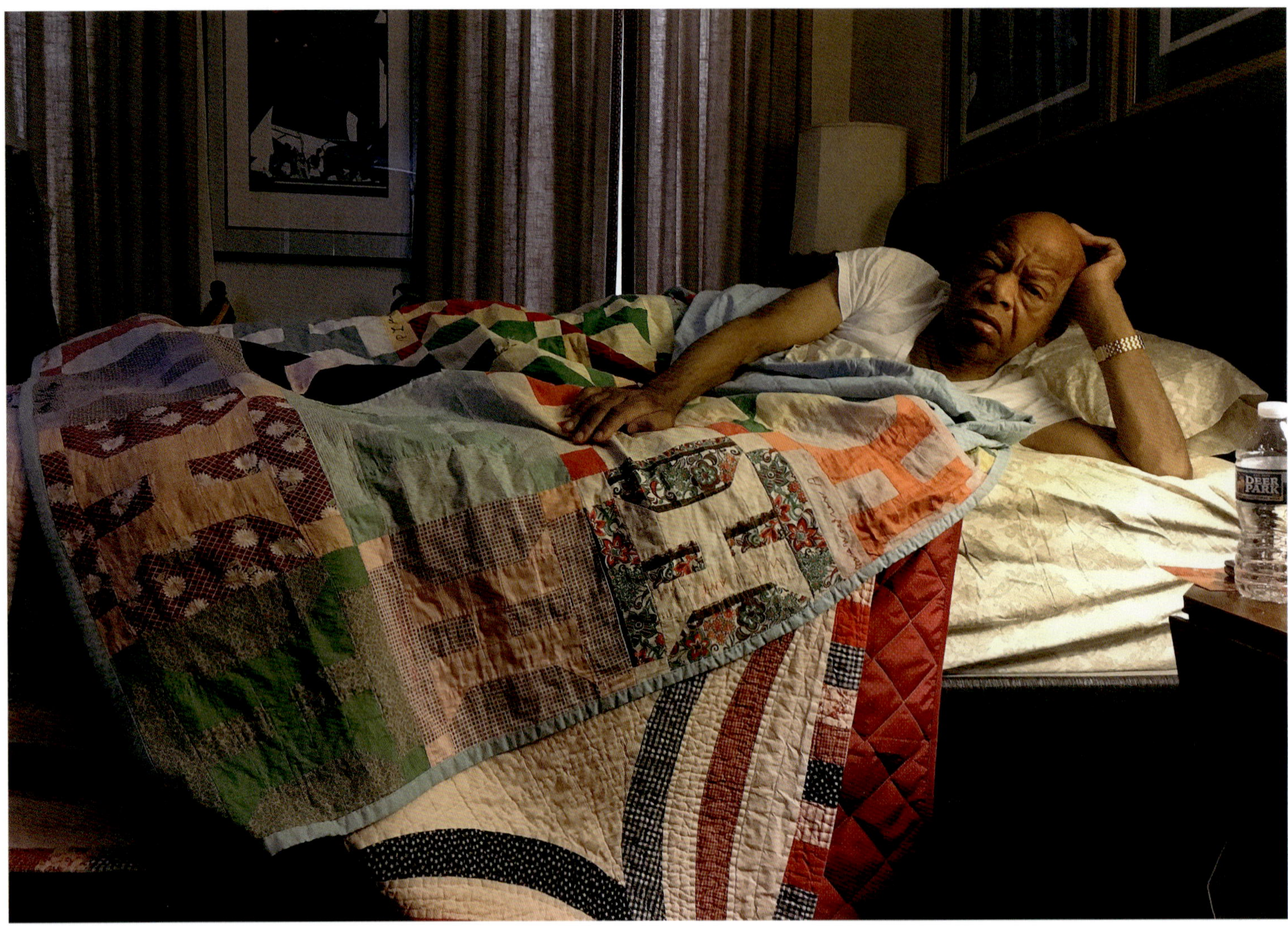

Fig. 1 **Congressman John Lewis covered by quilts, 2020. iPhone picture by Danny Lyon for his film** *SNCC*.

existence as a cycle that moves continuously through a series of realms and states of being. With the forced movement of Africans in the Americas, these same geometric forms became foundational to African American decorative arts, manifested most vividly in African American quilting. Geometric patterns in both Africa and the American South signify ideas about cycles of life, language, sound, and spirituality as well as individual and communal values.

Understood in this context, the African American quilt is like a cultural palimpsest, its origins on the African continent still visible to those who look closely, knowingly. The African American quilt is a tradition linking those disconnected by land, sea, and centuries of bondage. In the photograph of Lewis in his bed, the quilts draped over his body are sacred coverings, a tangible prayer, both American and African in visual language, ushering him peacefully into the next realm.

For longer than I can remember, quilts have embodied the duality of function and sacredness. In my home, old quilts from past generations were treated reverently,

CASSEL OLIVER

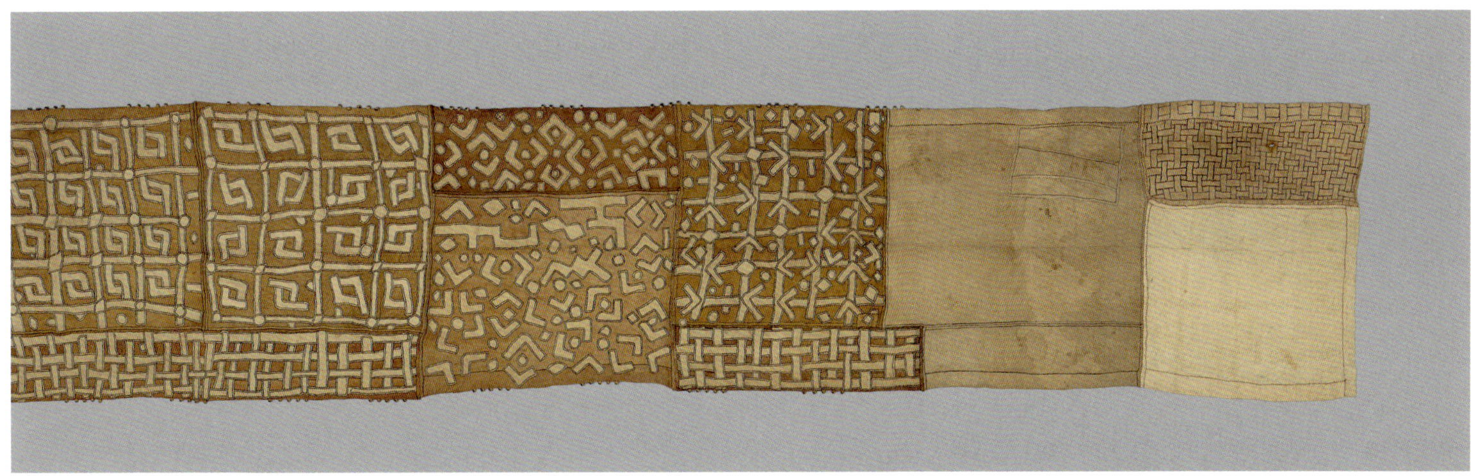

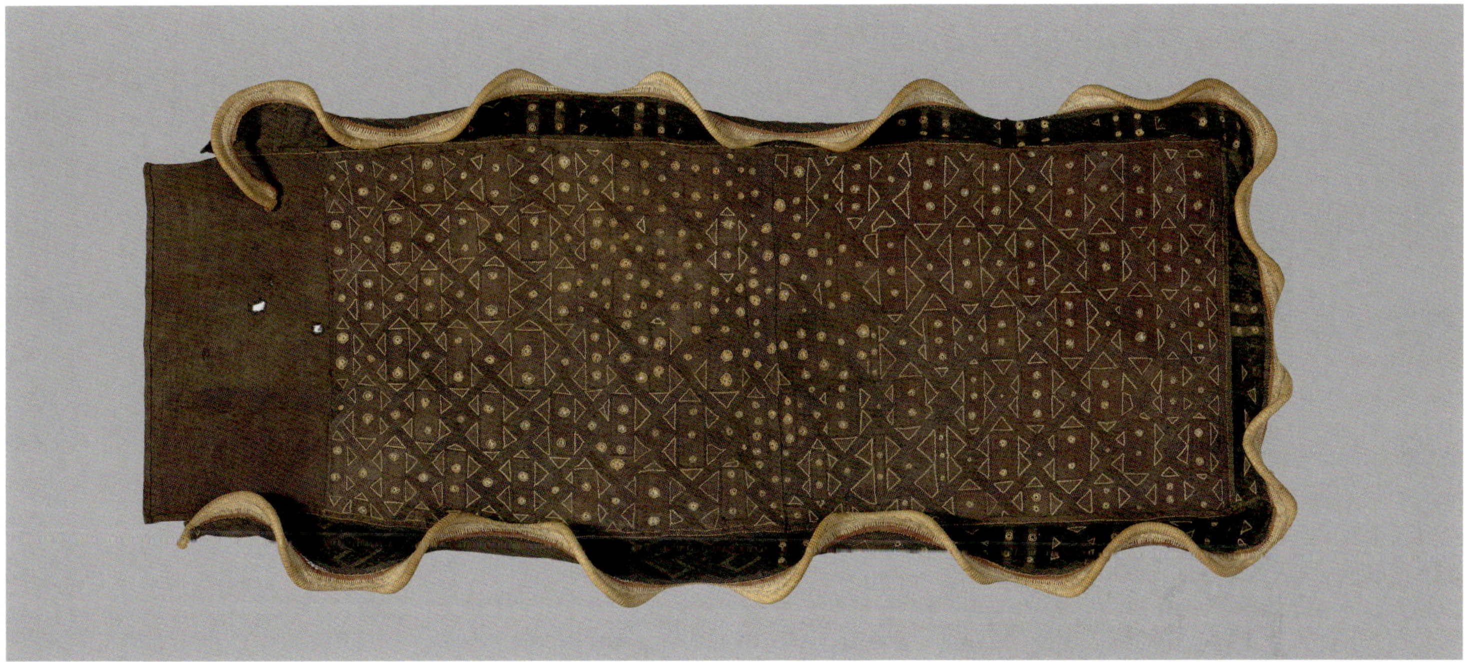

Fig. 2 Noblewoman's Skirt (detail), late 19th–early 20th century. Possibly Ngeende or Ngongo, Kuba; Kasaï Province, Democratic Republic of the Congo. Raffia, plain weaves; pieced; appliquéd with plain weaves; embroidered in pearl stitches; edged with pom-poms; 80.7 × 555.2 cm (31¾ × 218½ in.). The Art Institute of Chicago, Edward E. Ayer Endowment, a memorial to Charles L. Hutchinson by his great friend and admirer; Samuel P. Avery and Maurice D. Galleher endowments, 1985.200.

Fig. 3 Woman's Ceremonial Skirt, late 19th–early 20th century. Kuba; Democratic Republic of the Congo. Raffia, plain weave; embroidered with raffia in buttonhole, pearl, and stem stitches, and running stitches cut to form pile; edged with raffia and hemp, plain weave, 2:2 oblique interlacing, and raffia-wrapped raffia cord; 78.8 × 165.2 cm (31 × 65 in.). The Art Institute of Chicago, gift of Richard Faletti, the Faletti Family Collection, 1993.490.

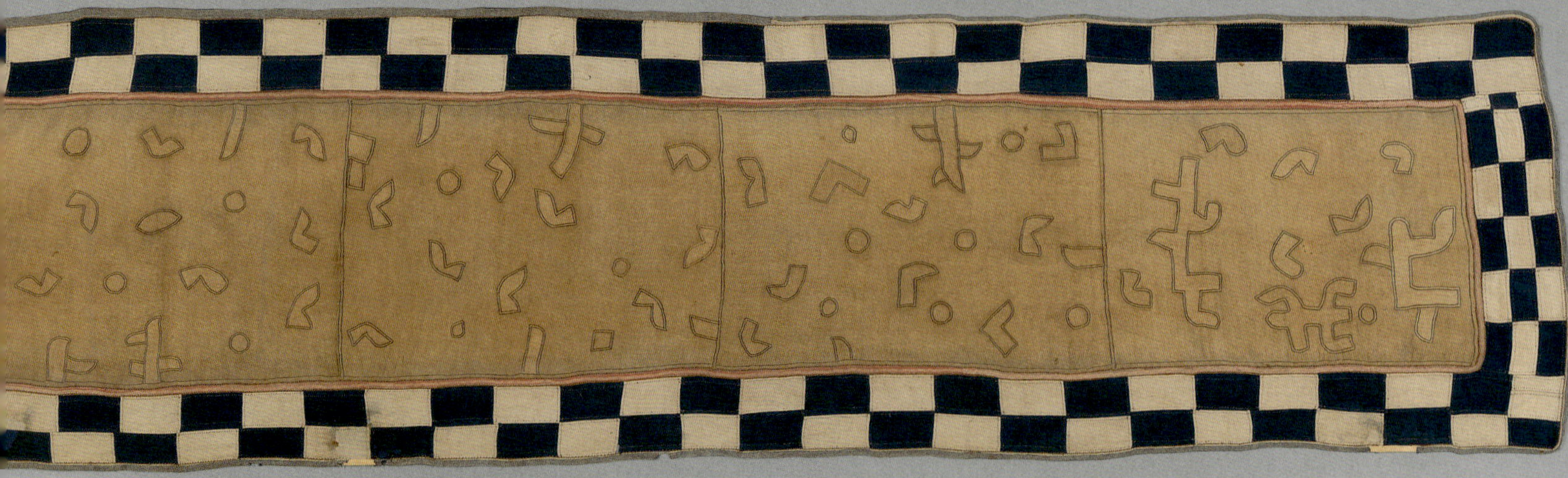

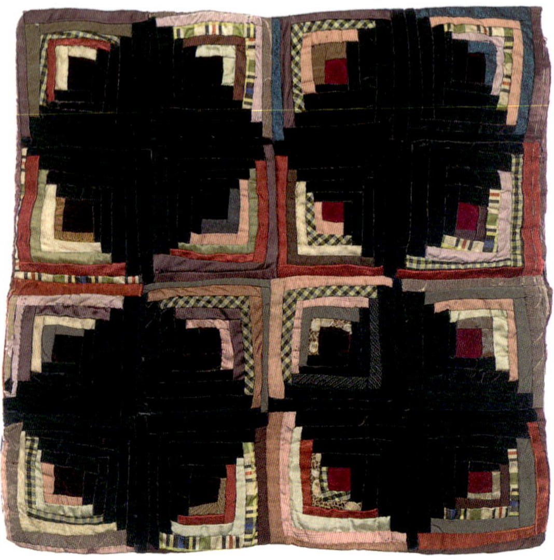

Fig. 4 Ceremonial Skirt (detail), late 19th century. Bushong, Kuba; Mushenge, Kasaï Province, Democratic Republic of the Congo. Raffia, plain weaves; pieced; appliquéd with plain weaves in pearl stitches; embroidered in pearl stitches; edged with bands of cotton, warp-stripe warp-float faced twill weave; cotton, plain weave; pieced and hemmed in slip and pearl stitches; and cotton, warp-float faced alternating float weave; joined with raffia in pearl and twisted insertion stitches; 77.1 × 475.4 cm (30 3/8 × 187 1/8 in.). The Art Institute of Chicago, Edward E. Ayer Endowment, a memorial to Charles L. Hutchinson by his great friend and admirer; Samuel P. Avery and Maurice D. Galleher endowments, 1985.198.

Fig. 5 Quilt Block, 1875–1900. United States. Silk, plain, twill, and satin weaves, some with supplementary patterning warps or wefts, some self-patterned, and some with cut solid velvet; pieced; 44.7 × 46 cm (17 5/8 × 18 1/8 in.). The Art Institute of Chicago, bequest of Martin A. Ryerson, 1943.763.

ritually, brought out in times when illness overwhelmed the body. Their weighted batting wrapped and warmed us as if they had the power to expel the sickness; they at least brought us comfort until it passed. My mother also made quilts, pieced together from old clothes and remnants from the fabric store, creating new, beautiful patterns from cast-offs, a common practice in the American quilting tradition (see fig. 5). She sewed these both by hand and with a sewing machine, singing and humming as she worked. I like now to think that her soft vocalizations were prayers that somehow penetrated every fiber. She is gone now, but her quilts are still here, still bringing comfort, a testament to the resilience of a woman born of a people who persevered against all odds. And still, we persevere. Congressman John Lewis urged us to "carry on" in his absence. How do we go on? I give his answer: We grieve, we endure, we agitate, then we do more of the same.

Hands Up, Don't Shoot

Perhaps even more profound than the image of Lewis in living repose is one from his last public appearance, in Washington, DC, during which he stood beside the city's mayor, Muriel Bowser, on Sixteenth Street, with its massive mural of the words *BLACK LIVES MATTER* inscribed directly on the blacktop (fig. 6). George Floyd's death, the immediate catalyst for the Black Lives Matter movement, was just one in a series of on-camera murders of Black men and women at the hands of police and vigilantes who saw themselves as keeping the streets safe through the unprecedented upheaval of the COVID-19 pandemic. When journalist Gayle King asked Lewis about the protests in response to Floyd's death, he observed, "This feels and looks so different. It is so much more massive and all inclusive." He further noted that it was "very moving to see hundreds of thousands of people from all over America and around the world take to the streets—to speak up, to speak

CASSEL OLIVER

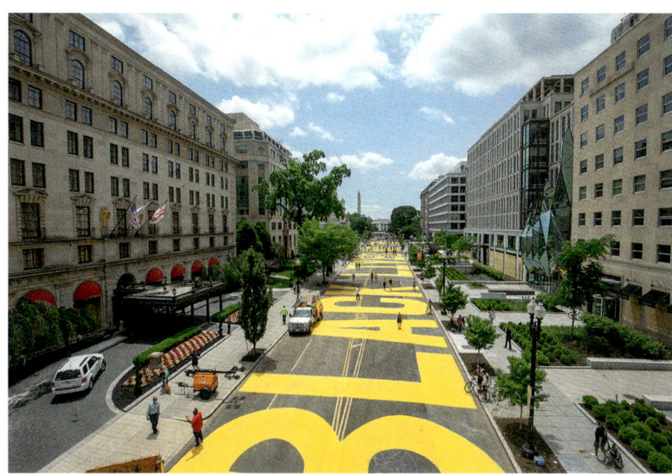

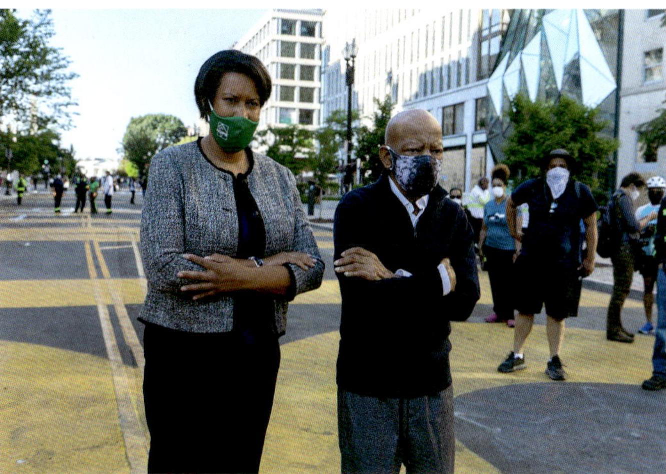

Fig. 6 **Top: The Black Lives Matter street mural, formerly at Sixteenth Street in Washington, DC. Bottom: Congressman John Lewis and Mayor Muriel Bowser visiting the mural in 2020.**

out, to get into what I call 'good trouble.'" When King asked Lewis about his own legacy in relation to the protests, he responded, "I believe that . . . if it becomes necessary to use our bodies to help redeem the soul of a nation, then we must do it."[2] Indeed, the congressman put his own body on the line numerous times. He was beaten, along with more than fifty others, by state troopers during the 1965 march from Selma to Montgomery in support of civil rights. His words—along with his life and work—testify that the violence one encounters in the fight for justice is not endured in vain.

On March 3, 1991, another infamous incident of police violence was caught on camera: the brutal beating of Rodney King at the hands of several officers of the Los Angeles Police Department. Filmed by George Holliday, who lived nearby, the footage aired on local and subsequently national and international news outlets, leading to public outcry and local riots. Excessive use of force against Black people was not a new phenomenon even back then, although such events were rarely captured on tape as King's beating had been. The incident served to make visible and undeniable what Black people had long known: that police frequently dismissed their humanity, as Jamaican writer Sylvia Wynter noted in her essay "No Humans Involved: An Open Letter to My Colleagues."[3] Wynter took the essay's title from the acronym *N. H. I.*, which stands for "no humans involved," used in police reports involving mostly young Black males. The essay, published in the Fall 1994 issue of *Forum*, shed light on the stark disregard for Black humanity as framed by police reports. This disregard was most likely forged by the logic of slavery and the parallel rise of militias created to maintain control over huge populations of enslaved people; cases like King's and Floyd's show how little such thinking had abated by the twentieth and twenty-first centuries.

Artist Nick Cave was moved by the coverage and discourse around King's beating. Trained as a dancer and visual artist, Cave was keenly aware of his body and—queer, Black, and male—of the perception of his body in American

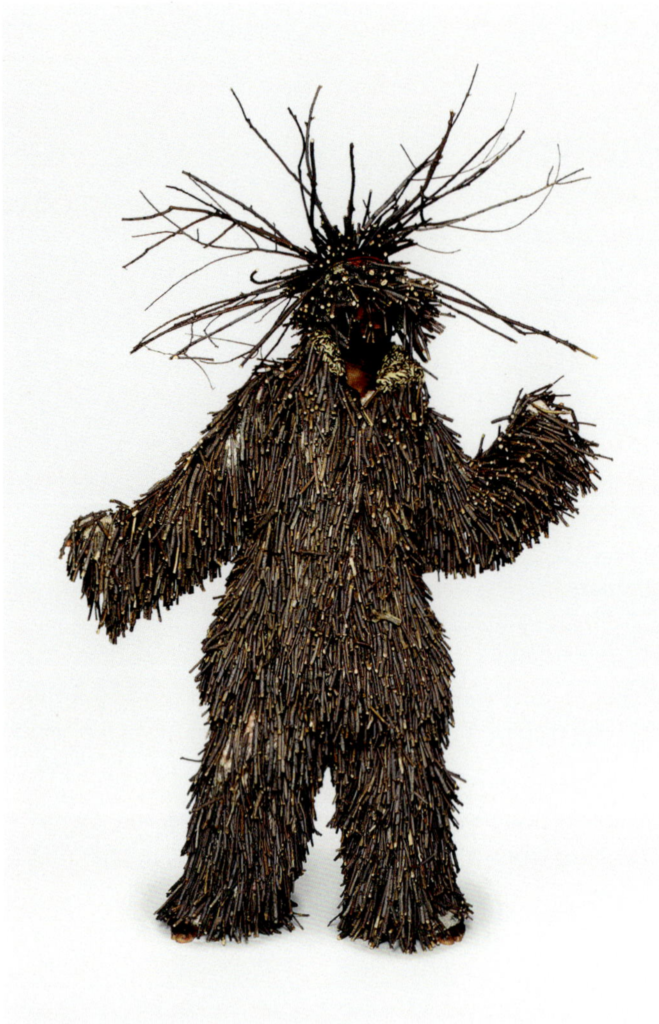

Fig. 7 **Nick Cave (American, born 1959).**
Soundsuit, 1992. Mixed media including
twigs, wire, metal, and mannequin; approx.
243.8 × 121.9 × 63.5 cm (96 × 48 × 25 in.).
Collection of the artist.

society. To stem the trauma of continuously viewing footage of King's attack, Cave conceived fantastical means to keep himself safe. He created a "soundsuit" (fig. 7), a second skin and protective layer that would ostensibly shield Black bodies from racial profiling and violence in encounters with police and similar entities. The endeavor blended his training in the visual arts with fiber and found objects and utilized his work as a dancer with the legendary Alvin Ailey, setting him on an artistic course that gave birth to decades of material explorations and revolutionary performances and installations. He has since made hundreds of soundsuits, each one a unique assemblage of different everyday objects.

Nearly thirty years later, Cave is still grappling with what it means to live in a society where the unrelenting scrutiny of and disrespect for Black bodies regularly leads to explosions of aggression. His large-scale installations and discrete sculptures have moved away from crafting protective spaces amid a tide of violence that seems inexhaustible and instead toward creating memorials and spaces for grieving. These projects gained new relevance as the artist addressed the losses of the COVID-19 pandemic, which disproportionately affected Black and Brown communities.[4] Seeking to restore individual humanity to mass casualties and statistics, Cave invited viewers into installations of his wall-mounted sculptures featuring cast hands and arms extending into the room and holding funerary wreaths and other meaningful objects.

Using his own body as a stand-in for the deceased, Cave offered sculptures of his arm—cast in bronze to denote his Black skin—extending from the wall with his palm turned upward and open to receive, for example, cascading white cloth that descends from above (fig. 8). The white cloth evokes not only purity but also a new beginning for the dead. The color white is also used in African and African American syncretic religious traditions to aid in the ritual crossing of thresholds between life and death, as shown in the Kongo cosmogram (fig. 9), a core symbol in Kongo religion that explains the organization of the physical and spiritual world.[5]

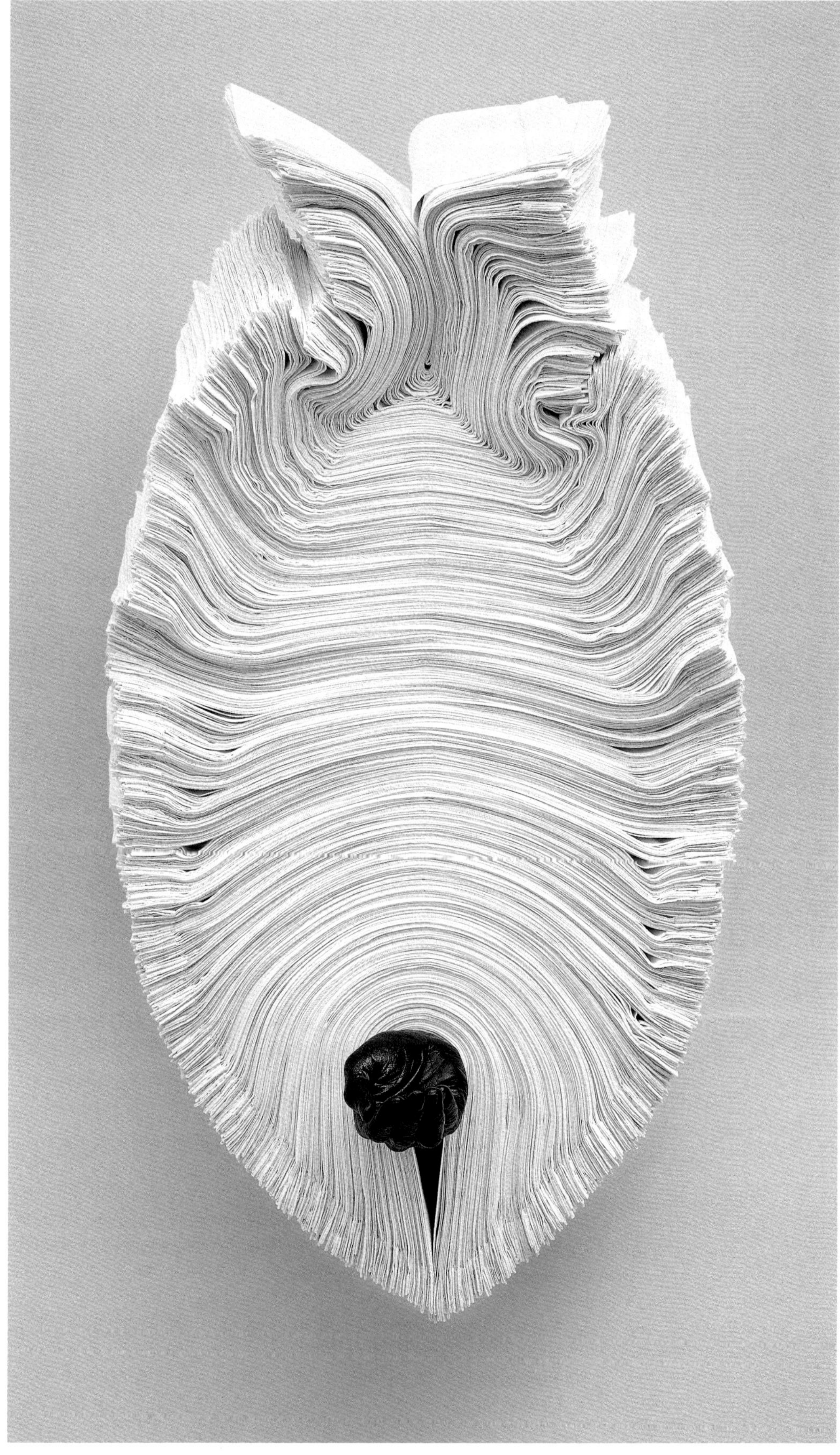

Fig. 8 Nick Cave (American, born 1959). *Untitled*, 2017. Cast bronze and cotton; 104.14 × 55.9 × 39.4 cm (41 × 22 × 15½ in.). Collection of the artist.

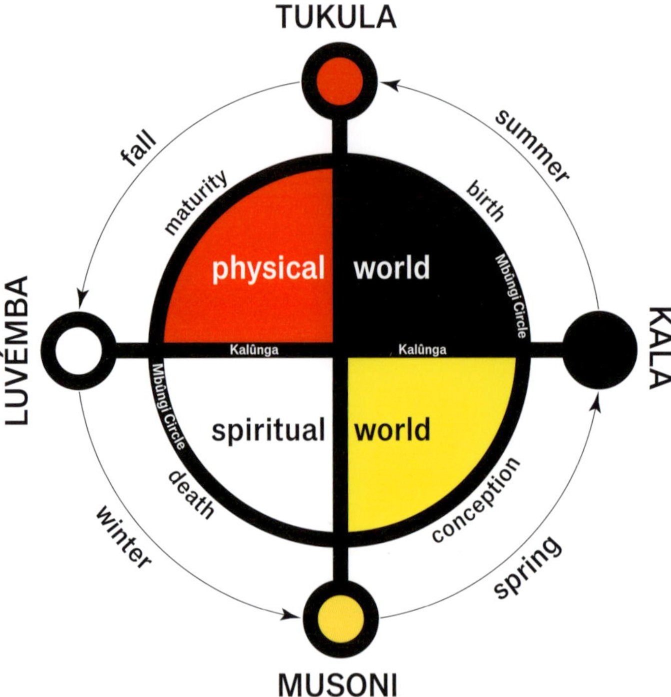

Fig. 9 The Kongo cosmogram (also known as the Dikenga or Yowa) is a sacred Kongo symbol representing the cyclical journey of life, death, and rebirth. Key elements include the crossroads (Dikenga) between the spiritual and physical worlds; the Kalûnga Line, symbolizing the river of transition; and the Mbûngi circle, which encircles the four life stages of conception (Musoni), birth (Kala), maturity (Tukula), and death (Luvémba). Simbi spirits guide souls along this path, highlighting the deep connection between the living and ancestral realms. Illustration by Isaac Facio.

The diagram is composed of a cross encased by a circle. The cross functions to delineate the four quadrants that, in a counterclockwise movement, denote maturity, death, rebirth, and early life. The upper quadrants signify life and the earth, while the lower quadrants signify death and the underworld. Dying and death occupy the upper- and lower-left quadrants, with the threshold of death represented as submersion in water and by the color white, both of which are associated with purification and rebirth.[6] Just as the tradition of Kuba cloth is carried forward in African American quilts, the ideas and philosophical underpinnings of the Kongo cosmogram, however fragmented, are part of African American culture. Cave is well aware of African American textile traditions, especially quilting, as well as the use of white in African and African American funerary traditions. His sensitive use of the white cloth—the handling of its many strips laid one by one over the forearm—is a kind of religious performance, an offering to and a memorialization of the dead. Furthermore, Cave's work interprets death not as the end of life but rather as a portal to the next realm, which promises a release from the infinite threats and violence that attend Black lives in this world.

As part of this series of wall-relief works incorporating textiles and bronze, Cave also created a sculpture of his arm extending through a wreath of flowers, his hand holding up a black-bristled brush that resembles a head and face (fig. 10). In this work, Cave memorializes the many anonymous men and women affected by police violence. The brush's vague allusion to a Black face underscores this anonymity, and yet by again offering his own cast arms and hands as stand-ins Cave provides a visual representation of a body to mourn. He invokes a presence onto which the viewer might project specifics. This is an act of love, a gift, an offering to Black people. Author bell hooks said that loving Blackness is a political act of resistance that can "transform our ways of looking and being, and thus creates the conditions necessary for us to move against the forces of domination and death and reclaim black life."[7] In the wake

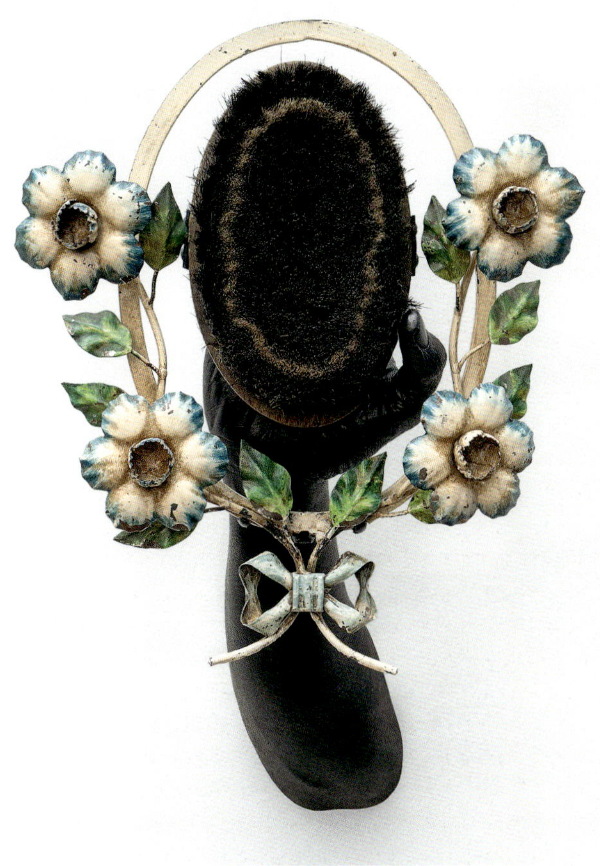

Fig. 10 **Nick Cave (American, born 1959).**
Untitled, 2023. Found hairbrush, cast bronze,
and found metal; 61 × 30.5 × 20.3 cm (24 × 12 ×
8 in.). Collection of the artist.

of such transformation, hooks argues, we are able to see beyond the specificity of Blackness and into the greater landscape of humanity to embrace all—particularly those who, like the Black community, are still struggling against the backdrop of oppression.

Speaking Their Names, Remembering Their Legacy

It is said that every man has two deaths: one when he is buried in the ground, the other the last time someone utters his name. Versions of this idea have been voiced in cultures around the world and throughout human history. Saying someone's name is an act against erasure, a guard against forgetting a person's imprint on the world, however large or small. In the Black Lives Matter movement, the phrase "say their names" has become a rallying cry protesting the senseless deaths.

Artist Carina Yepez resists a similar form of erasure by making quilts to preserve her Mexican American family's story in a country that consistently undervalues the contributions of immigrants. Yepez's quilts use images from the past to retain the identities, knowledge, language, and traditions of those no longer present on earth. Her work emanates from a deep repository of familial history, a migration story that begins in Guanajuato, Mexico, and unfolds in her native Chicago. Using digital technology, Yepez takes vintage photographs shared by familial and communal networks and reproduces them in vibrant, quilted form. In so doing, the artist aims to combat the loss of these histories and traditions, which can fade as older family members pass away and younger generations feel the pressure to assimilate in order to find success.

Yepez initially learned to sew from her grandmother, and mother. As they imparted these techniques, they also shared the stories and traditions that sustained them as they migrated from a small town in Mexico to the sprawling urban landscape of Chicago. Yepez was inspired by her

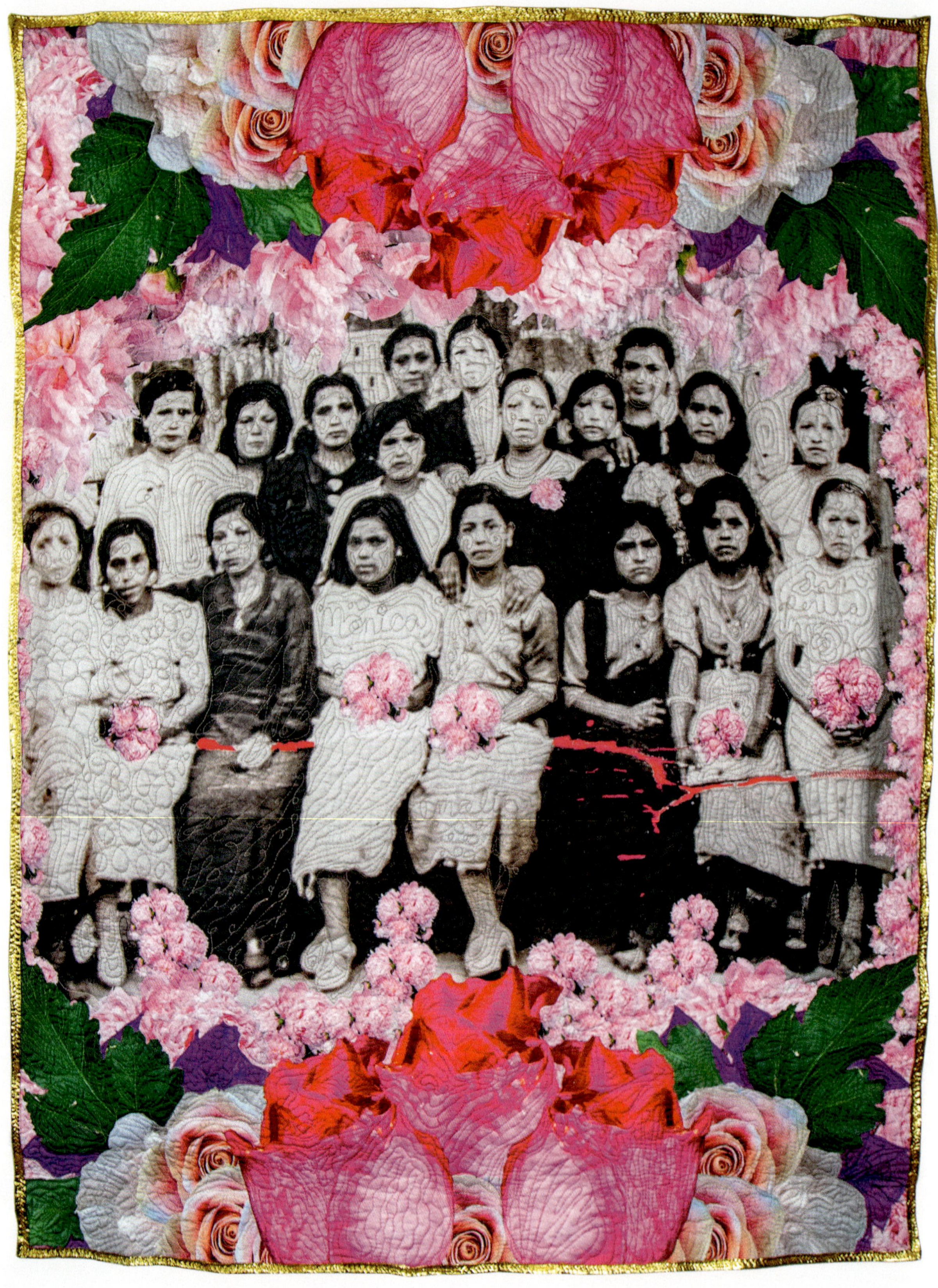

CASSEL OLIVER

grandmother's sewing group to create her own version of a safe space for women to sew and share. She began by engaging with women she encountered through her job in a fabric store and later in the cooperative Puntadas del Alma (Stitches of the Soul). Yepez participates in this circle of sisterhood, connected by sewing as a means of healing. Through the sharing of stitches and stories, these women are able to unburden themselves within a communal and even sacred space that offers a kind of resurrection from the shame and stigma that oppression and prejudice engender. Together, they celebrate their resilience, creating beauty using the traditions of their foremothers.

In her work *Mujeres* (*Women*) (fig. 11), Yepez re-created a photograph shared with her by her grandmother's friend Amalia. Made in Guanajuato, Mexico, it shows twenty women and young girls. Amalia sits in the center of the front row; Yepez's grandmother, then just a girl, is on the far right of the quilt at the right end of that same row. The women and girls were members of the informal crochet and embroidery group that inspired Yepez's own cooperative. By translating the image to a quilt, Yepez visually recited a moment from her grandmother's childhood, using techniques related to those that her grandmother learned and practiced through the group the photograph captures. Those people are now long gone, including Amalia, who was the last living person in the photo when she showed it to Yepez. For the artist, the work was an act of reclamation and a disavowal of erasure: The quilt imbues new life into the image, searing it into cloth and thereby preserving the stories of the other women pictured, just as they were preserved in Amalia's memory.

As retold to Yepez, Amalia's own story and those of the women in her family were tales of immeasurable joy and immense pain, as they navigated a society that weaponized their femininity and womanhood. In a world that often devalues women, racism and misogyny are a double-edged sword that often hampered their ability to achieve their ambitions. Thus, they often passed down their hopes and dreams to their children and grandchildren, generations with a better

chance of breaking away from constricting traditions. Inspired by family members, including her grandmother, Yepez created a quilt that honors the past while also looking forward to a future where women freely pursue their creativity and express their full being.

Before he departed this realm, Congressman John Lewis insisted that we—all of us Americans—are in a battle for the soul of the nation. Cave and Yepez offer us the stories of those who have too often borne the brunt of this battle. Their work insists, too, that we remember. They memorialize the dead not as victims but as people whose lives and deaths are testaments to the persistent need to fight and endure. We must find the determination not only to endure but to thrive. We must look to the stories embedded in the cloth whose fragments we hold close as pieces of our own humanity.

Notes

1   The picture was made by the congressman's friend Danny Lyon, the former SNCC photographer, on his iPhone. Lyon had come to film Lewis and say goodbye after a friendship of sixty years. In the interview, Lewis talks about his childhood on his father's farm in Troy, Alabama. Lyon's film *SNCC* is free to watch on Vimeo.

1   Jelani Cobb, *John Lewis: The Last Interview and Other Conversations* (Melville House, 2021), xiii.

2   "Rep. John Lewis Says Video of George Floyd's Death Moved Him to Tears: 'The Madness Must Stop,'" *CBS News*, June 4, 2020, cbsnews.com/news/george-floyd -video-death-john-lewis/.

3   Sylvia Wynter, "'No Humans Involved': An Open Letter to My Colleagues," *Forum N.H.I.:*

Knowledge for the 21st Century 1, no. 1 (1994): 42.

4   See, for example, Don Bambino Geno Tai, Irene G. Sia, Chyke A. Doubeni, and Mark L. Wieland, "Disproportionate Impact of COVID-19 on Racial and Ethnic Minority Groups in the United States: A 2021 Update," *Journal of Racial and Ethnic Health Disparities* 9, no. 6 (2021): 2334–39.

5   See Robert Farris Thompson, *Flash of the Spirit* (Vintage Books, 1984), 107–58.

6   On the Kalûnga Line, the watery divide between the earthly and spiritual realms, see Folayemi Wilson's essay in this volume.

7   bell hooks, *Salvation: Black People and Love* (HarperCollins, 2001), 66.

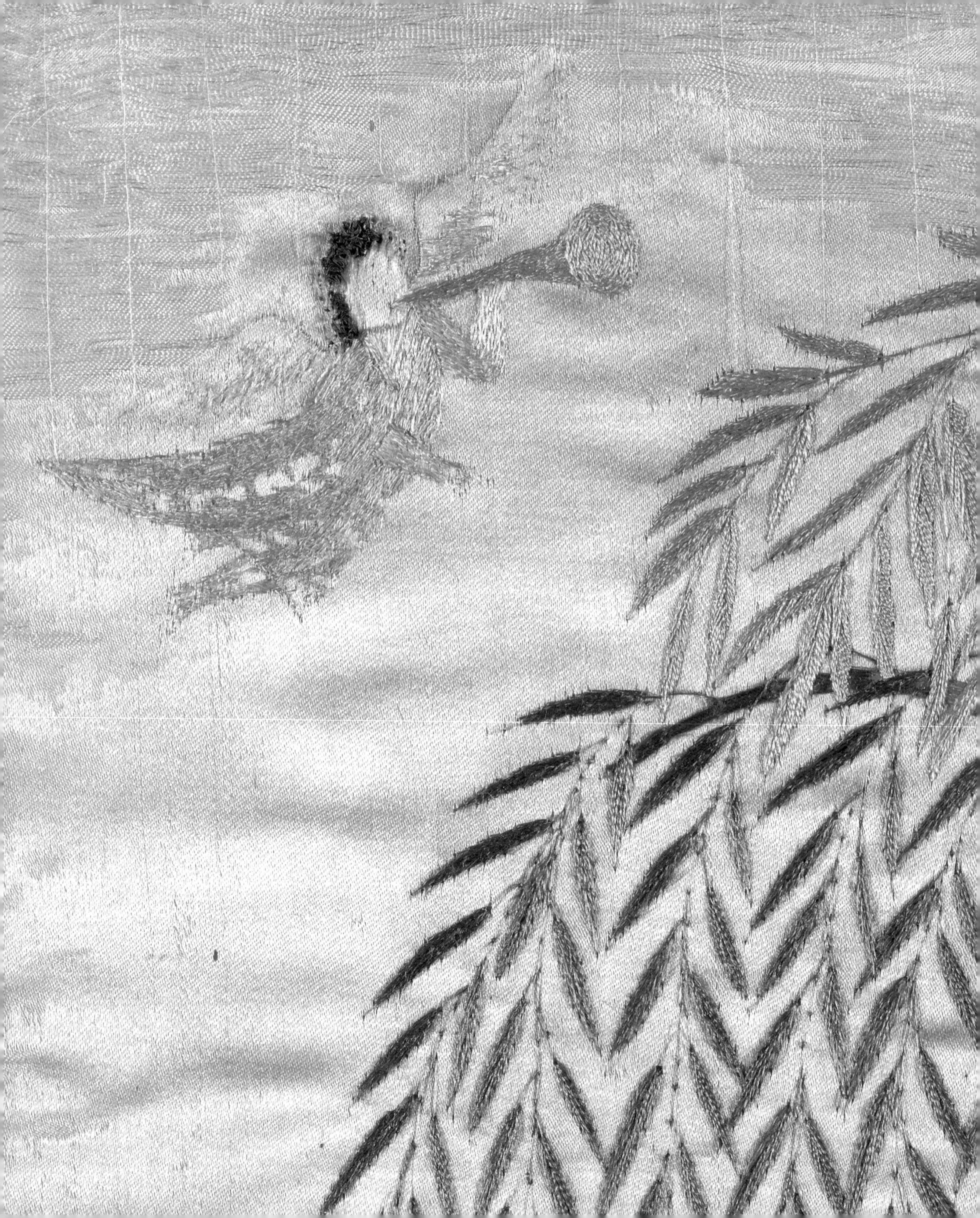

Grief and Disconsolate Forgetting

Objects of Mourning in the Context of Empire and Slavery

Jenni Sorkin

Art historian

Mourning jewelry is having a minor resurgence. Today, we can commemorate a loved one by transforming their body into a wearable object, such as a lab-grown diamond or ceramic stone made from cremated remains.[1] But this is an old art form, linked most closely to Victorian-era Britain and the monarch Queen Victoria, who became a marathon mourner after the death of her husband, Prince Albert, in 1861. The Victorians, too, incorporated elements of the human body into their mourning jewelry, most often a lock of hair from the deceased. The use of human hair in American and British objects of mourning in the nineteenth century offered the tantalizing possibility of transfiguring the body into a revered object that signaled permanence.

The London Gazette published official directives for mourning Prince Albert on December 16, 1861, two days after his death. Historian Helen Rappoport has noted that drapers, milliners, and tailors were "besieged" with orders for mourning outfits in black crepe, silk, and wool for upper- and middle-class people, while the lower classes wore simple black armbands. Among the Christmas gifts Victoria gave to women in her household that year were lockets with Albert's portrait. The queen went one step further for herself, sending locks of his hair to the best craftspeople in Berlin for them to turn into jewelry.[2]

Victoria's personal bereavement lasted forty years, until her own death in 1901. During that same time, she expanded and entrenched British imperial rule in Africa and India. For instance, she and Albert had influenced the 1858 Government of India Act, through which the Crown supplanted the East India Company's de facto government. Victoria began styling herself as the "Empress of India" in the 1860s, a title officially bestowed on her by Parliament in 1876, and she incorporated jewels looted from the continent into her crown.[3]

Simultaneously, Victoria popularized mourning garb—black veils, dark clothing, and hair jewelry, including bracelets, lockets, pendants, pins, pocket watches, and rings that preserved a single lock of the deceased's hair as a way

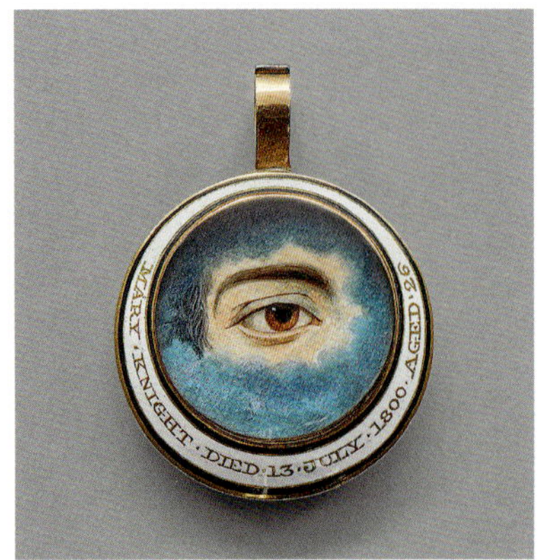

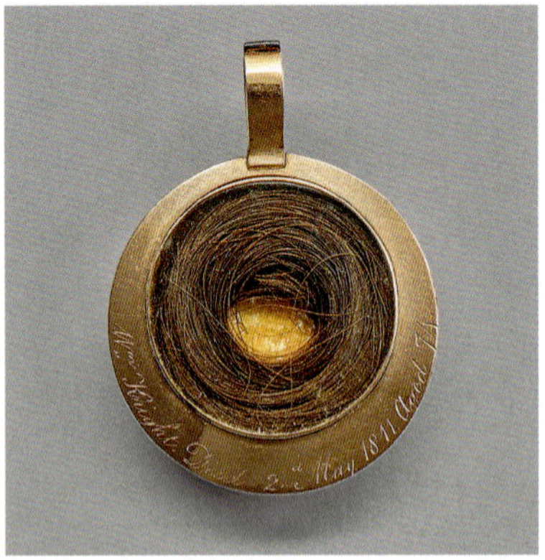

Fig. 1 Memorial Pendant, 1800. England. Gold, enamel, painted porcelain, glass, and hair; 4.3 × 3.2 × 0.7 cm (1 11/16 × 1 1/4 × 1/4 in.). The Art Institute of Chicago, bequest of Elizabeth H. Rosenak, RX15306/2. Top: The front of the pendant, with a painting of an eye in the sky, surrounded by an inscription: *MARY KNIGHT DIED 13 JULY 1800 AGED 26.* Bottom: The back of the pendant, with a coil of hair behind glass and an engraved inscription: *Wm. Knight. Died 2nd May 1811. Aged 74.*

Fig. 2 Memorial Pin, 1827. England. Gold, silver, diamonds, glass, and hair; 2.4 × 2 × 1 cm (15/16 × 3/4 × 3/8 in.). The Art Institute of Chicago, bequest of Elizabeth H. Rosenak, RX15306/33. Left: The front of the pin, with woven hair behind glass, surrounded by diamonds. Right: The back of the pin, with an engraved inscription: *Robert Muirheid / Natus 1st May / 1748 / obiit 25th Nov. / 1827.*

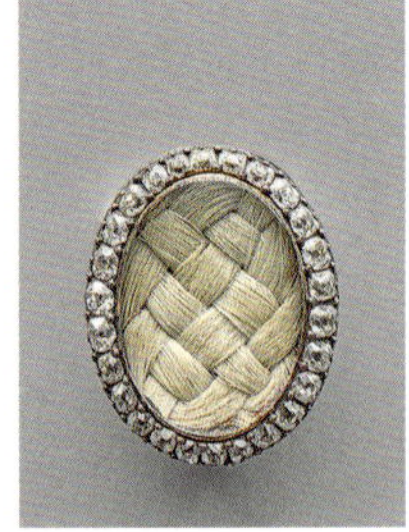

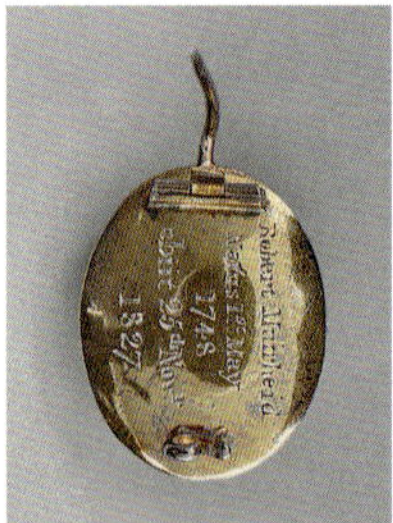

to hold them close in perpetuity. Also known as hairwork, these objects offered mourners a constant, immediate, and sensory experience of the departed. The lock of hair was often intricately braided, woven, or coiled and encased in glass, sometimes set behind a traditional mourning scene of angels, urns, or pious women rendered in enamel or carefully painted on ivory, perhaps surrounded by seed pearls or precious stones. Further into the nineteenth century, the significant labor of painted or enameled hair jewelry was, in part, supplanted by photographic portraiture. Commissioned as bespoke luxury objects by and for an elite white audience, hairwork became an important marker of propriety and public grief in the triangulation of fashion, empire, and the proximity of death, at a time when infant mortality was high, women died frequently in childbirth, and infectious disease was rampant, particularly in the British colonies with illnesses like malaria.

The scale of these sacred objects is both intimate and bodily. Encircling a finger, resting on a woman's décolletage, worn atop the beating heart, or pressed to a fluttering pulse, mourning jewelry functioned as a constant affirmation of connection. Worn against the body, hair jewelry was a vestige of skin-to-skin contact between the mourner and the beloved—or, put another way, a permanent perception of touch between the living and the dead. The hair itself inhabited a phantom space as a corporeal presence representing an otherwise absent body. Stemming from an older tradition of the Georgian period, which Victoria popularized and disseminated widely, hair jewelry can be seen as a more personalized form of the Catholic reliquary, with the relic serving individual, secular contemplation and display rather than communal, religious pilgrimage and prayer.

Hair jewelry often incorporated decorative representations of other body parts, as in a British memorial pendant from the Georgian period in the Art Institute of Chicago's collection (fig. 1), which includes a painting of a human eye. Inlaid against a background of blue enamel, it is as if the beloved's fixed gaze represents a watchful

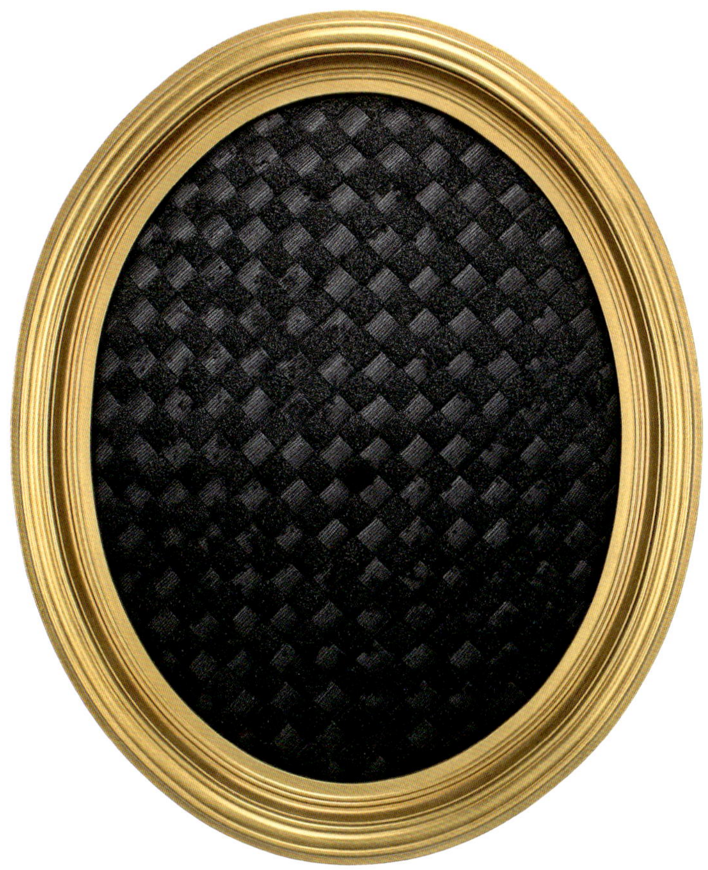

Fig. 3 Angela Hennessy (American, born 1971). *Mourning Weave*, 2014. Woven Velcro, velvet fuzz, and frame; 61 × 50.8 cm (24 × 20 in.). Courtesy of pt.2 Gallery, Oakland, California.

apparition in a heavenly sky, who remains the mourner's constant guardian even in death. An inscription below this image reads MARY KNIGHT DIED *13 JULY 1800 AGED 26*. The other side of the pendant contains a coil of hair, with another name engraved below it: William (abbreviated as *Wm.*) Knight, along with the inscription *Died 2nd May 1811. Aged 74*. It is unclear if the relationship between the Knights was filial, perhaps father and daughter, or if William was Mary's widower, albeit with a significant age gap.

The hair in the aforementioned pendant is coiled like a tiny wreath, but hair is presented in many different ways in mourning jewelry: coiled, braided, or sometimes woven in a plain-weave pattern, with strands tucked under and over each other, as with the bright-white hair interlaced and set behind an ovular piece of glass in a memorial brooch at the Art Institute (fig. 2). Surrounded by diamonds, the hair belonged to Robert Muirheid, whose birth and death dates are engraved in Latin on the back of the badge: *Natus 1st May / 1748 / obiit 25th Nov. / 1827*. White wigs, made of horse or goat hair and powdered with flour and tallow, were one of the primary markers of status for European men of the late eighteenth century.[4] Given Muirheid's age, it is possible that the hair contained in the brooch was not his own; his being commemorated in such a fashion suggests that he was a man of means.

While hair has light-reflective properties, its preparation under glass alters the way light refracts. Woven or braided hair maximizes surface area, offering more abundant sheen, while knotted hair absorbs light. Like silk, hair is a protein-based fiber, but it is far less smooth, as it has microscopic scales that give it a distinctly woolly appearance when viewed under magnification. Discussions of hair texture invoke the complexities of race. Artist Angela Hennessy's *Mourning Weave* (fig. 3) embraces these tensions in two ways, remaking a traditional hair-jewelry brooch using woven Velcro and velvet fuzz to represent jet-black hair at outsized proportions in a two-foot-tall gold frame. Hennessy utilizes the term *weave* as a double entendre, referring simultaneously to the object's construction and to the common hairstyle in which hair extensions are sewn to braided natural hair. She enlarged the miniature size of mourning jewelry, inviting its consideration as sculpture, while also offering a pointed critique of the medium's historic whiteness through her chosen materials, intended to approximate the texture of Black hair.

Rarer than its use in mourning jewelry is the incorporation of hair in mourning samplers, including one in the Art Institute's collection (fig. 4). The creators of this example, made around 1810 in Providence, Rhode Island, used human hair to represent the hair of the angels in each corner. Such samplers offer a window into the world of girlhood in the colonial and early national periods in America, in which needlework was a mandatory part of female education. The need for teachers of needlework also opened doors for enterprising single women to establish private schools for girls in their homes, as indicated by the Boston sampler made by members of the Smith and Humphrey families under the tutelage of an instructor at "Miss Field's School" (fig. 5).[5] Historian Kate Silbert argues that samplers were not merely aesthetic exercises but rather functioned as a form of social mobility, tastemaking, and authorship, offering young white women a sense of belonging and status.[6] Needlework is also inextricable from literacy, not only as a pedagogical tool for writing instruction but also as a form of writing; indeed, Silbert regards samplers themselves as literary sources and historical records. They were also often used for religious instruction, giving girls an opportunity to memorize the Lord's Prayer or the Ten Commandments as they stitched them. Mourning samplers were distinct in their sentimental and symbolic tropes, such as angels, urns, and weeping willow trees.

Samplers also reveal economic concerns. Care was often taken to conserve silk floss, for instance, wasting as little as possible on the back of the piece. According to conservator Lucinda Pelton, that was not the case for the Art Institute's Providence sampler. As she writes, "there are

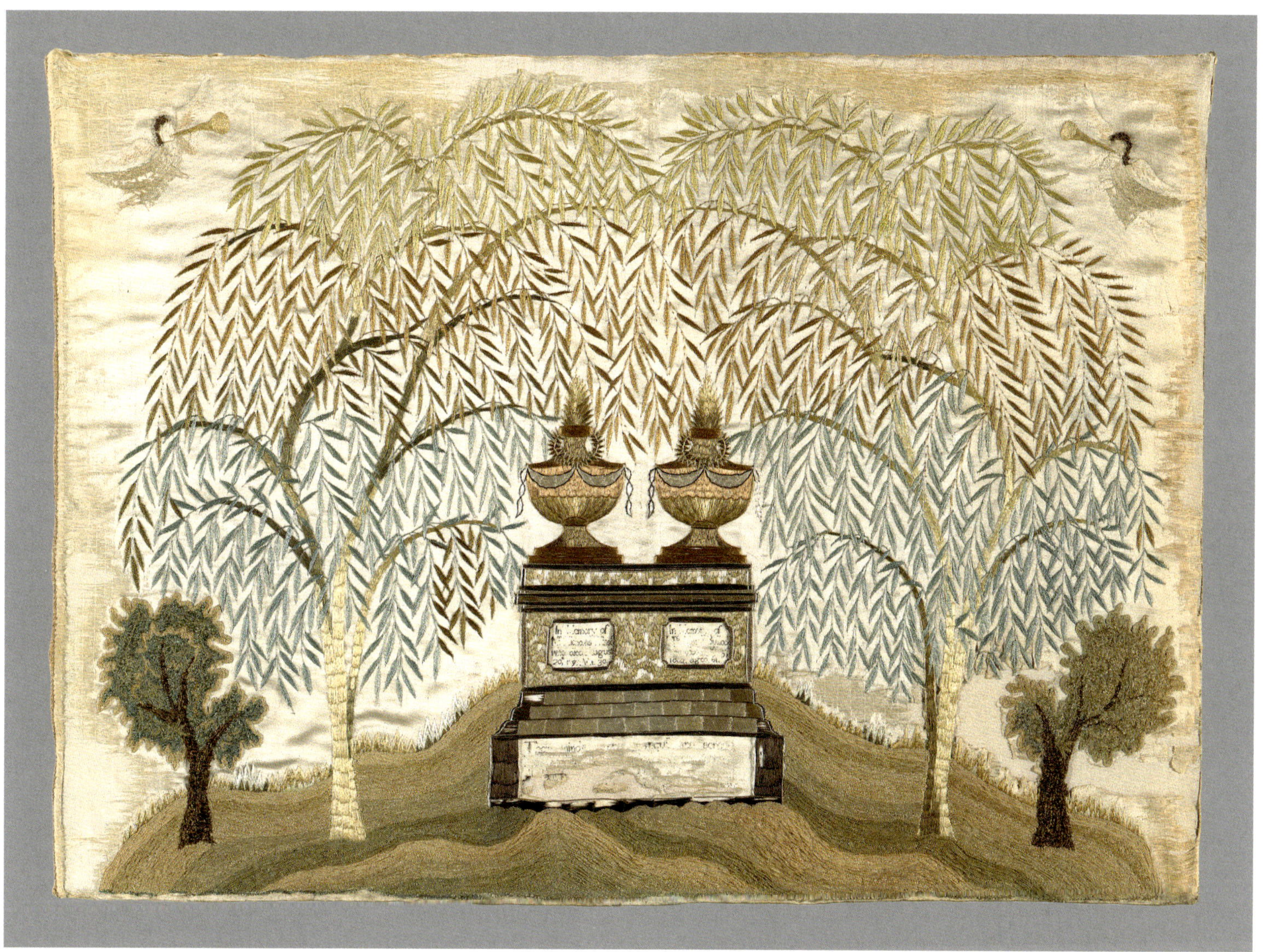

Fig. 4 **Mourning Sampler**, about 1810. Mary Blach's School, Providence. Silk, warp-float faced 4:1 satin weave, embroidered with silk, silk chenille, and human hair in split, surface satin, and stem stitches; couching; 42.2 × 58.8 cm (16½ × 23⅛ in.). The Art Institute of Chicago, Department of Textiles Collection, 1971.146.

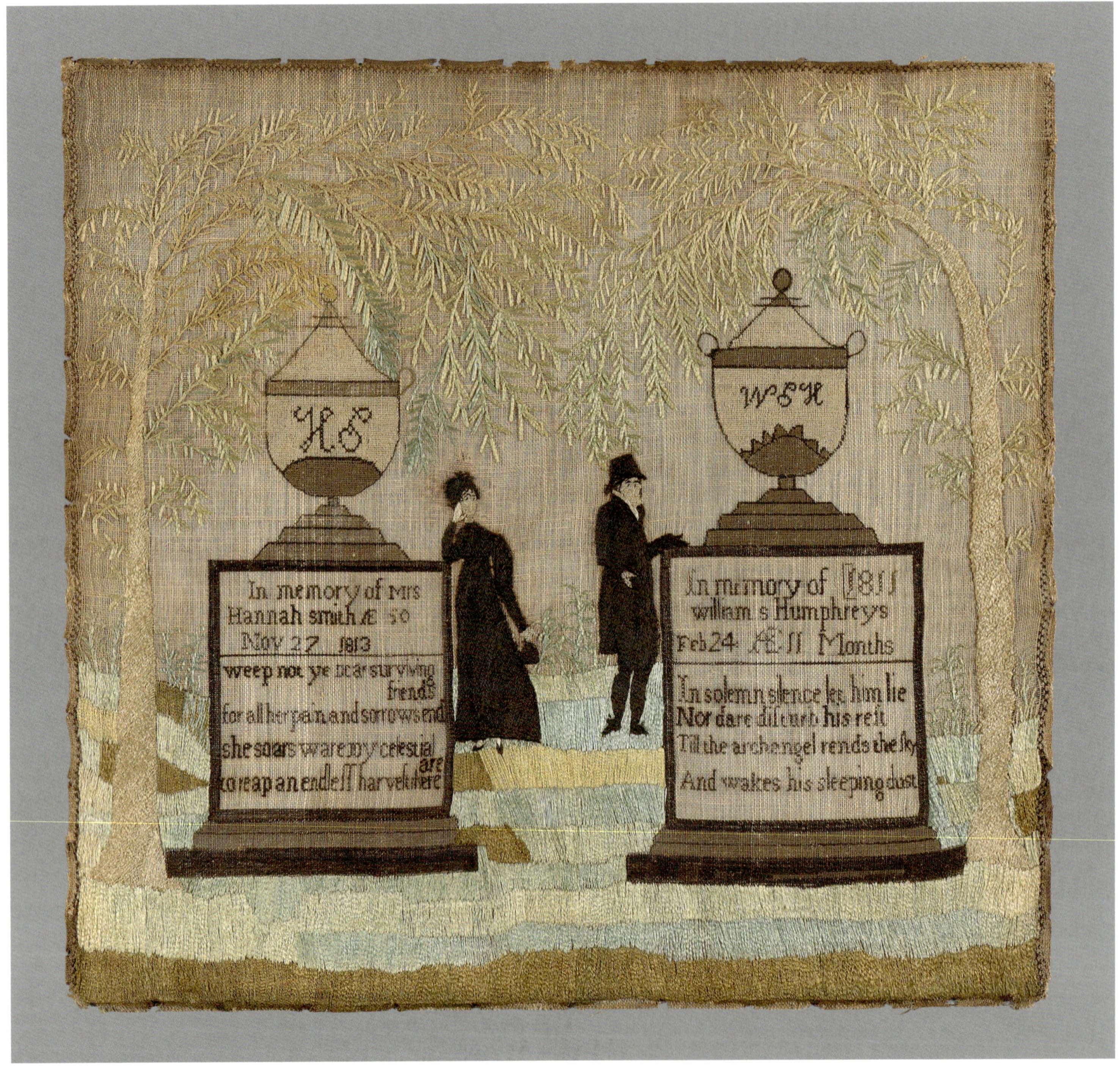

Fig. 5 Mourning Sampler, about 1815. Made by members of the Smith and Humphreys families at Miss Field's School, Boston. Linen, plain weave; embroidered with silk floss in tent, cross, long and a mixture of stem, whip, and couching stitches; 50.2 × 53.7 cm (19¾ × 21⅛ in.). The Art Institute of Chicago, Barbara Notz Hines Memorial Fund and Elizabeth M. Schultz Endowment, 2008.134.

many long floats to carry the silk floss to the next needle
hole [on the back], instead of making knots and trimming the
floss to save precious inches of silk."[7] That this liberal use
of silk might indicate a relatively wealthy maker invites us
to consider their economic environment. Rhode Island was
the New England colony most implicated in the transatlantic
slave trade. According to Brown University's *Slavery and
Justice Report*, over the course of the eighteenth century
"Rhode Islanders had mounted at least a thousand voyages,
carrying over one-hundred thousand Africans into New
World slavery."[8] Providence was a wealthy port city fully
entrenched in this economy of human misery, which may
have afforded, directly or indirectly, such liberal use of silk
and the leisure and education to embroider it so beautifully.
Such luxuries were not possible for the enslaved people of
Providence, the vast majority of whom remain unnamed,
while the white people who stole their lives and labor commemorated their own names and lineages in samplers. This
inquiry into the milieu from which samplers emerge suggests how we might approach them as historical objects and
works of art. The mourning samplers discussed observe the
deaths of specific, named white deceased; by recontextual-
izing them within larger histories of American slavery, might
we make space for shared grieving?

Recovering the art of mourning is speculative work at
best: Aside from the names and dates stitched or engraved
on objects, information about either the honored dead or
the living maker or wearer is often scarce. Any hair included
in mourning jewelry or samplers is only a partial reclamation, a preserved fragment of the body, obscured by fogged
glass or buried in the corners of a sampler. Hairwork is an
art form in which the material and its narrative presence are
equally fragmented—simultaneously fraught and compassionate symbols of the past, with the certainty of death as
the primary bond between the wearer and their beloved.

Notes

1   See Abigail R. Esman, "Mourning Jewelry Leaves the Victorian Era Behind," *New York Times*, May 26, 2023, nytimes.com/2023/05/26/fashion/jewelry-mourning.html.

2   See Miles Taylor, "Queen Victoria and India, 1837–61," *Victorian Studies* 46, no. 2 (2004): 264–74.

3   See Helen Rappaport, *A Magnificent Obsession: Victoria, Albert, and the Death that Changed the Monarchy* (St. Martin's Press, 2012), 123.

4   See "The Rise and Fall of the Powdered Wig," American Battlefield Trust, May 26, 2020, battlefields.org/learn/head-tilting-history/rise-and-fall-powdered-wig.

5   Recently, Kelli Racine Coles has worked to identify samplers made by Black schoolgirls in Philadelphia. See Kelli Racine Coles, "Schoolgirl Embroideries and Black Girlhood in Antebellum Philadelphia," in *Hidden Stories/Human Lives: Proceedings of the Textile Society of America 17th Biennial Symposium, October 15–17, 2020*, doi.org/10.32873/unl.dc.tsasp.0086.

6   Kate Silbert, "Needle, Pen, and the Social Geography of Taste in Early National Providence," *New England Quarterly* 92, no. 2 (2019): 219.

7   Lucinda Pelton, email message to author, July 8, 2024.

8   See "Slavery, the Slave Trade, and Brown University," in *Brown University's Slavery and Justice Report*, 2nd ed., ed. Anthony Bougues, Cass Cliatt, and Allison Levy (Brown University, 2021), 19–64.

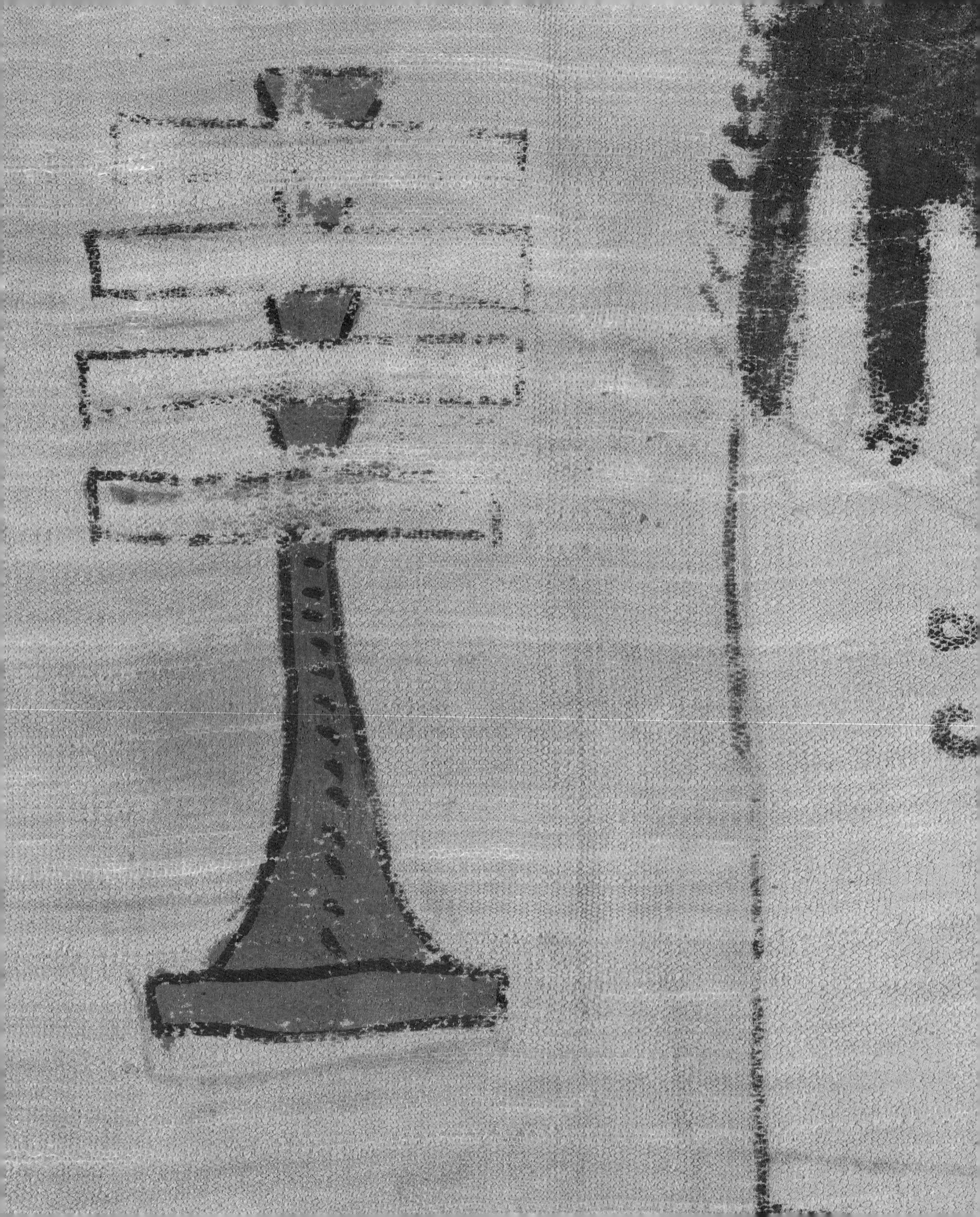

Silent Witness

Ancient Textiles as Biocultural Archives of Disease and Human History

Gustavo Da Silva
Biomedical scientist

Isaac Facio
Conservator

Cristian Koepfli
Microbiologist

Lucinda Pelton
Conservator

An Egyptian child's tunic in the Art Institute of Chicago's collection (fig. 1) is more than one thousand years old, yet it still bears traces of its wearer (or wearers) in every crease and fold—much more than is visible to the naked eye. Such textiles are more than relics; they are time capsules, preserving not just patterns and dyes but the very molecules of past lives. By analyzing ancient DNA (aDNA)—DNA from specimens that died decades, hundreds, or even thousands of years ago—scientists can decode stories of disease that shaped civilizations.[1] Textiles may be particularly rich sources of aDNA.

Textiles embody the technological advancements, artistic expressions, and daily lives of the societies that created them. Textiles have served countless purposes throughout human history: clothing and wrapping bodies in life and death; providing shelter, comfort, and decoration in homes and other spaces; and serving as markers of affiliation and status that transmit and uphold cultural structures and values. Beyond these practical uses, textiles have also held deep symbolic significance, playing integral roles in ceremonies, rituals, and other expressions of celebration and mourning throughout our lives and even through our deaths and afterlives. In ancient societies textiles often transcended their materiality to become vehicles of memory and cultural transmission, and burial practices provide a particularly rich example of this phenomenon. Textiles used in these contexts, whether as shrouds, wrappings, or funerary offerings, carried meanings beyond their visible patterns or textures. Their wearers or users imbued them with personal, familial, and societal significance; they often communicate the identity of the deceased as well as cultural beliefs about the afterlife. Such textiles are some of the most evocative remnants of the past, their fragile fibers bearing silent witness to lives—and deaths—of long ago.

Every moment of these experiences and events is embedded in textiles, including—quite literally—the blood, sweat, and tears of the people whose bodies they touched (see fig. 2). While their physical features—colors, patterns,

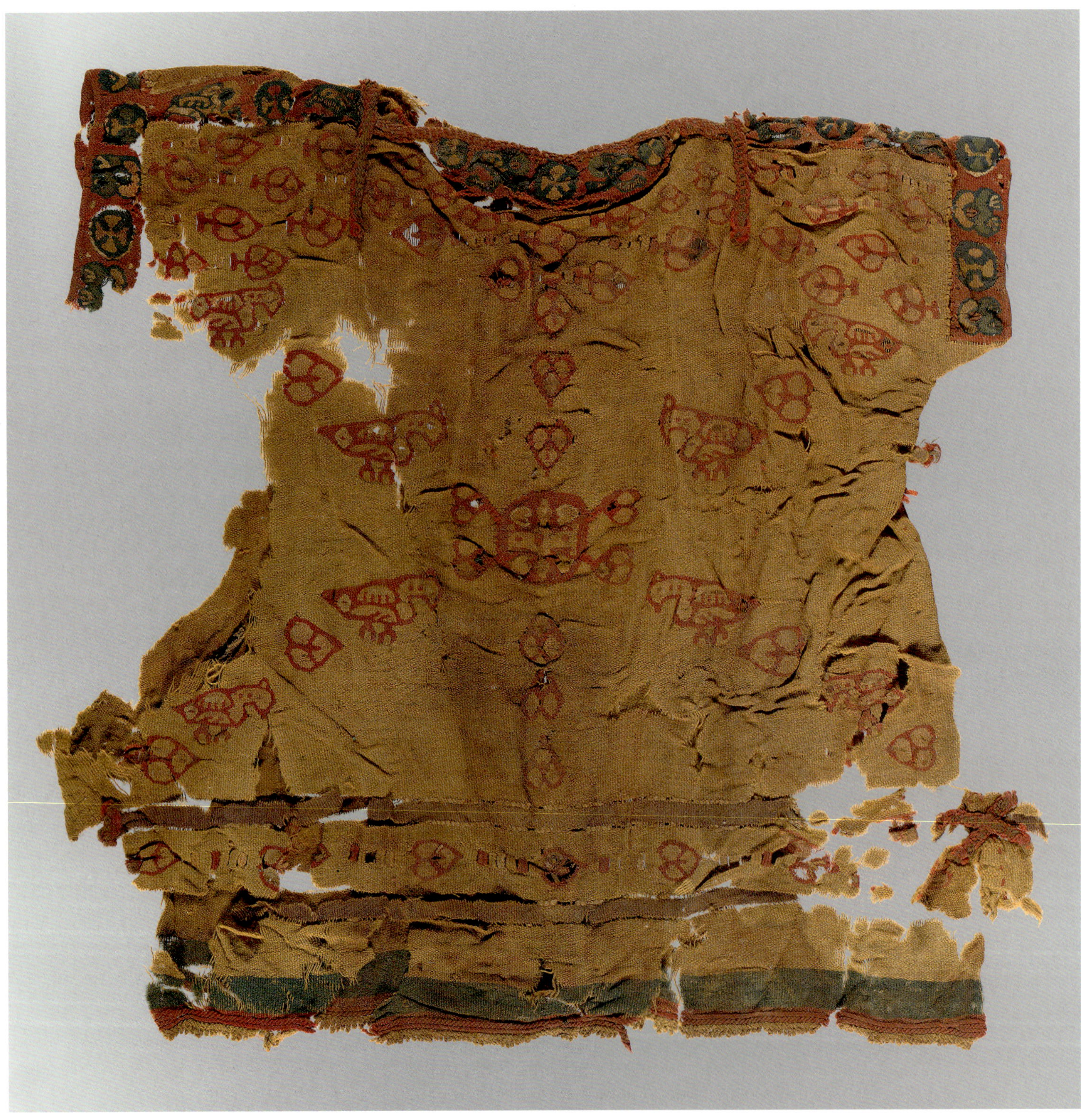

Fig. 1 Child's Tunic, 6th–8th century. Egypt. Wool and linen; slit tapestry weave; edged with braided binding and plied warp fringe; embellished with woven cord; 48.3 × 47 cm (19 × 18 ½ in.). The Art Institute of Chicago, gift of Martin A. Ryerson to the Antiquarian Society, 1914.713.

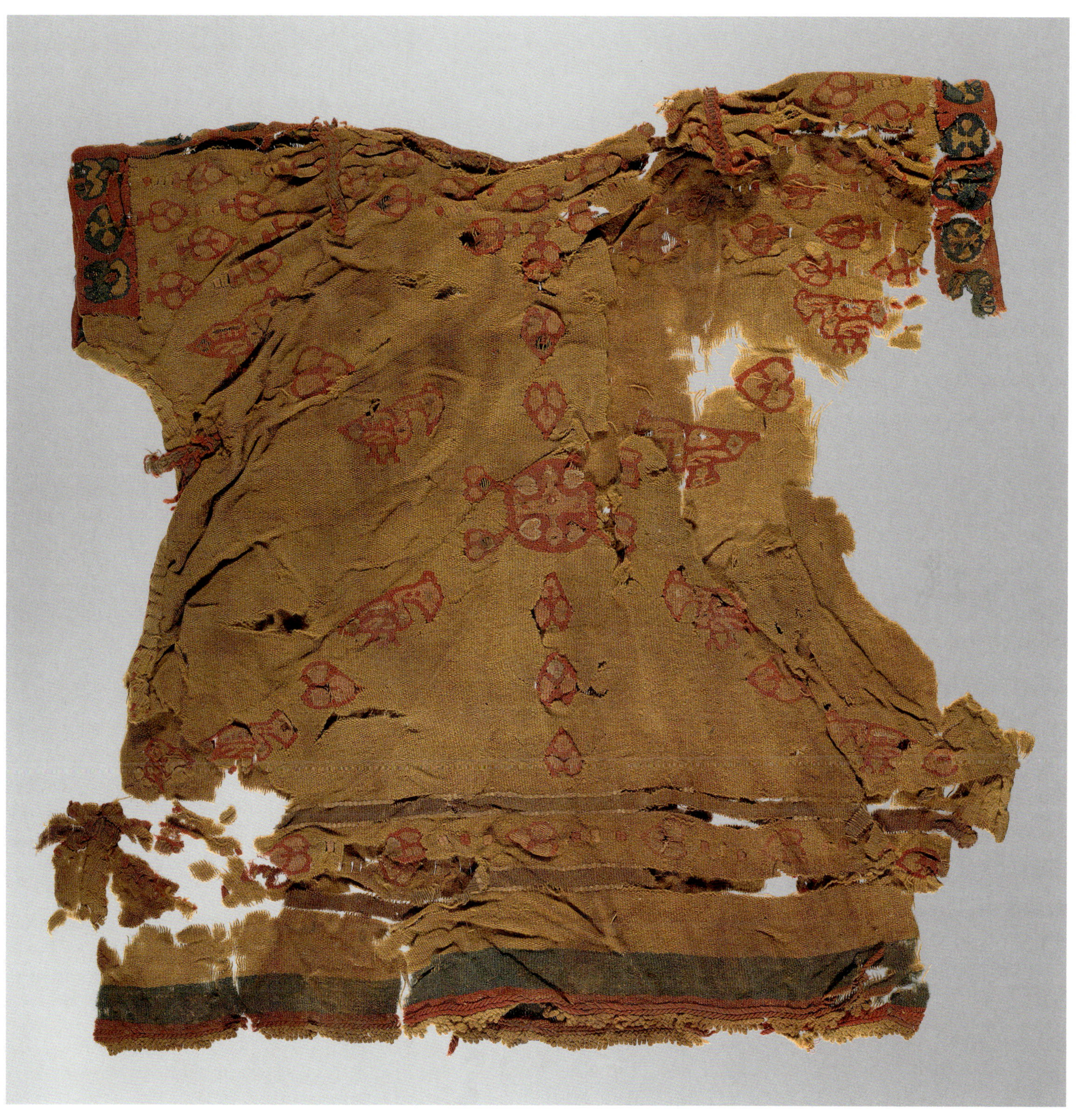

and textures—tell part of their story, textiles also preserve microscopic evidence of their histories. Fibers act as repositories for molecular and biological data, absorbing residues from the people and environments they encounter. Sweat, skin cells, blood, and even microbial communities can become embedded in the fabric, creating an archive of the interactions between textiles, humans, and their surroundings—what researchers term "biocultural archives," combining material and biological histories.[2]

The exhibition *On Loss and Absence: Textiles of Mourning and Survival* presented a unique opportunity to consider how conservation techniques for investigating evidence left behind on textiles might apply to the extraction of aDNA. The Art Institute's textile holdings include ancient Egyptian and pre-Hispanic Andean artworks dating as far back as the first millennium BCE. These objects demonstrate creasing, decay, fragmentation, and staining that visualize their past lives, including the bodies that once made contact with them. Among these are textiles from ancient Egyptian burial contexts—shrouds, tunics, and fragments—dating to the first millennium CE.[3] These artifacts, preserved for thousands of years in the arid climate of Egyptian burials, offer remarkable insights into the practices and values of the people who made and used them.

This essay details a pathbreaking study by researchers from the Koepfli Lab at the University of Notre Dame in Indiana, which sought to extract and analyze aDNA from textiles and other objects in the Art Institute's collection.[4] The project aimed to demonstrate potential for textiles and their associated conservation techniques to connect the cultural and scientific threads of history. This interdisciplinary effort merges archaeology, conservation, and molecular biology to offer new perspectives on textiles as biocultural archives.

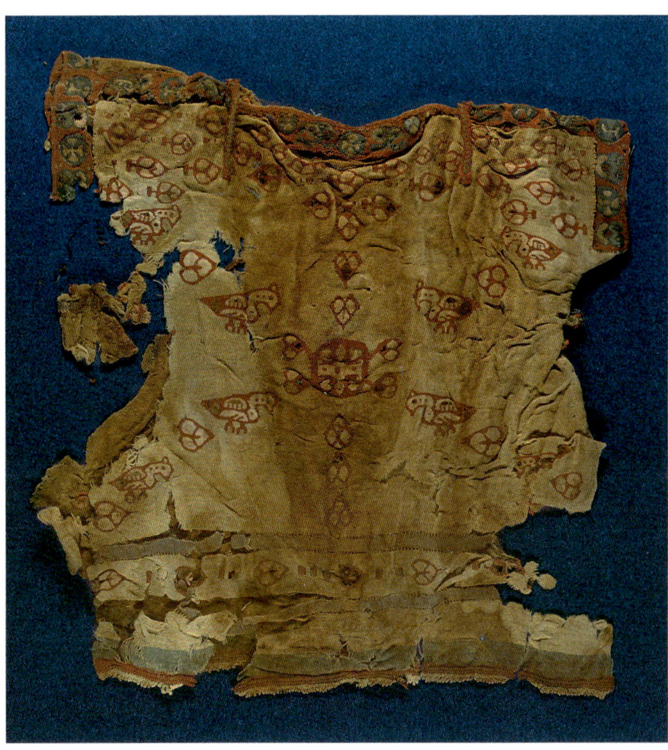

Fig. 2 **This image of the child's tunic (fig. 1) under UV light highlights staining and decay.**

The Fragility and Resilience of Ancient Textiles: Environmental Survival and Decay

Textiles are among the most fragile materials in the archaeological record, yet they are also among the most revealing. Their organic composition, typically derived from plant fibers like linen and cotton or animal fibers like wool and silk, makes them highly susceptible to decay. Microorganisms such as bacteria and fungi, environmental factors like moisture and fluctuating temperatures, and exposure to ultraviolet light can all degrade textiles over time. Without careful preservation or unique burial environments, many ancient textiles deteriorate beyond recognition, leaving behind only faint traces of their original form. Consider your own clothing and the kind of wear it sustains as your body moves around in it over time: the buildup of stains around a collar, heavy abrasion between pant legs, residues and discoloration from chemical deodorants and perfumes, and so on. These changes are like a record of your activities, captured in the fabric.[5]

The process of decay begins as soon as a textile is created, with environmental exposure gradually breaking down its structural integrity. For example, plant-based fibers like linen, a staple of ancient Egyptian textiles, are composed of cellulose, which is vulnerable to hydrolysis and oxidation—chemical degradation by the action of water or oxygen, respectively. Microorganisms thrive in humid or wet conditions, using enzymes to degrade cellulose and consume the fibers. Similarly, animal-based fibers like wool and silk, which are composed of protein, are prone to hydrolysis and microbial activity. These vulnerabilities mean that textiles rarely survive in environments that lack stable, dry conditions.[6]

Egypt's arid desert climate, however, provides an advantage when it comes to the preservation of ancient textiles. Tombs and burial chambers, often sealed from external elements, create microenvironments that slow down microbial activity and protect textiles from light and moisture; in Egypt, this can be true even for textiles buried directly in the ground, as was the case for the objects in this study. Many Egyptian burial textiles (see fig. 3) have survived for millennia, providing modern researchers with a window into ancient life. These textiles are not only remnants of material culture but also records of the environments in which they were used and stored.[7]

Textiles' fragility makes their conservation a delicate and complex task. At institutions like the Art Institute, conservators use noninvasive techniques to stabilize textiles and prevent further deterioration. Storage environments are carefully controlled, with temperature and humidity maintained at levels that inhibit microbial growth and minimize physical stress on fibers. Conservators use acid-free materials to store and mount textiles, ensuring that harmful chemicals do not accelerate degradation. They also keep handling to a minimum, wearing gloves and taking other precautions to prevent oils and residues on their bodies from transferring to the objects.[8]

This research on aDNA was designed to be minimally invasive, ensuring that the structural and visual integrity of the textiles remained intact. The sampling methods, including swabbing and the application of agarose gels, were novel in DNA recovery but typical in textile conservation treatments such as cleaning.[9] The balance between preservation and scientific investigation reflects the interdisciplinary nature of this research, merging conservation protocols with molecular biology. By navigating the challenges of the objects' fragility and cultural value, this study underscores the importance and resilience of these artifacts as carriers of history: Their preservation is not merely a matter of maintaining aesthetic and physical form but also of safeguarding the stories and knowledge embedded within their fibers. These efforts ensure that textiles can continue to inform and inspire future generations of researchers, scholars, and museum visitors.

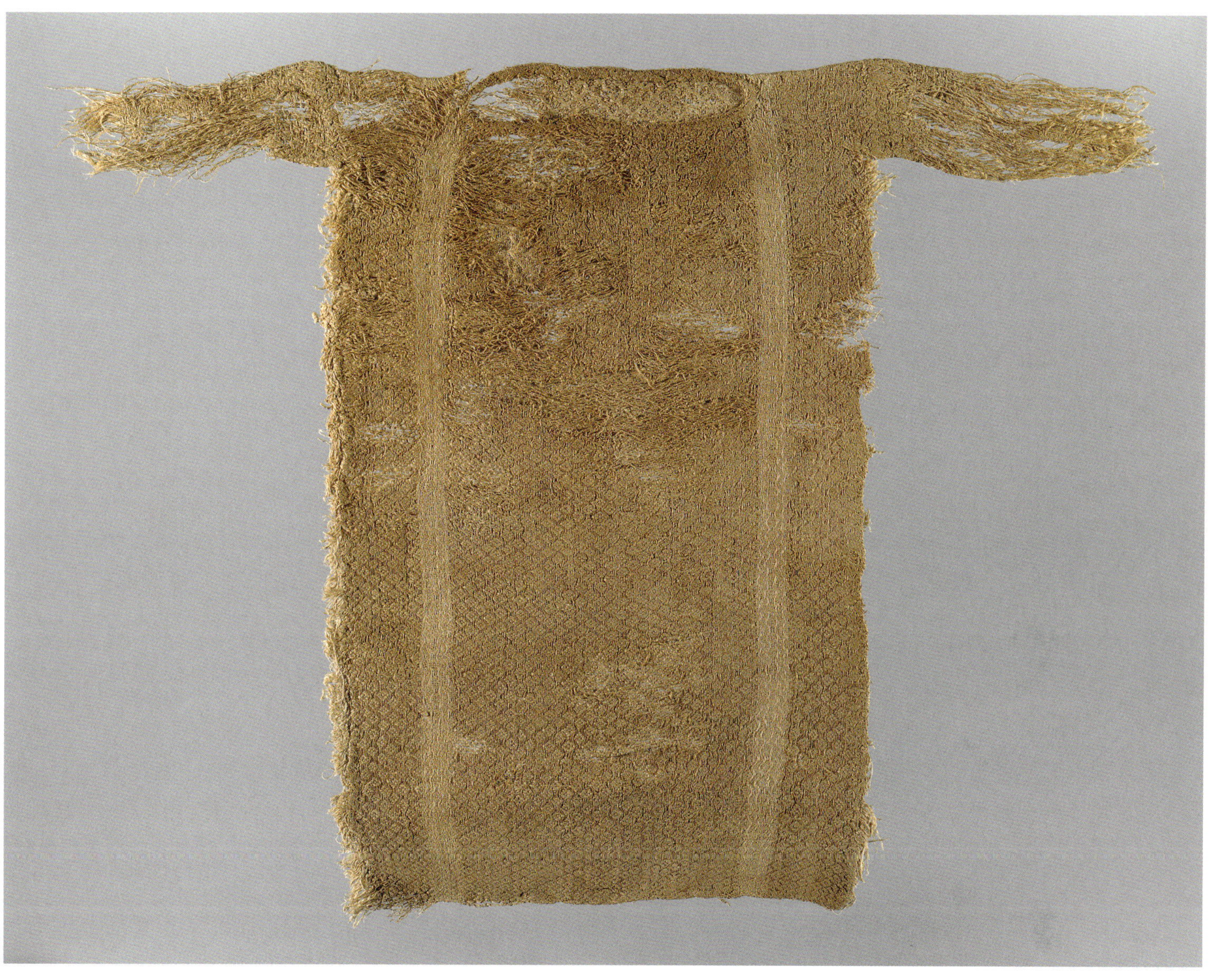

Fig. 3 Child's Tunic, 6th–8th century. Egypt.
Linen, diamond twill weave; 52.8 × 71.8 cm
(20 ¾ × 28 ¼ in.). The Art Institute of Chicago,
gift of Martin A. Ryerson to the Antiquarian
Society, 1914.714.

Curating the Past: Artifact Selection

The textiles analyzed in this study were initially considered for their connection to the exhibition's themes; all are objects from burial and funerary contexts, found at archaeological sites, made of natural fibers, that maintain residues from their original burials. To the best of our knowlege, all have been used—that is, they served the purpose for which they were made, bringing them into contact with human remains. Based on Art Institute object records, they have all had minimal conservation intervention since they have been in the Art Institute's care; the selected objects retain their creasing and staining, thus increasing the possibility that they have also retained genetic material from their original use and environment, in addition to any DNA that they may have accumulated post-excavation.

The objects in the study include: burial shrouds used to wrap the deceased, which are often well preserved in sealed burial environments; children's tunics, smaller garments selected for their direct association with individuals; and additional textiles and burial objects, namely a yoke tunic (fig. 4) and canopic jars, chosen to complement the analysis and broaden the scope of potential biological insights. These artifacts—a total of eleven ancient Egyptian and Andean objects, with the six Egyptian objects having undergone analysis at the time of this publication—represent a variety of burial contexts and preservation conditions, two environmentally distinct parts of the world, and a range of materials including cotton, linen, and wool fibers and bird feathers.[10]

Innovations in DNA Recovery: Swabbing and Agarose Gel Applications

To safeguard these fragile artifacts, we employed gentle methods that combine scientific precision with conservation ethics. Two noninvasive techniques—swabbing and agarose gel applications—extracted DNA while preserving the textiles' integrity.

Swabbing techniques are a regular part of the delicate work of archivists, with moistened rayon swabs gliding over visible stains or discolored areas (see fig. 5).[11] These zones, akin to biological hotspots, may be signs of human interaction. Once collected, swabs were sealed in sterile containers, protecting their genetic cargo for lab analysis.

For broader spans of coverage, we turned to a surprising ally: agarose gels, which, as noted above, are regularly used in textile conservation but have not been used for aDNA collection. Conservators applied thin films of agarose gel to textiles; as the gels dry, they act like molecular sponges, absorbing invisible residues—skin cells, microbes, and even pathogens—all while leaving the textiles undisturbed.[12] Remarkably, this method outperformed swabbing, yielding more abundant DNA from artifacts, including in areas that showed no visible staining or residues. The gels became silent collaborators, extracting hidden histories without compromising a single thread. The noninvasive sampling techniques employed—particularly the use of agarose gels—represent a significant innovation in aDNA research. Agarose gels allowed us to extract DNA without introducing physical stress to the textiles, making them an ideal method for fragile artifacts.[13]

From Fabric to Lab: Challenges and Innovations in Processing Ancient DNA

Samples were next processed in the laboratory to extract, purify, sequence, and analyze DNA, ensuring that the resulting data were reliable and representative of historical material.[14] One of the challenges in the study was the variability in DNA preservation across the objects. While some textiles yielded sufficient DNA for sequencing, others produced only trace amounts. These differences likely reflect variations in burial or subsequent storage environments,

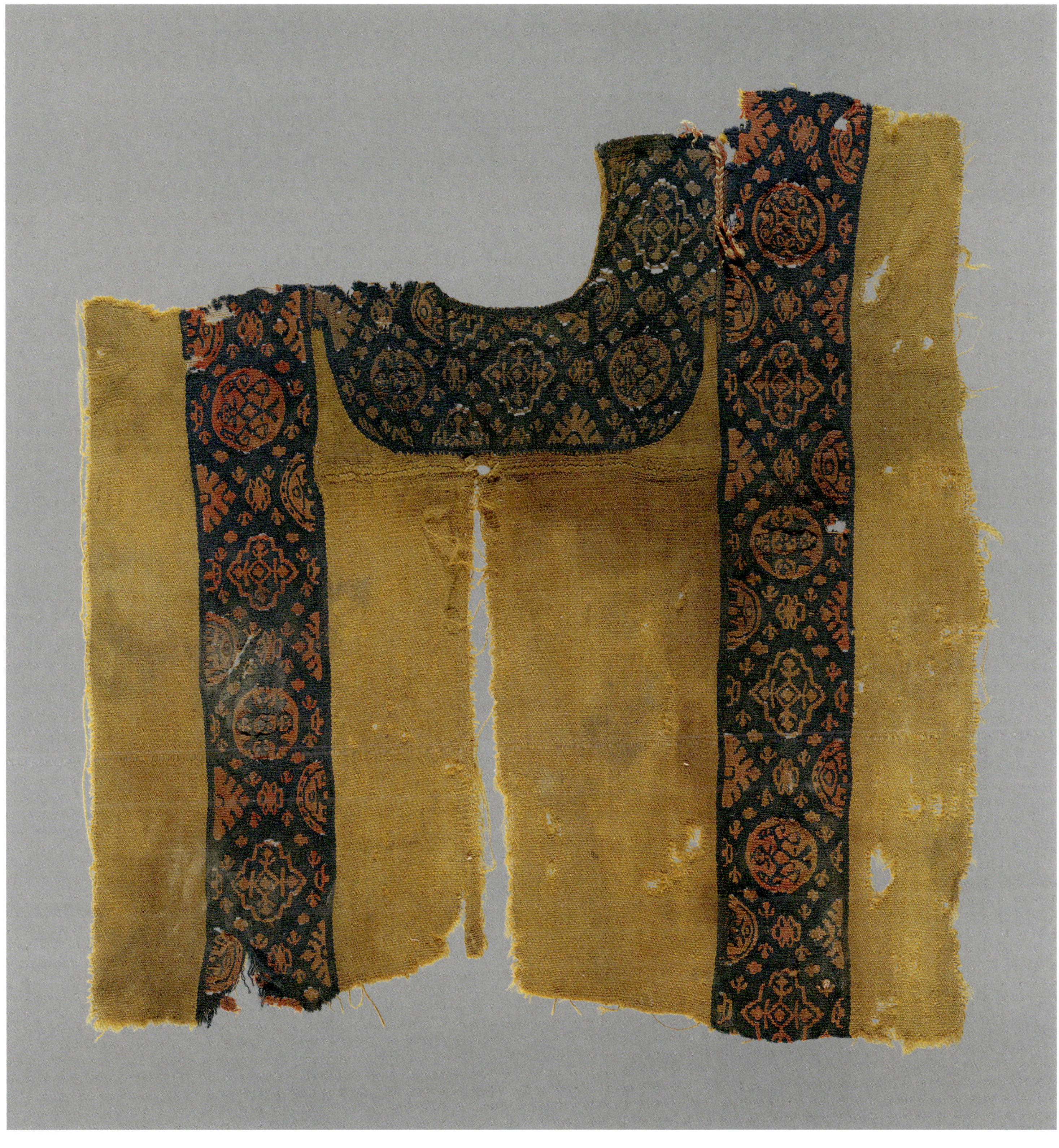

Fig. 4 Tunic Fragment, 6th–8th century. Egypt. Wool, plain weave with bands of slit tapestry weave; linen braided cord; 44.2 × 43.2 cm (17⅜ × 17 in.). The Art Institute of Chicago, gift of Martin A. Ryerson through the Antiquarian Society, 1914.701a.

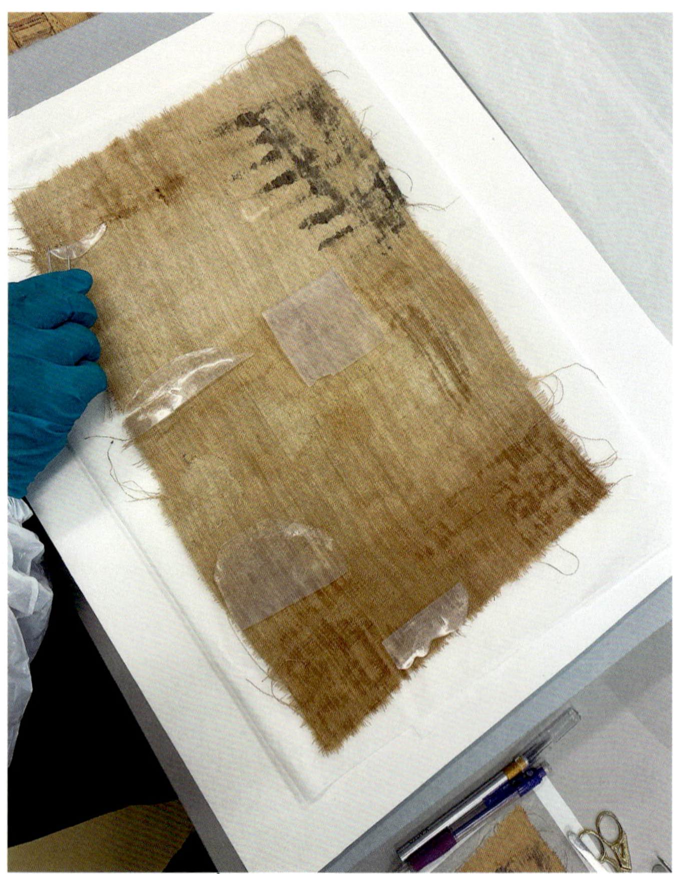

Fig. 5 **Conservator Lucinda Pelton cutting and applying gels to the surface of the fragment of a funerary shroud (fig. 6).**

Fig. 6 **Fragment of a Funerary Shroud, 2nd–3rd century. Egypt. Linen, plain weave; painted; 46 × 29 cm (11 × 18 in.). The Art Institute of Chicago, gift of Mrs. Edward C. Sonnenschein, 1946.184.**

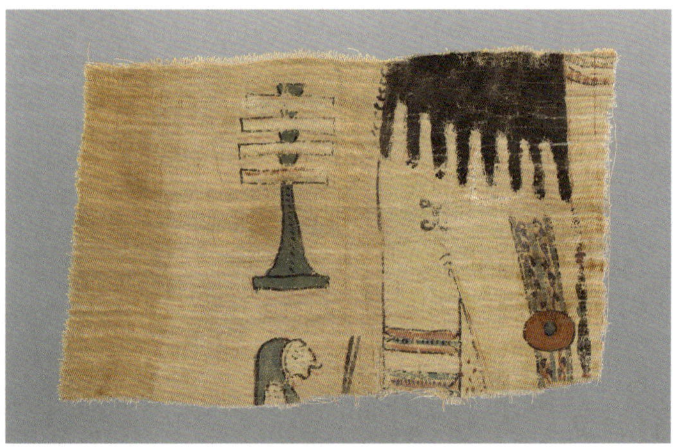

handling histories (including undocumented cleaning treatment), residues from human interaction, and the molecular composition of the fibers themselves.

Contamination is a significant challenge in aDNA research, especially for objects in museums, which often have long histories of excavation, handling, and storage. Textiles are particularly vulnerable to contamination due to their porous and absorbent nature, which allows them to capture residues such as dust, moisture, and DNA from their surroundings. Conservators often think of textiles as sponges and filters. They are highly absorbent, and they can act like a sieve filtering out ambient material like dust and moisture. These same qualities make textiles compelling records: They are relatively easily altered by contact with other materials. Textiles absorb material from excavation sites, where soil microorganisms interact with fibers, and from museums, where human contact can introduce recent DNA.

To minimize these risks during the sampling process, stringent precautions were implemented throughout the study. Personal protective equipment, including gloves, masks, and lab coats, were employed to prevent the transfer of contemporary DNA. Water and agarose gel controls that had not come into direct contact with the artifacts were processed alongside the textile samples to serve as baselines for detecting contamination. The absence of significant DNA in these controls provided reassurance that the sequences identified in the textiles were not significantly contaminated during sample collection. Furthermore, aDNA is typically fragmented due to degradation over time, so focusing on short sequences allowed us to distinguish our targets from contemporary DNA. Any long, intact DNA fragments—lacking the degradation typical of aDNA and therefore likely from contemporary sources—were excluded, and bioinformatics tools filtered out sequences matching known contemporary genomes.

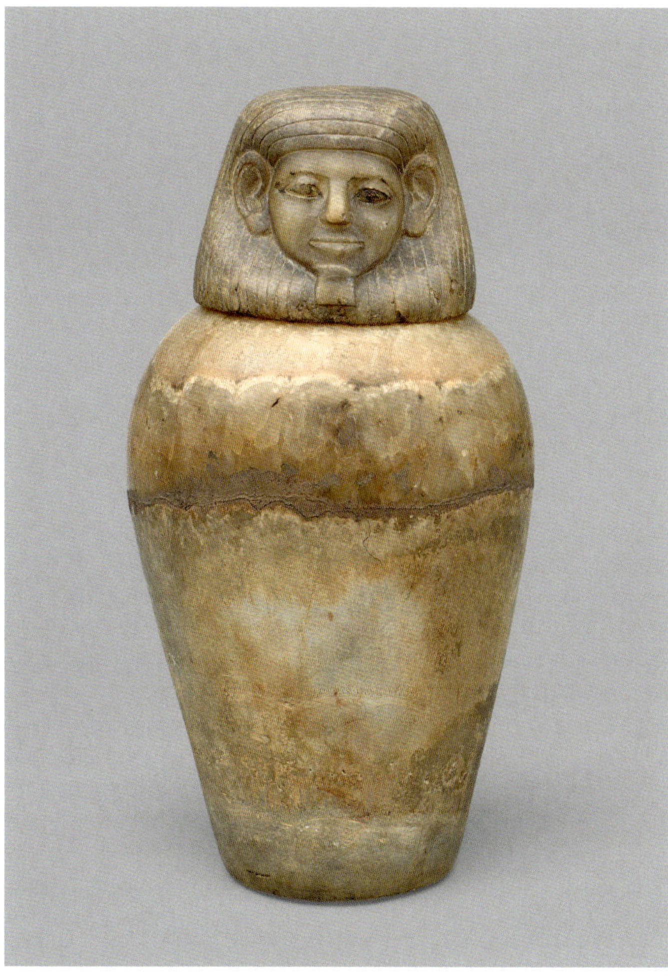

Fig. 7 Canopic Jar, Middle Kingdom, Dynasty 12 (about 1985–1773 BCE). Egypt. Travertine (Egyptian alabaster); 35.5 × 17 × 17 cm (14 × 6¾ × 6¾ in.). The Art Institute of Chicago, purchased with funds provided by Henry H. Getty, Robert H. Fleming, Norman W. Harris, and Charles L. Hutchinson, 1894.360a–b.

Unearthing Disease: Pathogen DNA in Burial Textiles

DNA analysis identified tuberculosis (TB) pathogens in a fragment of a funerary shroud (fig. 6) and a child's tunic (fig. 1), along with DNA from other sources. The fragment yielded DNA from *Mycobacterium tuberculosis*.[15] The degraded state of the DNA fragments aligns with expectations for historic (over one hundred years old) sequences. DNA from *Mycobacterium avium* was identified in the child's tunic. While typically associated with animals, *M. avium* can infect humans under specific conditions, particularly in cases of weakened immune systems.[16] Its presence highlights the complex interactions between humans and zoonotic pathogens in ancient to modern societies. In addition, another tunic fragment (fig. 5) contained trace amounts of *M. tuberculosis*, highlighting the prevalence of TB at various stages in the history of this object. One of the canopic jars (fig. 7) also tested positive for DNA sequences consistent with *Yersinia pestis*, the bacterium responsible for the plague. However, the fragments were too short for definitive identification, and their nature did not allow us to determine their precise source, leaving this finding inconclusive.

These results emphasize textiles' potential as repositories of biological data, capable of preserving microbial DNA for extended periods of time. The findings also raise important questions about the preservation of disease-related DNA in different contexts. The term *historical DNA* describes more recent aDNA (around one to two hundred years old), offering a distinction between modern historical periods and the distant past.[17] Artifacts excavated during the eighteenth and nineteenth centuries pose particular challenges of distinguishing aDNA from a textile's original use from more recent historical DNA—introduced during excavation, curation, or other past interactions. While the DNA recovered in this study is clearly not modern as it exists in short fragments, its exact temporal origin cannot yet be fully determined. Contamination management is not merely a technical consideration but a fundamental requirement in DNA analysis. By implementing strict contamination controls, protective measures, and analytical methods that filter out recent sequences, this study can only ensure control of contamination during the sampling process; it cannot control for everything that has occurred since the objects were excavated. This is the greatest challenge in interpreting the data to distinguish ancient, historical, and recent DNA.

Tuberculosis and Society: A Pathogen's Cultural Footprint

The detection of *Mycobacterium tuberculosis* underscores its longstanding presence as a public health concern but also raises important questions about the timeline of its preservation. TB has shaped human societies for centuries, with evidence from skeletal remains, ancient medical texts, and records from different historical periods attesting to its widespread impact. Archaeological findings indicate that TB was present in ancient Egypt, as skeletal deformities consistent with advanced TB—such as spinal lesions associated with Pott's disease—have been observed in mummified remains. Ancient medical texts, such as the Ebers Papyrus, describe symptoms resembling TB, suggesting an early understanding of the disease and attempts at treatment.[18]

TB's long role in human history also makes it challenging to determine the precise origin of aDNA extracted from textiles. While Egypt's arid climate and burial practices may have contributed to the preservation of biological residues, TB was highly prevalent worldwide in the eighteenth and nineteenth centuries, when many objects were excavated and handled.[19] Indeed, TB was the defining public health crisis of the period, thriving in the overcrowded and unsanitary conditions of newly industrialized cities. Given the widespread occurrence of TB during the era when these textiles were recovered, the detected DNA could originate from individuals who came into contact with these objects long after their initial burial.

Thus, while burial textiles provide valuable biological and cultural insights, further research is needed to disentangle ancient infections from more recent historical contamination. Advances in bioinformatics and contamination controls continue to refine methodologies, ensuring that textiles remain credible sources for understanding past disease environments. These advances must be complemented by historical understanding of TB's role in shaping social structures, medical advancements, and even cultural attitudes toward illness and mortality throughout human history.

Woven Histories: Tracing Disease and Time Through Textiles

This study demonstrates that burial textiles are more than silent artifacts or works of art—they are molecular vaults preserving genetic echoes of past lives. Through noninvasive sampling, we successfully recovered aDNA from these fragile materials, proving that textiles can serve as viable sources for genetic research. The use of agarose gel extraction emerged as a breakthrough technique, surpassing traditional swabbing by yielding richer DNA without compromising the objects' integrity.

Yet the discovery of *M. tuberculosis* and *M. avium* in these textiles presents an intriguing challenge: While we can confirm that the recovered DNA is not recent, its exact historical origin remains uncertain. The enduring presence of TB in both ancient and historical periods complicates efforts to pinpoint whether this DNA stems from the original wearers or from individuals who later handled these objects. This uncertainty underscores the importance of expanding bioinformatics approaches to unravel the precise timelines encoded in these fibers.

Despite these challenges, the implications of this research are vast. Burial textiles are both biological and cultural archives, capturing the interplay between human health and social forms. As techniques advance, textiles could unlock new narratives about diseases, resilience, and daily life. This study is just the beginning: By bridging archaeology, conservation, and molecular science, we move closer to decoding the histories woven into fabric, waiting to be read.

Notes

1   On ancient DNA, see Michael Hofreiter, David Serre, Hendrik N. Poinar, Melanie Kuch, and Svante Pääbo, "Ancient DNA," *Nature Reviews Genetics* 2, no. 5 (2001): 353–59, doi.org/10.1038/35072071; and Nicolas Arning and Daniel J. Wilson, "The Past, Present and Future of Ancient Bacterial DNA," *Microbial Genomics* 6, no. 7 (2020), doi.org/10.1099/mgen.0.000384. On recent studies using ancient DNA, see Jifeng Zhang, Kun Shi, Han W. Paerl, Kathleen M. Rühland, Yanli Yuan, Rong Wang, et al., "Ancient DNA Reveals Potentially Toxic Cyanobacteria Increasing with Climate Change," *Water Research* 229 (February 2023), doi.org/10.1016/j.watres.2022.119435; and Alessandro Achilli, Anna Olivieri, Ornella Semino, and Antonio Torroni, "Ancient Human Genomes—Keys to Understanding Our Past," *Science* 360, no. 6392 (2018): 964–65, doi.org/10.1126/science.aat7257. See also "International Society of Genetic Genealogy Wiki," International Society of Genetic Genealogy, isogg.org/wiki.

2   Ludovic Orlando, Robin Allaby, Pontus Skoglund, Clio Der Sarkissian, Phillip W. Stockhammer, María C. Ávila-Arcos, et al., "Ancient DNA Analysis," *Nature Reviews: Methods Primers* 1, no. 1 (2021), doi.org/10.1038/s43586-020-00011-0.

3   Our thanks to Ashley Arico and Stephanie Caruso at the Art Institute for their assistance and contributions during this process.

4   The Koepfli Lab at the University of Notre Dame, Indiana, focuses on genomics to understand infectious diseases, particularly malaria. In collaboration with the Eck Institute for Global Health, also at Notre Dame, the lab uses advanced genomic technologies to study disease transmission dynamics and support global health initiatives. Their research includes developing tools for diagnosing and tracking parasites, with the aim of improving health standards and informing strategies for disease control and elimination.

5   For more on how different stresses affect textiles, see J. W. S. Hearle, B. Lomas, and W. D. Cooke, *Atlas of Fibre Fracture and Damage to Textiles*, 2nd ed. (Woodhead, 1998).

6   See Hearle, Lomas, and Cooke, *Atlas of Fibre Fracture and Damage to Textiles*, 377.

7   See, for example, Hearle, Lomas, and Cooke, *Atlas of Fibre Fracture and Damage to Textiles*, 390.

8   Conservators are bound to the guidelines of ethical practice set by the American Institute for Conservation Code of Ethics, which states that conservators must avoid damaging cultural property or affecting its future use. See "Our Code of Ethics," American Institute for Conservation, accessed May 9, 2025, culturalheritage.org/about-conservation/code-of-ethics.

9   Poultice treatments, the application of aqueous solutions or solvents to specific areas, are commonly used to clean textile objects when immersion cleaning is too dangerous, such as when fugitive dyes are present. Poultices work through diffusion and capillary action, pulling out grime, staining, and other foreign products as they dry. At present, agar/agarose and gellan gum are two of the most frequently used physical gels in art conservation. Both are natural polysaccharides. Agarose is obtained from the cell walls of red algae species like *Gelidium* and *Gracilaria*, or from the seaweed *Sphaerococcus euchema*. See "Gels," American Institute for Conservation Wiki, accessed May 9, 2025, conservation-wiki.com/wiki/Gels; and R. Armisén and F. Galatas, "Agar," in *Handbook of Hydrocolloids*, ed. Glyn O. Phillips and Peter A. Williams (Woodhead, 2000), 82–107.

10   Six ancient Egyptian objects from the Art Institute's collection were analyzed for this project: Two canopic jars (1894.360a–b and 1894.361a–b), two children's tunics (1914.713 and 1914.714), a tunic fragment (1914.701a), and a fragment of a funerary shroud (1946.184). The selections for testing also included five Andean textiles that have not been analyzed at the time of this publication: 1955.1711, 1955.1777, 1955.1806, 1956.63, 1957.75 (p. 120, fig. 6).

11   Swabs were moistened with Tris-EDTA, a biological buffer commonly used in molecular biology to maintain pH stability and protect nucleic acids.

12   The films are composed of 2% agarose gel, which conservators typically use in a variety of textile cleaning treatments. See Lora V. Angelova, Bronwyn Ormsby, Joyce Tonsend, and Richard Wolbers, eds., *Gels in the Conservation of Art* (Archetype, 2017).

13   See James A. Fellows Yates, Thiseas C. Lamnidis, Maxime Borry, Aida Andrades Valtueña, Zandra Fagernäs, Stephen Clayton, et al., "Reproducible, Portable, and Efficient Ancient Genome Reconstruction with nf-core/eager," PeerJ, March 16, 2021, doi.org/10.7717/peerj.10947.

14   Samples were initially treated with proteinase K to degrade proteins while preserving DNA, then purified via silica spin columns to remove debris. DNA quantification was performed by fluorometry, which measures fluorescence from DNA-binding dyes. Sequencing was carried out on the portable Nanopore MinION platform, optimized for reading short, degraded fragments typical of ancient samples. Sequence analysis employed the Eager pipeline to correct age-related damage and filter modern contaminants using comparative databases, with stringent controls (e.g., water, unused gels) to ensure data integrity. See Yates et al., "Reproducible, Portable."

15   Using tools that compare DNA sequences, we found that our sample's sequence is a much stronger match—a higher score and a lower chance of error—to *M. tuberculosis* than to other *Mycobacterium* species, supporting its identification as *M. tuberculosis*.

16   See Vishwanath Venketaraman, "Editorial: Non-Tuberculous Mycobacteria Infections and COVID-19," *Frontiers in Cellular and Infection Microbiology* 15 (February 2025), doi.org/10.3389/fcimb.2025.1550277.

17   See, for example, Shawn M. Billerman and Jennifer Walsh, "Historical DNA as a Tool to Address Key Questions in Avian Biology and Evolution: A Review of Methods, Challenges, Applications, and Future Directions," *Molecular Ecology Resources* 19, no. 5 (2019): 1115–30, doi.org/10.1111/1755-0998.13066.

18   On Pott's disease in ancient Egypt, see Eric Crubézy, Betrand Ludes, Jean-Dominique Poveda, John Clayton, Brigitte Crouau-Roy, and Daniel Montagnon, "Identification of Mycobacterium DNA in an Egyptian Pott's Disease of 5,400 Years Old," *Comptes rendus de l'Académie des sciences, Series III, Sciences de la vie* 321, no. 11 (1998): 941–51; and Lisa Sabbahy, "An Overview of the Evidence for Tuberculosis from Ancient Egypt," in *Palaeopathology in Egypt and Nubia: A Century in Review*, Jenefer Cockitt, A. Rosalie David, and Ryan Metcalfe (Archaeopress, 2014), 51–55. On tuberculosis in ancient Egyptian medical texts, see "Tuberculosis Through the Ages," Museum of Health Care, accessed November 25, 2024, museumofhealthcare.ca/explore/exhibits/breath/tuberculosis-through-the-ages.html; and Tim Sandle, "Pharaohs and Mummies: Diseases of Ancient Egypt and Modern Approaches," *Journal of Ancient Diseases and Preventive Remedies* 1, no. 4 (2013), doi.org/10.4172/2329-8731.1000e112.

19   See Thomas M. Daniel, "The History of Tuberculosis," *Respiratory Medicine* 100, no. 11 (2006): 1862–70, doi.org/10.1016/j.rmed.2006.08.006.

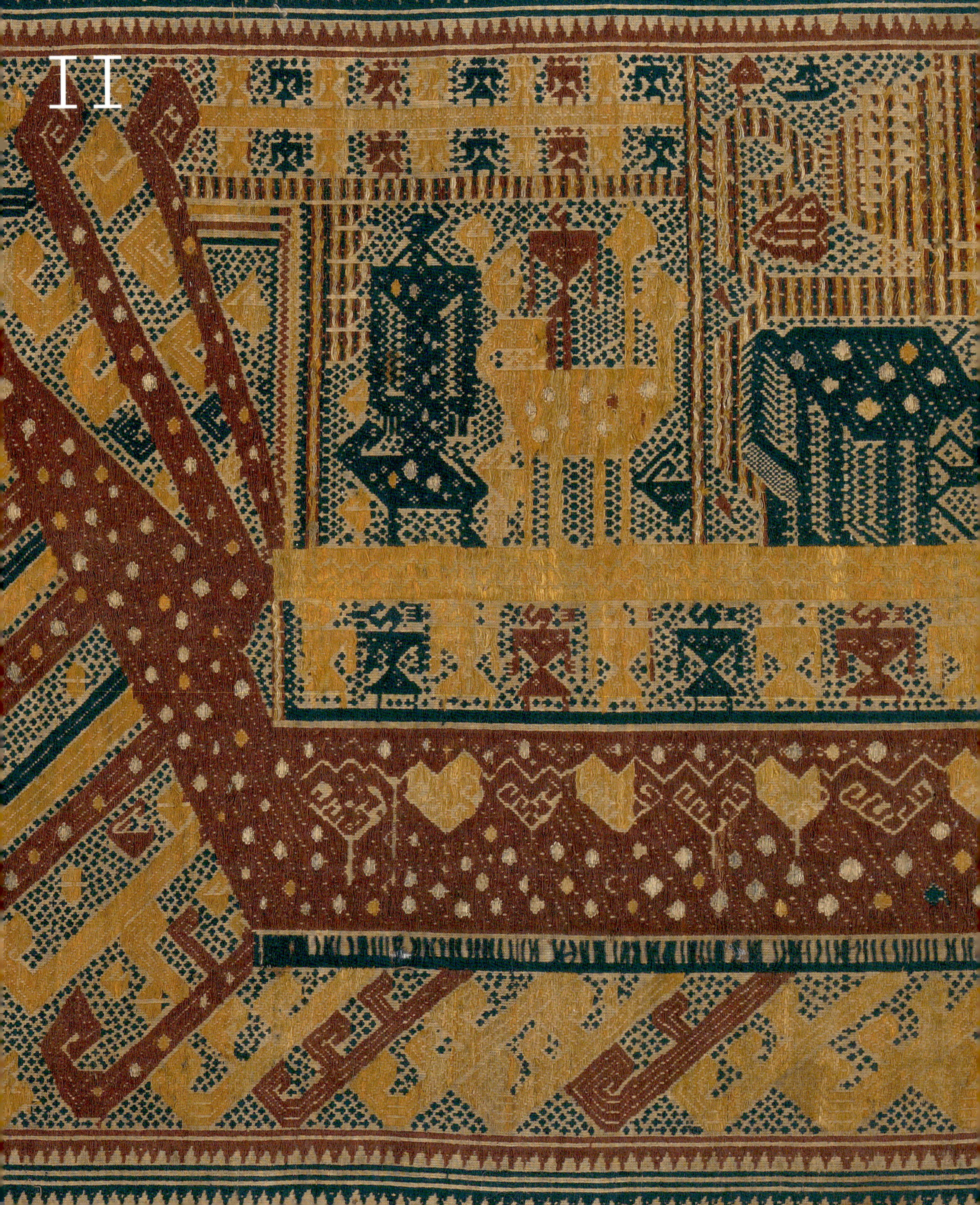
II

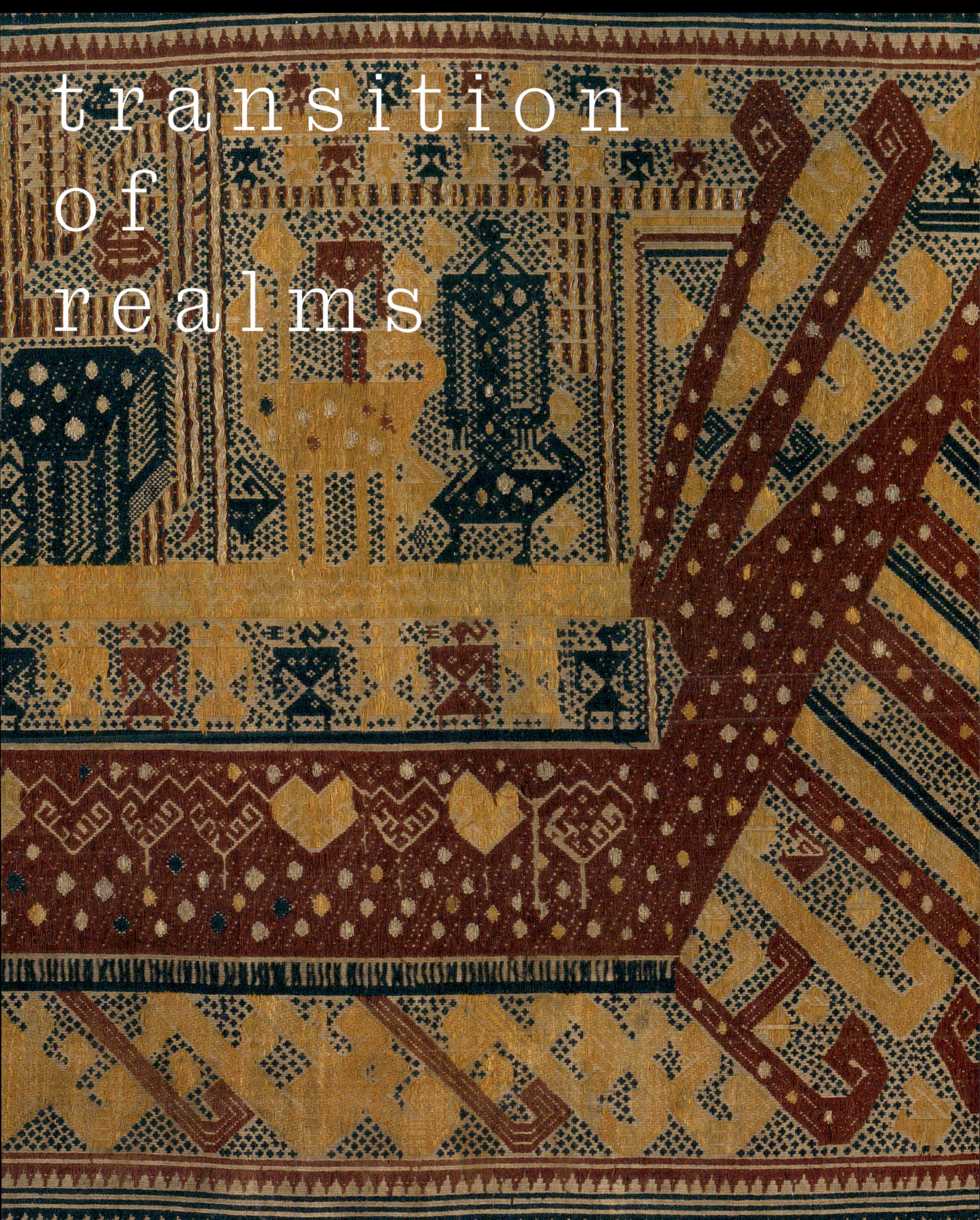
transition
of
realms

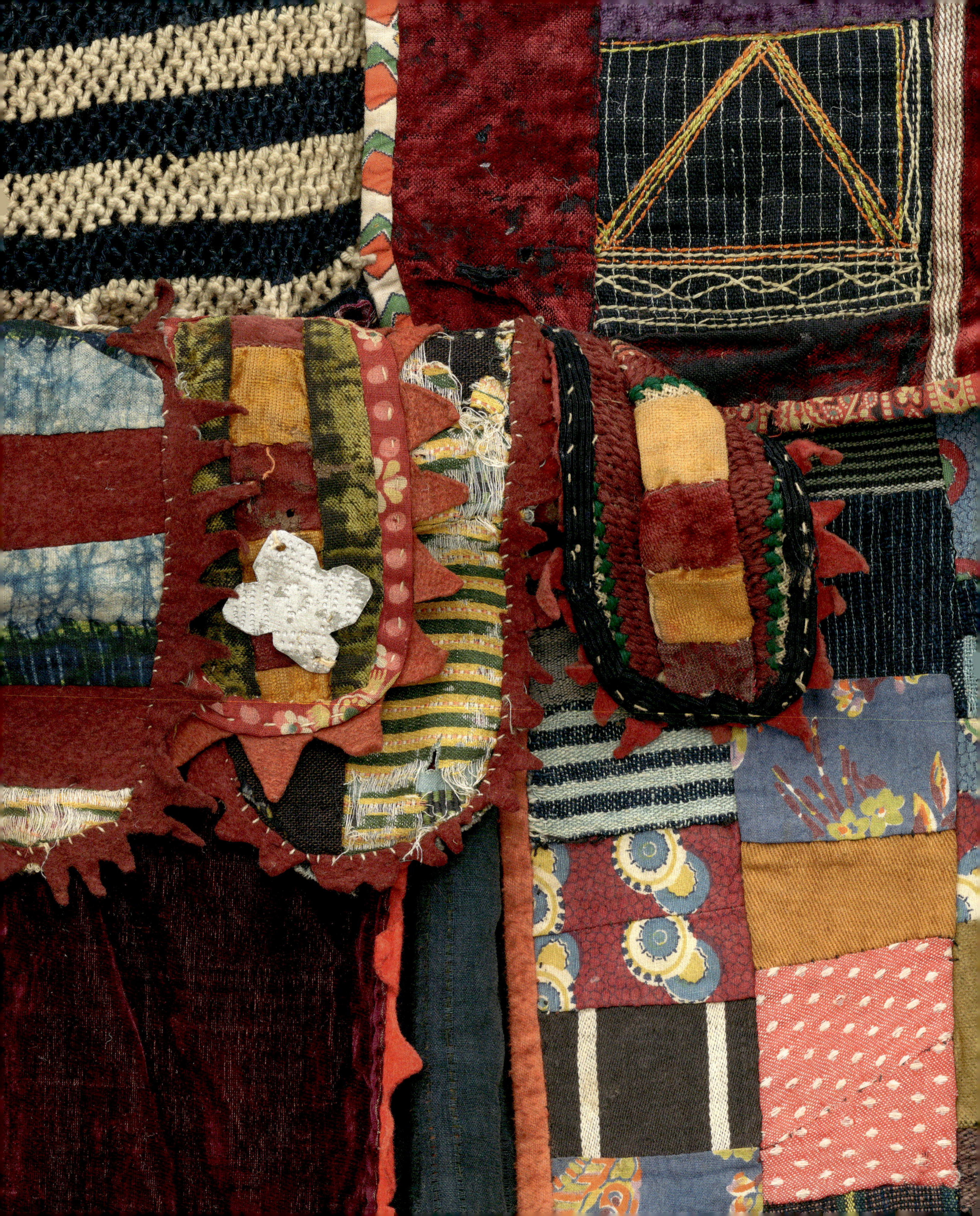

Of Water and Sky Along a Fibered Path

Folayemi Wilson
Artist, designer, educator, and writer

The sea and sky—two vast forces of nature that serve as backdrops to our earthly existence—play prominent roles in the metaphysical beliefs about life and death of several cultures represented by objects in the exhibition and book *On Loss and Absence: Textiles of Mourning and Survival*. Often connected to themes of travel and transition, the sea and sky are frequent elements of aesthetic and cultural narratives, conveyed through textiles, about earthly life, the afterlife, and the liminal space in between.

Art historical scholarship and museum exhibitions are increasingly considering such objects in the context of the beliefs, narratives, and traditions that informed their making and their relationship to life in the communities from which they come. Many academics and museum professionals to this day were trained to focus on the aesthetics, condition, and provenance of works and to emphasize their technical mastery and exceptional nature. This tendency has been undergirded by the Western points of view that often prevail in museums. Today, many institutions are making efforts to deconstruct their own history of applying a hierarchical, Western lens to works from non-Western contexts. Although most societies globally operate within some form of hierarchy, the values expressed by those hierarchies may be very different.

By approaching objects from an understanding of the social structures from which they emerge, as projects like *On Loss and Absence* attempt to do, we may avoid imposing Western values or viewpoints. Many of the textile objects highlighted in this volume are considered exceptional or of the highest quality (and thus worthy of being in a museum collection) and were used by chiefs, royalty, and other privileged members of their respective societies. When we look beyond the aesthetic beauty or rarity of fine embroidery and impressive weaving, we may begin to ask questions about the object's cultural meaning: Who used it? Who made it? Why was it made? How do all the people who have interacted with this textile over the course of its long life fit into the fibered path of the culture from which

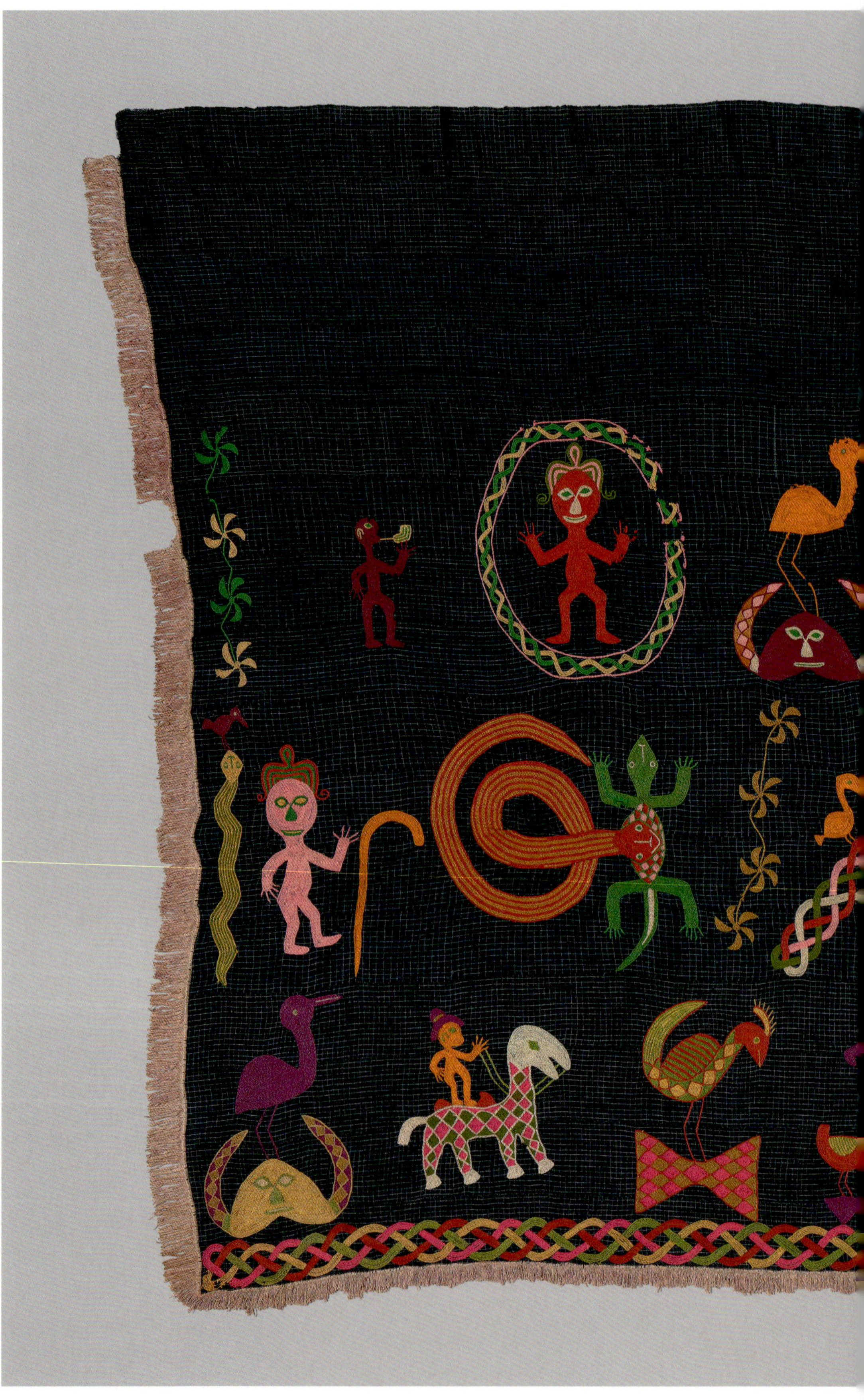

Fig. 1 Ogboni Chief's Textile, early–mid-20th century. Iwo Yoruba; Nigeria. Cotton, indigo dyed; sixteen strips of plain weave, joined by hand stitching; embroidered with wool in chain stitches; edged with cotton, button-hole stitched uncut fringe; 162.5 × 275.6 cm (64 × 108½ in.). The Art Institute of Chicago, O. Renard Goltra Fund, 1995.424.

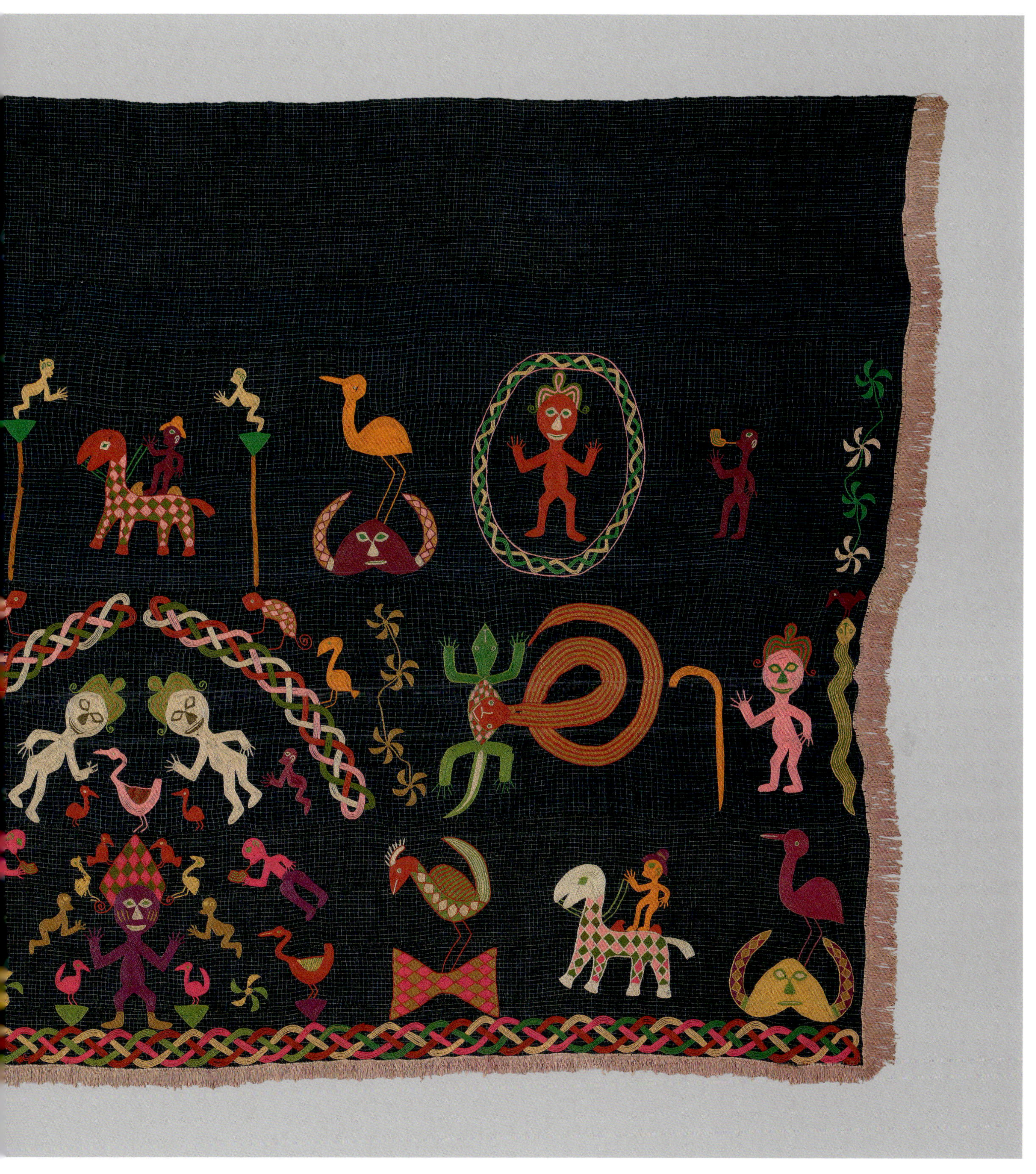

it comes? This essay explores the symbolic language of water and sky shared broadly by the textile traditions of the Yoruba of western and southern Nigeria, the Paminggir peoples of Indonesia, and the ancient Egyptians. Attention to these objects' different cultural contexts reveals the similarities and differences in their ideas of metaphysical boundaries and in how each uses the language of cloth as a material mediator embodying and even effecting the transition between life and death.

The Watery Boundary of the Kalûnga Line

While I was traveling as a young girl in Benin City, Nigeria, on a research trip with members of the National Black Theatre of Harlem, our group encountered a stunning man almost seven feet tall. I will never forget watching him dance. Barefooted, he was elegant and stately. His skin was a glistening blue-black, and, to my young eyes, his feet alone seemed to be the length of my forearm. On this particular excursion, we were learning about the metalwork traditions in that part of the country.[1] This gentleman, an iron worker adorned with beautiful textiles, danced for us in celebration of our homecoming as African Americans. When he moved, it was as if he was floating well above the ground with the grace and agility of a much smaller man.

His image is seared in my memory as one magical moment among many from that trip during which I was able to get in touch with a piece of my spiritual ancestry. Like the places in the Americas populated by diasporic Africans—Brazil, Charleston, Gullah Geechee country off the coast of the Carolinas, and New Orleans, among others—the air in Benin City was alive and thick with a predominantly ancestral presence. The primordial and the beyond conjoined with the present; all three seemed to exist simultaneously. This was my inauguration into an awareness of the Kalûnga Line and the potent forces that reside between this world and the next. In Central African Kongo cultural beliefs, the

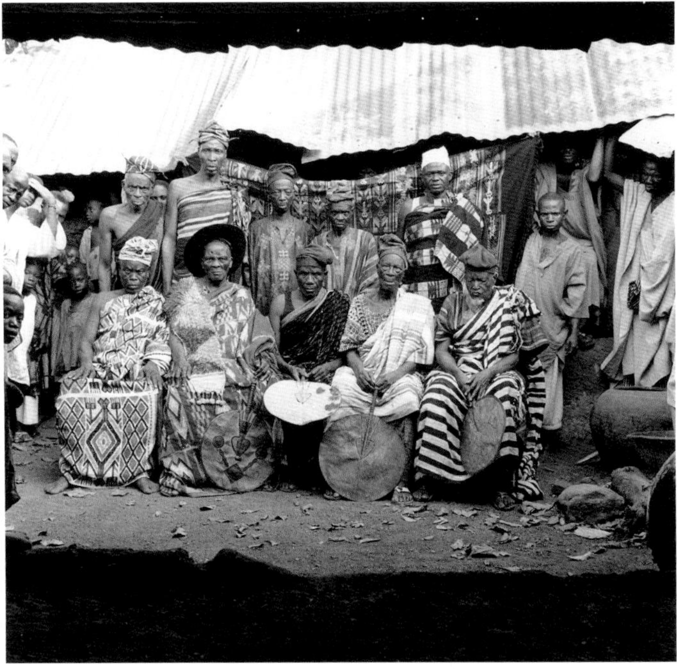

Fig. 2 **Ogboni chief's council, Ijebu Igbo, Nigeria, 1950s.**

Kalûnga Line is a watery and traversable boundary that divides the realm of the living from the realm of the dead—the ancestral realm—and connects the two worlds through a complex system of mediation that allows spiritual energy to inhabit and empower both (see p. 38, fig. 9).

Yoruba social and political systems explicitly involve moving between the human and spiritual realms, each of which functions as part of a cosmology managed by the *oba* (king), who channels the *orisha* (deities), as well as by elders, chiefs, and their councils. From the Yoruba perspective, many ritual and traditional objects, including the kinds of textile objects included in the present volume, are imbued with *asé*.[2] Asé is a Yoruba concept of power that can be manifested in objects and in turn commanded by those authorized and trained to wield it, including *babalowos* (spiritual leaders and healers), obas, and elders, as well as artists. The metaphysical energy of asé moves between and can travel on both sides of the Kalûnga Line.[3] Historian and anthropologist William Fagg noted that traditional Yoruba art and objects should be considered through a fourth-dimensional perspective, which views such cultural productions as "objects in which the fourth or time dimension is dominant and in which matter is only a vehicle, or the outward and visible expression, of energy or life force. Thus it is energy and not matter, dynamic and not static being, which is the true nature of things."[4]

This concept of energy can be applied to an Ogboni chief's textile in the Art Institute of Chicago's collection (fig. 1). While in a museum context such objects are typically presented two-dimensionally, this textile was designed to be "activated" by being worn. When it is donned by a chief during ceremonies and rituals, its symbolism comes potently alive, its meaning animated by a spiritual perspective. The Ogboni (see fig. 2) is a sociopolitical society that works in coordination with the oba and functions like a legislative branch; it can be thought of as holding the asé of governance. This colorful wrapper would have enlivened an Ogboni chief's role as an elder citizen of very high standing

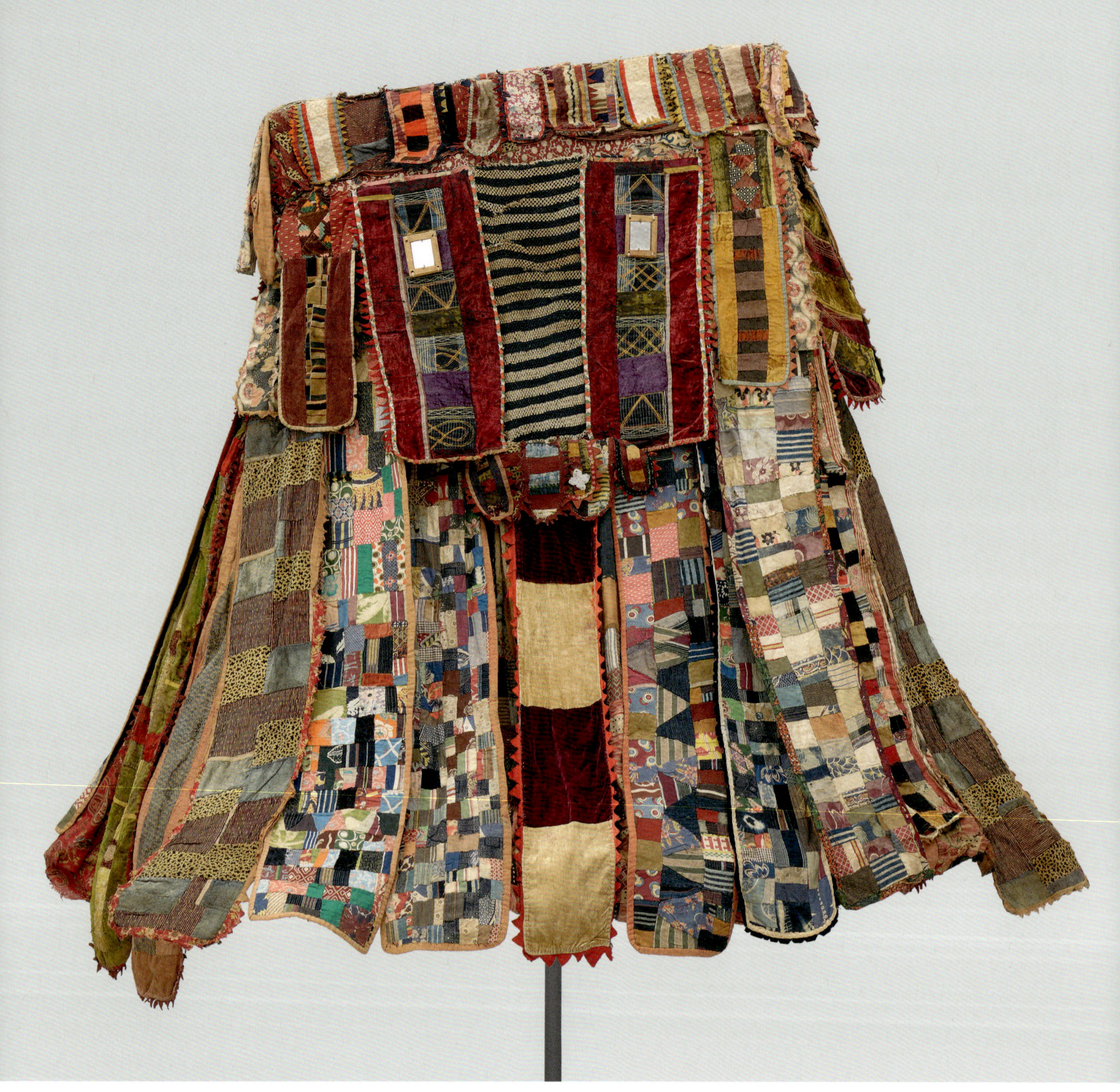

Fig. 3 Masquerade Costume for Egúngún (*Paka*), late 19th–early 20th century. Yoruba; Ọ̀yọ́ State, Nigeria. Natural and synthetic fiber, wood, mirror, metal, and shell; pieced panels and sections of appliqué, quilted, felted, knotted, velvet, printed, and woven fabrics; embellished with trim and embroidery; 154.9 × 160 cm (60 × 63 in.). The Art Institute of Chicago, gift of Deborah Stokes and Jeffrey Hammer, 1994.709.

and would have been worn in important ceremonies. The sixteen narrow bands of indigo, plain-weave cloth with embroidered sections show the oba in the bottom center flanked by *iyami*, often represented as birds, who personify the "secret and mysterious powers of women" elders; iyami were often revered by the king, who depended on their power and influence.[5] The uniformly coiffed women above the king could stand in for a sense of beauty (a form of asé) being offered to the king, as symbolized by their outstretched hands. Warriors on horseback protect the king. The colorful chains forming an arch near the center resemble intertwining snakes; the lizards walking on the arch, along with many kinds of birds and other animals with spiritual resonance, have the ability to move through worlds seen and unseen. More literal snakes along the left and right edges symbolize rebirth as well as the power to terminate life. The snakes biting the lizards to the left and right of the arcing chains may signify the king's ability to take life.[6]

Elders with smoking pipes and canes represent both sides of the Kalûnga Line; both realms are within this king's domain.[7] Like the oba and Ogboni, Yoruba ancestors also play an important role in maintaining bonds across the Kalûnga Line. They commune with the living through masquerades such as the Egúngún, in which deceased members of the community revisit and speak with their people by possessing initiates trained in ancestral communication. The initiates dress in elaborate costumes made of multiple layers and fragments of cloth (see fig. 3) meant to hide their identities as they perform rituals serving to cleanse, reconnect their communities to righteous ways of living, and bestow blessings.

Miami-based contemporary artist Yanira Collado uses an aesthetic and conceptual framework similar to the Egúngún masquerade costume in her work *Untitled* (fig. 4). The fragments in Collado's work similarly represent the bonds that traverse the Kalûnga Line and unite ancestral agency and asé with earthly life. Referencing her Dominican heritage, Collado uses fragments in an attempt

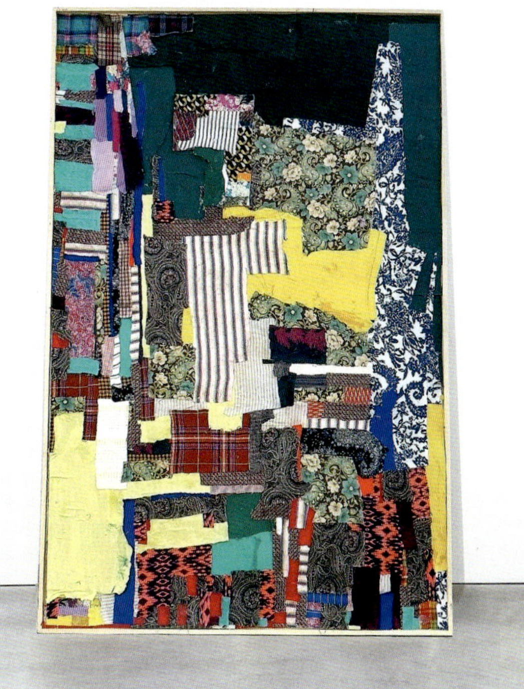

Fig. 4 Yanira Collado (Dominican and American, born 1975). *Untitled*, 2024. Found textile fragments; collaged and adhered mounted on wooden frame; 181.6 × 119.4 cm (71½ × 47 in.). Collection of the artist.

to "assemble a visual language that reconciles the process in which the history of this information is recorded, stored, and retrieved." Collado is also "interested in the labor inherent in these materials and the shapes taken during their transitions, which conjure up invocations, ritual, a transcendence of presence, and in many ways, fragments becoming whole."[8]

Sailing to the Afterlife

Since at least antiquity, cultures around the world have imagined ships as mechanisms of travel between worlds and vessels transporting the living to the realm of the dead. In Megalithic times, bodies were not buried in the earth but were rather entombed in stone shrines or urns with small replicas of boats enclosed among other artifacts, such as bones or wooden dolls representing ferrymen. These "ships of the dead," as they are sometimes known, also appear in the textiles of the Paminggir peoples of southern Indonesia.

At one time, the departed in Indonesia actually set sail on boats traveling east to west in ship funerals; later, they were buried in coffins or whole tombs fashioned into the shape of a boat.[9] These customs were "based on the belief that the ghosts of the ancestors live in the hereafter in a country which all returning ghosts try to reach across the sea."[10] These same beliefs gave rise to the ship cloths used in funerary rituals and other important life events, such as births and weddings, in Southeast Asian cultures. Rather than being worn on the body, these textiles were displayed on the house or dwelling of the person central to the ceremony. Ship motifs in these cloths include architectural details typical of the kinds of structures, such as shrines or houses, meant to commemorate ancestors. Funerary ship cloths often depicted the transition of the deceased through a watery bardo.

Of the two major kinds of ship cloths used in Indonesia, *palepai*—the Indigenous name for the longer form—held greater prestige, as they were owned by elite members of Sumatran society. The smaller, squared *tampan* was more common and was used by broader classes of people. Tampan were used in various communal rituals to announce important life events and stages, such as births, circumcisions, promotions to a new civic role or title, readiness for marriage, and marriage itself, in addition to deaths and funerals. A pregnant mother might have commissioned a weaving once she knew a baby was on the way, or a bride's family might have had one made as part of the prepations for her marriage.

Sometimes these two types of cloths were used in conjunction with each other: For example, in elaborate wedding ceremonies, a bride might sit under the groom's family's hanging palepai on a tampan from her own family's collection. Food and gifts might be offered wrapped in a small tampan during ceremonies. Regardless of the occasion, these cloths were woven with consistent motifs of ships, architecture, birds, horses, and trees (like the tree of life), which all served as metaphors of transition, whether for a baby being born or given a name, a bride entering a new phase of responsibility or joining another family, or the dead journeying to the afterlife.[11]

The style and arrangement of motifs in ship cloths is key to interpreting their meaning. A double-ship example (fig. 5) at the Art Institute features two large, red ships alongside animals, architectural elements, and figures. The double ships could denote the joining of two clans or families. Red ships in these textiles represent the revered realm of the ancestors, while blue ships represent the human, earthly realm. The conical architectural elements on staffs in palapai are thought to be abstractions of shrines or religious structures built to commemorate the departed; like birds, they only appear on red-ship palepai, while blue-ship versions illustrate secular, domestic structures and architectural elements.[12]

The religious structures in the red-ship example suggest a strong connection to ancestral heritage. This ship

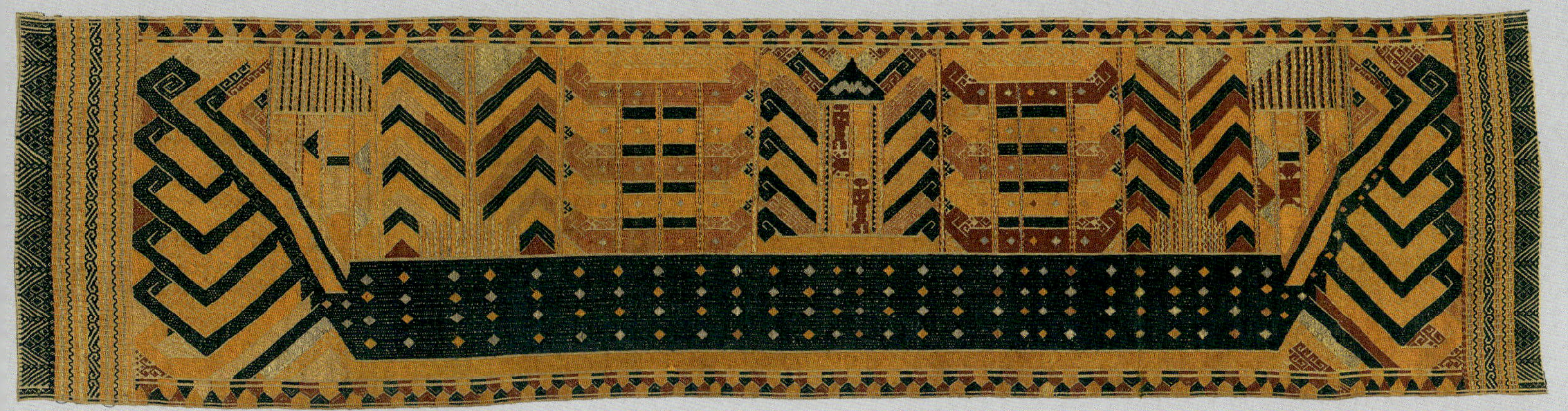

cloth was likely displayed at funerary events to symbolize the support the departed needed to make it to the other side: The animals may be familiars, and the figures may represent ancestors, who welcomed and perhaps protected the deceased on their journey to the next realm. The blue-ship example (fig. 6) from the collection includes an abundance of motifs reminiscent of houses in the Kenali region, which feature projections and extensions of wooden beams at right angles in each corner. Although some blue-ship cloths include many figures and other motifs, this example is simpler, predominately adorned with buildings, indicating that it was likely used on occasions more concerned with earthly matters.

The Sky as a Refuge for the Newly Departed

Beliefs and rituals related to death in ancient Egypt combined watery imagery of boats and rivers with symbols of the sky. Depictions of boats in royal tombs and illustrated funerary literature such as the Book of the Dead allude to the belief that the departed sail through the sky with the sun god Re after transitioning from life to the afterlife.[13] Wings, a symbol of supernatural ascension, are prominent in the iconography painted on a cartonnage panel (fig. 7), once part of mummy trappings. The painting, applied to the surface of a plaster layer with a woven-textile support, depicts the goddess Isis, another major Egyptian deity who aided the dead, kneeling with outstretched wings and the sun as a crown on her head. Symbols like the ankh, the hieroglyph for life; a scale, used to weigh the heart of the dead; and jackals, protectors of the dead, are all elements in the process of a funerary transition from the land of the living to the realm of the blessed dead.

References to ascension and the sky may also be present in a delicate bead net funerary shroud in the Art Institute's collection (fig. 8). It would have been placed over the chest of the mummified individual in preparation for

Fig. 5 (opposite) **Ceremonial Hanging (*Palepai*), 19th century. Paminggir people; Lampung area, South Sumatra, Indonesia. Cotton, silk, and silver-leaf-over-lacquered-paper-strip-wrapped bast fiber (probably ramie), plain weave with supplementary patterning and brocading wefts, main warp fringe; without fringe: 67 × 296.6 cm (26 ⅜ × 116 ¾ in.). The Art Institute of Chicago, gift of E. M. Bakwin Indonesian Textile Collection, 2002.914.**

Fig. 6 (above) **Ceremonial Hanging (*Palepai*), 19th century. Paminggir people; Lampung area, South Sumatra, Indonesia. Cotton, silk, gold-leaf-over-lacquered-paper-strip-wrapped bast fiber (probably ramie), and silver-leaf-over-lacquered-paper-strip-wrapped cotton, plain weave with supplementary brocading wefts; 60.8 × 246.3 cm (23 ⅞ × 97 in.). The Art Institute of Chicago, gift of E. M. Bakwin Indonesian Textile Collection, 2002.920.**

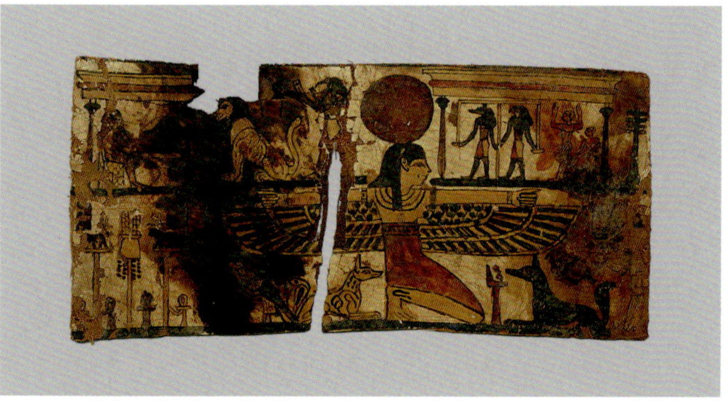

Fig. 7 Cartonnage Chest Panel, Roman
Period (30 BCE–395 CE), 1st–2nd century.
Egypt. Cartonnage (plaster and textile)
and pigment; 18.4 × 38.7 cm (7¼ × 15¼ in.).
The Art Institute of Chicago, gift of Mrs.
Joseph L. Valentine, 1948.244.

Fig. 8 Bead Net Funerary Shroud with
Amulets, Third Intermediate Period, Dynasty
23–25 (about 818–656 BCE). Egypt. Faience
beads and amulets, with modern cotton
fiber; 58.4 × 30.5 × 1.9 cm (23 × 12¹⁄₁₆ × ¾ in.).
The Art Institute of Chicago, purchased
with funds provided by Henry H. Getty and
Charles L. Hutchinson, 1894.968a–e.

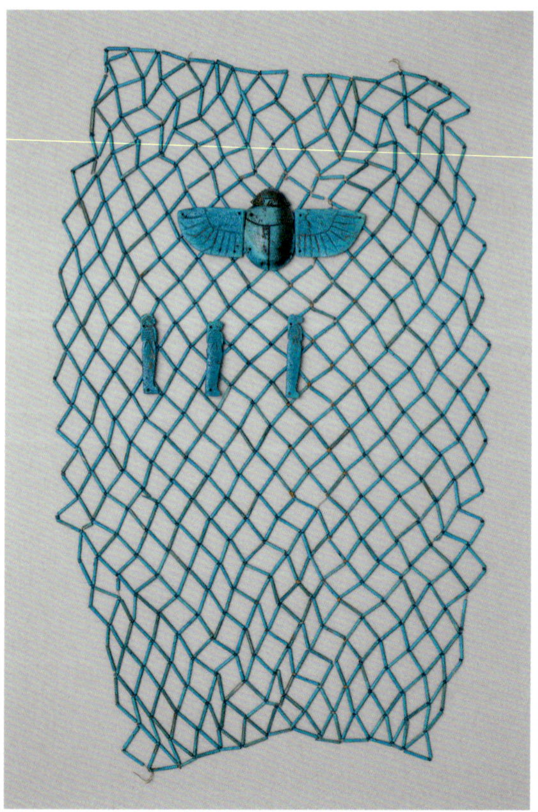

their journey to meet Osiris, god of the afterlife and resurrection, among other things. Osiris is present at the final
judgment and is introduced to the deceased if they receive
a favorable verdict and are granted rebirth. This shroud,
reassembled in the present day from ancient beads and
amulets, is believed to be missing one of four amulets representing the four Sons of Horus, god of the sky. Horus's sons
were a group of deities thought to protect the deceased as
they transitioned to the afterlife.[14] Among the net of faience
beads—brilliant blue, the color of the sky—occasional small,
yellow beads, somewhat faded through time, may represent
stars, their scattered placement approximating constella-
tions. The scarab, with its broad wings adept at flight, was
a symbol of rebirth, a talisman meant to bring blessings to
the departed as they ascended to reconcile their life and
achieve immortality.

People throughout time and around the world—
from ancient Egypt to nineteenth- and twentieth-century
Indonesia and Nigeria to contemporary artists in the
Americas—have used textiles to explore the idea of transition between realms and express understandings of life and
death. In many cultures, textiles have even played a role in
effecting these transitions through their use in traditions
and rituals celebrating life events, invoking the ancestors,
and sending loved ones safely to the afterlife. Through
masterful technique, inventive manipulation of materials,
and symbolic use of color and form, makers and their communities evince their belief not only in the existence of an
afterlife but also in its connection to the human world. Their
imagination and craft make the Kalûnga Line tangible, not
least of all by showing us how to honor ancestral legacies.

Notes

1   Benin City, part of the Edo kingdom, is well known for its Benin Bronzes, bronze sculptures looted by the British during their raid on Benin in 1897. Although several museums plan to return these treasures, controversy still abounds about who can rightfully claim these works.

2   See Babatunde Lawal, "Aworan: Representing Self and Its Metaphysical Other in Yoruba Art," *Art Bulletin* 32, no. 3 (2001): 498.

3   On the manifestation of asé in the visual arts, Nigerian historian Rowland Abiodun notes: "Functioning essentially as a kind of 'oriki,' visual art forms also carry condensed, highly charged and direct visual messages—'ase'—which are powerful and efficacious as their verbal equivalents. The visual artist uses his or her 'oju-inu' (inner eye) and 'oju-ona' (design consciousness), important aesthetic attributes, to select, combine, and represent specific colors, patterns, motifs, and aspects of the subject matter in order to communicate its 'ase' with the maximum visual impact." Rowland Abiodun, "Understanding Yoruba Art and Aesthetics: The Concept of Ase," *African Arts* 27, no. 3 (1994): 76. *Oriki* is a form of praise poem that is meant to evoke someone's inner asé.

4   William Fagg, "In Search of Meaning in African Art," *African Arts* 7 (July 1973): 164.

5   Moyo Okediji, "Art of the Yoruba," *Art Institute of Chicago Museum Studies* 23, no. 2 (1997): 170.

6   Okediji, "Art of the Yoruba," 172.

7   For more on Yoruba symbolism, see Sunday James, "Art Language Through Selected Signs and Symbols of the Yoruba People of Nigeria," *European Journal of Philosophy, Culture and Religious Studies* 7, no. 1 (2023): 79–87.

8   Yanira Collado, "Introduction," Emerson Dorsch, accessed February 18, 2025, emersondorsch.com/artist/yanira-collado.

9   See A. Steinmann, "The Ship as Represented in the Art of South East Asia," *Ciba Review* 52 (September 1946): 1880.

10   Steinmann, "The Ship as Represented," 1881.

11   Steinmann, "The Ship as Represented," 1887. For more on ceremonial uses of palapei and tampan ship cloths, see Mattiebelle Gittinger, "Ship Textiles of South Sumatra: Functions and Design Systems," *Bijdragen tot de Taal-, Land- en Volkenkunde* 132, no. 2 (1976): 207–27.

12   Gittinger, "Ship Textiles of South Sumatra," 225.

13   See A. Steinmann, "The Ship in Prehistoric Art," *Ciba Review* 52 (September 1946): 1870–74. See also Steve Vinson, "Boats (Use of)," in *UCLA Encyclopedia of Egyptology*, ed. Willeke Wendrich (UCLA, 2013).

14   My thanks to Ashley Arico, Katie Shulman, and Ruth Rolfsmeyer at the Art Institute of Chicago for their contributions and discussions during research for this essay.

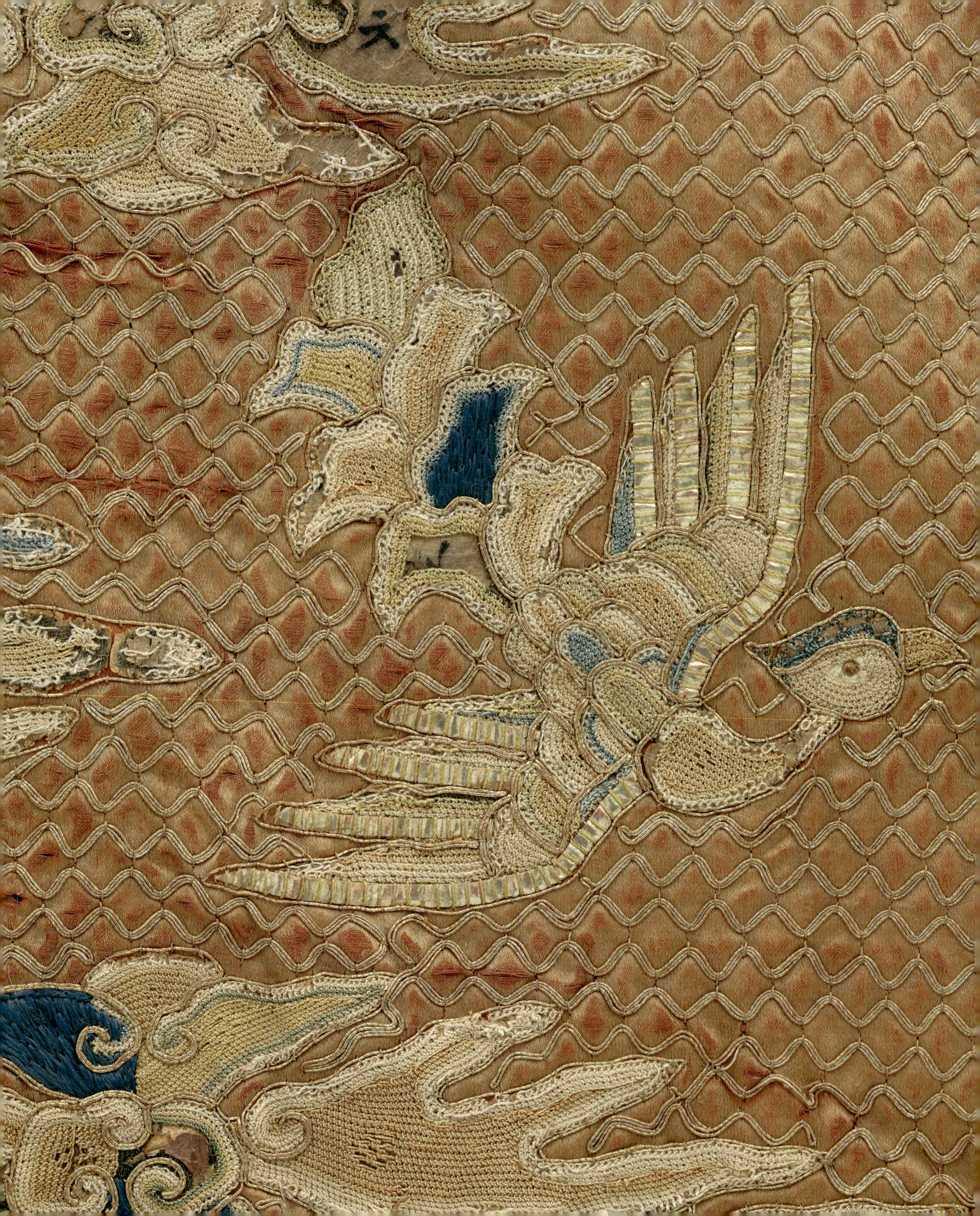

For Eighteen Looped Clouds

Jen Chen-su Huang

Artist and writer

i. Sparse clouds traverse the shoulders on the front of this vestment (fig. 1), forming into ovular clusters near each edge. These eighteen cloud clusters—two on the vestment's front and sixteen on the back—are a means of meditating on the robe; they walk me through how it was made, where it has been, what it has gone through, all the while evoking in me personal memories and free associations. Like fingers moving through prayer beads, my eyes contemplate each cluster, traveling from the front-left cloud formation to the rift at the shoulders where tailoring must have occurred, down the rear of the robe to the lowest peak, and back up again, over the hill of the shoulders to the clouds on the right. Through this looped pilgrimage, I attempt to shift from a distanced position of observation to one of entangled observance.[1]

ii. Sand clinging to every crevice, I lie on my belly, palms propping up my eyes as they follow the clouds above, drifting with no sense of urgency. At my feet a cerulean sky meets clear seas. The tide draws the crystalline blue closer to me as the waves come rolling in only to recede again. Within minutes the water returns, surpassing the foamy traces of its last journey onto the shore.

iii. On the back of the robe, sixteen clusters of needle-loop-embroidered clouds surround the Palace of Heaven (fig. 2), a glistening pagoda assembled from carefully gilded paper and silk thread. This tower sits atop saffron-colored silk that would have rested along the spine of the highest-ranking Taoist priest. Two white cranes mirror one another as they kiss at the wearer's shoulder blades, and many more cranes with gilt wings can be found interspersed among and within blossoming mushroom (*lingzhi* 靈芝) clouds. This vestment is known as a *jiangyi* 降衣, which translates literally to "the robe of descent," wherein heaven and earth meet through the body of the priest.

iv. Clouds, fungi, birds—all are composed of needle-looped stitches, with each loop neatly nestled in the previous row.

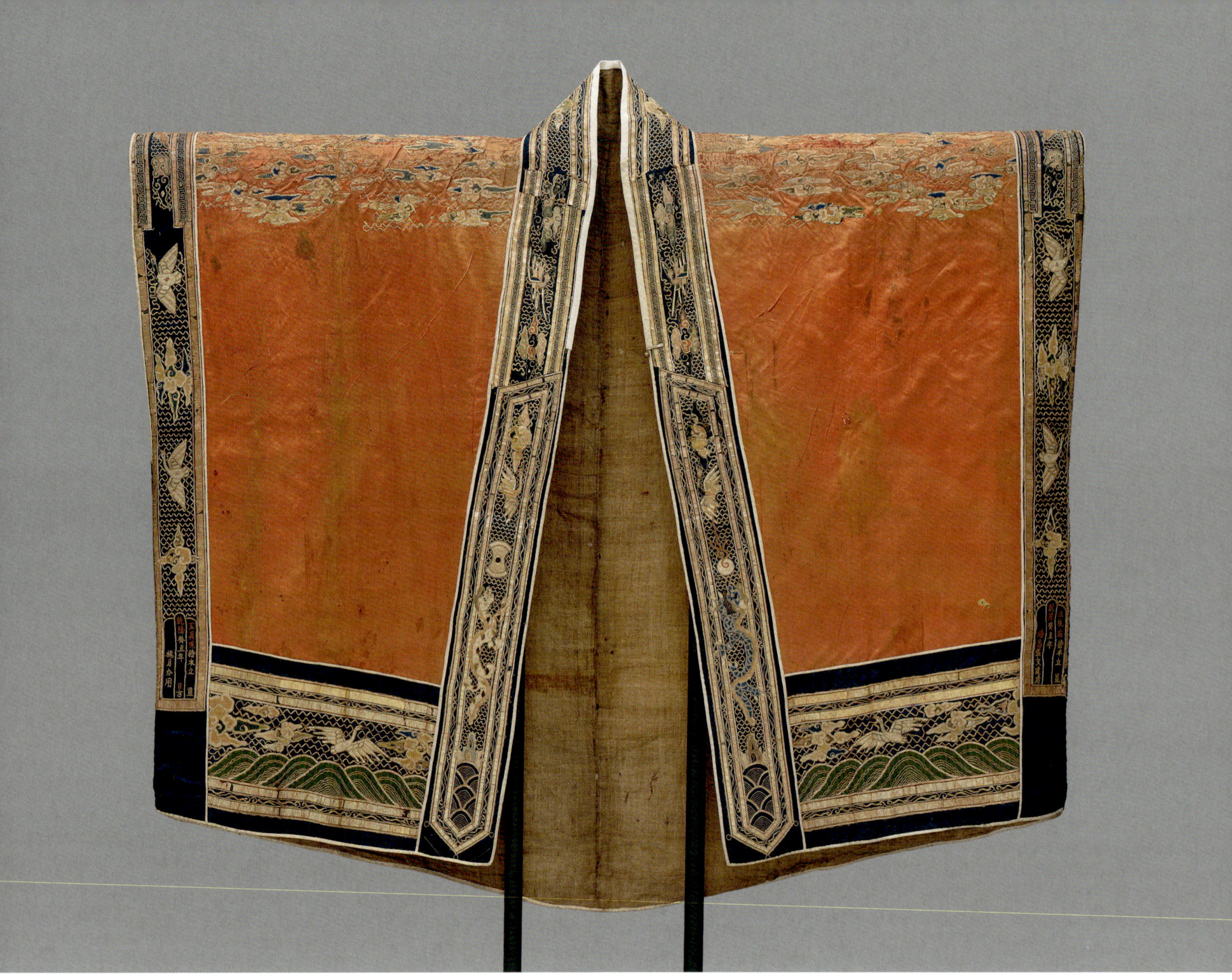

Fig 1 Vestment for a First-Degree Taoist Priest, Qing dynasty (1644–1911), 18th century. Han-Chinese. Silk, warp-float faced 7:1 satin weave; embroidered with silk, peacock-feather-wrapped silk, gold-leaf-over-lacquered-paper-strip-wrapped silk, and gold-leaf-over-lacquered paper in surface satin stitches; laid work and couching; appliquéd with forms of silk, plain weaves between two layers of paper, some with gold- and silver-leaf-over-lacquered paper, and embroidered with silk in chain and knot stitches, needle looping with laid thread and darned bars, and silk and gold-leaf-over-lacquered-paper-strip-wrapped silk, laid work and couching; edged with cotton, plain weave; lined with ramie, plain weave; metal button; 139.6 × 156.2 cm (55 × 61½ in.). Inscribed: *Zheng Wuda of Hai-chang, 1793*. The Art Institute of Chicago, gift of Mrs. Alexander F. Stevenson through the Antiquarian Society, 1907.322.

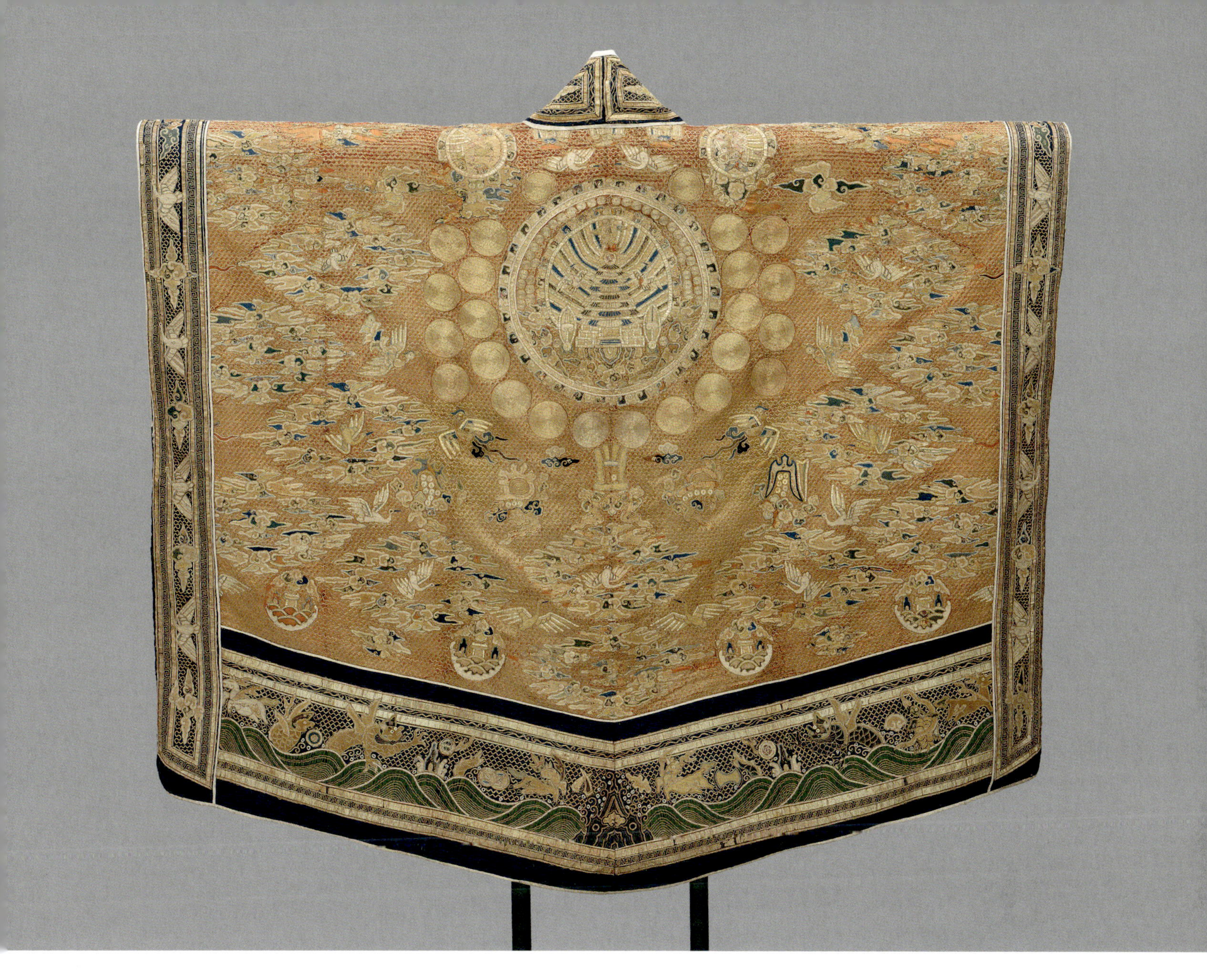

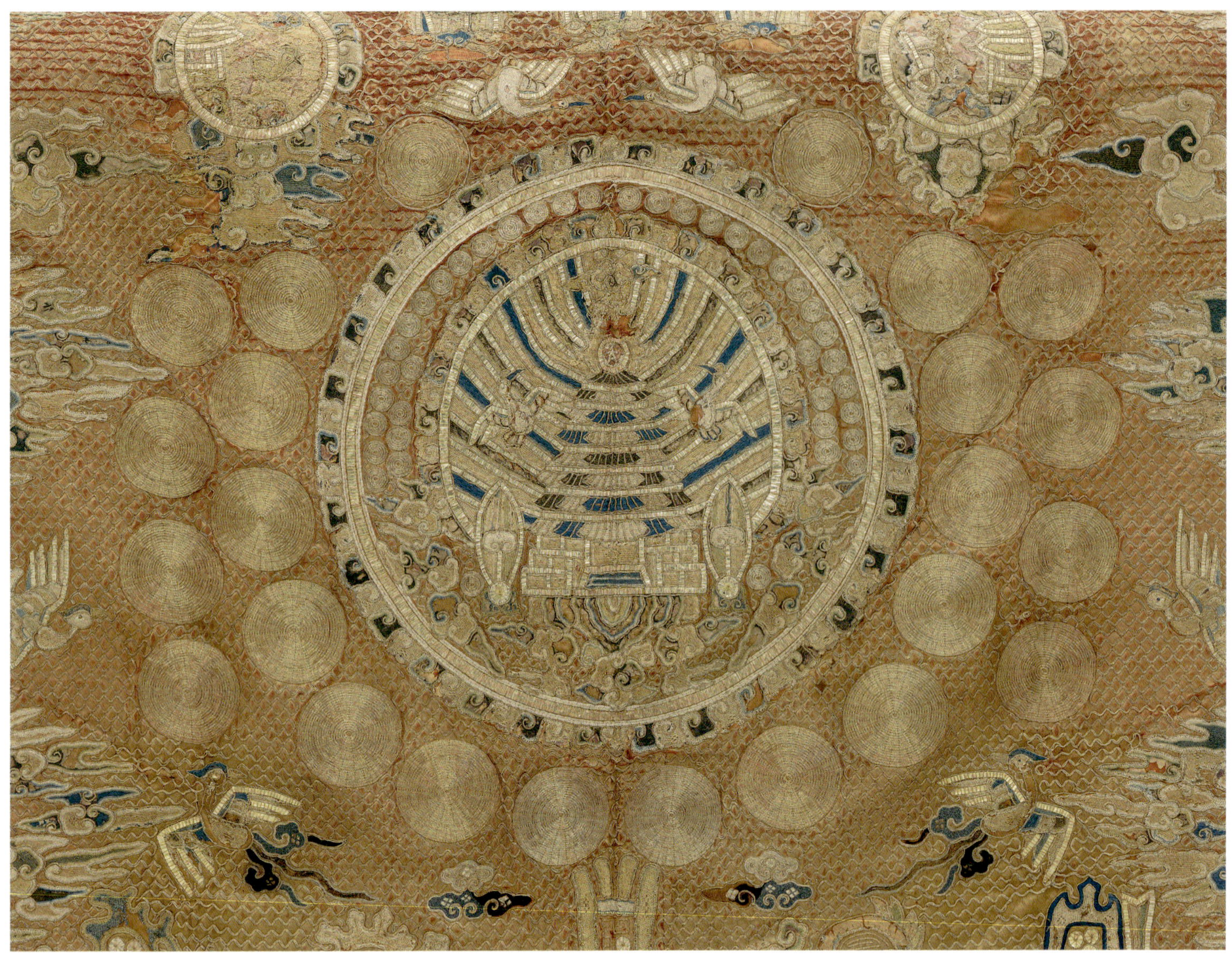

Fig. 2 The "Palace of Heaven" on the center
back of the vestment.

Upon a close inspection of the delicate embroidery on this particular jiangyi, my aunt and uncle tell me that this is certainly not the robe of any ordinary neighborhood priest; its abundance of decadent embellishments would not have been seen parading the dusty streets of their hometowns in rural Taiwan. But they have seen religious garments such as these while participating in funerary rituals, during which relatives of the deceased walk in a circle while chanting, ushering the soul from this life into otherworldly realms. Round and round they go, miming the motion of looped stitches.

v. Lost in the dazzling imagery of Chinese cosmology, I cannot turn away from these needle-looped stitches. Tracing the movement of shimmering silk thread, they guide me to sites of decay. In numerous areas, the looped threads composing the voluminous clouds are beginning to unravel, revealing black characters on yellowing paper underneath (see fig. 3). Perhaps these obscured notations were inscribed by the garment's maker to indicate a change in thread color or technique. Or one might let their mind wander—maybe the calligraphy hidden beneath the stitches holds spiritual meaning like lines from a mantra. The purpose of this hidden, talismanic text will remain unclear until the embroidery further decays.

vi. Having studied these unfurling stitches, I try my hand at needle-loop embroidery to imagine a way of mending them. Could they be rewound like a recording, a kind of time travel? Scholar Saidiya Hartman coined the term "critical fabulation" as a way to write into history's omissions.[2] Recognizing the way archives reinscribe losses and absences brought about by historical injustices, critical fabulation works into irretrievable gaps, holding space for perspectives that have been rendered invisible or deliberately erased. It is a contemplative process that perceives unknowing as a precondition and relies on speculation and imagination more than objective facts. Hartman makes clear that "the outcome of this method is a 'recombinant

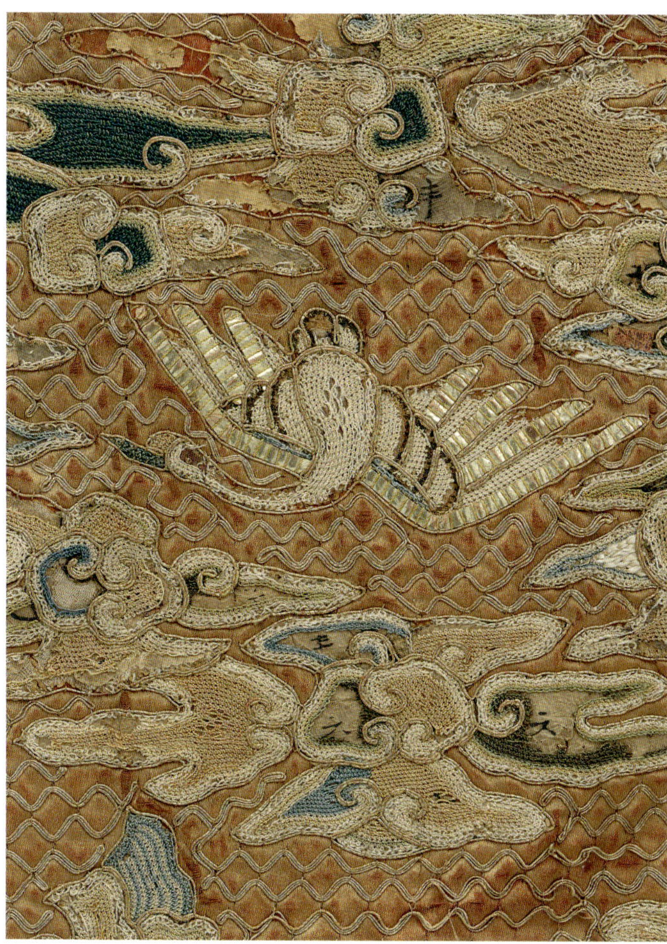

Fig. 3 **Areas of worn needle-loop embroidery reveal a layer of paper with notations.**

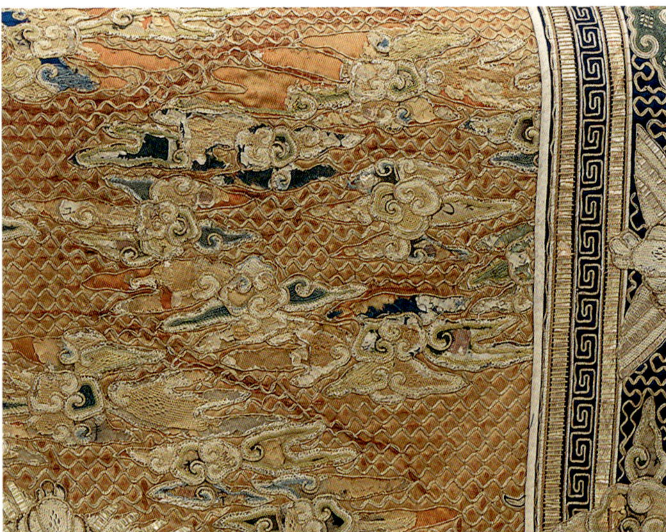

Fig. 4 Detail of the top-right edge of the back of the vestment, showing clouds filled in with vibrant-blue satin stitches in areas where the original needle-loop stitches wore away. This type of repair is used throughout the vestment. The cloud cluster is cut off by the garment's border trim, likely a sign of alteration.

Fig. 5 Detail of a cloud cluster on the back of the vestment with a crane in the center. The crane's body includes needle-looping and diamond-shaped eyelets. Some clouds feature a mushroom instead of a crane (see figs. 4 and 6).

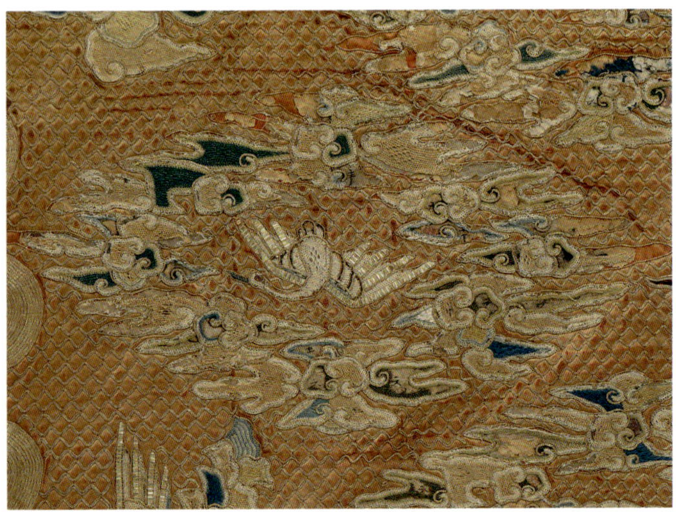

narrative,' which 'loops the strands' of incommensurate accounts and which weaves present, past, and future"—just like the pathway of a needle as it loops backward in order to move forward.[3] Stitch upon stitch, the structure relies on what came before. Textiles cannot be made without bringing the past along.

vii. The classic Taoist text *Tao Teh Ching* 道德經 notes, "a great tailor does little cutting," and likewise, the jiangyi refuses the individuation of sleeves and veils the silhouette of the human figure within.[4] Cutting is beside the point. Spirituality does not operate under the splicing logics of the scientific method, which strives toward the separability and singularity of known objects. Rather, this robe of descent folds heaven and earth, collapsing what is high and low into the same plane, onto layered and stitched fabric.[5]

viii. These eighteen ogival clouds are made up of smaller, petaled forms, primarily cream colored, sometimes pale orange, and other times more golden yellow. Occasionally their edges are outlined in needle-looped sky-blue and algae-green silk stitches. Interspersed with these subdued tendrils are rare areas of vibrant cobalt blue. Abraded threads have been repaired with satin stitches in this new brilliant-blue hue (see fig. 4). So tight and thick are these azure stitches that no inky calligraphic curl can be seen peeking through this conservation measure.[6]

ix. Surrounding the central palace on the back of the robe, sixteen needle-looped clouds are staggered in an orderly formation. At the iris of each of these eye-shaped cloud clusters is either a mushroom or a crane (see fig. 5), both featuring diamond-shaped eyelets that reveal tiny slivers of the underlying material. Three clouds are vertically stacked along the sleeves at the right and left sides, each of which includes a looped lingzhi cloud at the center. These bordering cloud clusters are just barely cropped at the seams. Positioned next to them, although slightly lower, three

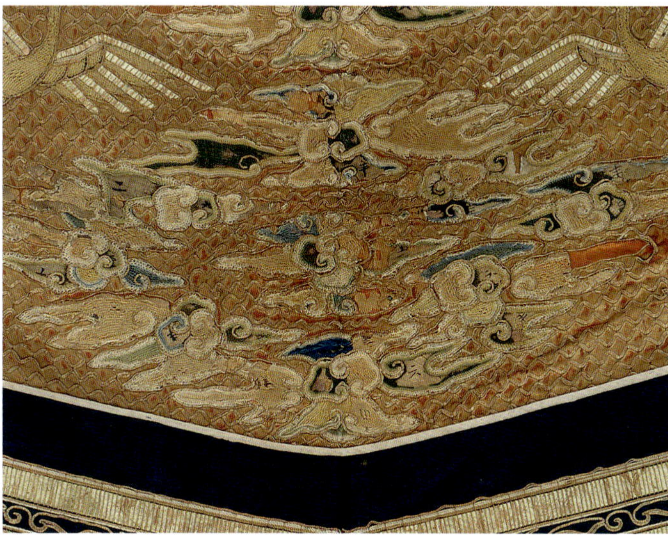

Fig. 6 Detail of the bottom-most cloud cluster on the back of the robe, with a *lingzhi* (mushroom) at the center.

more cloud formations flank the gilded pagoda on each side. A golden-yellow or white needle-looped crane is embroidered in the center of each of these six inner clouds. Directly above the row of clouds with cranes are two severed clouds, one each at the right and left shoulders. The eyes of these clouds are no longer visible; just the fraying lower edges of the clouds remain.

x. What had this most prestigious jiangyi endured that led to its eroding embroidery? How many priests—and later British or American collectors—have developed an intimate understanding of its ramie-lined interiors?[7] Clearly, the robe was beloved, worn, and later modified to hide or repair losses or tailored for a new, more petite person. To shorten the robe, the clouds were cropped at the shoulder seams where the three rectangular panels composing the garment meet. The width was also reduced, with the bordering mushroom clouds abruptly cut off where they meet the heavily embellished navy trim along the left and right edges of the robe (see, again, fig. 4). When the vestment is viewed from the front, one notices the awkward repair made to the neckline: To minimize the length and width of the vestment, the continuous navy-blue border had to be trimmed at the lapels.

xi. All that remains uncut lies at the bottom. Beneath the central Palace of Heaven, there are two more cloud clusters, one stacked atop the other directly along the center crease of the garment. A white, needle-looped crane with holes forming a small lace diamond on its belly floats in the eye of the top cloud cluster. Below this cloud, where the robe comes to a slight point at the middle, sits the last cloud formation (fig. 6). This cloud contains another lingzhi mushroom at its iris.

xii. The lingzhi cloud is a symbol of immortality. In Taoist funerary rites, the priest helps facilitate the transition of the spirit of the deceased from this life into otherworldly realms. Even after the death of the body, the immortal soul continues to dwell in the universe.

xiii. Meandering clouds guide me to recollections of my devout Taoist-Buddhist grandmother. My father recalls her daily routine: waking up in the morning to worship and light incense at the family altar and thank the ancestors and the heavens, immediately followed by preparing breakfast for the family. After finishing her work as a skilled seamstress, her hands would shift to the task of sliding prayer beads, one hundred and eight in total, while reciting mantra after mantra. This vision of her fingertips journeying from sphere to sphere recalls the ordinary, everyday practices that draw heaven to earth and enable women like my grandmother to move between realms. Her devotion was a means of finding peace amid the harsh conditions of political upheaval and poverty in the aftermath of World War II.

xiv. Ah-ma passed away two decades ago, but my family credits my early pull toward the needle and thread to her. Even if she is no longer with us, I feel her presence as I journey through these eighteen looped clouds and when I recreate their needle-looped stitches in my studio. This meditative motion of looping brings heaven onto earth, where she is beside me.

xv. With its fraying clouds and areas of repair, the Taoist robe is like a palimpsest. It is made of more than a dozen materials ranging from cotton, ramie, and silk to gilded paper and delicate threads wrapped in peacock feathers. Each individual element evokes its own associations and memories that together imbue the robe with an other-worldly aura. Composed of a looped alchemy of animal, mineral, and plant matter, the robe of descent envelops the human priest and augments his power.

xvi. Clouds can contain both mushrooms and cranes; they are of earth and sky. These eighteen clouds are situated in a glimmering field of waves. The rectangular vestment scintillates with the undulating movement of silk threads wrapped in lacquered paper strips covered with gold leaf.

xvii. Somewhere in the early morning skies above Brandenburg, Germany, I look out from the airplane window to greet the lake below. Reflecting the golden clouds in all their opalescent splendor, the water becomes the sky. Heaven and earth are no longer separate planes of existence; rather, they are that same sea of blue crashing onto the shore, creating inlets at my feet.

xviii. Just like the clouds floating on the surface of the lake, the robe of descent closes the distance between heaven and earth. Swimming and soaring are not so different in this realm of looped lingzhi clouds. After all, for mycelial networks there is no distinction between earth and sky.[8]

Notes

1   This essay is largely indebted to Shin-yuan Huang, Kung-shiuh Huang, Tsae-mei Huang, and King-long Lin and inspired by conversations with Fred Moten. See "Solomon Fellow Visiting Artist Talk and Reading by Fred Moten: Observance and Observation," April 13, 2023, Carpenter Center, Harvard University, Cambridge, MA, Vimeo, 1 hour, 47 min., 40 sec., posted May 10, 2023, vimeo.com /825549357.

2   Saidiya Hartman, "Venus in Two Acts," *Small Axe*, no. 26 (June 2008): 11.

3   Hartman, "Venus," 12.

4   Lao Tzu, *Tao Teh Ching,* trans. John C. H. Wu (Shambhala, 1989), 57.

5   Worn exclusively by the highest-ranking priest, the jiangyi represents the cosmos. Its rectangular shape symbolizes the earth, which is depicted as a square in Chinese cosmology. When the priest outstretches his arms, the array of motifs symbolizing the heavens becomes visible. The priest who wears this robe thus embodies the meeting of heaven and earth. For more information, see Kate Irvin, "From the Land of the Immortals: Chinese Taoist Robes and Textiles," RISD Museum, accessed October 18, 2024, risdmuseum.org /exhibitions-events/exhibitions/ land-immortals.

6   This robe bears evidence of various conservation measures from different time periods, such as the satin stitches filling in some of the unfurling needle-looped embroidery. There is no documentation regarding exactly when these blue satin stitches may have been introduced. Many thanks to Isaac Facio and Lucinda Pelton for their conservation insights.

7   For more information on the popularity of vintage Chinese robes in British and American markets, see Sarah Cheang, "Dragons in the Drawing Room: Chinese Embroideries in British Homes, 1860–1949," *Textile History* 39, no. 2 (2008): 223–49; and Elinor Pearlstein, "Color, Life, and Moment: Early Chicago Collectors of Chinese Textiles," in "Clothed to Rule the Universe: Ming and Qing Dynasty Textiles at the Art Institute of Chicago," special issue, *Art Institute of Chicago Museum Studies* 26, no. 2 (2000): 80–93, 106–12.

8   In various scientific studies, including those conducted by NASA, it has been shown that fungi can survive surprisingly well in space, including in zero-gravity and high-radiation environments.

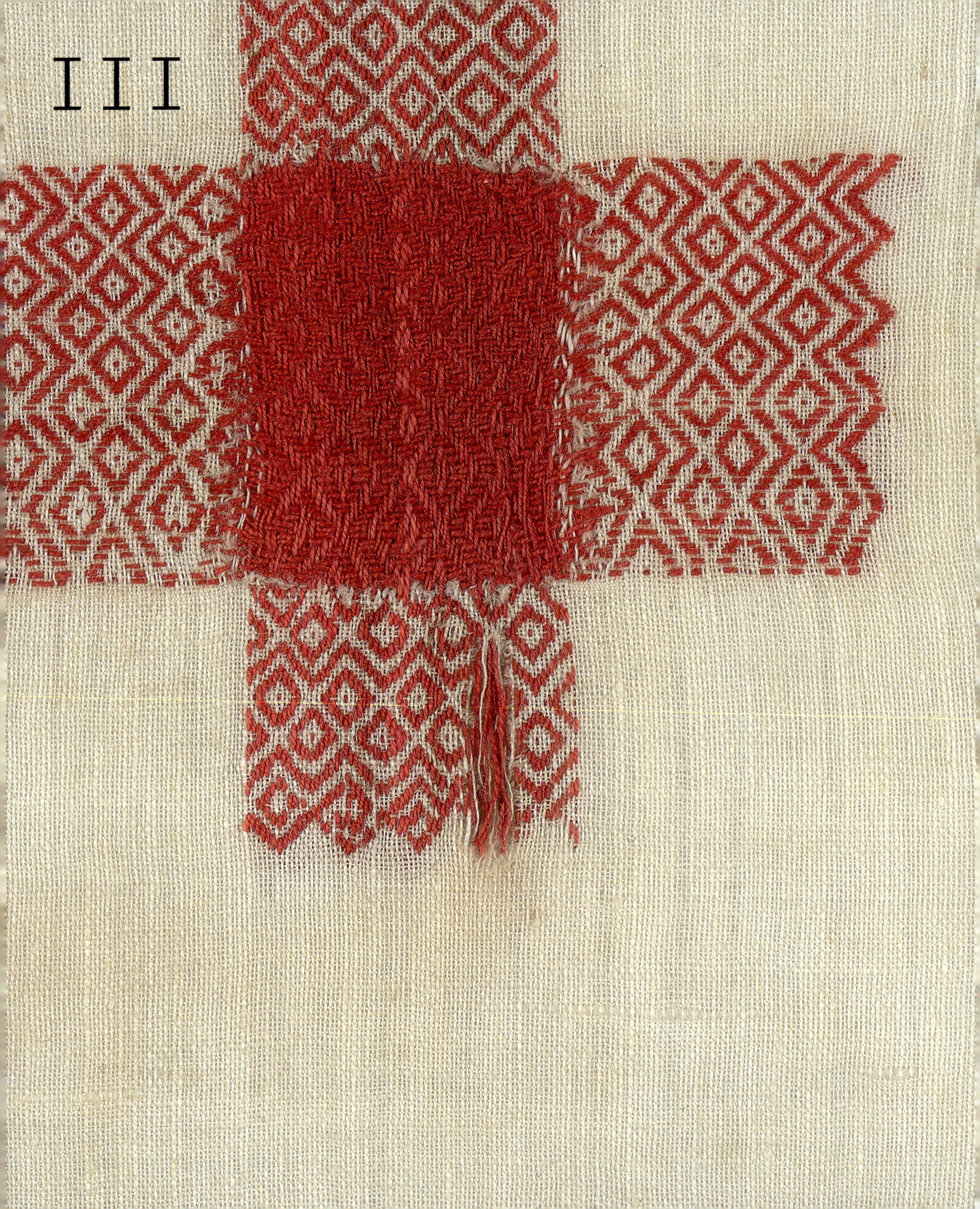

III

care
and
repair

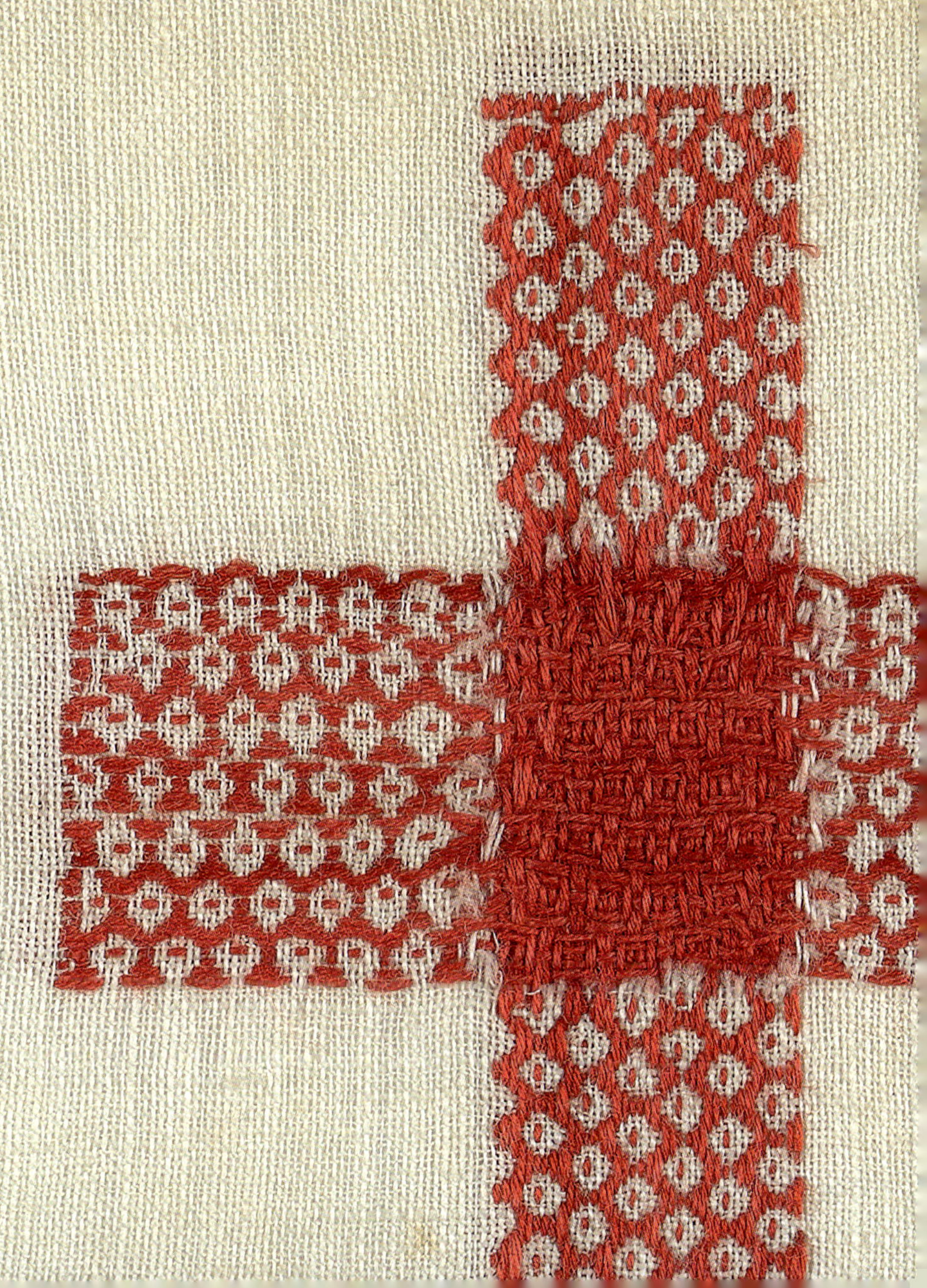

Fragmentary Understanding

Textiles in the Encyclopedic Museum

Melinda Watt
Curator

The stranger who arrives in Chicago from a moderate-sized European city and gets his first vision of this metropolis at the center of business, is prodigiously impressed by the swarm of humanity, wagons, carriages, automobiles, electric, surface and elevated cars. There is a touch of harshness, almost of brutality, in this surging mass, and the individual is made to feel, here you must go along or go under. Everything appears concentrated on the idea of gain, and one might suppose that the sense for the ideals of life did not exist. But how charmingly the stranger is undeceived when he reaches the shore of the almost boundless Lake Michigan, for there he beholds a temple of art, the Art Institute, facing the foot of Adams Street, which is a central artery, as one might behold an oasis in the desert.

—Paul Schulze, 1909[1]

In 1894 Chicagoans Martin A. Ryerson and Edward E. Ayer traveled to Europe together on a buying trip for two of the city's newest museums. Ryerson was buying for the Art Institute of Chicago, while Ayer was buying for the Field Museum. Both returned with hundreds of textile samples and fragments for the collections they supported.[2] At the time, Ryerson was reputedly Chicago's richest citizen and one of the most generous patrons of the city's cultural institutions. His family owned the only lumberyard to survive the city's devastating fire of 1871, and they were therefore indispensable to rebuilding Chicago, profiting handsomely in the process. Ayer was the first president of the Field Museum, one of the largest natural history museums in the world.[3] Twelve years after he donated the cache of textiles he gathered on the 1894 buying trip, the museum eliminated the Department of Industrial Art where they were housed, and the Art Institute acquired the collection.[4] The *Bulletin of the Art Institute of Chicago* reported that the collection numbered "about 900 specimens" and would "fill approximately 75 swinging frames."[5] This method of presenting groups of small, two-dimensional works, samples, or fragments using frames was promoted as early as 1868 by Henry Cole, founding director of the Victoria and Albert Museum in London, and it was widely adopted, with variations, by a number of European and American museums.

Displaying these small and fragmentary textiles grouped on frames was a convenient way to combine storage and display (see fig. 1). These new "swinging frames" adopted by the Art Institute were hailed for their compactness, accessibility to visitors, and ability to protect objects from light and dust.[6] However, the system was not considered aesthetically pleasing, as the *Bulletin* noted: "It is a matter of regret that so many of these old time fragments of fabrics and embroideries have to be mounted on cards, not precisely helter-skelter, but too often, nevertheless, with considerable detriment by conflict of color, texture, shape, etc., to their intended artistic values. The taste of qualified customers, architects and interior designers must be relied

"

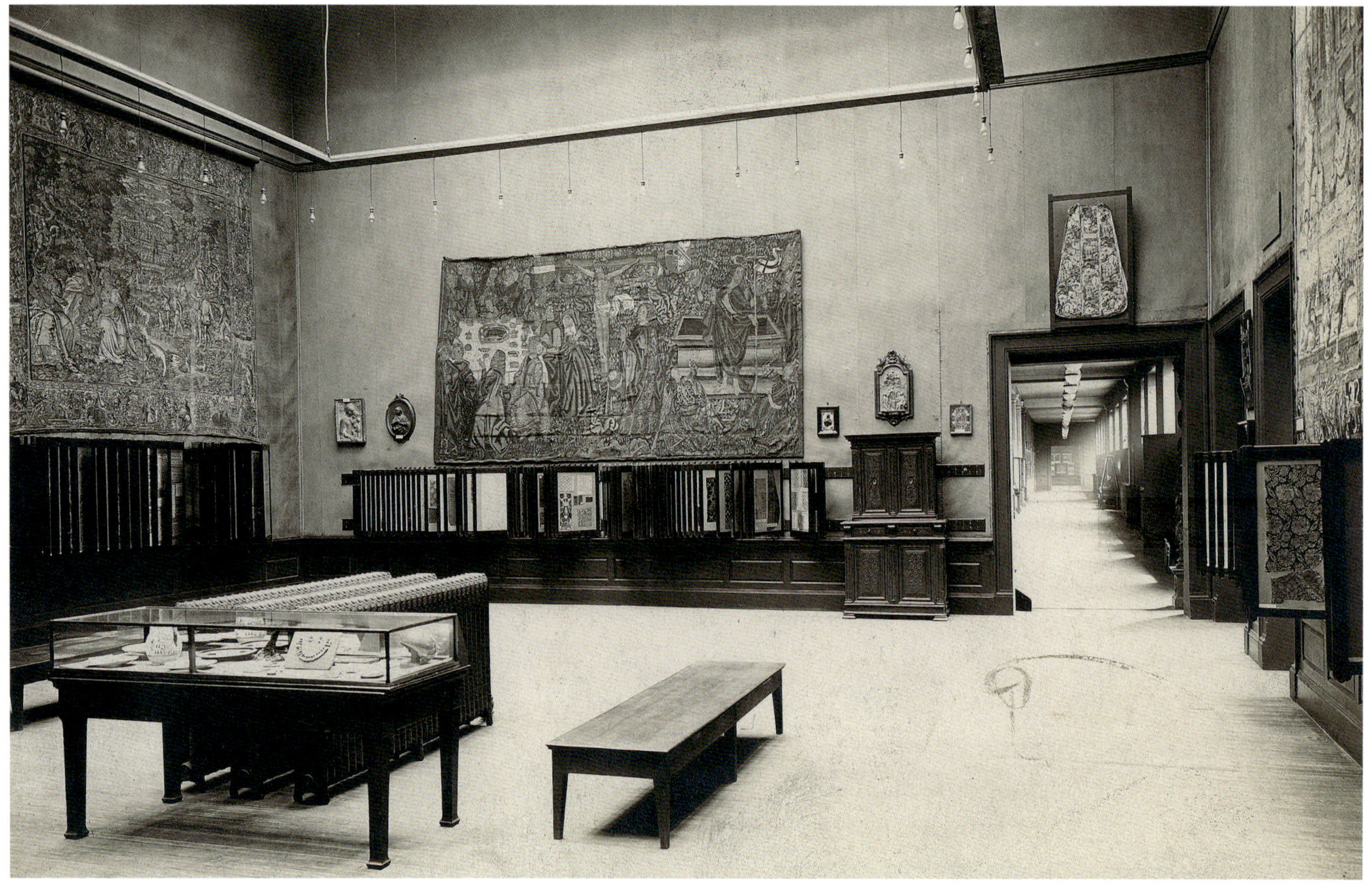

Fig. 1 **Room 45 at the Art Institute of Chicago, 1908. Swinging frames, used to display small textile fragments, line the walls.**

Fig. 2 (opposite) **Frame with Sixteen Mounted Fragments, Pharaonic Period (2600–1070 BCE). Egypt. Linen; plain weave, some extended warp fringe, and other variations; some pieced; 71.5 × 58.8 cm (28⅛ × 23⅛ in.). The Art Institute of Chicago, gift of Martin A. Ryerson through the Antiquarian Society, 1909.152.1–3, .11, .32, .36, .40, .42–43, .45, .51, .56–57, .63, and .65–66.**

upon to restore the textile arts to honor."[7] Very quickly, it seems, cataloging this "series of specimens" proved beyond the capabilities of Art Institute staff, and they sought expert assistance.[8] Ryerson invited Paul Schulze, then director of the Royal Textile Museum in Krefeld, Germany, and a professor of art and textile technologies, to "arrange, classify, and catalogue" the museum's textile collection, as well to deliver several public lectures on historical fabrics and fashion.[9] In addition to providing these services, Schulze also sold seventy fragments, purportedly of Egyptian wrappings for mummified remains (see fig. 2), as well as one extraordinary collage created by the professor himself (fig. 3). The latter is a stunning exercise in verisimilitude: Schulze adhered a small piece of fourteenth-century Italian woven silk to a support board, then used pen, ink, and watercolors to extend the image and complete a pattern repeat of the textile's design. This singular work embodies the multiple purposes of textile fragments in museum settings: It is simultaneously a representation of an important early European woven pattern, an exercise in drawing and understanding repeating woven design, and a pedagogical tool for scholars of history and technology. Throughout his museum career, Schulze also acted as a dealer of historical textiles, woven

WATT

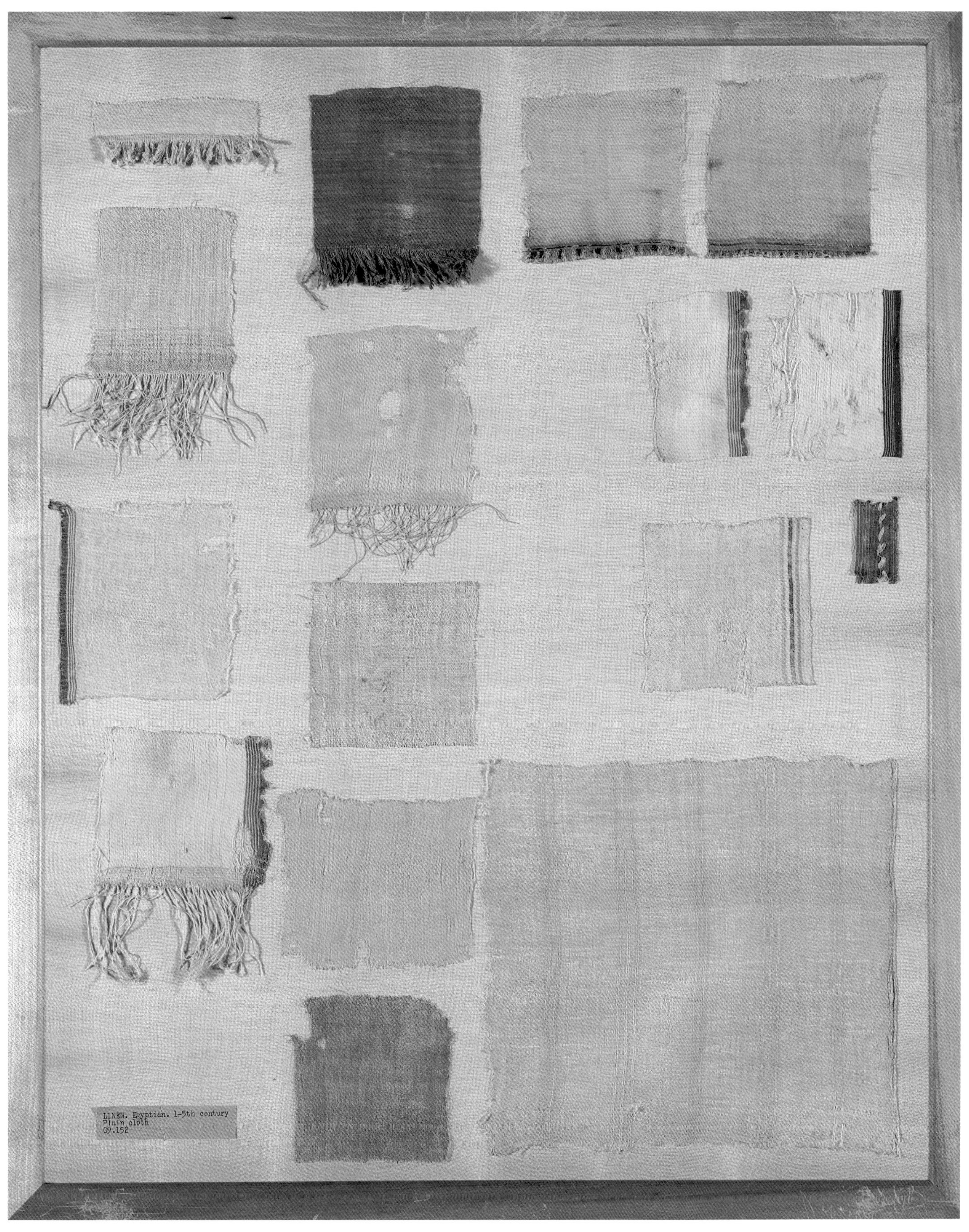

LINEN. Egyptian. 1-5th century
Plain cloth
09.152

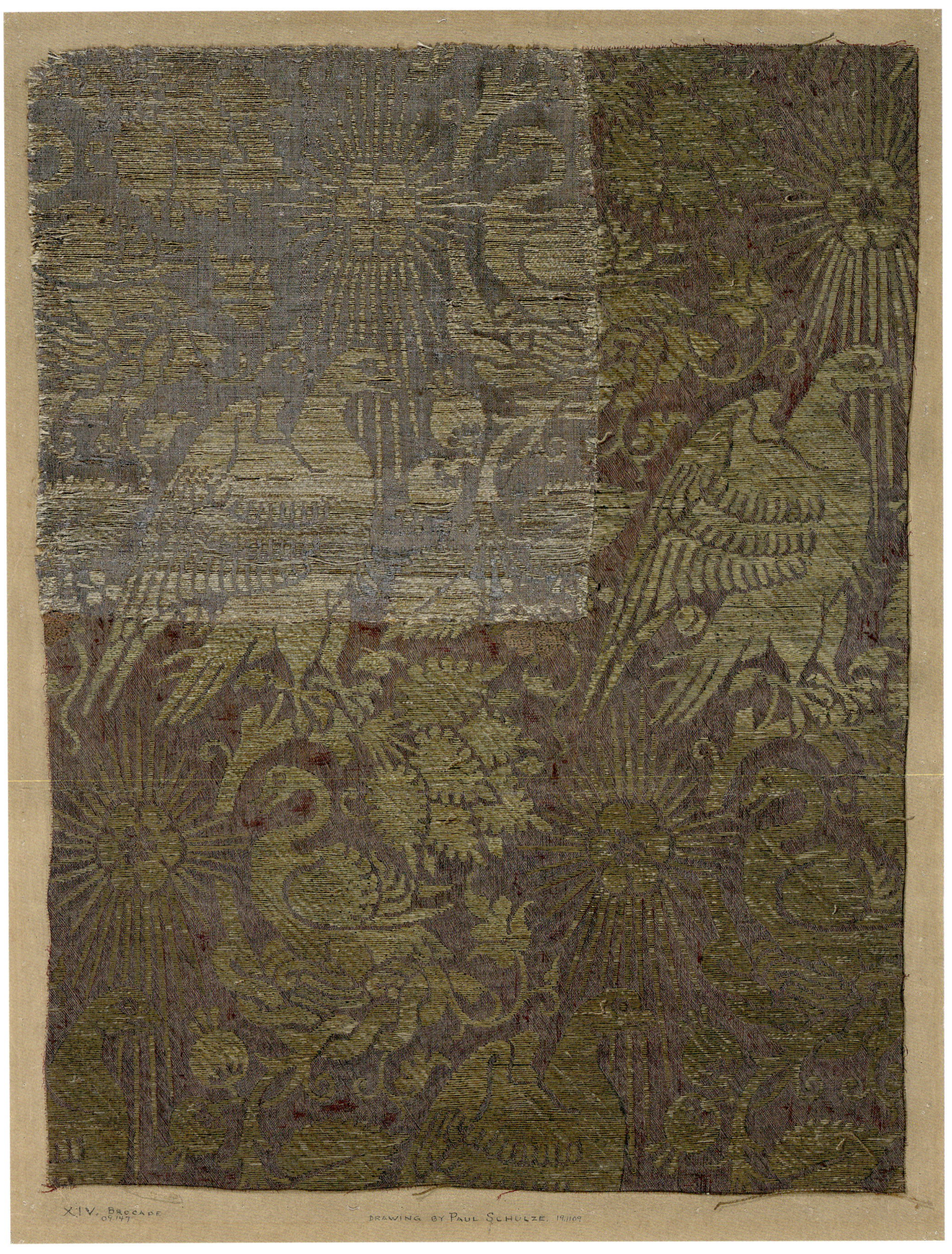

WATT

reproductions of historical patterns, and similar collages. The Victoria and Albert Museum, the Metropolitan Museum of Art in New York, and the Kunstgewerbemuseum in Berlin also have collages by Schulze.[10]

In this age of instant and accurate digital reproduction, Schulze's virtuoso performance may seem merely quaint. But many fragments that were part of this rich and diverse group at the Art Institute still inform scholarly discourse to this day, as researchers identify relationships among fragments scattered across European and North American museums. For example, a Byzantine-era Egyptian woven silk at the Art Institute has analogous fragments in the Victoria and Albert Museum, the Badisches Landesmuseum in Karlsruhe, Germany, and eleven other collections, requiring researchers to engage in something like a long-distance game of Concentration.[11] That these fragments are scattered across Western museums illustrates one of the results of museum collecting at its height during the late nineteenth and early twentieth centuries: Collectors like Ryerson and Ayers helped create a market for historical textiles that encouraged dealers to separate groups of related fragments—or, even worse, to deliberately cut them into smaller pieces to sell to more clients. It is no coincidence that the aforementioned group of seventy Egyptian fabrics are all neat squares and rectangles.[12]

A twenty-first-century museum visitor may reasonably question the value of fragile and incomplete pieces of fabric: Why expend resources on the physical care of such objects? In fact the practice of collecting textile fragments has a long history, and fragments that may seem insignificant to some actually hold great value for the study of art, culture, history, and technology. Private collectors and dealers began amassing fragments, especially woven examples, in the mid-nineteenth century, in an effort to develop a chronology of design and technique as a resource for textile-industry professionals. Two figures stand out in this history: first, Canon Franz Bock, a German priest who, via his access to church treasuries, acquired obsolete

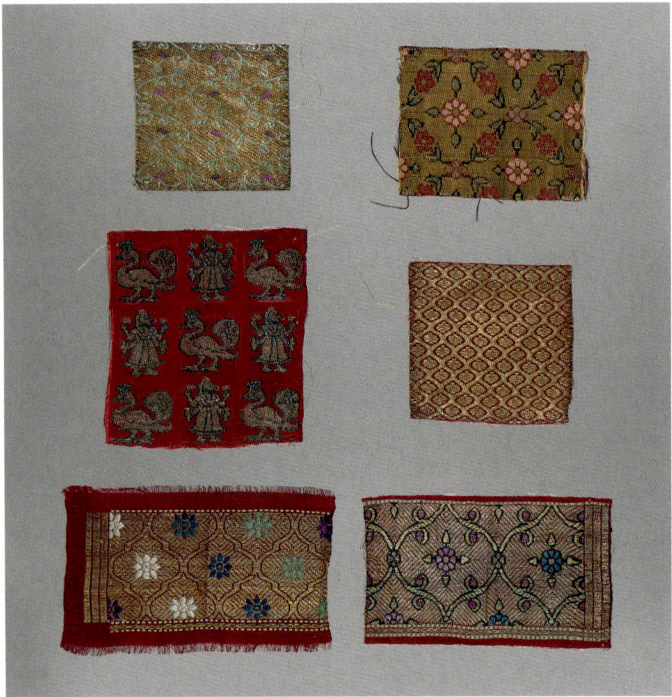

Fig. 4 **Six Woven Textile Fragments, probably 1870s. Probably Varanasi (Benares), India. Silk and metal-wrapped thread; various weave structures; various dimensions. The Art Institute of Chicago, gift of Martin A. Ryerson through the Antiquarian Society, 1907.863a–f.**

vestments and sold them to museums; and, second, Friedrich Fischbach, a German textile designer, professor, and collector who amassed and then sold collections of textiles to major museums. Bock published several of the first Western textile histories in the form of studies of European ecclesiastical vestments and imperial regalia.[13] Fischbach's lavishly produced and widely influential books mark some of the first attempts at a chronology of Western textiles, with illustrations taken from objects in his own collections.[14]

The so-called encyclopedic Western museum has been referred to as the "most Victorian of institutions."[15] Today, museums like the Art Institute resist the *encyclopedic* designation, recognizing both its entrenchment in colonial aims and the impossible standard it sets. The idea of museums as repositories of art and objects that can inform the public about the vast sweep of history has held sway into the twenty-first century, even as the museum community grapples with the troubling ways many objects were acquired in pursuit of the unattainable goal of being truly "encyclopedic." Such pursuits reflect distinctly nineteenth-century preoccupations with collecting and classifying objects acquired through colonial exploits. Henry Cole of the Victoria and Albert Museum was also a key organizer of the Great Exhibition of 1851, and the museum's initial holdings were drawn from this agglomeration of both mass-produced and handmade objects from countries that were then part of the British Empire, among other places. This accumulation of design objects was intended to educate and inspire the British public, industrial designers, and artists, one of the founding goals of the Victoria and Albert Museum.[16] Thus the Western concept of an encyclopedic museum was established in Victorian Britain.

Most encyclopedic museums in Western Europe and North America followed the lead of the Victoria and Albert Museum, including by making significant efforts to acquire historical textile fragments from around the globe to serve as pedagogical tools for artists and designers. The Art Institute, among other newly founded museums in the

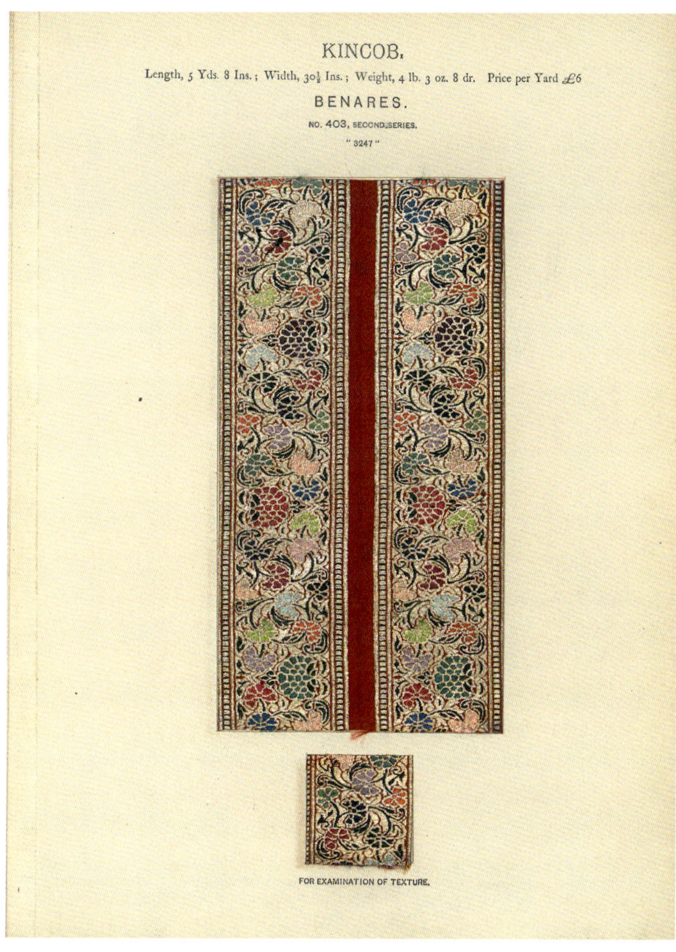

Fig. 5 Plate 403 from John Forbes Watson's *Collection of Specimens and Illustrations of the Textile Manufactures of India,* second series, *Kincobs, Nos. 401 to 458*, 1873. Thomas J. Watson Library, Metropolitan Museum of Art, New York.

United States at the turn of the century, placed an emphasis on collecting small but representative examples of textiles. Today, an internal database search of the Art Institute's textiles collection for objects identified as "fragments" yields over two thousand results out of the department's approximately fourteen thousand objects.

The Victoria and Albert Museum's stellar collection of textiles from the Indian subcontinent was drawn from the former India Museum, a collection of goods amassed by the East India Company (EIC) during its long domination of trade in the most populous and profitable region of the British Empire. Soon after the company was dissolved in 1874, the collections were divided between the British Museum, Kew Gardens, and the Victoria and Albert Museum.[17] The textile collection in particular served as a repository of designs and techniques to inspire industrial designers and artists in Great Britain. A group of six small fragments (fig. 4) at the Art Institute dated to the 1870s and attributed to the centuries-old weaving center of Varanasi in northern India may have once been part of the group collected under the auspices of the EIC. Very similar patterns also appear in the seventeen-volume work *Collection of Specimens and Illustrations of the Textile Manufactures of India* (1873–80; fig. 5), compiled and organized by John Forbes Watson. According to Watson, the publication's goal was to ensure that British textile manufacturers understood the technical characteristics of each fabric sample in the books well enough to duplicate it: "Each sample has been prepared in such a way as to indicate the character of the whole piece from which it was cut, and thus to enable the manufacturer to reproduce the article if he wishes to do so."[18] Watson's publications embody the British attitude toward global empire as the culmination of its colonialist enterprise to create and expand global markets. Watson and a coauthor also sought to catalog the people of the Indian subcontinent, just as they had its textiles, in *The People of India* (1868–75), an eight-volume work, illustrated with photographs, that was intended "fairly to represent the different varieties of the Indian races."[19]

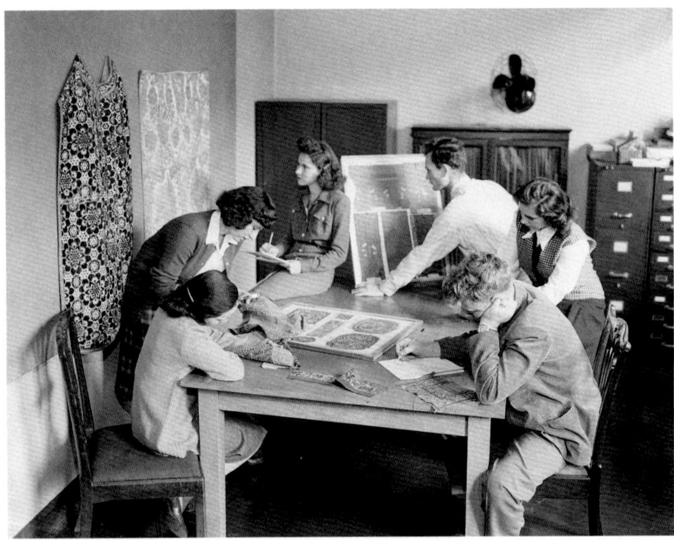

Fig. 6 **Students in the Art Institute of Chicago's Textile Study Room, 1947.**

Although Watson intended to distribute *Collection of Specimens and Illustrations of the Textile Manufactures of India* to manufacturers, we know of one individual who invested in a set of the books: Edward C. Moore, silver designer for Tiffany, who personified the late nineteenth-century global collector, educator, and artist, all rolled into one prodigious talent. Moore traveled frequently to London and Paris researching educational models for aspiring industrial designers, visiting international expositions, and acquiring decorative arts for his own design inspiration. In the early 1860s he founded a vocational training program at Tiffany where his growing collection of objects and books was at the disposal of students.[20] At the time, American encyclopedic museums such as the Met, the Museum of Fine Arts Boston, the Philadelphia Museum of Art, and the Art Institute were still a decade or more away from being founded, so it was no exaggeration when *Scientific American* declared that "the work which Messrs. Tiffany & Co. are now carrying on is of national importance; for their establishment is not only a great business concern but a school of art … and already many superior workmen and artists have in this way been made."[21] It is not known exactly when Moore acquired Watson's volumes, but he bequeathed them to the Met along with his art collection and reference books. Initiatives such as Moore's that emphasized teaching via objects contributed to the idea of the museum study room. In 1940 the Art Institute opened its Textile Study Room, which was filled with framed fragments as well as complete textile objects. It was open to the general public and actively promoted the idea that the museum was not just for scholars and specialists (see fig. 6).[22]

While many study collections focused on historical woven textiles, it was a popular activity among educated American women with disposable income in the late nineteenth and early twentieth centuries to collect examples of handmade European lace. An underappreciated category today, lace was highly valued as a fashionable accessory for both men and women from the early seventeenth century

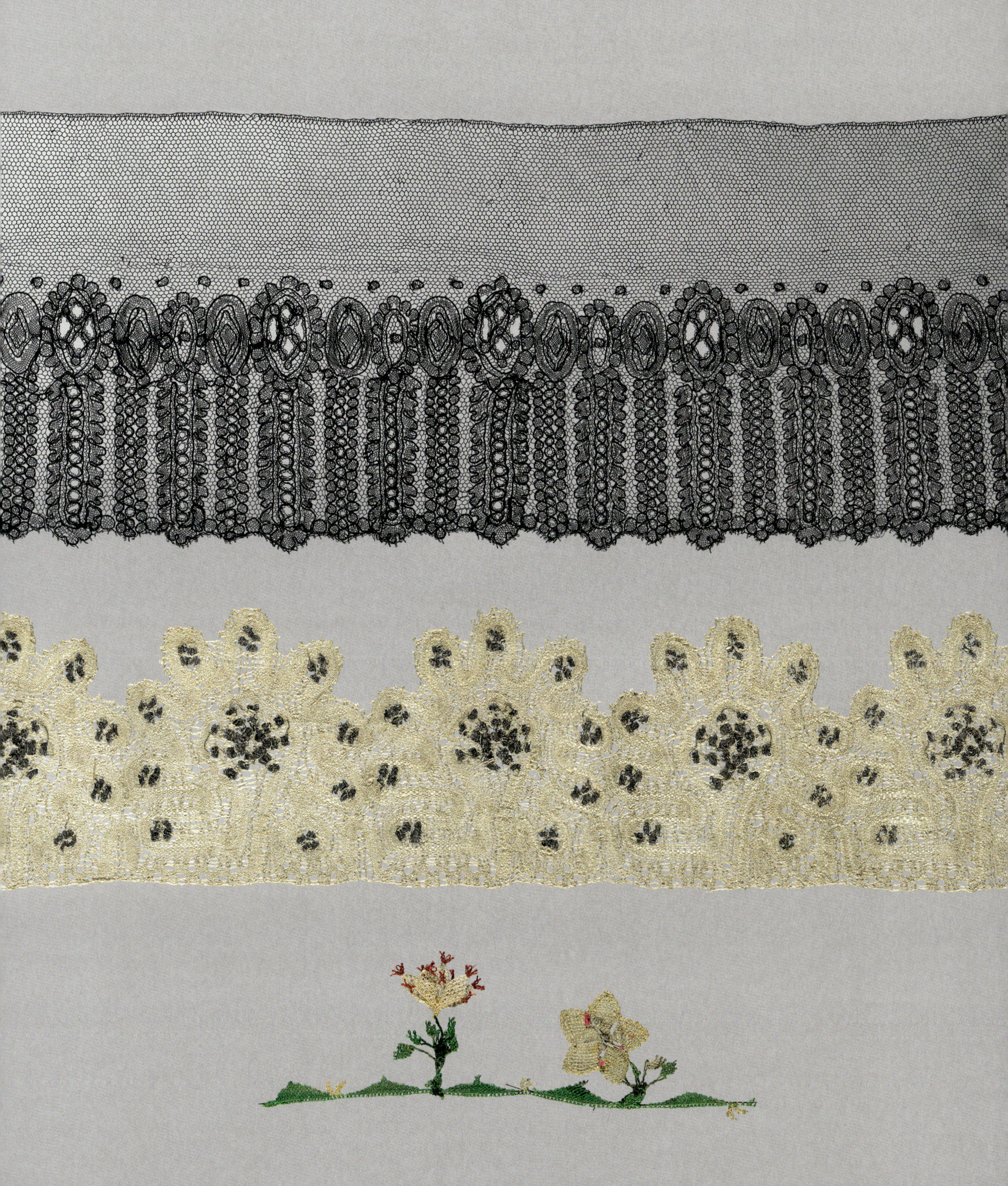

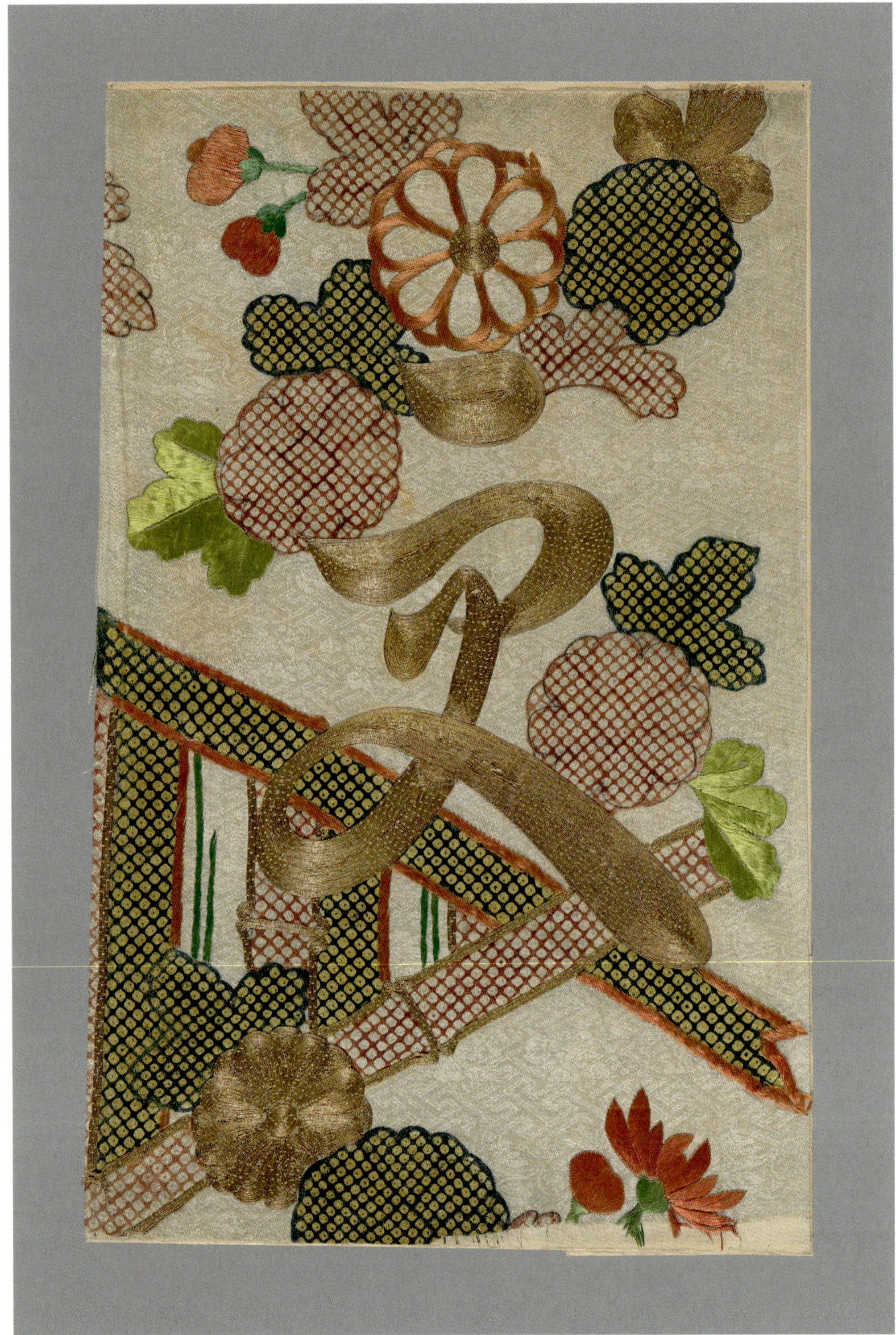

Fig. 8 Fragment of a Kimono, Edo Period (1615–1868), 1675–1725. Japan. Silk, gilt-lacquered-paper-strip-wrapped thread; stenciled; embroidered; mounted to wove paper; 36.8 × 23.5 cm (14½ × 9¼ in.). The Art Institute of Chicago, gift of Martin A. Ryerson, 1922.4248.

WATT

until well into the nineteenth century. Lace's slow decline in popularity coincided with the invention of machine-made varieties that all but destroyed the handmade industry. A Bohemian example (fig. 7, top) is one of more than one hundred pieces of lace donated to the Art Institute by the influential Antiquarian Society in 1900. The donation signaled the museum's dedication to preserving specimens of this dying art, the collecting of which can be seen as an exercise in nostalgia not only for the craft but also for the class distinctions that ownership of the highest-quality lace conferred.

Other fragmentary items of dress have particular evocative power. The technical prowess and unique design aesthetics of Japanese traditional dress are well represented by a fragment of kimono fabric (fig. 8) donated by Ryerson in 1922 with a group of ninety Japanese textiles and designs.[23] The fragment is typical of the refined fabrics for dress produced in Japan: a monochrome, textured woven silk embellished with resist dyeing, silk embroidery, and couched metal-thread embroidery. The full pattern of stylized flowers has been lost, and the precise meaning of a Japanese character embroidered in the center of the piece cannot be interpreted without the rest of the text.[24]

Historian Carol Breckenridge argued that "displayed objects must be textualized, and, therefore require verbal and written explanation in the form of signs, guides, and catalogues—if they are to be anything other than a mere accumulation of disoriented curios and wondrous artifacts."[25] Fragments such as a thirteenth-century Spanish silk (fig. 9) illustrate this point.[26] The appearance of the woven, golden interlace belies the complex history of attributions based on Catholic legend as well as evidence based on scrupulous scientific investigation. Commonly referred to as a fragment of the dalmatic of San Valero (or Valerius) of Saragossa, a Spanish saint who died around 315 CE, the fabric in fact derives from a group of luxurious thirteenth-century textiles likely made by Muslim artisans and used to create a sumptuous set of religious vestments

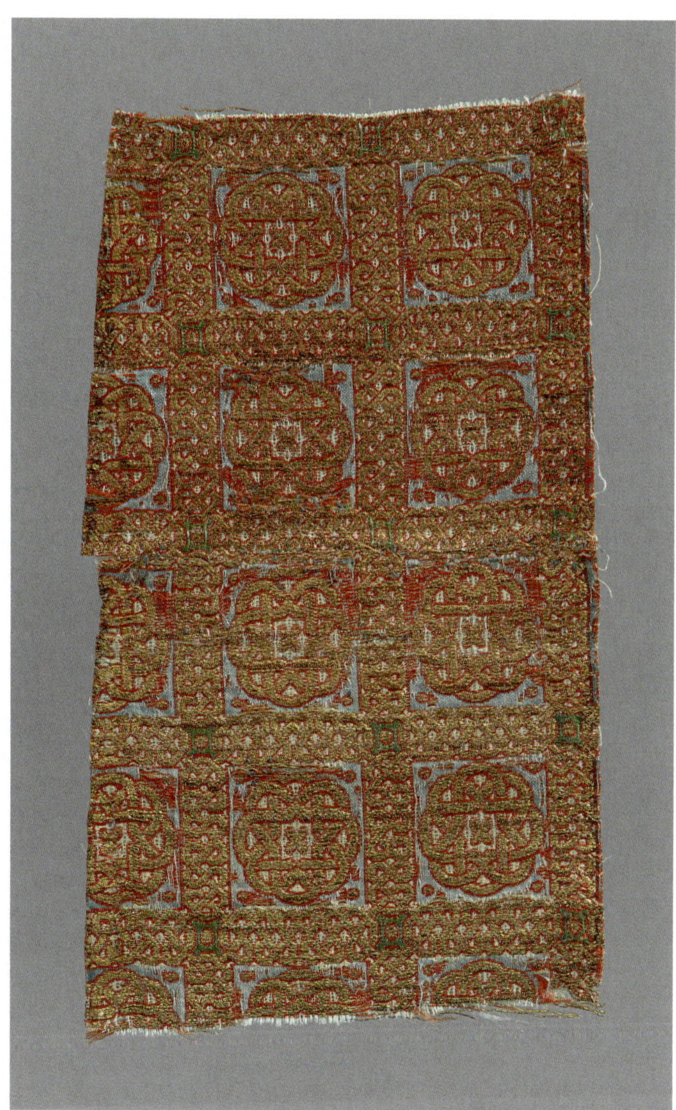

Fig. 9 Fragment from the Dalmatic of San Valero, 13th century. Islamic; Spain. Silk and gilt-animal-substrate-wrapped silk, weft-faced four-color complementary weft plain weave with inner warps and areas of detached plain interlacing of inner warps with complementary ground wefts; 13.5 × 7.8 cm (5⅜ × 3⅛ in.). The Art Institute of Chicago, purchased with funds provided by Mrs. Howell B. Erminger, Jr., Potter Palmer, R. T. Crane Jr., and Florence D. Bartlett, 1945.167.

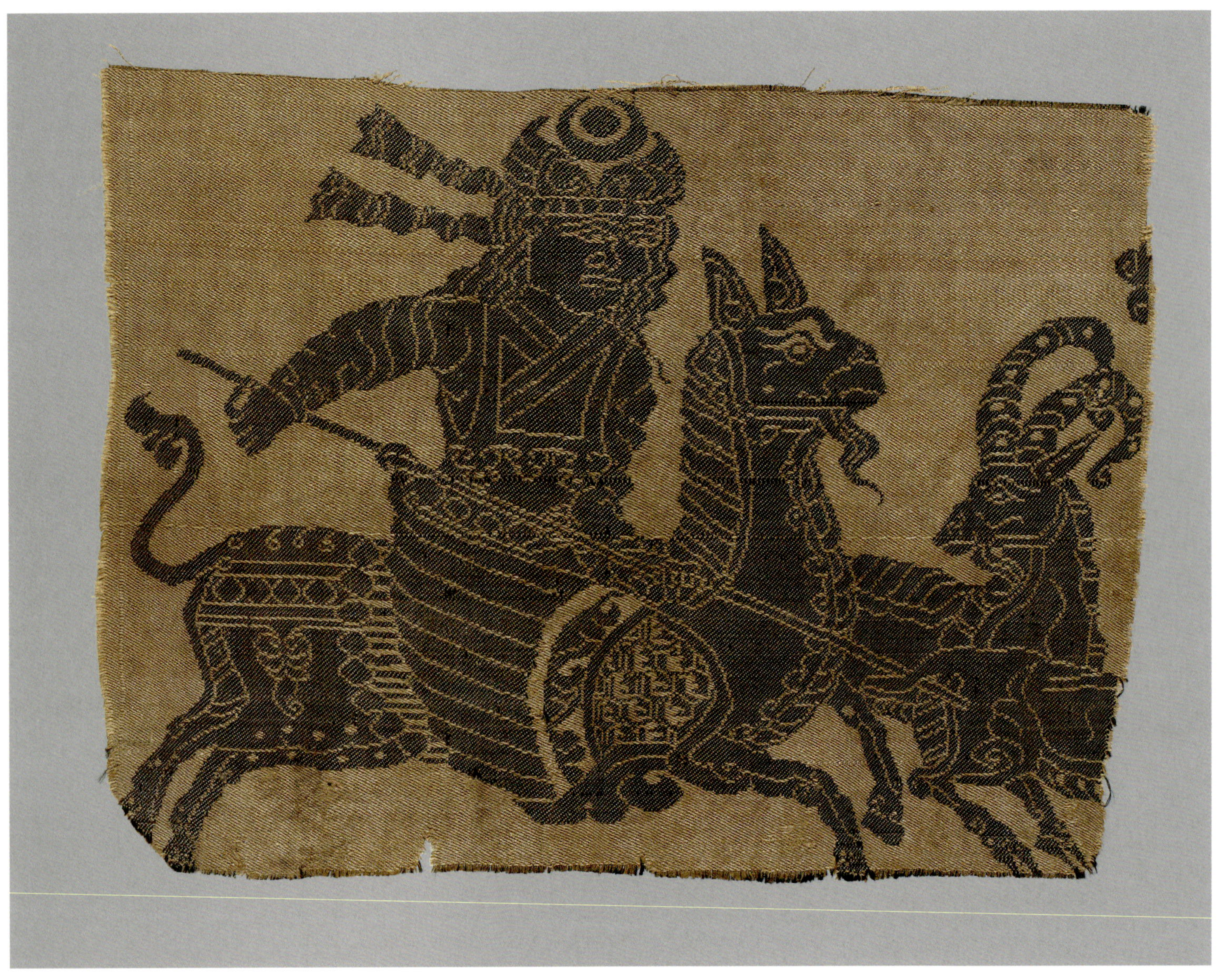

Fig. 10 Woven Silk Fragment, about 1930–50, imitation of a 10th- or 11th-century pattern. Iran. Silk, twill compound weave; 21.6 × 27.9 cm (8½ × 11 in.). The Art Institute of Chicago, purchased with funds provided by Harold T. Martin, Mrs. Noah Van Cleef, and Mrs. Daniel Green, 1983.527.

worn specifically during worship of the long-dead saint.[27] Although the textile's creation was far removed from the life of the saint, its status as a religious relic is nonetheless a part of its history.

Relics of another kind—those that purport to stand in for entire lost cultures—are also represented in the Art Institute's collection, such as a figural fragment of woven silk (fig. 10) formerly attributed to the Abbasid Caliphate and believed to be from the tenth or eleventh century. The fragment is about the size of a sheet of printer paper and carries a woven illustration of what appears to be a snapshot of a royal hunt: A king riding a winged quadruped (a symbol of dynastic divinity) wears a headdress adorned with a crescent moon and streamers that flow behind him in an indication of speed.[28] Armed with a spear, he pursues a ram with large, curved horns. But this glimpse of a thousand-year-old royal hunt is an illusion: scholars and scientists since the 1950s have debated the origins of the entire corpus to which this fragment belongs, concluding that many are early twentieth-century fakes.[29] The forger, taking into account that no scholar would believe that a fabric or garment of such age could survive intact, created fragments as part of their strategy to deceive.

Conversely, two pieces of an embroidered border (fig. 11) are genuine examples of imagery from a culture that flourished during the first millennium BCE and then declined due to environmental devastation. Made between about 100 BCE and 800 CE, the fragments are by members of the Nasca society that lived on the southern coast of what is now Peru. The repeating image of pampas cats, each holding a nut or seed in its mouth, reveals an important aspect of Nasca culture: These cats were revered because they controlled the population of rodents that would otherwise have destroyed food crops, and therefore they were essential to the success of Nasca agricultural practice. Symbolic felines on Nasca textiles and ceramics represented what they considered the most powerful category of predator on land.[30]

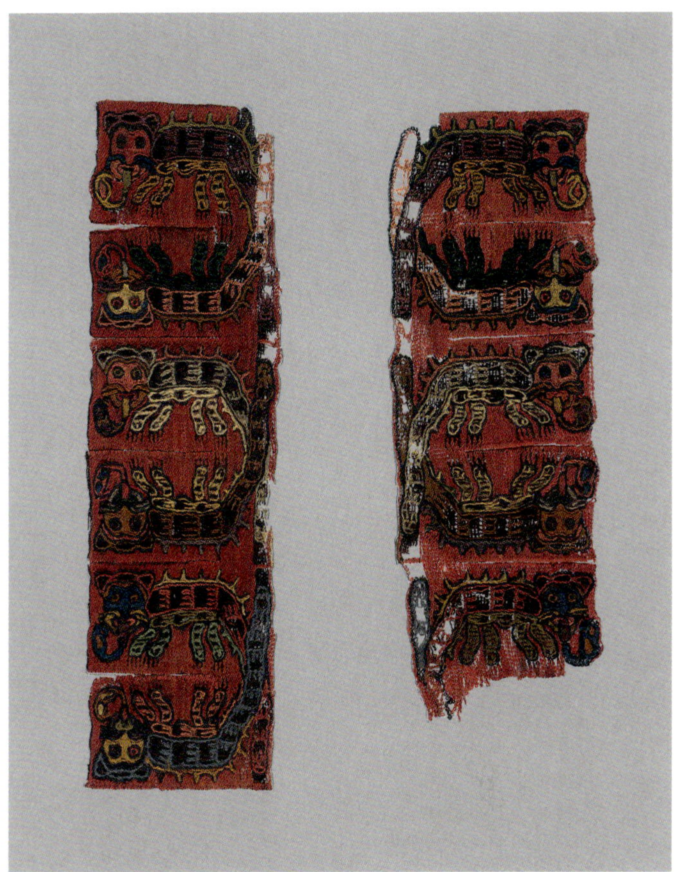

Fig. 11 Border Fragments, 100 BCE–200 CE. Nasca; south coast Peru. Cotton, plain weave; embroidered with wool (camelid) in stem stitches; left: 32.7 × 9.2 cm (12⅞ × 3⅝ in.); right: 27.3 × 10.5 cm (10¾ × 4⅛ in.). The Art Institute of Chicago, purchased with funds provided by Mrs. Chauncey B. Borland, 1956.403a–b.

Why do museums still collect and preserve fragmentary textiles in the twenty-first century? There are as many answers as there are textiles, for each has its own story to tell. The narrative value of objects like these is of renewed interest for museums that seek to interrogate their institutional pasts. Recent projects like *Fragmentary Visions: Grinnell College's Kelekian Collection* (Grinnell College Museum of Art, Iowa, 2023) have shown the pedagogical value of studying the objects themselves as well as the context of the modern art market. That exhibition used just a small group of ceramic, manuscript, and textile fragments donated to the college museum in the 1980s and 1990s to raise broader questions about categorization, contextualization, and ancient and modern networks of commerce and value.[31] Notable American collectors Banoo and Jeevak Parpia have been studying and buying textiles from the Indian subcontinent and South Asia for decades. Their own philosophy regarding less-than-perfect examples is based on these years of experience: "An important factor [in the development of the collection] was our acceptance that fragments were equally if not more worthy of a second look, and they often exert a heightened aesthetic appeal that is not found in complete extant objects."[32]

The practice of fragment collecting is strongly rooted in Victorian attitudes toward colonialism and encyclopedic museums, but these objects—and, we hope, our institutions—have value that transcends these origins, not least of all because of the new perspectives that conservators, curators, historians, visitors, and others continue to bring to these enigmatic works. A fragment can be like a little window, giving the susceptible viewer a glimpse of another time and place.

Notes

1   Paul Schulze, "Collection of Textiles at the Art Institute," *Bulletin of the Art Institute of Chicago* 3, no. 4 (1910): 58. The museum is built on landfill, and in 1909 the amount of land that had been reclaimed from the lake was much smaller than today, so the original 1893 building was much closer to the water when Schulze saw it for the first time.

2   Throughout this essay, I use the word *fragment* to denote a textile with an incomplete pattern that was once complete, part of a larger whole diminished over time through use. *Sample* denotes a textile that was deliberately cut into a small piece to represent a larger whole, usually made soon after the textile's creation for the purpose of marketing. Many textile "fragments" collected and dispersed by dealers in the late nineteenth and early twentieth centuries, however, were deliberately cut into smaller pieces so that private collectors and museums could each have representative pieces of a particular pattern.

3   Ayer worked tirelessly to convince a reluctant Marshall Field to support the museum and lend it his name, finally telling Field, "You can sell dry goods until hell freezes over … but in twenty-five years, you will be absolutely forgotten." Jon Anderson, "May 2, 1921," *Chicago Tribune*, May 20, 1997, chicagotribune.com/1997/05/20/may-2-1921/.

4   Christa Charlotte Mayer, *Masterpieces of Western Textiles from the Art Institute of Chicago* (Art Institute of Chicago, 1969), 9.

5   "A Supplementary Collection of Brocade Patterns, Pressed Velvets, etc.," *Bulletin of the Art Institute of Chicago* 2, no. 2 (1908): 28. Note that the current number is just over six hundred.

6   "Rearrangement of the Collection of the Antiquarians," *Bulletin of the Art Institute of Chicago* 2, no. 2 (1908): 28, *29*. My thanks to Elizabeth Pope for drawing my attention to this image.

7   "A Supplementary Collection," 30.

8   Schulze, "Collection of Textiles at the Art Institute," 59. The word *specimen* alludes to the scientific aspirations of this kind of mass collecting of any fragmentary material.

9   "Visit of Prof. Paul Schulze," *Bulletin of the Art Institute of Chicago* 3, no. 1 (1909): 12. The museum is now the German Textile Museum (Deutsches Textilmuseum Krefeld). Schulze was director from 1883 to 1926.

10   My thanks to Dr. Annette Schieck of the German Textile Museum and Silvija Banic of the Victoria and Albert Museum for sharing their collection information and ongoing research regarding Schulze's career.

11   My thanks to Stephanie Caruso for alerting me to ongoing research on this group of fragments that includes ten verified examples. The others are: Victoria and Albert Museum, 338-1887; Staatlich Kunsthalle Karlsruhe, Germany, T.169; Musée des Tissus et des Arts Décoratifs, Lyon, France, 891.III.6; Hungarian National Museum, Budapest, IM 8616; Germanisches Nationalmuseum, Nuremberg, G2145; Musées royaux d'art et d'histoire, Brussels; Museum im Andreasstift, Worms, Germany, T 565; Museo Nazionale del Bargello, Florence, 601.3; and Museum für Kunst und Gewerbe, Hamburg, Germany, 1889.8.

12   It is unclear how many different campaigns of mounting fragments in this format there have been over the last century.

13   Lisa Monnas, *Merchants, Princes and Painters: Silk Fabrics in Italian and Northern Paintings 1300–1550* (Yale University Press, 2008), 272.

14   For a summary of Fischbach's life, work, and influence on textile designers such as William Morris, as well as a discussion of his contemporaries, see Monnas, *Merchants, Princes and Painters*, 269–93.

15   Lara Kriegel, "After the Exhibitionary Complex: Museum Histories and the Future of the Victorian Past," *Victorian Studies* 48, no. 4 (2006): 681.

16   Originally called the South Kensington Museum, the Victoria and Albert Museum was founded in 1852 on the heels of the 1851 International Exhibition in London, often referred to as the Crystal Palace Exhibition or simply the Great Exhibition.

17   See "India Museum," British Museum, accessed October 30, 2024, britishmuseum.org/collection/term/BIOG10900.

18   Felix Driver and Sonia Ashmore, "The Mobile Museum: Collecting and Circulating Indian Textiles in Victorian Britain," *Victorian Studies* 52, no. 3 (2010): 370.

19   Driver and Ashmore, "The Mobile Museum," 367.

20   Medill Higgins Harvey, ed., *Collecting Inspiration: Edward C. Moore at Tiffany & Co.* (Metropolitan Museum of Art, 2021), 22.

21   Harvey, *Collecting Inspiration,* 22.

22   See "The Textile Study Room," *Bulletin of the Art Institute of Chicago* 41, no. 1 (1947): 6–8. The Met opened a textile study room prior to 1915; see "The Textile Collection and its Use," supplement, *Metropolitan Museum of Art Bulletin* 10, no. 5 (1915): 1–10, 12.

23   According to database and accession records 1922.4156–248 in Textiles at the Art Institute of Chicago.

24   My thanks to Janice Katz for her translation assistance. The paper to which the fragment is attached has an inscription that indicates this is one of a collection of kimono fragments and that it dates to the Kyōhō era (1716–36).

25   Carol Breckenridge quoted in Driver and Ashmore, "The Mobile Museum," 381.

26   Acquired in 1945 from the important dealer Dikran Kelekian.

27   Another fragment of this pattern is in the Met (46.156.4), along with three other fragments associated with the cult of San Valerius, 46.156.2, 46.156.3, and 46.156.10.

28   For the use of actual and mythical creatures in royal hunting scenes, see Louise W. Mackie, *Symbols of Power: Luxury Textiles from Islamic Lands, 7th–21st Century* (Cleveland Museum of Art, 2015), esp. 132–51.

29   For a summary of this debate and the relevant literature, see Mackie, *Symbols of Power*, 154–55.

30   My thanks to Elizabeth Pope for her interpretation of this object and its significance. See also Alan R. Sawyer, *Early Nasca Needlework* (Lawrence King, 1997), 102–3.

31   See Anne F. Harris, foreword to *Fragmentary Visions: Grinnell College's Kelekian Collection* (Grinnell College Museum of Art, 2023). I am grateful to Lal Verda Karaoğlu for bringing this project to my attention. The collection was donated by Nanette Kelekian, who was devoted to museums, art history, and sharing the legacy of her grandfather, preeminent art dealer Dikran Kelekian.

32   Banoo and Jeevak Parpia, introduction to *Traded Treasure: Indian Textiles for Global Markets*, ed. Ellen Avril (Herbert F. Johnson Museum of Art, Cornell University, 2019), 8.

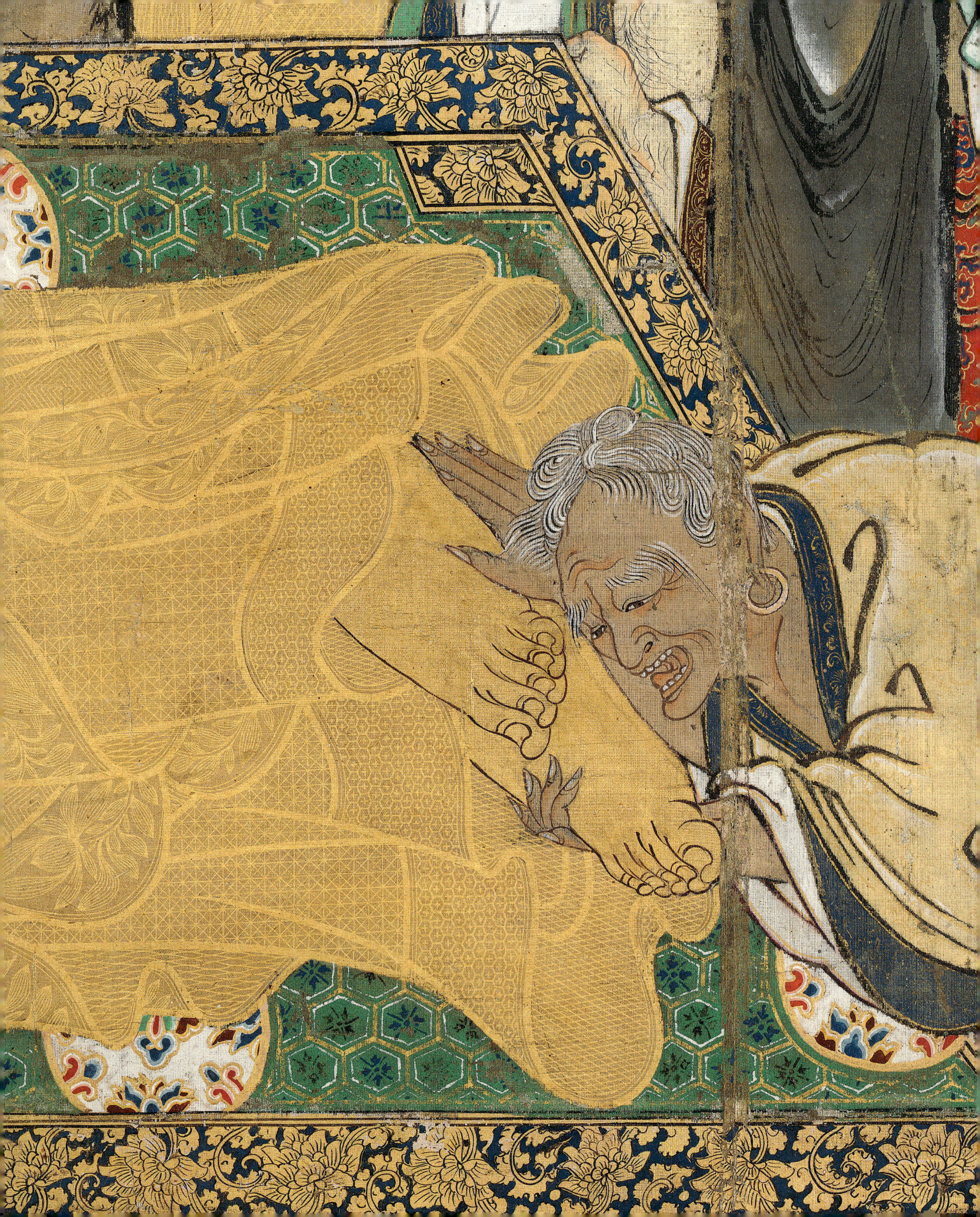

Wounds, Scars, and a Bandage

Jerry Bleem
Artist, educator, writer, Franciscan friar,
and Catholic priest

Losses, whether minor or major, shift relationships and alter futures. They mark lives irreversibly, forcing adjustments and leading us to seek strategies for coping and healing. No one lives without being wounded, carrying scars, or needing to be bandaged, either literally or figuratively. Death, the ultimate human loss, can be understood as both an ending and the beginning of a new—if unknown—reality. Two objects in the Art Institute of Chicago's collection from disparate cultures, geographies, and religions, *The Holy Shroud of Besançon* (fig. 1) and *Nehan: Death of the Buddha* (fig. 2), encapsulate this latter view. Both Christians and Buddhists believe in an existence after death, and both works depict religious leaders who have died. Rather than portraying Jesus's resurrection or the Buddha's enlightenment, however, these objects convey their fragile humanity just after their earthly demises, focusing on a transitory yet formative moment for each of these revered figures and their followers.

The Holy Shroud of Besançon belongs to the tradition of contact relics, textiles that reportedly touched Jesus at the end of his earthly life and were miraculously marked with visible evidence of that touch. The Veil of Veronica and the Shroud of Turin are two famous examples. The former is said to retain an image of Jesus's face after Veronica stopped to wipe sweat from his brow on the road to Calvary; the latter, like the Shroud of Besançon, bears an imprint of Christ's entire body, which was wrapped in the shroud after his crucifixion. The actual Shroud of Besançon, named for the French cathedral and town where it was kept, no longer exists. Judged as inauthentic, the cloth was torn apart to be used as bandages on May 24, 1794, by order of the National Convention.[1] Its destruction during the French Revolution reflects the period's anti-Catholic sentiment. Our visual knowledge of the shroud relies on prints, like the one in the Art Institute's collection by Jean de Loisy. Worshippers who traveled to Besançon to view the supposed burial cloth would have purchased such prints as souvenirs or as gifts for those unable to make the journey. Then as now, vendors at pilgrimage sites offered keepsakes of various designs,

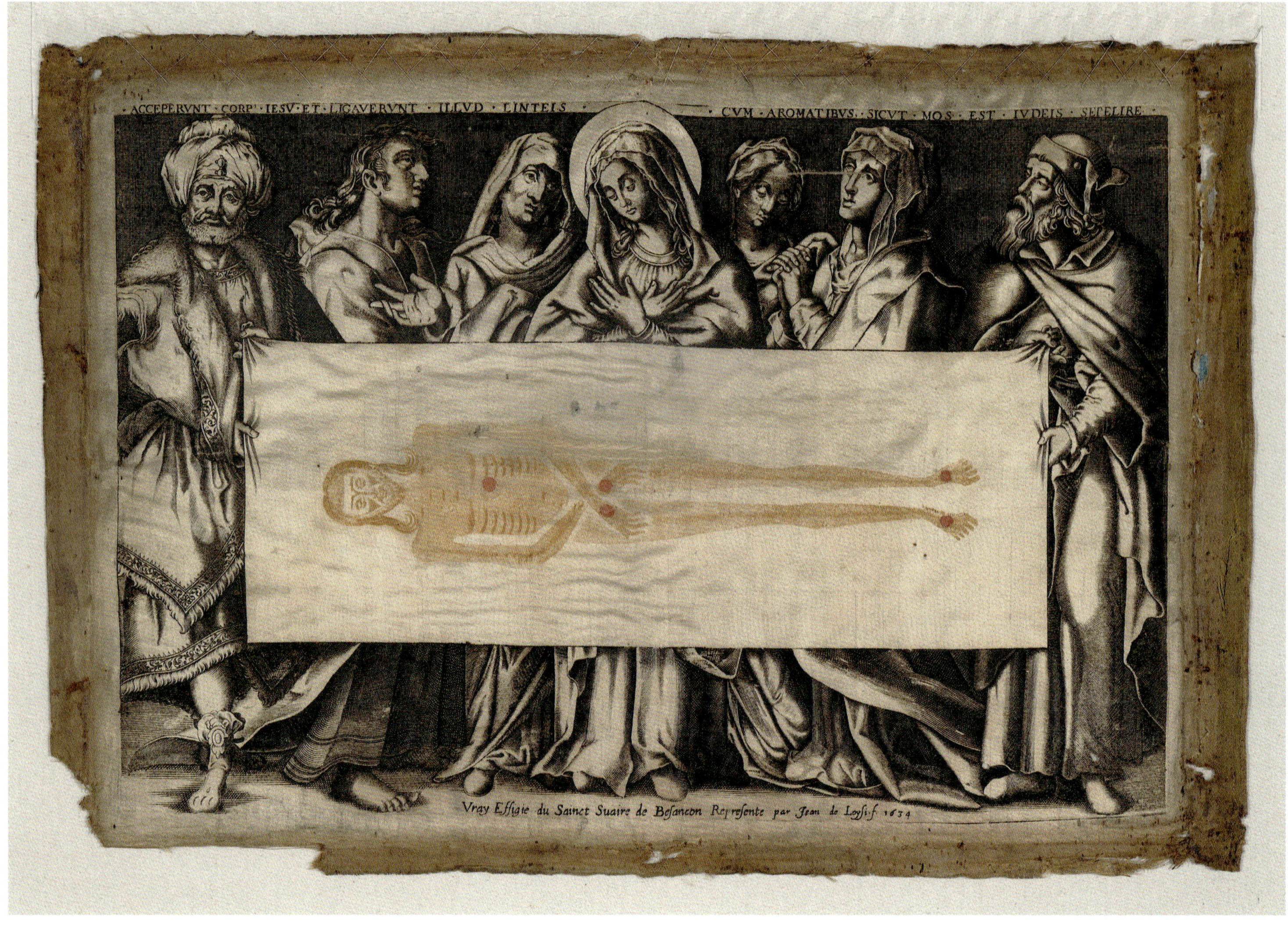

Fig. 1 Jean de Loisy (French, 1603–after 1660). *The Holy Shroud of Besançon*, 1634. Engraving in black and yellowish brown, with hand additions in red gouache on cream, silk satin weave; 32.4 × 48.3 cm (12¾ × 19 in.). The Art Institute of Chicago, the Amanda S. Johnson and Marion J. Livingston Fund, 2013.162.

Fig. 2 (opposite) *Nehan: Death of the Buddha* (涅槃図), late 17th–early 18th century. Japan. Hanging scroll; ink, colors, and gold on silk; painted image: 351.8 × 250.6 cm (138½ × 98⅝ in.); full scroll: 461.7 × 270.1 cm (181¾ × 106⅜ in.). The Art Institute of Chicago, Martin A. Ryerson Collection, 1921.161.

price points, and sizes as a way for visitors to remember their trip or share the experience once they returned home.

Loisy's intricate print on silk was produced for those able to afford a quality memento. It and other extant prints of various designs suggest that the original Shroud of Besançon included a frontal image of the dead Jesus—half of what is imprinted on the Shroud of Turin, which also shows the back of the body. While Turin's shroud resembles an X-ray, Besançon's suggests a drawing. This particular print—there were other compositions featuring different people—follows the Gospel of John in showing Joseph of Arimathea and Nicodemus presenting the Shroud of Besançon as the cloth used to carry Jesus's body to his burial tomb (see John 19:38–39). Standing behind the shroud—depicted in the same black ink suggesting their solid, earthy presence—are Jesus's mother, Mary; his apostle John; and Mary Magdalene. Gospel accounts name four women, as shown in the print, but do not agree on the identity of the other two who were present.[2] The residue of Jesus's body on the shroud is rendered in pale-yellow tones—the lightest in the print, as if to express the void

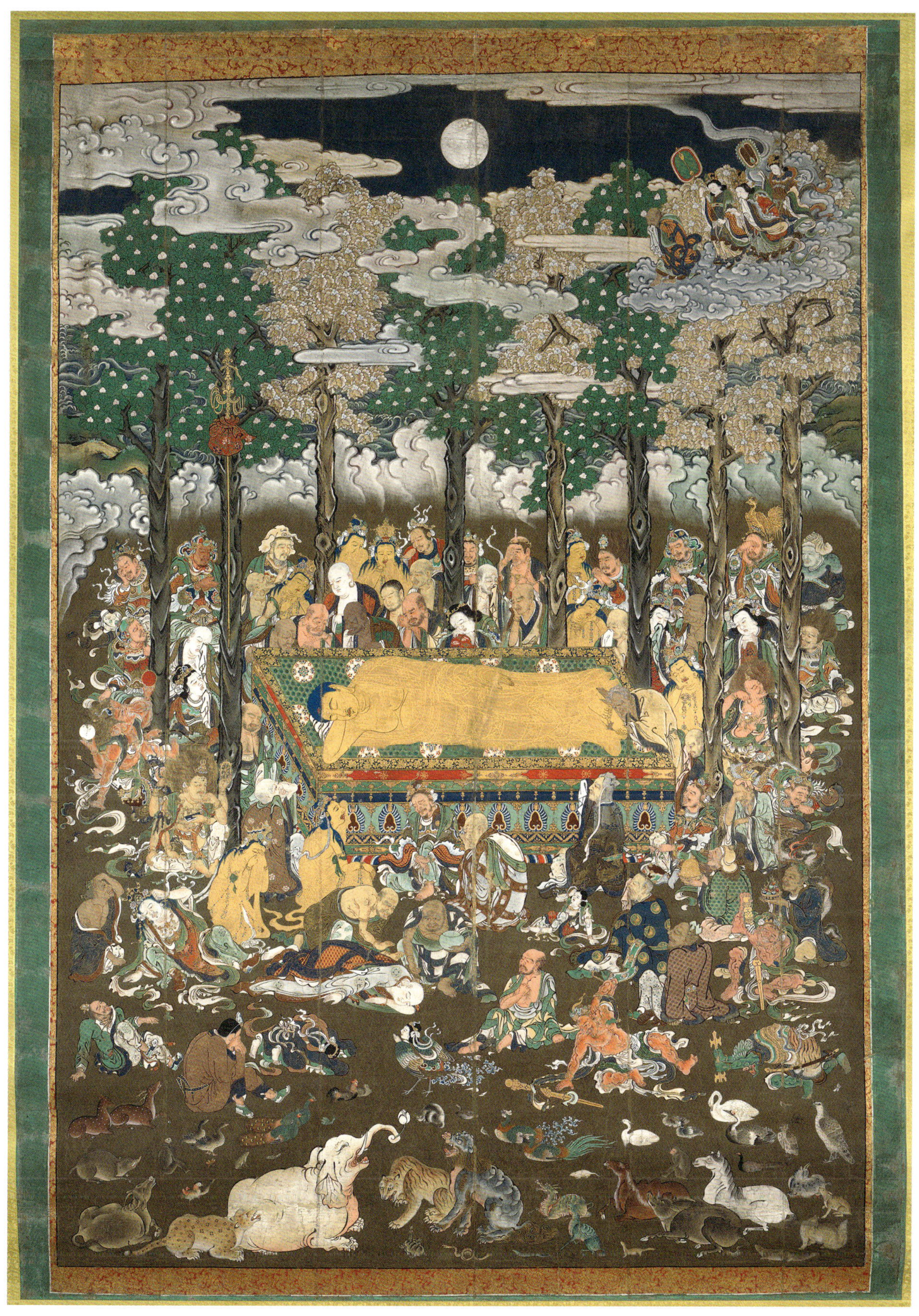

left by the passing of a beloved. Red, the print's third and final color, highlights the traditional five wounds of Christ: on his hands and feet, where he was nailed to the cross, and near his ribs, where his body was pierced to ensure that he was dead. As evidence of Jesus's violent death, these ruptures of the body's fabric chronicle human suffering, focusing the viewer's attention on the voids left by nails and a lance. Another Besançon memento makes the wounds even more obvious by punching out the nail holes in the print's substrate.[3]

The original Shroud of Besançon could be seen as representing the sorrow not only of those who witnessed the Christ's death but also of those who traveled to view the cloth. The Bible characterizes Jesus as both divine and human, but the story of his suffering and public execution emphasizes much more the vulnerability of his flesh. It is easy to identify with his despair and the pain of his death as well as with the grief of those who loved him. His death has been used to console those facing their own mortality as well as those mourning a loss. For those who carried Loisy's image home with them, it might have been more than a souvenir; it might also have been a balm for personal wounds.

The scene of mourning in *Nehan: Death of the Buddha* is no less solemn but far less intimate. Monumental and strikingly colorful, this painting on silk was likely used in a temple or some other public space on the annual remembrance of the death of Siddhartha Gautama, the historical Buddha, who died upon achieving *nehan*, or nirvana. Unlike Loisy's print presenting a small group of grief-stricken family members and disciples, *Nehan* gathers representatives of all living beings at the Buddha's deathbed. Animals, people of every social class, mythological beings, Hindu deities, and guardians gather as witnesses to this pivotal moment—not only the Buddha's death but also his attainment of nirvana. The variety and complexity of their reactions mirror the diversity of responses when anyone dies. The bodhisattvas, enlightened beings who have delayed nirvana to help others, no longer suffer or have desires; most of these figures, cognizant of what has been achieved, respectfully and tranquilly observe the dead Buddha with a depth of understanding that eludes others. Their golden bodies and attire, like the Buddha's, indicate their enlightened state.[4]

Others, however, are heartbroken; they cover their faces with their hands or use handkerchiefs to wipe away tears. In the upper-right corner of the scroll, the Buddha's distraught mother, Maya, and her attendants hurry to her son. With her hand to her mouth, she responds as a parent devastated by the death of a child. Before the deathbed's left side, a monk, overwhelmed by sorrow, has fainted; two of the assembly compassionately console him with soothing pats and reviving water. Another mourning disciple, perhaps faithful Ananda, sets aside all he has learned about detachment and shamelessly expresses his grief, tenderly holding the Buddha's feet in a gesture of respect and bowing in a posture of blessing that movingly declares the depth of his loss. Their wounds, although not physical, are undeniable.

Cloth, as the material we wear against our bodies, has been used as a metaphor for skin. This analogy extends to the way fabric is repaired: as mending restores the wholeness of cloth, so torn bodies and psyches may be sewn up over time. And just as there are many ways to heal wounds and trauma, there are also many ways to renew and care for garments. Nineteenth-century darning (or mending) samplers illustrate an array of techniques for repairing damage to a woven surface by replicating its structure. An example dated 1808—probably created in the Netherlands by Maria de Bruÿn—uses red thread on a white cotton background to illustrate how to replace absent warp and weft threads to reconstruct a damaged or missing area of a garment or other fabric item (fig. 3). Here, the high-contrast colors serve to instruct a future mender, but it is likely that actual repairs would have matched as much as possible the color of the cloth being mended, so that the restoration would be inconspicuous. In an era when handmade cloth was too precious to discard even when it was showing signs of wear, the ability to disguise these reconstructed areas was a prized skill. And yet the sampler shows repairs themselves as artful designs of unique beauty.

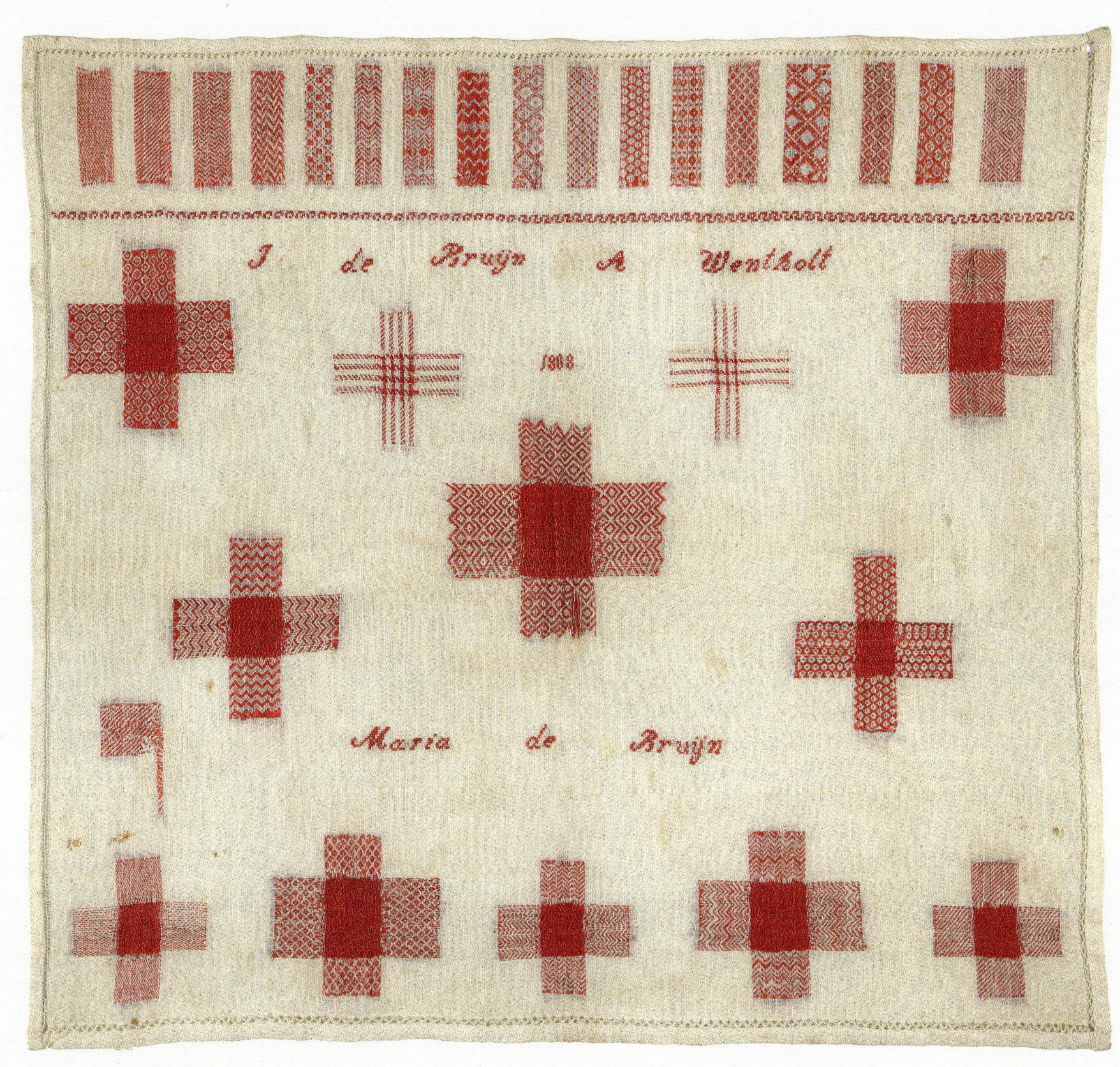

Fig. 3 Darning Sampler, 1808. Possibly Maria de Bruÿn (Dutch, active early 19th century). The Netherlands. Cotton, plain weave; embroidered in darning and cross stitches; 33.5 × 36.7 cm (13⅛ × 14½ in.). The Art Institute of Chicago, gift of Mrs. Harold Keele through the Needlework and Textile Guild, 1976.129.

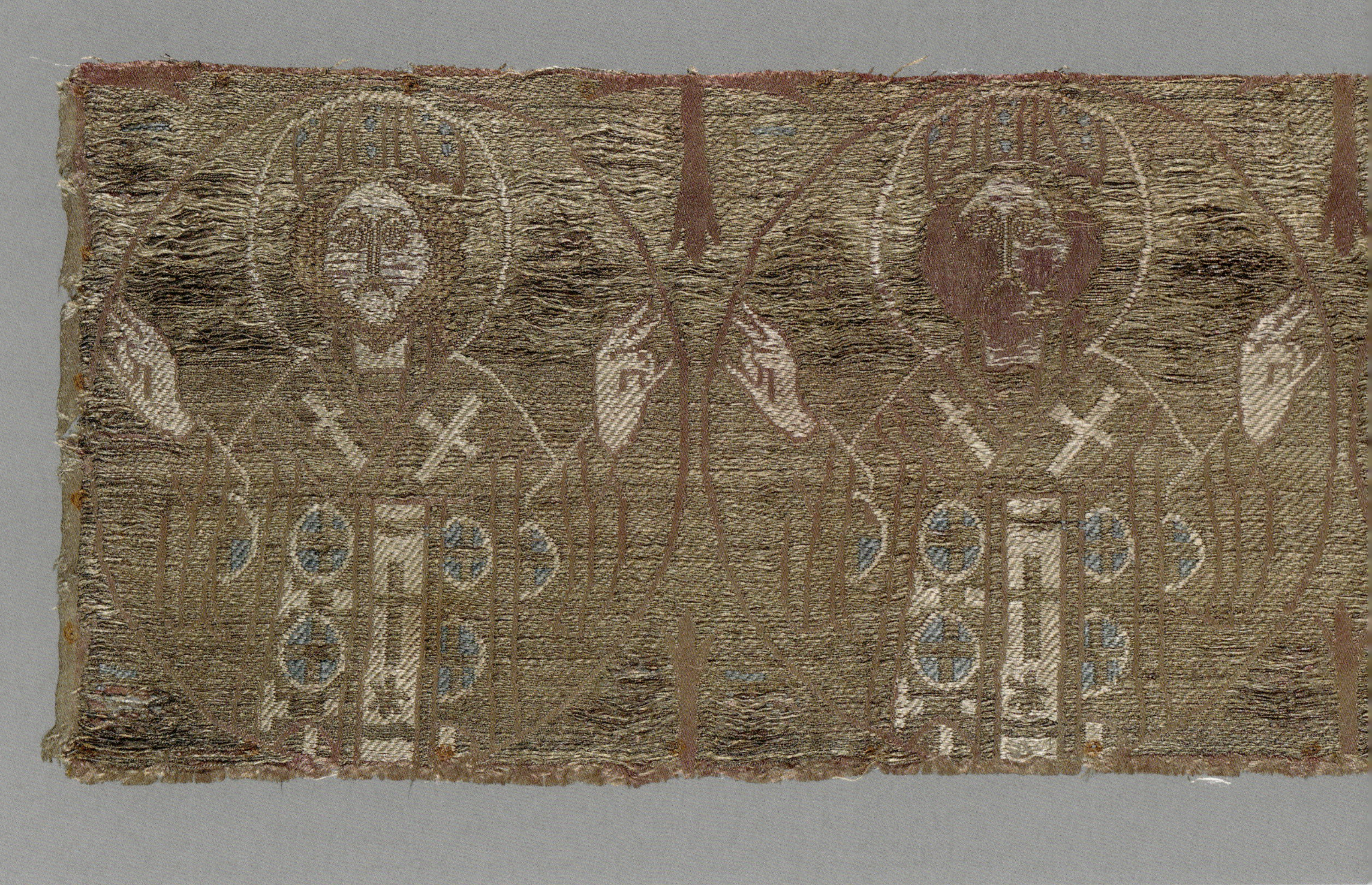

Departing from the thriftiness exemplified by a darning sampler, the most sumptuous of the textiles discussed
here exists today as a small fragment containing three rondels,
each with an image of a cleric at prayer (fig. 4). It almost certainly came from an Armenian liturgical garment; collected
by Art Institute patron Martin A. Ryerson (who also acquired
Nehan: Death of the Buddha), its complexly woven surface
of silk and gilt-metal threads attests to its affluent origin.
Even in its current state, it documents how vesture functions as a display of class and theology. Its material richness
ignores the biblical passages questioning wealth that
impoverishes others (a debate that continues to this day) in
favor of a spiritual logic maintaining that the accoutrements
of communal prayer should be the finest the congregation
can afford. In effect, nothing is too good for God.[5]

What wounds does such reasoning bandage? Many
religions encourage their members to strive for a degree
of generosity, goodness, and wholesomeness that sometimes slips into perfectionism. Even the evangelist Matthew
recorded Jesus as saying, "Be perfect, just as your heavenly
Father is perfect" (Matthew 5:48). The inevitable falling
short of this mark provokes a variety of responses. In the

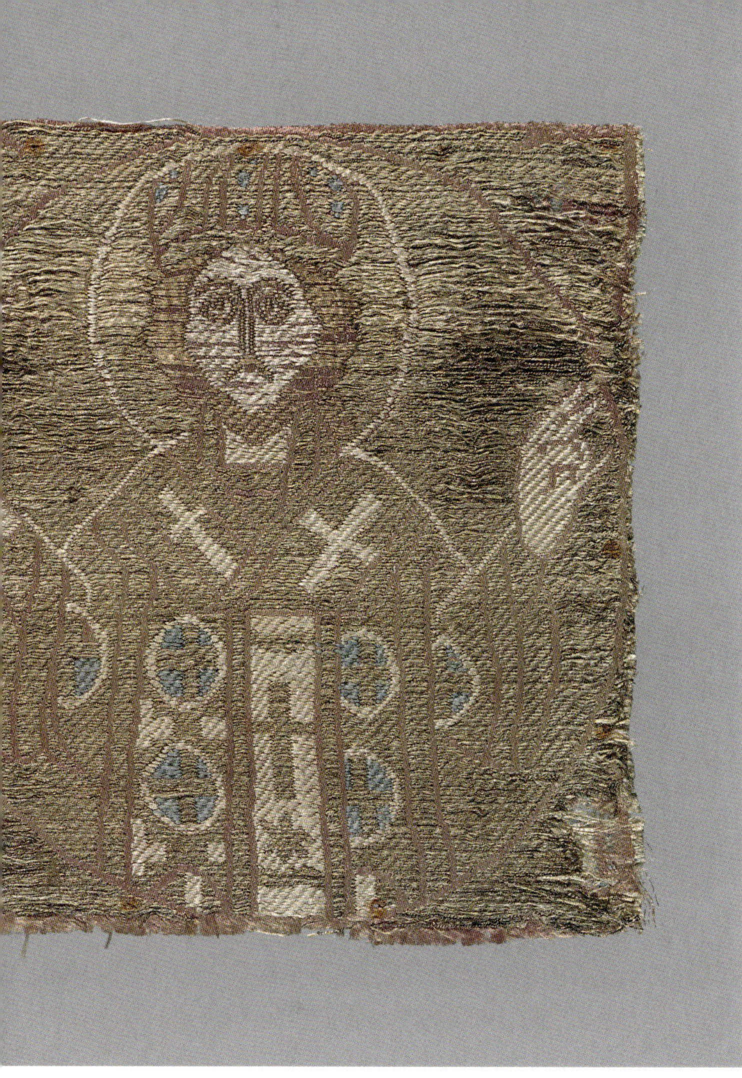

absence of a solid provenance for this fragment, one can only speculate: Was it originally part of a vestment donated as an expression of faith or as restitution for real or perceived failures? Does it represent a wealthy donor's attempt to enhance their status in the community? What reduced it to a snippet of what must have been a dazzling garment?

These four objects could be labeled a print, a painting, instructions, and a scrap. I have considered them as wounds, scars, and a bandage. Like all textiles, they have complicated histories; these fabrics of our lives carry not only our blood and sweat but also our beliefs, our challenges, and our failures. Catholic Christians would view *The Holy Shroud of Besançon* as more than a high-end souvenir; Buddhists will see *Nehan: Death of the Buddha* as more than an exquisite decoration for a special day; the darning samplers tell us more than just how to make our ragged clothes presentable; and a largely forgotten story of an Armenian community and its worship is hidden in the small, intricately woven, tarnished remnant of a vestment.

The same is true of us. We are more than our wounds and scars. We are more than our fragments.

Notes

1   See Suzanne Karr Schmidt, "Printing the Body of Christ on Fabric," Medium Study, *Conversations: An Online Journal of the Center for the Study of Material and Visual Cultures of Religion* (2016), mavcor.yale.edu /conversations/medium-studies /printing-body-christ-fabric; and Dorothy Crispino, "Doubts Along the Doubs," *Shroud Spectrum International* 4, no. 14 (1985): 11.

2   John 19:26–27 identifies "the disciple Jesus loved" as presented to Jesus's mother as her "son," her legal protector. He has traditionally been conflated with the apostle John. In that same gospel, the other women are named as Jesus's "mother's sister, Mary the wife of Clopas, and Mary of Magdala." Matthew 27:56–57 names them as "Mary Magdalene, and Mary the mother of James and Joseph, and the mother of the sons of Zebedee." Mark 15:40 calls them "Mary Magdalene, Mary the mother of the younger James and of Joses, and Salome."

3   See Karr Schmidt, "Printing the Body of Christ on Fabric."

4   Thanks to Janice Katz for her insights.

5   For example, see James 2:2–4: "For if a man with gold rings on his fingers and in fine clothes comes into your assembly, and a poor person in shabby clothes also comes in, and you pay attention to the one wearing the fine clothes and say, 'Sit here, please,' while you say to the poor one, 'Stand there,' or 'Sit at my feet,' have you not made distinctions among yourselves and become judges with evil designs?"

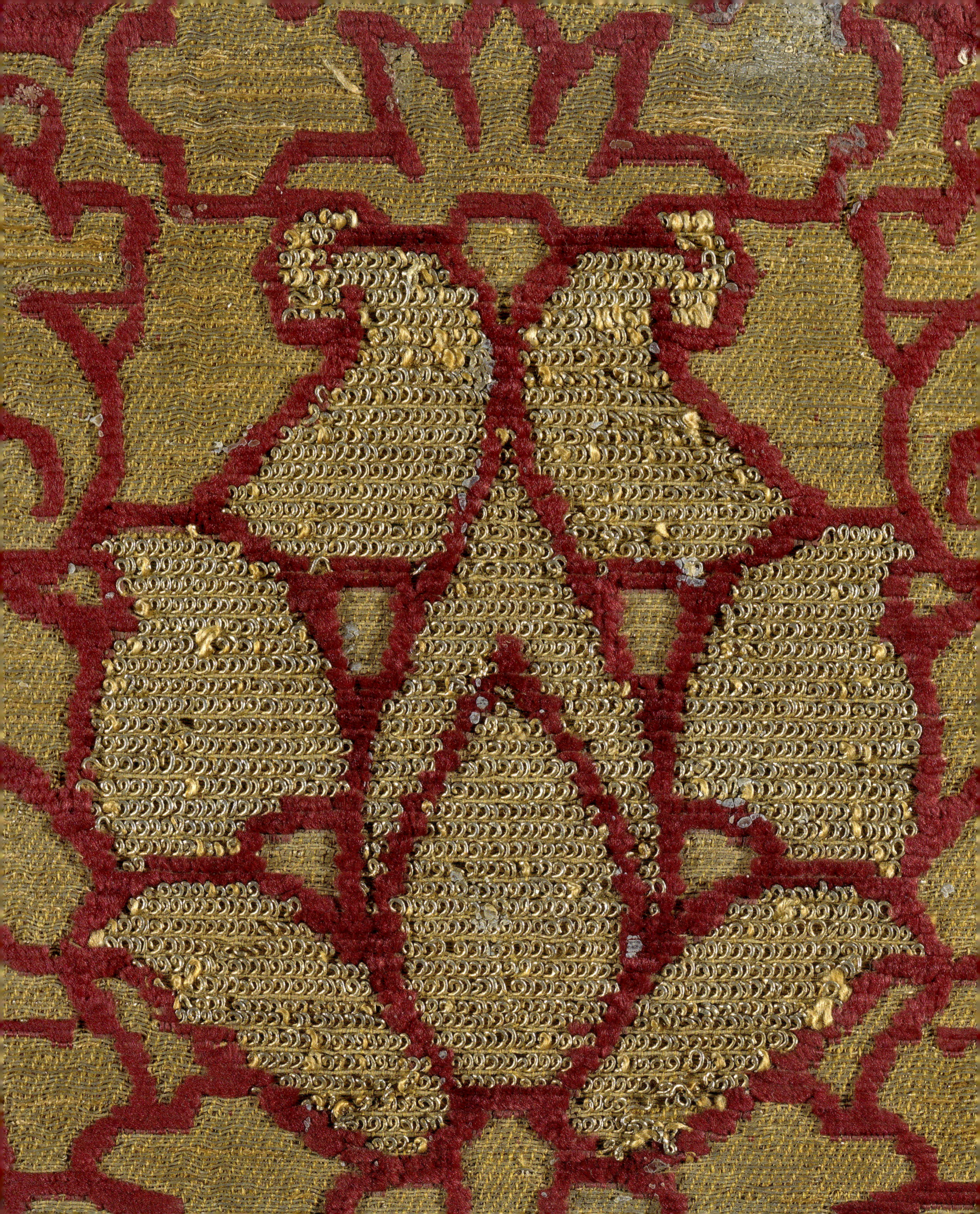

Representing and Re-Presenting Textiles

Sarah Molina
Art historian

Cybele Tom
Conservator and art historian

The desire to refer to oneself reverberates throughout the history of art. Self-portraits, signatures, monograms, colophons, and owner seals are some common ways the self-referential desire manifests. Somewhat rarer is the genre of paintings that internally stage painting—so-called metapictures—which art historians have often viewed as artists' commentary on the medium itself.[1] But self-referential devices are not exclusive to the arts of the pen and the brush. This essay centers meta-textiles, selecting examples from the Art Institute of Chicago's collection that explicitly refer to their own textile medium. All have been separated from their original contexts and functions; several survive only as fragments. Nevertheless, their materials and structures endure, offering revelatory clues to their makers' intentions, their uses, and their histories, including what has been lost through age and damage. Paying close attention to the relationship between imagery and construction, this essay re-presents textiles as dynamic objects that physically index their own histories. Specifically, it interprets these works as products of artists consciously negotiating the strictures and possibilities of their medium and thereby addressing the nature of textiles as a theme in their work. Close examination of textile microstructures and materials—even and perhaps especially their losses—can guide us in their present-day care, display, and interpretation.

Representing Textiles in Other Media

When textiles have been included in art historical scholarship, they have usually been treated as decorative or functional objects, a categorization that often preempts the kinds of formal and conceptual considerations given to the "high arts" of painting and sculpture. In addition, textiles displaced from their original contexts, as most pre-modern examples are, were often studied through their representation in other media of the period. Comparison of a fifteenth-century brocaded velvet and contemporary

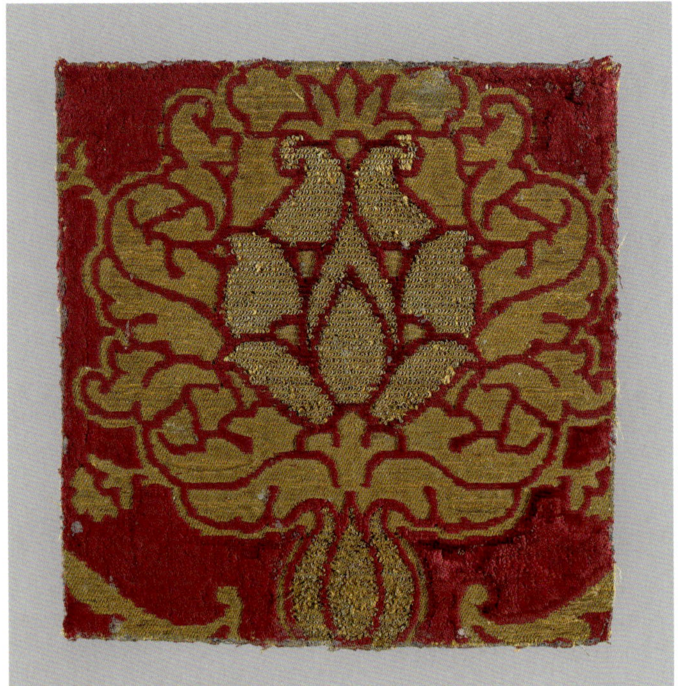

Fig. 1 **Fragment of Velvet, 1450–1500. Italy. Silk, warp-float faced 3:1 twill weave with weft-float faced 1:3 twill interlacings of secondary binding warps and gilt-metal-strip-wrapped silk supplementary facing wefts and supplementary brocading wefts forming weft loops in areas and with supplementary pile warps forming pile-on-pile cut voided velvet; 24.5 × 24.1 cm (9 ⅝ × 9 ½ in.). The Art Institute of Chicago, gift of Martin A. Ryerson through the Antiquarian Society, 1895.773.**

depictions of similar textiles in painting and sculpture, however, reveals important differences between the textile's actual appearance and structure and its representation in another art form.

A small square of brocaded velvet in the Art Institute's collection bears a single gold palmette delicately outlined in red (fig. 1).[2] A complex underlying structure (see fig. 2) enables its three-dimensional texture and glittering appearance: It features two different heights of pile—a lower pile for the thin lines outlining the palmette leaves, a higher pile in the thick red band surrounding the palmette—and supplementary wefts of silk thread, densely wrapped in gilt silver, to make parallel floats and loops in the palmette.[3] The pattern is cut at the edges, indicating that this piece once formed part of a larger textile. In fact we know from larger extant examples with very similar designs, such as a velvet altar frontal in the Art Institute's collection (fig. 3), that the palmette would have repeated. The technological requirements for achieving pattern repeats, or figures, of this scale and complexity in fifteenth-century Italy were considerable, demanding a specialized loom, called a drawloom, that allowed individual warp threads to be raised in groups as dictated by the pattern. Two people—the weaver and a "drawboy" to handle the figure harness—were needed to operate the drawloom.[4] When rendered in velvet, which required six times as much silk as a non-pile silk fabric like lampas, and complemented with precious-metal brocading, pattern repeats of this intricacy became symbols of high social status and material opulence throughout the late medieval and early modern world.[5]

These coveted fabrics were depicted in paintings and on polychrome sculpture, particularly as clothing for holy and powerful figures. Many painted representations of brocaded velvet not only feature a complex repeat but also seek to replicate a variety of visual effects unique to the fabric. Jan van Eyck, for example, rendered Saint Donatian's blue cope (see fig. 4) in both light- and dark-blue tones to capture the way cut silk velvet shimmers between sheen and shade.

MOLINA AND TOM

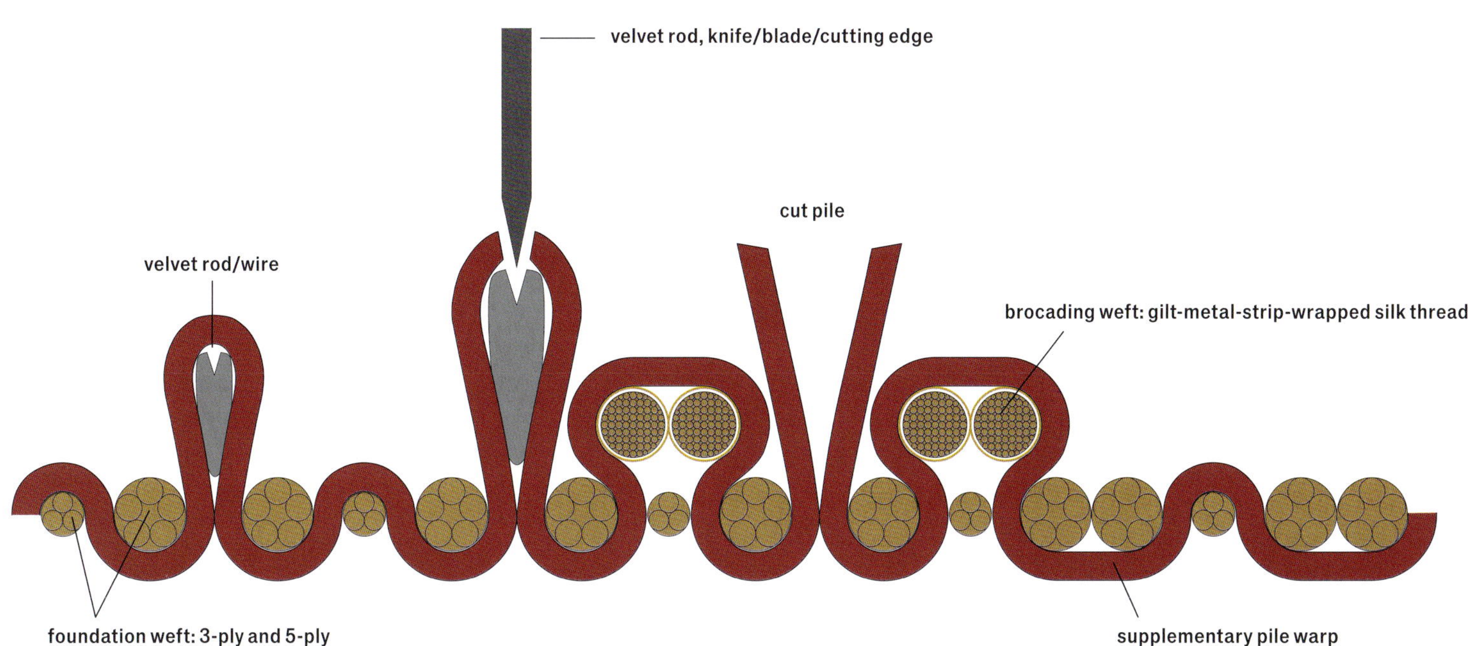

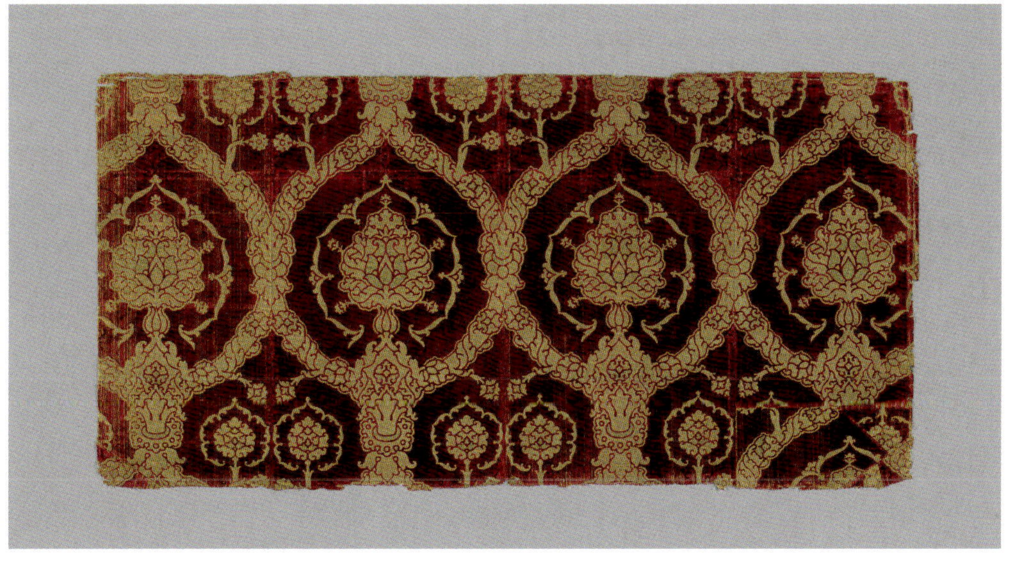

Fig. 3 Altar Frontal, 1480–1550. Spain or Italy. Silk, warp-float faced 3:1 *Z* twill weave with supplementary discontinuous facing brocading wefts forming areas of weft loops (known as bouclé) tied by secondary binding warps in weft-float faced 3:1 twill interlacing and supplementary pile warps forming pile-on-pile cut voided velvet; 100.8 × 203.4 cm (39¾ × 80⅛ in.). The Art Institute of Chicago, Kate S. Buckingham Endowment, 1944.403.

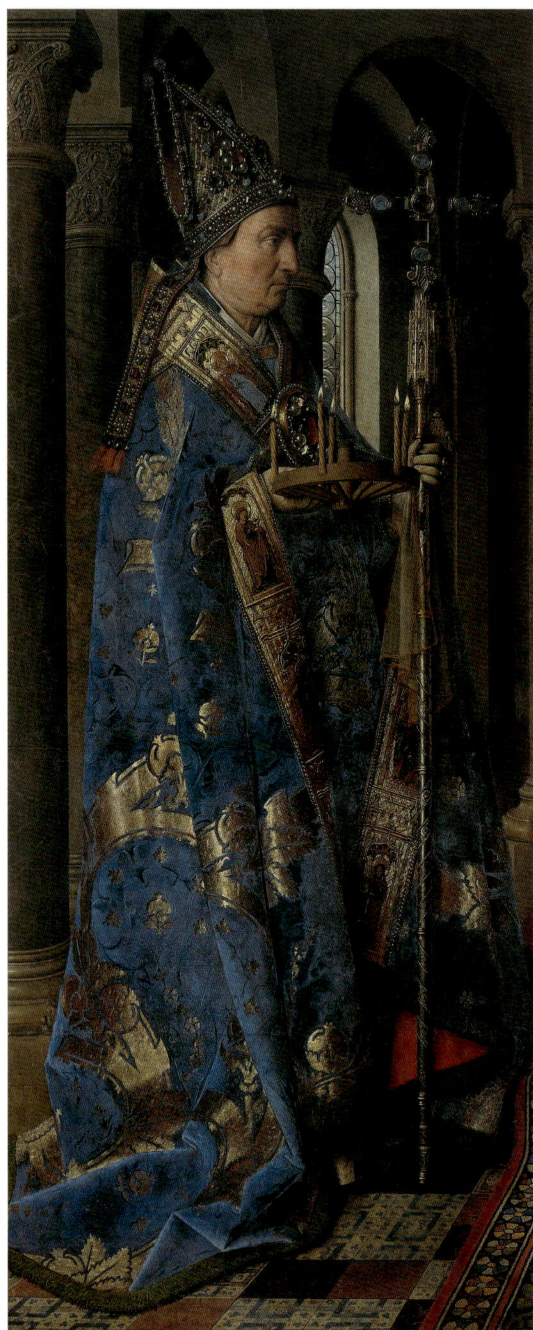

Fig. 4 Jan van Eyck (Netherlandish, about 1390–1441). *The Virgin and Child with Canon Joris van der Paele* (detail), 1434–36. Oil on wood; framed: 141 × 176.5 cm (55½ × 69½ in.). Groeningemuseum, Bruges, Belgium, inv. no. 0.161.1. The painter interspersed the cope's lighter-blue sheen with intermittent passages of darker, more saturated blue to imitate velvet pile's characteristic shimmer.

Depending on the direction of pile, which shifts with every fold and movement, light is absorbed or reflected, resulting in the appearance of brighter or darker color. Other artists evoked long brocade floats and bouclé (loops)—like those seen, respectively, in the outer leaves and inner artichoke of the aforementioned Art Institute fragment—by scratching parallel lines and loops into a paint layer to reveal a specially laid golden surface below. Painters often used real gold leaf to match the glittering effects of gold-wrapped thread. Furthermore, there is overwhelming evidence of painters going beyond the flat surface of a canvas or panel in their attempts to represent the structure, texture, and three-dimensionality of the fabrics. For instance, some painters employed a technique called applied brocade, in which a pliant material was formed in a mold based on a textile pattern, glued to the painted or sculpted surface, and then gilded to reproduce the texture and gleam of brocades in three dimensions (see fig. 5).[6] In some cases, the applied brocade was further worked by hand in order to replicate the varying levels of relief often found on real brocades.[7]

At the same time, these artists working in paint and sculpture purposefully disrupted their hard-earned illusions, calling attention to the true media of their creations. For example, applied brocade elements were almost always arranged in such a way that their parallel striations (meant to imitate the supplementary wefts of actual brocade) ran diagonally, vertically, or in multiple directions, all impossible for actual loom-made brocades.[8] Similarly, while gold leaf was initially used lavishly in applied brocades, use of real gold in painted surfaces had fallen out of favor in large parts of western Europe by the late fifteenth century: imitation of gold through paint alone was seen as more desirable.[9] That is, imitation (of gold) within the imitation (of brocade) replaced the only material that applied brocade and real brocade shared (gold), in a move away from the material characteristics of textiles and, arguably, toward more emphasis on the virtuosic achievements of paint alone.

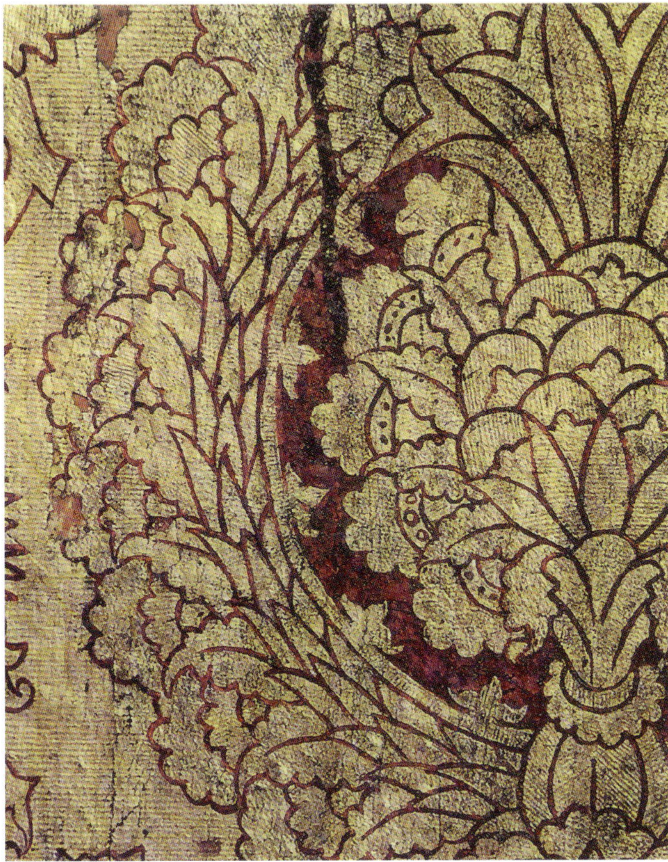

Fig. 5 **This detail of Giovanni Martini's altarpiece in the Church of St. Stephen in Remanzacco, Italy, shows an area of applied brocade on a flat surface. The fine parallel striations imitate brocade floats, but they run horizontally from the left edge of the image and vertically and diagonally in the center of the palmette, a technical impossibility for actual brocades woven on a loom. Courtesy of Teresa Perusini.**

When artists seek to imitate one medium in another, they must contend with the unique affordances and limitations of their own art form. Such instances become opportunities to redefine the boundaries and nature of their craft; the imitated medium, here textiles, becomes pretext for self-referential commentary. Thus, when art historians look to representations of textiles in other media for contextual reference, they must bear in mind how those images mediate and manipulate textiles. One way to balance these external perspectives on textiles is to attend closely to how textiles are represented and depicted in the textile medium itself, an approach we highlight in the following examples.

Picturing Microstructures in Paracas Textiles

Andean textiles from antiquity to today depict and interpret aspects of their facture—that is, motifs drawn from the object's structures and microstructures often appear in its design and iconography.[10] A tunic at the Art Institute from the Paracas people (fig. 6), who lived on the southwest coast of Peru from 800 from to read: 100 BCE, features a striking geometric design of vertical zigzags that seem to intertwine: regular gaps in the lines' continuity create the illusion of spatial depth, such that the lines appear to twist around each other. The off-white zigzag lines on either side of the neck opening twist in the Z direction, while the dark-purple zigzag lines twist in the S direction, like the ply and spin of yarn; a single yarn can be spun in an S or Z direction, while multiple yarns can also be plied together ("twisted") in either direction to create a thread. Since the yarns that make up the tunic are themselves Z spun and S plied (see fig. 7), the design visually magnifies the structure of its own threads—that is, the macro design pictures a fundamental aspect of the tunic's physical microstructure.[11] What at first seems to be a mere aesthetic pattern is in fact a deliberate act of self-reference, one with implications for the tunic's meaning and function.

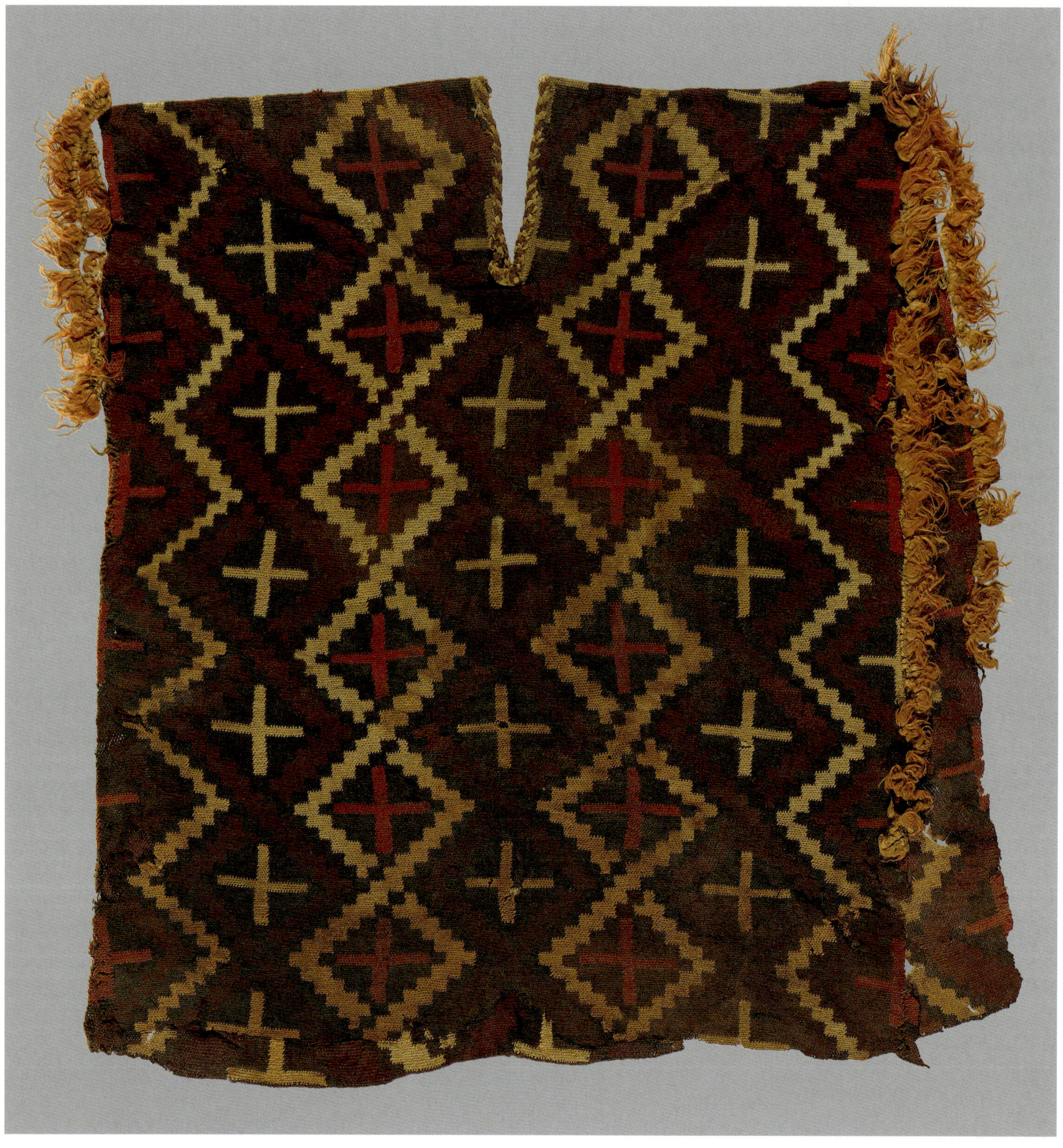

Fig. 6 Tunic, 2nd–1st century BCE. Paracas; south coast, Peru. Wool (camelid), simple looping; applied wool (camelid) braided collar edging; and unspun wool fringe; 76.8 × 74.4 cm (30¼ × 29¼ in.). The Art Institute of Chicago, Simeon B. Williams Fund, 1957.75.

In picturing its own microstructure, the tunic assumes agency and sets up a hierarchy among viewers. Recognition of the tunic's mode of self-representation presupposes specialized knowledge: Viewers are separated into those who understand its facture, who speak its fiber language, and those who do not. The privileged viewer not only sees the tunic but also, crucially, experiences the tunic as being seen; in the latter stage of this encounter, the tunic moves from perceived object to a self-aware entity, returning the viewer's gaze. Indeed, traditional Andean textiles are conceived as living beings, as the Noqanchis weaving collective explains in their essay in this volume. This understanding can be seen in the tunic's seamless construction: First, it was created as one continuous fabric rather than assembled of two identical halves sewn together. Second, rather than cutting a slit in the fabric for the head opening, which would have compromised the textile's integrity, the maker incorporated an edge-finished lacuna as part of the process of making the fabric.

The twisting elements in the pattern would have been enhanced by motion when the tunic was worn. Mounted flat in a museum display, the tunic seems stiff and the zigzags rigidly vertical. But draped over shoulders, the fabric would have curved downward, setting the outer zigzags rippling at slight diagonals, enhancing the optical illusion of inter-twined threads. The tunic offers protection and the wearer lends animacy; like yarn, they are bound in an interdependent, life-giving relationship.

Other motifs on the Paracas tunic reflect charac-teristics of the textile medium more broadly. The style of the zigzag pattern on the tunic adopts a stepped angularity, recalling the warp-weft grid that is the basis of all woven fabric. This tunic, however, was not woven on a loom but rather made by looping: Using a threaded needle, the maker wrapped a loop around the space between two adjacent loops of the previous row, creating offset rows of loops.[12] The offset is most visible in the tunic at the interface between the brown and white yarns, and gives a "toothed" contour to the white passages (see fig. 8). This micro feature is deliberately

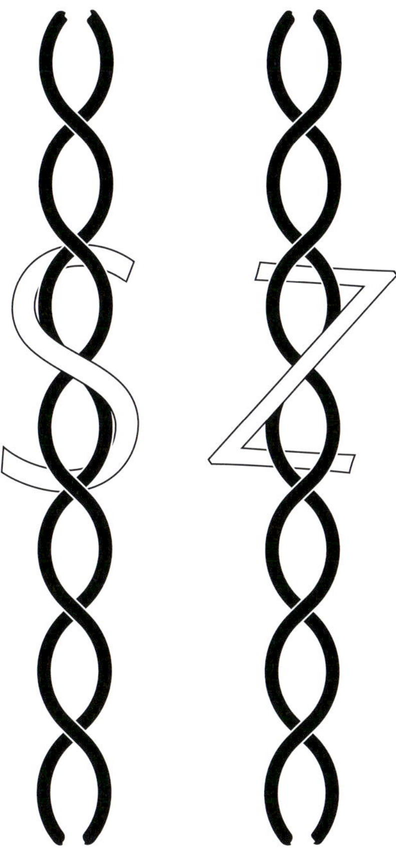

Fig. 7 Diagram showing the direction of spin and ply. A single yarn can be spun in an *S* or *Z* direction, while multiple yarns can also be plied together ("twisted") in either direction to create a thread. Designed and drawn by Isaac Facio.

Fig. 8 This magnified detail of the Art Institute's tunic (fig. 6) reveals how its larger, stepped pattern of off-white and dark-brown areas echoes its microstructure: A similar toothed contour emerges where the different colors of yarn meet, a product of the looping technique.

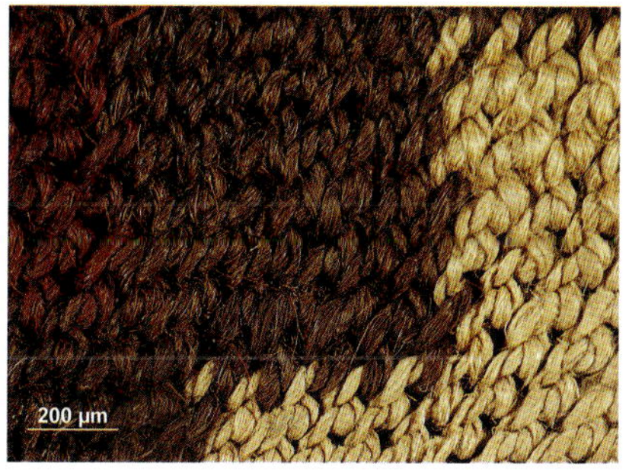

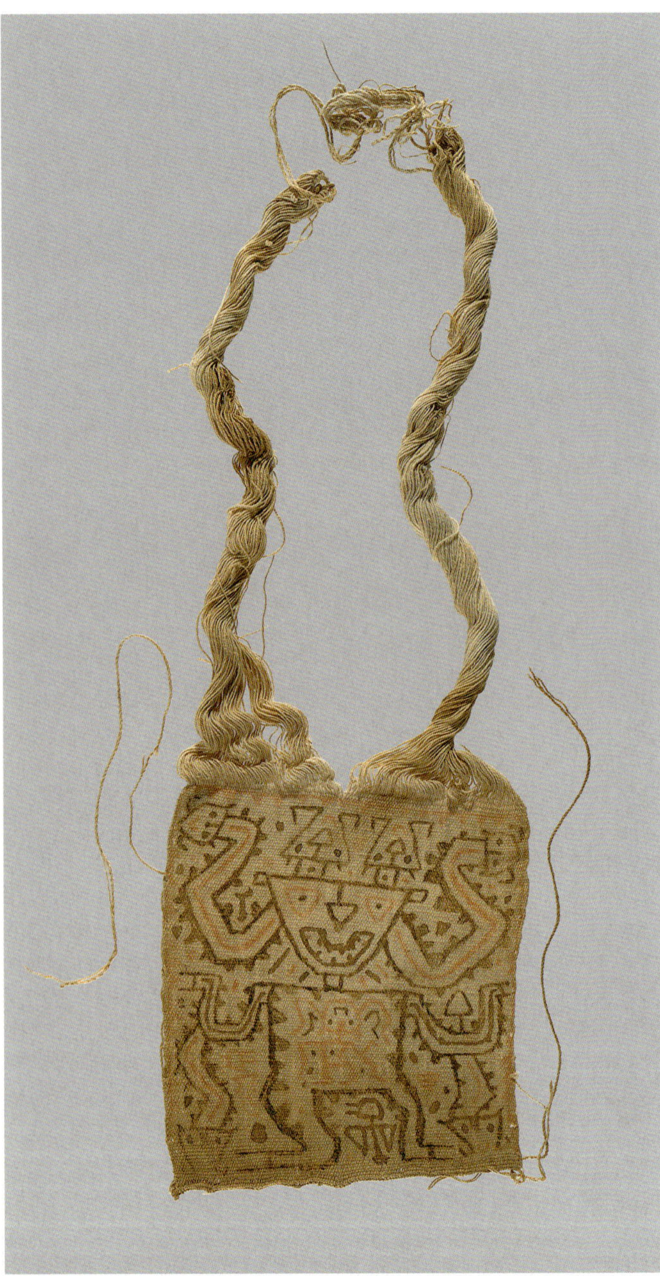

Fig. 9 Funerary Bundle Mask, 1st century
BCE. Paracas; probably Ocucaje, Ica Valley,
south coast, Peru. Cotton, plain weave with
bundles of extended warps; painted; 75.6 ×
23.2 cm (29¾ × 9⅛ in.). The Art Institute of
Chicago, Simeon B. Williams Fund, 1957.76.

visualized—and, again, magnified—in the stepped contours of the zigzag lines.[13]

A funerary bundle mask (fig. 9) from the same period and culture adopts similar angular contours to depict a full-frontal image of a supernatural being with serpents coming from its head.[14] Depicted on this figure's chest is a miniature version of the same being, its head upside-down as if it is looking up at itself. The sharp geometry in the forms of the figure and serpents is augmented in places by similar contour lines that appear lined with teeth or spikes. In this case, however, the image on the mask was not created in the textile structure but instead painted on it. The angular forms and lines, features derived from woven structures, have been deliberately carried over into the medium of paint, testifying to the textile medium's status as something to be emulated with other techniques and in other media. Just as painted imitations of brocaded velvet sought to re-create the luxury fabric's prestige, the mask's painted figure, with its toothed contours, alludes to a more labor-intensive version in which the image is composed of yarn.[15] Both examples point us back to the primacy and cachet of the textile and suggest an alternate hierarchy to the modern western framework that has privileged painting and sculpture.[16]

Visualizing Luster in a Medieval Spanish Fragment

Another fragment (fig. 10), made of silk and metal threads, demonstrates the unique synergies that can arise from representational images rendered in the textile medium. The fragment, a piece of a larger textile woven in thirteenth-century Spain, retains part of a pattern repeat: a depiction, contained within a roundel, of a white lamp hanging between a pair of richly dressed musicians holding tambourines. The hanging lamp and repeat roundels reflect the motifs and compositions of ivory carving, metalwork, and other textiles produced for the courts of the medieval Islamic world. Although fabrics like this one were woven in workshops

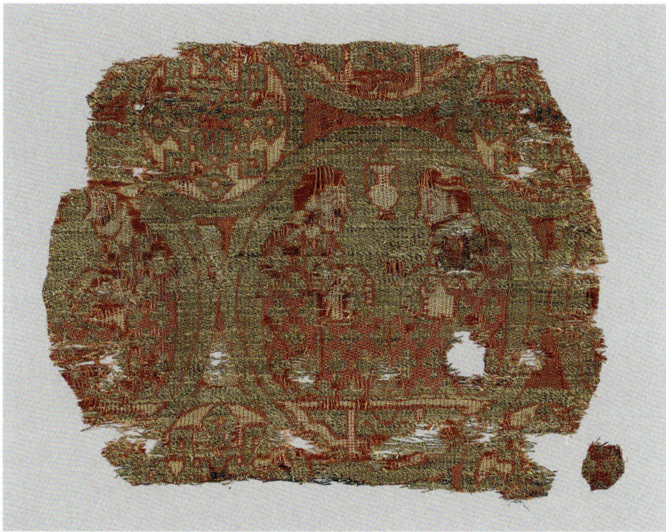

Fig. 10 **Fragment with Roundel Pattern,
13th–14th century. Spain. Silk and gilt-
animal-substrate-wrapped silk, weft-faced
three- and four-color complementary weft,
plain weave with inner warps and areas
of detached plain weave of inner warps and
complementary ground wefts; 10.3 × 13.2 cm
(4⅛ × 5⅛ in.). The Art Institute of Chicago,
purchased with funds provided by Mrs.
Walter Byron Smith, 1950.1.**

Fig. 11 **This magnified detail of the Art
Institute's 13th-century Spanish fragment
(fig. 10) shows the plain-weave binding structure of white-silk warps and largely unspun
white-silk wefts used to create the motif of the
lamp, as well as the luster of the metal threads
beyond the lamp's red outline.**

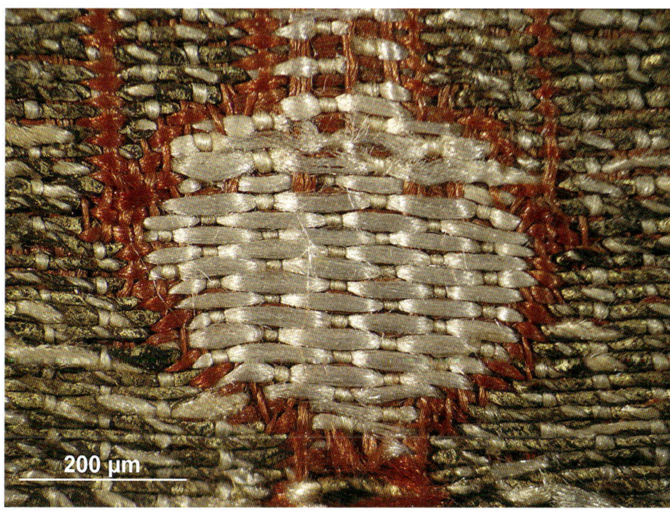

administered by the Islamic kingdoms of Spain, their secular subjects and luxurious materials appealed to a wide
range of audiences, including the Catholic Church.[17] This
fabric belongs to a group of at least fourteen other fragments, all cut from the same textile and found in the pages
of a thirteenth-century manuscript in the Vic Cathedral in
Catalonia.[18] Some were cut in circular shapes, possibly to fit
under the round bosses of choir books.[19]

The analysis of other surviving fragments indicates
that at least five different colors of silk wefts—black, blue,
green, red, and white—and metal threads were used to
make this weft-faced, compound weave.[20] The metal threads
compose the background of each roundel, the cross-shaped
pattern of the musicians' dresses, their tambourines, and the
interlaced, eight-pointed stars. During this period in Spain,
metal threads and silk were prized elements in fabrics that
likely appealed to a wide swath of elite consumers.[21] The
extensive use of metal threads would have created a shimmering surface activated by light and movement when worn
on the body or hung as a curtain.[22]

Abrasion and tarnish to the metal threads have
considerably dulled their visual effect today such that they
appear darker and gray at times. But photomicrographs
reveal traces of gold that would have produced a striking
radiance (see fig. 11). The metal threads were made from
gold applied to animal gut or membrane, which was cut into
strips and wrapped in a *Z* direction around a white, *Z*-twisted
silk core. While the metal threads produce a golden sheen,
the silk threads were also carefully manipulated to create a
radiant finish. The hanging lamps, for instance, were woven
so that white-silk weft threads are crossed with white
warps in a plain-weave structure to produce the body of the
vessel, with red-silk wefts bound by red warps to create its
outline (see, again, fig. 11). The white weft threads running
horizontally across the lamp are largely unspun, creating a
particularly shiny surface for both the lamp and the textile.
The depicted lamp illuminates the lively scene both figuratively and literally. Similar globular oil lamps would have lit

such festive scenes in real life; as a pictorial device in the textile, the lamp highlights the patterns of the musicians' robes. But these robes are wrought from the same material that would be used to create such robes in real life: metal threads that physically glimmer. Thus, this fragment does not simply represent textiles by depicting the musicians' robes—it also simulates the effect of such textiles under light. Executed in textile form, the representational and material effects of woven luster are united, showing us even now how the once-whole fabric would have glimmered.

When this object is displayed in a museum context, visitors can simultaneously see both the depicted scene of light cast upon metal-thread-and-silk robes and the physical luster of these same materials constituting the fragment. In its current state, however, the fragment does not display its original shine, and the crucial equivalence between image and material is less obvious. In such situations, photomicrographs that reveal the traces of gold and the structure of the textile can be enlightening pedagogical tools when integrated into gallery displays. The micro is fundamental to understanding the macro: namely, the aesthetics of luster that culturally and materially imbue this small fragment with multiple layers of meaning.

The Story of Silk in a Persian Textile

A silk fragment in the Art Institute's collection (fig. 12), also featuring extensive metal-wrapped, silk-core threads, narrates a history of its materials. It depicts a lively scene of human figures steering boats surrounded by swimming ducks and fish. This fabric, likely made in Iran in the sixteenth or early seventeenth century, illustrates two types of boats: a simpler model occupied by three men in rounded caps and a more elaborate ship with a large crest atop its mast and figures, possibly passengers, seated in compartments. On the latter type, pairs of men drop the oars and stand on the deck wearing wide-brimmed hats often used to

distinguish Europeans in paintings and drawings produced by court artists in Safavid Iran (see fig. 13). The Safavids ruled parts of greater Iran from 1501 to 1722; under the patronage of the shahs, the arts of painting and weaving flourished. Because of the highly stylized figures in the fragment, it is difficult to distinguish the specific origins of the men in wide-brimmed hats, but they have often been identified as Portuguese sailors.[23] Similar hats were worn by Portuguese figures in paintings, and the type of dress, with its baggy sleeves and loosely tied sash around the waist, resembles that illustrated, for example, in a portrait of explorer Ferdinand Magellan engraved by André Thevet (fig. 14).

The Portuguese were so closely associated with the seas that they were often depicted on boats in paintings made in the neighboring Mughal empire.[24] Their maritime prowess was also closely linked to the story of the early modern textile trade, augmented in the late fifteenth century by the Portuguese discovery of a new sea route directly connecting Europe and Asia, which enabled the raw-silk and finished-textile trade that flourished under Shah ʿAbbas I in the early seventeenth century.[25] Thus, although this fragment does not explicitly depict the trade of silk textiles, it indirectly references the silk trade by representing dress textiles that distinguish the foreigners integral to the industry and by illustrating the seas on which trade was borne.

The fabric is a double cloth made entirely of silk and metal-wrapped silk. It is composed of two sets of warps and wefts that produce two layers of cloth (see fig. 15), which connect at the selvedges and areas where they cross due to the pattern.[26] Both layers of cloth are plain weaves—one formed from red-silk warps and wefts and the other by white-silk warps that bind alternating white-silk and metal-wrapped wefts. These metal threads are composed of high-purity silver hammered into thin strips that were wrapped in an *S* direction around an untwisted white-silk core.[27] Because of similarities between Safavid and Mughal textiles and a general lack of information about their provenance, textiles from this period are difficult to attribute. But the striking

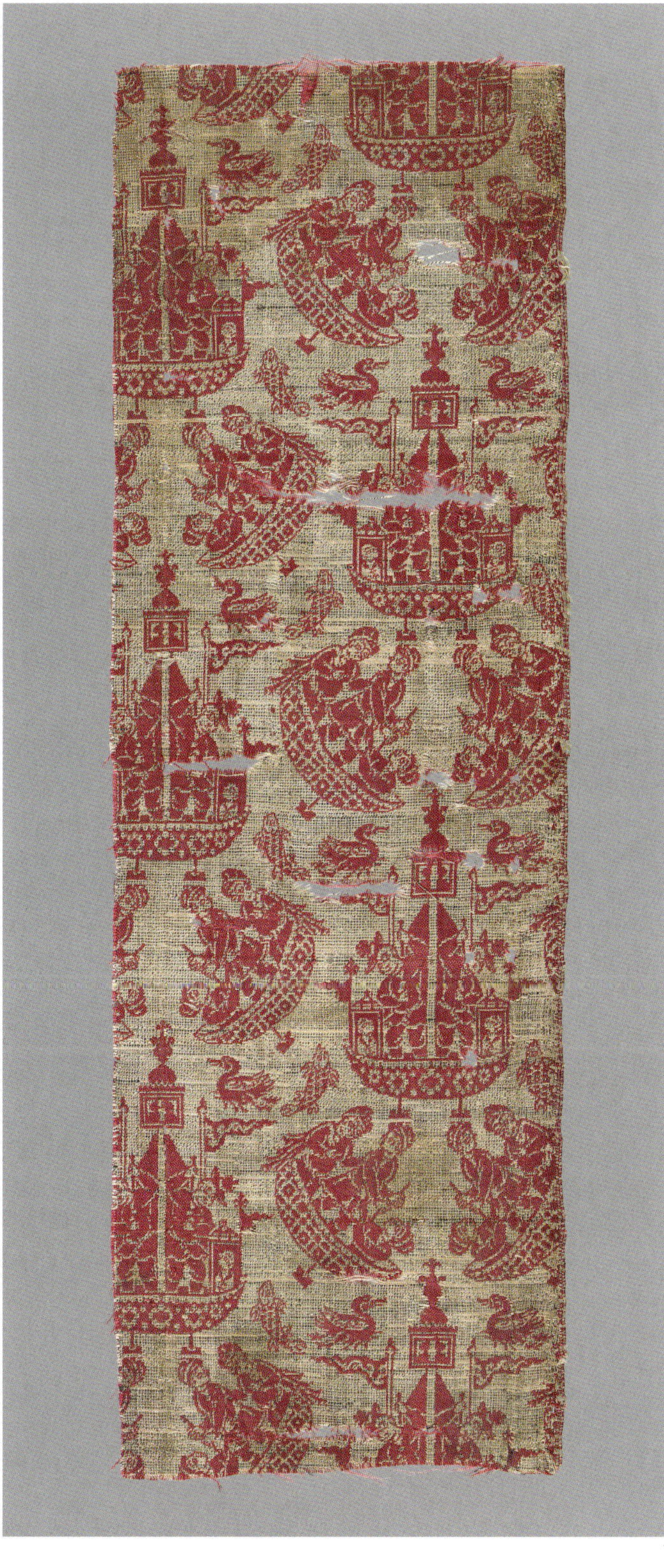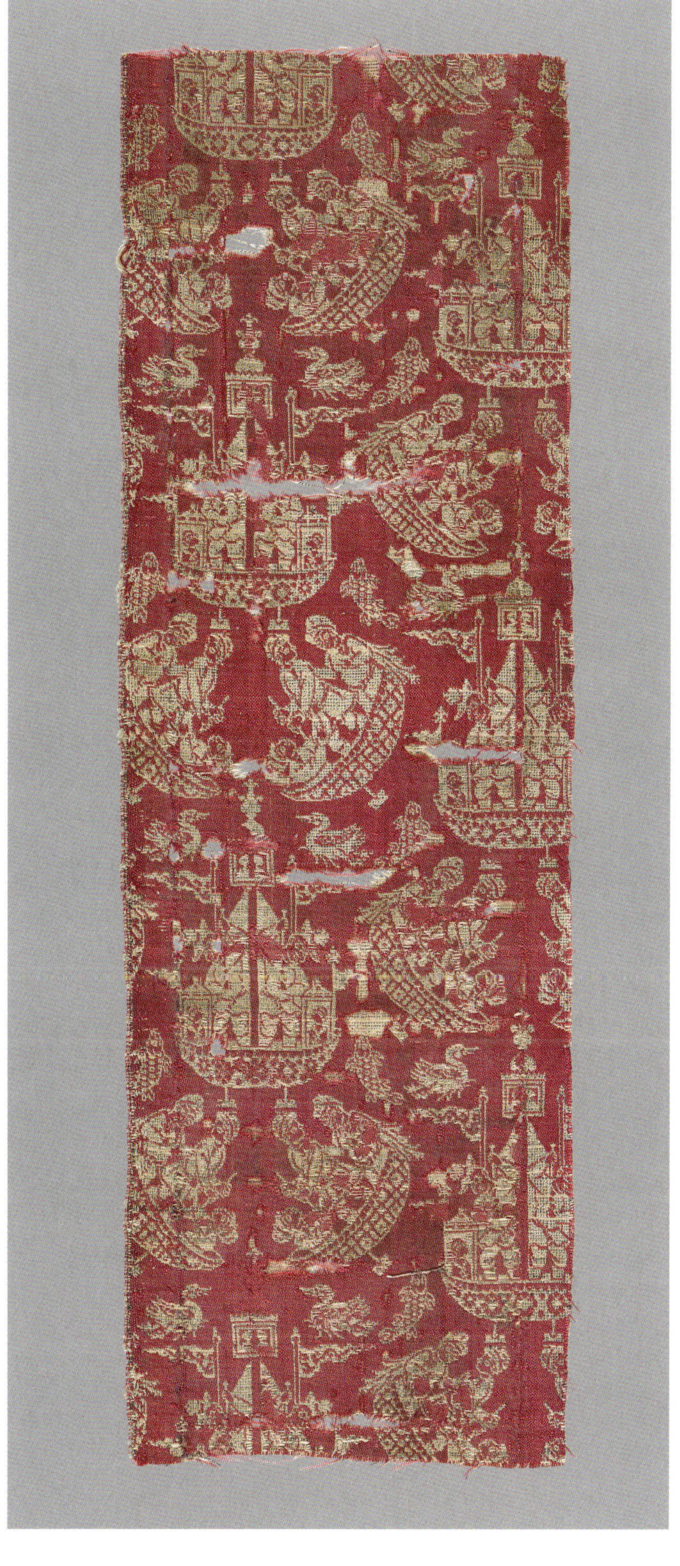

Fig. 12 Fragment of a Dress Fabric, probably
Safavid dynasty (1501–1722), 1601–25. Iran.
Silk and silver-strip-wrapped silk; double cloth;
24.1 × 7.9 cm (9½ × 3⅛ in.). The Art Institute of
Chicago, Oriental Art Sundry Fund, 1954.448.
Both sides are shown, as the textile is revers-
ible by design.

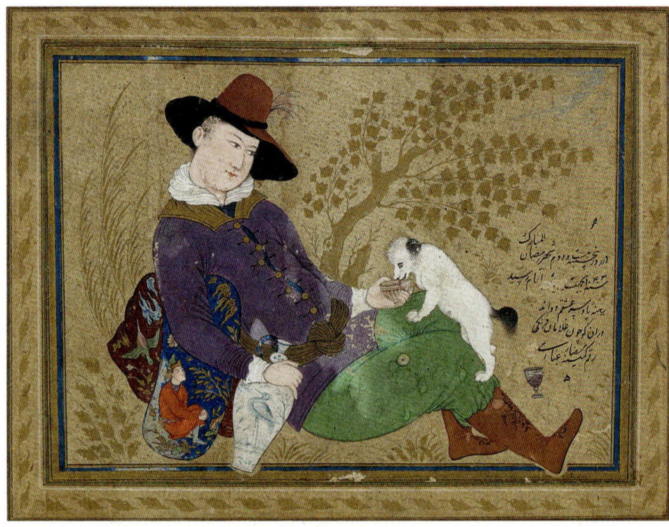

Fig. 13 Riza ʾAbbasi (Iranian, about 1565–1635). *Youth in European Clothing*, 1634. Opaque watercolor, ink, and gold on paper; 14.6 × 19.2 cm (5¾ × 7½ in.). Detroit Institute of Arts, gift of Robert H. Tannahill in memory of Dr. William R. Valentiner, 58.334.

Fig. 14 André Thevet (French, 1504–1592). *Fernand Magellan, Portugais*, from *Les vrais pourtraits et vies des hommes illustres*, 1584. Engraving and etching; 17.2 × 14.2 cm (6¾ × 5⁹⁄₁₆ in.). The British Museum, London, 1879, 1213.271. The shirt worn by the Portuguese explorer in this illustration is similar to those seen in the Art Institute's fragment of Safavid dress fabric (fig. 12).

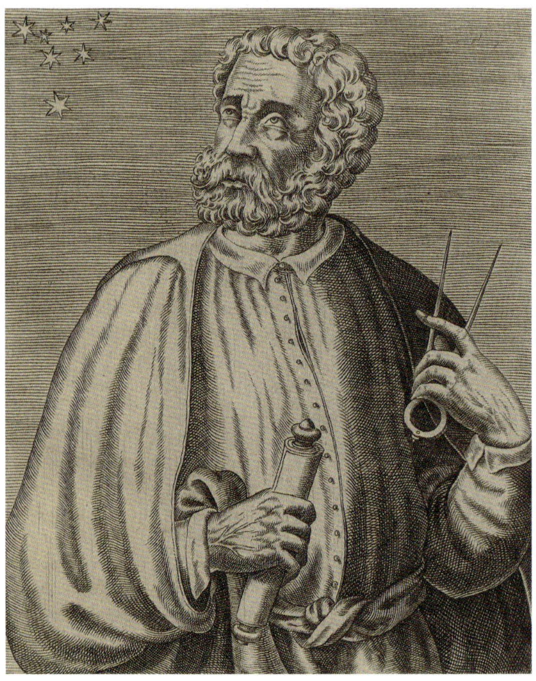

iconographic and structural similarities to other red-and-white double cloths featuring text and imagery from Persian poetry typical of Safavid court production suggest that this fragment was very likely produced in a Safavid workshop.[28] Additionally, the fragment's vibrant red color derives from the cochineal insect, a common insect dye source found in Safavid velvets.[29]

The structure of double cloths yields a reversible fabric. French traveler Jean Chardin, commenting on the textile workshops of Safavid Iran, referred to "the double [brocade], which is called d'ouroye . . . meaning two faces, because it has no back side."[30] While this fragment could have been fashioned into a fabric privileging either face, the textural effects of the alternating white-silk and metal-wrapped wefts on the side where the red weave forms the pattern engender an additional iconographic reading: they create the impression of rippling water. The two types of thread alternate every other weft, but sometimes three metal-wrapped wefts occur in a row—a mistake on the part of the weaver, perhaps, but one that enhances this rippling effect (see fig. 16). The nearly pure silver threads have kept their shine over time, but the silver wrapping varies in tightness around the white-silk core; the fragile metal has come loose in many areas, further dramatizing the impression of moving waves. Although unintentional, the disruption of the metal wrapping adds to the illusion of the metal-ground background as the sea. When displayed in the museum, a two-sided case would allow visitors to see both sides of the textile, encouraging them to compare the differences in overall effect caused by its materials and structure, even as they have changed over time.[31]

Loss as Storytelling

Textiles' various appearances, materials, and structures are often inextricably linked in ways that blend the physical with the representational. Textile artists throughout history have chosen to enhance this aspect in ways unique to the medium,

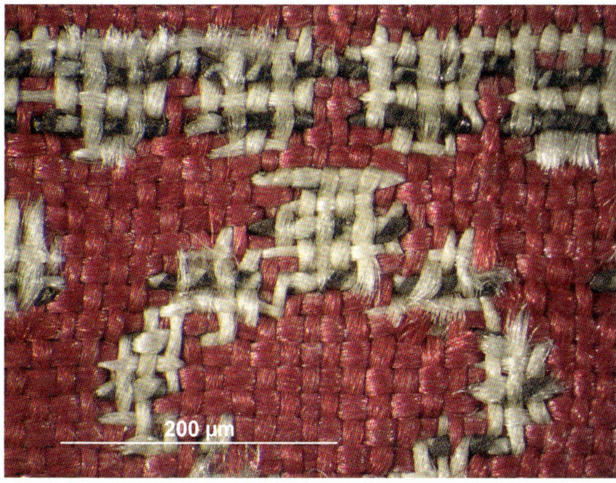

Fig. 15 **This magnified detail of the Art Institute's fragment of Safavid dress fabric (fig. 12) shows the plain-weave, double-cloth structure.**

Fig. 16 **This magnified detail of another fragment of the same Safavid dress fabric (fig. 12), this one from the Los Angeles County Museum of Art (inv. no. M.63.56.1), shows three metal-wrapped wefts in a row, which enhances the effect of rippling waves on the white-ground side.**

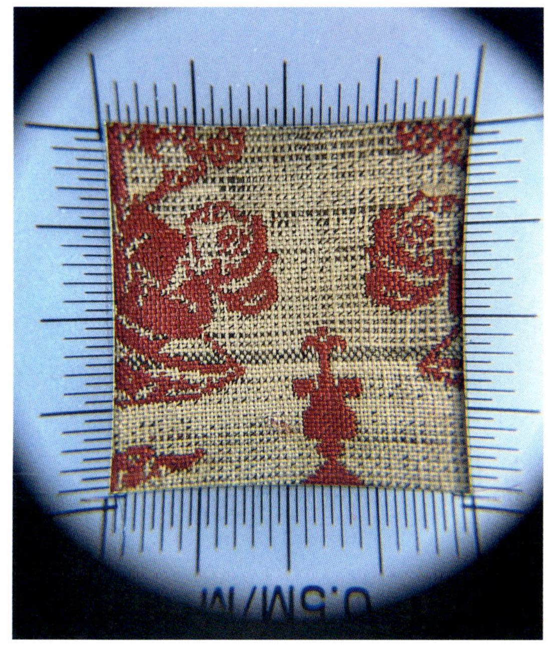

selecting among myriad materials and techniques to navigate the limitations and explore the possibilities of their art. For those tasked with studying these objects, examining and understanding the microstructures of textiles can yield rich narratives about their making, use, and significance—meanings that may be lost or altered over time, as objects become more distant from their original forms and functions. Ultimately, the painstaking work of analyzing the traces of textile makers' decisions and techniques is a form of care and conservation itself, work that helps preserve and translate the rich and multifaceted meanings of textiles for new viewers. In museums, these deeper understandings can inform enlighting displays for visitors faced with decontextualized fragments.

Textiles' capacity to index their own histories also invites us to reconsider how we define loss and our response to it. While we might inevitably privilege the intact object, lament fragmentation, and work to halt or minimize further degradation, we can also embrace the fact that loss often reveals the hidden work and choices underlying the whole or engenders new meanings. The abrasion of the metal threads in the silk fragment from Safavid Iran, for example, has added to its pictorial narrative of fibers traded along global sea routes. These losses not only heighten the overall visual effect but also speak to the textile's fragile materiality—is it not more valuable precisely for this quality? Narratives of loss are not concealed but instead can be revealed by the study of textiles; the stories encoded in these objects provide a model for reckoning with loss and absence by embracing them.

Notes

We are particularly grateful to two people at the Art Institute of Chicago who both read and edited multiple versions of this essay: Ken Sutherland and Kit Shields. Ken's eye for detail and Kit's considerable efforts with early drafts helped us realize our ideas in clearer, stronger writing.

1   See Victor I. Stoichita, *L'instauration du tableau: Métapeinture à l'aube des temps modernes* (Méridiens Klincksieck, 1993); the introduction to the English version of the same book, Lorenzo Pericolo, "What Is Metapainting? 'The Self-Aware Image' Twenty Years On," in *The Self-Aware Image: An Insight into Early Modern Metapainting*, trans. Anne-Marie Glasheen (Harvey Miller, 2015), 11–31; and Péter Bokody and Alexander Nagel, eds., *Renaissance Metapainting* (Turnhout, 2020).

2   The fragment is a pile-on-pile, cut-and-voided velvet. It can also be classed as an *a griccia,* a fifteenth-century term for velvets with a multi-lobed palmette; see Regula Schorta, "Trattato dell'arte della seta: A Florentine 15th Century Treatise on Silk Manufacturing," *Bulletin de liason du CIETA* 69 (1991): 57–83. This is a proper brocade in that it contains discontinuous supplementary wefts; these can be metal or another fiber, and in this textile they are gilt-metal-strip-wrapped silk supplementary facing wefts and supplementary brocading wefts forming weft loops.

3   The gilt-silver wrapping of the threads was confirmed by Ken Sutherland at the Art Institute of Chicago, using scanning electron microscopy with energy dispersive spectroscopy (SEM-EDS). Analyses were performed at the EPIC facility of Northwestern University's NUANCE Center, Evanston, Illinois, which has received support from the Soft and Hybrid Nanotechnology Experimental (SHyNE) Resource (NSF ECCS-2025633), the IIN, and Northwestern's MRSEC program (NSF DMR-2308691). For detailed results and analysis conditions, see reports on file in Conservation and Science at the Art Institute.

4   On the technological history of velvet production in fifteenth-century Italy, see Michael Peter, "Velvets of the Fifteenth Century: Art, Technique, and Business," in *Velvets of the Fifteenth Century* (Abegg-Stiftung, 2020), 9–20.

5   See Evelin Wetter, introduction to *Abbild, Nachbildung, Trompe-L'oeil: Textilien im Textil* (Abegg-Stiftung, 2024), 9. Indeed, it was this very coupling of luxury symbol with material and technical extravagance that ushered in the next phase in the life of this brocaded velvet: It was likely cut down to its present dimensions expressly to serve as a liturgical corporal bag, deemed a suitable manmade artifact to carry and protect the cloth upon which the Eucharistic host rested. A near identical fragment at the Abegg-Stiftung (inv. no. 2770) in Riggisberg, Switzerland, was trimmed at the same borders and bears similar dimensions. Both fragments may have come from the same original cloth. See Michael Peter, *Mittelalterliche Textilien IV: Samte vor 1500* (Abegg-Stiftung, 2019), 418–19, cat. 80.

6   On the history and technique of applied brocade, see Eike Oellermann, "On the Imitation of Textile Structures in Late Gothic Polychromy and Panel Painting," in Johannes Taubert, *Polychrome Sculpture: Meaning, Form, Conservation*, ed. Michele D. Marincola, trans. Carola Schulman (Getty Conservation Institute, 2015), 54–63. See also Ingrid Geelen and Delphine Steyaert, eds., *Imitation and Illusion* (Royal Institute for Cultural Heritage, 2011), 24–48.

7   On velvet types and their imitation in paint, see Wivine Williez, "Lampas, Velvet and Cloth of Gold: Criteria for Interpreting the Representation of Textiles by Applied Brocade," in Geelen and Steyaert, *Imitation and Illusion*, 140–50.

8   Brocaded fabric could always be cut and sewn so that the supplementary wefts ran vertically or diagonally to the axis of the dress fabric, but comparison of actual brocade patterns with their imitations shows that real wefts usually run horizontally through the palmette, while applied brocade striations usually run vertically through the pattern. In the example in fig. 5, the striations run in multiple directions within the piece of fabric depicted.

9   Geelen and Steyaert, *Imitation and Illusion*, 39.

10   For recent scholarship on the role of facture in interpreting Andean textiles, see Denise Y. Arnold and Elvira Espejo, *The Andean Science of Weaving: Structures and Techniques of Warp-Faced Weaves* (Thames and Hudson, 2015); Andrew James Hamilton, *The Royal Inca Tunic: A Biography of an Andean Masterpiece* (Princeton University Press, 2024); and Elena Phipps, *The Peruvian Four-Selvaged Cloth: Ancient Threads/New Directions* (Fowler Museum, 2013).

11   On visual representations of fabric structures, see Mary Frame, "Visual Images of Fabric Structures in Ancient Peruvian Art," in *The Junius B. Bird Conference on Andean Textiles, April 7th and 8th, 1984*, ed. Ann Pollard Rowe (Textile Museum, 1986), 47–80. Some scholars have suggested that certain spin and ply combinations served as a signature for a particular weaving community; see, for example, Phipps, *The Peruvian Four-Selvaged Cloth*, 25. However, conversations with contemporary practictioners Danitza Willka and María José Murillo indicate that it is possible to discern the weaver's "hand" by attending to yarn thickness, spin and ply combinations, color choice and variation, iconography, and style.

12   For an in-depth discussion of this technique, see the essay by Alipio Melo, María José Murillo, and Danitza Willka in this volume. Looping was used for utilitarian items such as fishing nets, but it was also pushed to dazzling three-dimensional effect: the border of the so-called "Paracas Textile" (inv. no. 38.121) at the Brooklyn Museum, New York, from the Nasca people features figures and flowers made entirely of cross-loop stitching.

13   See Anne Paul, "Multiple Layers of Meaning in a Paracas Necropolis Textile," in *Approaching Textiles, Varying Viewpoints: Proceedings of the Seventh Biennial Symposium of the Textile Society of America, Santa Fe, New Mexico 2000* (Textile Society of America, 2001), 211.

14   Variations of the figure appear frequently on ceramics and other types of burial textiles, such as cloaks. The consistent emphasis on the eyes has led scholars to call it an "oculate being." For a typology of similar mythological beings, see Mary Elizabeth King, "Mythological Figures in Textiles from Ocucaje, Peru," in *Atti del XL Congresso Internazionale degli Americanisti, Roma-Genova, 3–10 Settembre, 1972* (Tilgher, 1974), 521–29. Versions of the oculate being with a miniature figure pictured inside its torso are associated with renewal and fertility; see Phipps, *Four-Selvaged Cloth*, 16.

15   We know of no surviving Paracas funerary-bundle masks in which the image is woven; they are all painted textiles or painted ceramics.

16   There is at least one important difference between the Italian velvet and Paracas textiles: In the ancient Andean worldview, the textile medium, distinct from all other media, participates in the structure of the cosmos. Its emulation in other media like ceramic and paint speaks to textiles' generative role as the basis of life.

17   Maria Judith Feliciano has published extensively on these "Andalusi" textiles, focusing on their appeal to many audiences and their reuse in Christian contexts. See Maria Judith Feliciano, "Muslim Shrouds for Christian Kings?: A Reassessment of Andalusi Textiles in Thirteenth-Century Castilian Life and Ritual," in *Under the Influence: Questioning the Comparative in Medieval Castile*, The Medieval and Early Modern Iberian World, vol. 22 (Brill, 2005), 101–31.

18   Florence May discussed the discovery of these fragments in Florence Lewis May, *Silk Textiles of Spain, Eighth to Fifteenth Century* (Hispanic Society of America, 1957), 136–41. The fragments are currently dispersed throughout various collections, including: the Metropolitan Museum of Art, New York (28.194); Cooper-Hewitt, Smithsonian Design Museum, New York (1965-33-5); Boston Museum of Fine Arts (18-525); Wadsworth Atheneum, Hartford, Connecticut (1931.100); Cleveland Museum of Art (1932.137); Abegg-Stiftung, Riggisberg, Switzerland (4227); and Instituto Valencia de Don Juan, Madrid (2098). Some can still be found in the episcopal archive of the Vic cathedral. For a good summary of fundamental scholarship concerning this group of fragments, refer to Olga Bush, "47. Textile Fragment," in *Masterpieces from the Department of Islamic Art in the Metropolitan Museum of Art*, ed. Maryam Ekhtiar, Priscilla Soucek, Sheila Canby, and Navina Haidar (Metropolitan Museum of Art, 2011), 80, cat. 47.

19   Bush, "47. Textile Fragment," 80, cat. 47.

20   Technical analyses conducted on fragments at the Institute of Valencia de Don Juan, Madrid, and the Abegg-Stiftung, Riggisberg, Swizerland, note the remnants of black wefts. See Pilar Borrego Díaz, "Análisis técnico del ligamento en los tejidos hispanoárabes," *Bienes Culturales,*

no. 5 (2005): 107–8; and Karel Otavsky and Muhammad ʿAbbas Muhammad Salim, *Mittelalterliche Textilien, vol. 1: Ägypten, Persien und Mesopotamien, Spanien und Nordafrika* (Abbegg-Stiftung, 1995), 194–95, cat. 107.

21 Maria Judith Feliciano, "Muslim Shrouds for Christian Kings?," 118.

22 Elizabeth Dospěl Williams has argued that the large size of at least one fragment suggests that the original textile was a furnishing fabric, possibly a curtain. See Elizabeth Dospěl Williams, "Textile with Musicians," in *Jerusalem, 1000–1400: Every People Under Heaven*, ed. Barbara Boehm Drake and Melanie Holcomb (Metropolitan Museum of Art, 2016), 107–8, cat. 53.

23 Alternatively, these might be English or Dutch sailors. Both the English East India Company and Dutch East India Company were involved in the maritime trade of silk with the Safavids.

24 Marika Sardar, entry for cats. 91A and 91B, in *Interwoven Globe: The Worldwide Textile Trade, 1500–1800*, ed. Amelia Peck (Metropolitan Museum of Art, 2013), 255–56. A group of Safavid carpets featuring scenes of boats with Europeans have also been called "Portuguese carpets" by later dealers and collectors; see an example (44.63.6) at the Metropolitan Museum of Art, New York.

25 On the history of the Safavid silk trade, see Marika Sardar, "Silk Along the Seas: Ottoman Turkey and Safavid Iran in the Global Textile Trade," in Peck, *Interwoven Globe*, 66–81.

26 Refer to the published technical analysis of a fragment from the same textile (3.131) in the Textile Museum, Washington, DC, in Carol Bier, ed., *Woven from the Soul, Spun from the Heart: Textile Arts of Safavid and Qajar Iran, 16th–19th Centuries* (The Textile Museum, 1987), 242–43, cat. 57. Many fragments from this cloth can be found in various museum collections.

27 Lucinda Pelton and Ken Sutherland at the Art Institute of Chicago conducted SEM-EDS analysis on the metal threads to determine that they are composed of silver with only trace amounts of copper (quantitation could not be performed under the analytical conditions used). For details, see analytical report on file in the Department of Conservation and Science, Art Institute of Chicago.

28 This attribution is based on a reading of the iconography of a closely related textile that now survives in fragments—see an example (3.280) at the Textile Museum, Washington, DC. The similarities between the two include the minute scale of the design, the structure of plain-weave double cloth, the selvedge of two thin cords, the *S*-direction wrapping of the metal threads, and the alternation of metal-wrapped and white silk weft threads. The Textile Museum's fragment features scenes from a Persian poem, and the Art Institute's textile may also indirectly reference the same poem; for a discussion of these textiles, see Louise Mackie, *Symbols of Power: Luxury Textiles from Islamic Lands, 7th–21st Century* (Yale University Press, 2015), 362. While many qualities of the Art Institute's fragment point to a Safavid origin, the composition of the metal is silver of relatively high purity, a trait that has been attributed to Mughal textiles. The Art Institute's study, however, was not quantitative; only quantitative testing of a larger sample size of various textiles might tell us how frequently such metals occur in Safavid textiles. An important study concerning the dyes and metal threads of Mughal and Safavid velvets was undertaken at the Metropolitan Museum of Art, New York; see Nobuko Shibayama, Mark Wypyski, and Elisa Gagliardi-Mangilli, "Analysis of Natural Dyes and Metal Threads Used in 16th–18th Century Persian/Safavid and Indian/Mughal Velvets by HPLC-PDA and SEM-EDS to Investigate the System to Differentiate Velvets of These Two Cultures," *Heritage Science* 3, no. 12 (2015): 1–20.

29 Hortense de la Codre generously conducted dye analysis on a red fiber from the Art Institute's textile fragment using liquid chromatography tandem mass spectrometry (LC-MS/MS) and found high levels of carminic acid, indicating use of cochineal. Note that in the Metropolitan Museum of Art's study (see note 28 above), the authors found that cochineal was generally used to dye red Safavid velvets while lac was used in Mughal examples, with some exceptions; see Shibayama, Wypyski, and Gagliardi-Mangilli, "Analysis of Natural Dyes and Metal Threads," 3. In the Art Institute's fragment, components of soluble redwood dyes were also detected at low levels. Such dyes have been reported in other Safavid textiles, but further research needs to be conducted to determine the significance of their presence here. LC-MS/MS analysis was conducted at the IMSERC (RRID:SCR_017874) MS facility at Northwestern University, which has received support from the SHyNE Resource (NSF ECCS-2025633), the State of Illinois, and the International Institute for Nanotechnology (IIN). For detailed results and analysis conditions, see report on file in Conservation and Science, Art Institute of Chicago.

30 Jean Chardin, *Voyages du chevalier Chardin, en Perse, et autres lieux de l'Orient*, vol. 4 (Le Normant, 1810), 152.

31 In the exhibition, the textile was displayed using vertical pressure mountings so that both sides could be shown; this method is not always feasible.

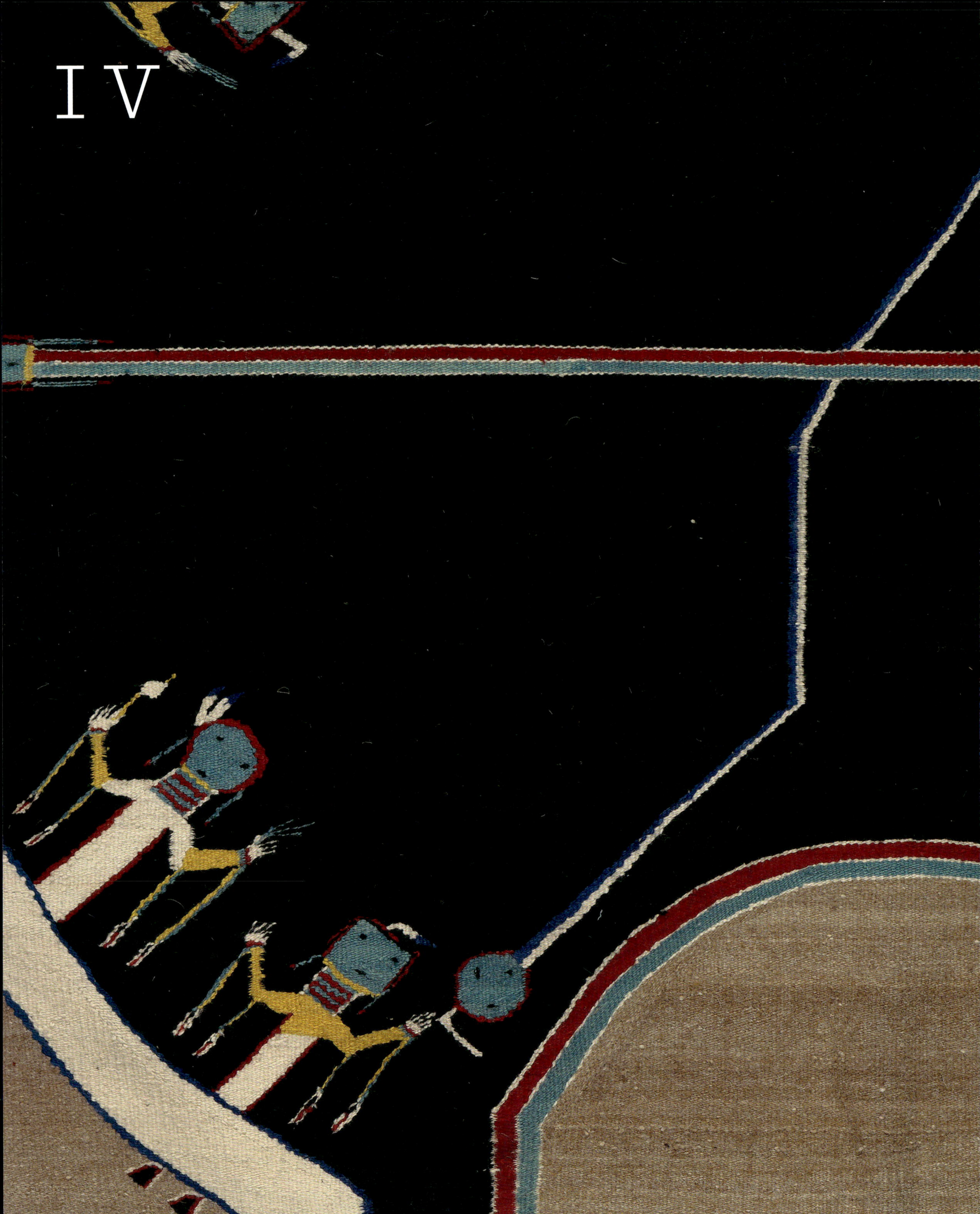
IV

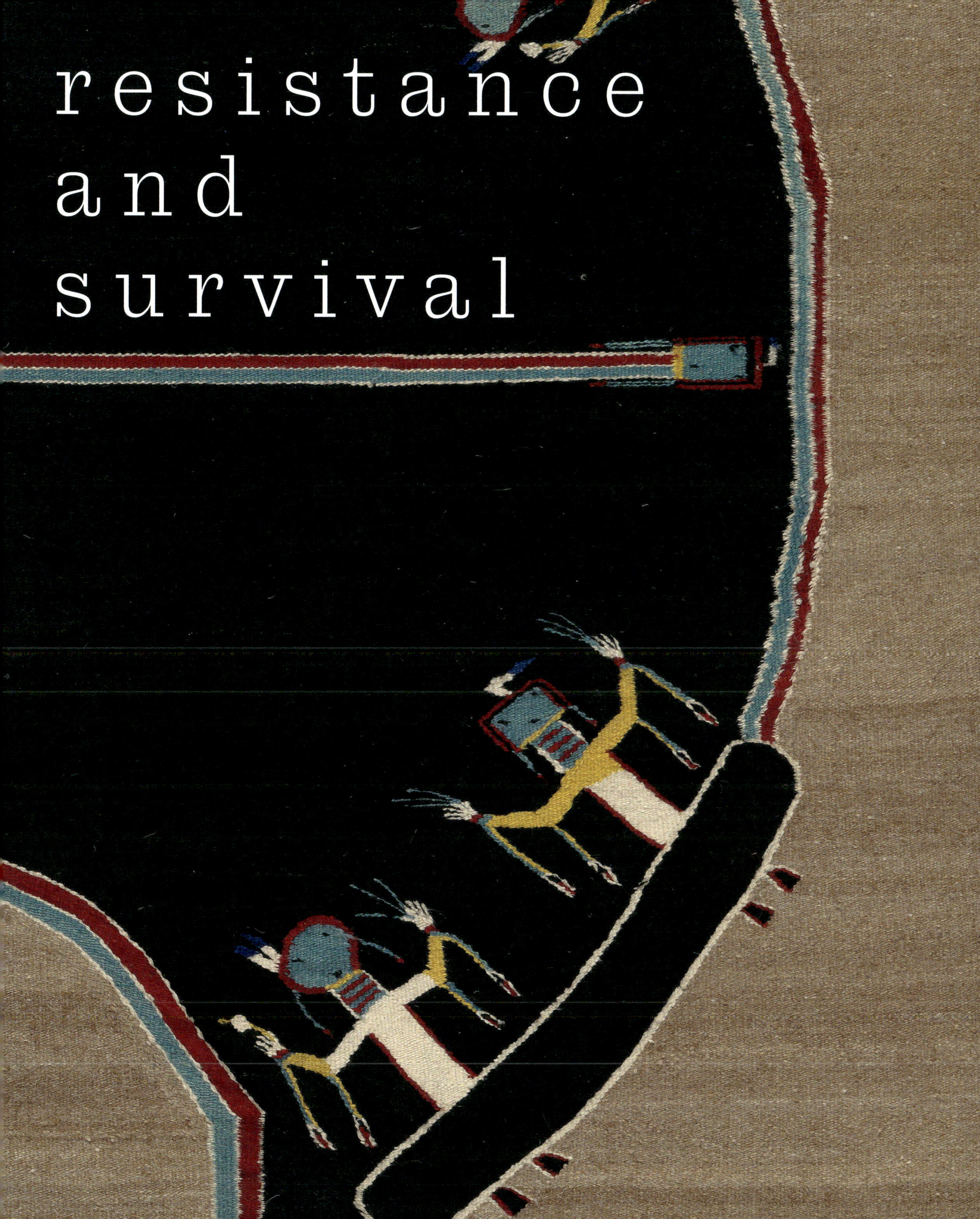
resistance
and
survival

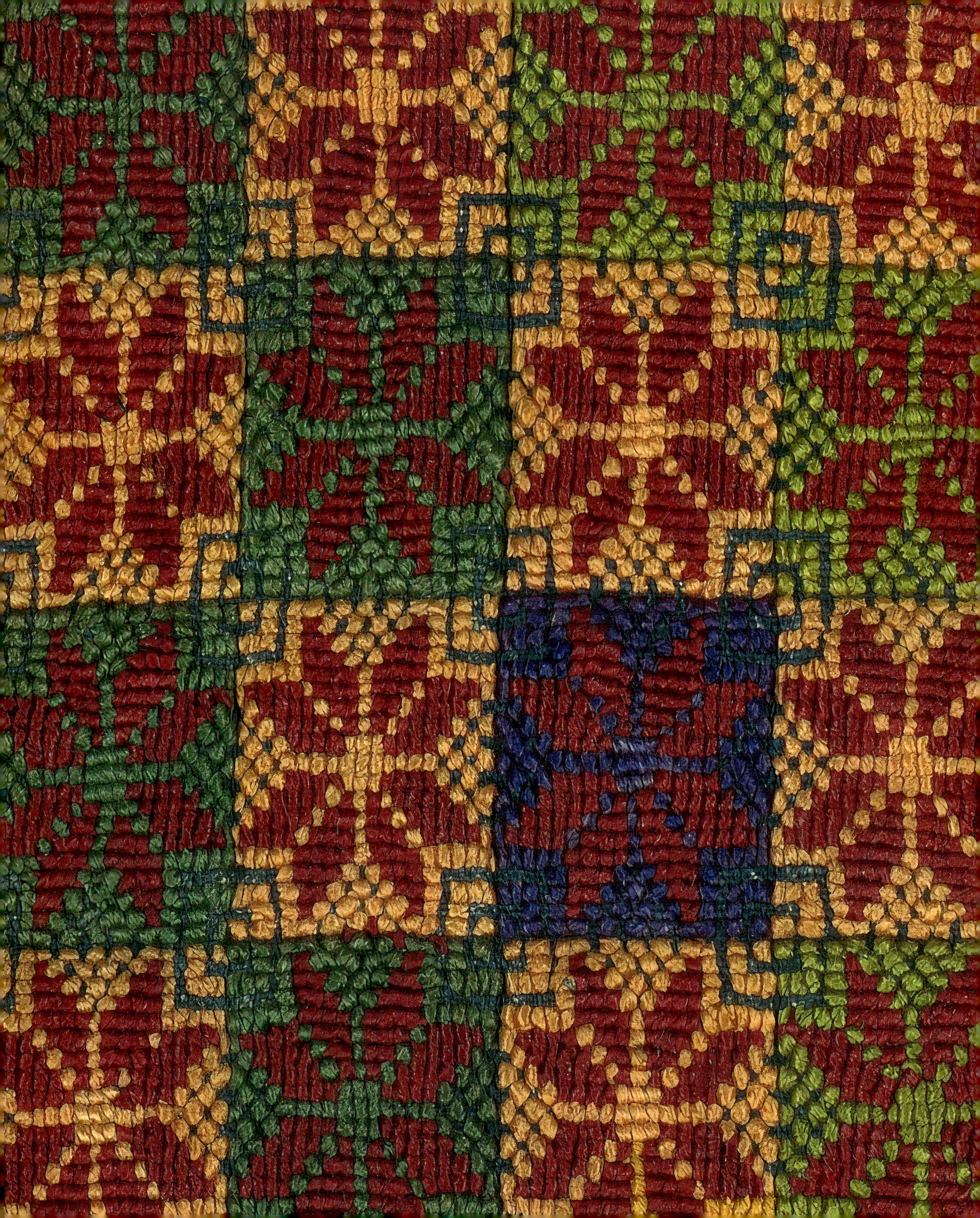

The Timelessness of *Tatreez*

Stitched Stories of Palestinian Makers Once Known

W a f a   G h n a i m
Author, educator, embroiderer, and researcher

فلسطينيةَ العينين والوشم
فلسطينيةَ الاسم
فلسطينيةَ الأحلام والهمِّ
فلسطينيةَ المنديل والقدمَين والجسم
فلسطينيةَ الكلمات والصمت
فلسطينيةَ الصوت
فلسطينيةَ الميلاد والموت

Her eyes and tattoos, Palestinian,
Her name, Palestinian,
Her dreams, and sorrow, Palestinian,
Her kerchief, her feet and body, Palestinian,
Her words and her silence, Palestinian,
Her voice, Palestinian,
Her birth and her death, Palestinian.

—Mahmoud Darwish, excerpt from "A Lover from Palestine"[1]

Once upon a *tatreez*, Palestinian women embroidered their lives with a medley of stitches, patterns, and fabrics on their beautiful, traditional *thobe*.[2] For centuries, the needle and thread were the pen and ink that documented the maker's biography, recording an "individual or a place: a wife, a mother, a daughter, a family, a house, a village, a town, a field, a market."[3] Through a dazzling tableau of colorful threads, glimmering coins, and exquisite silks, Palestinian women decorated their dresses with embroidered *tatreez* motifs reflecting their hometown, tribe, or village.[4] During the late nineteenth and early twentieth centuries, Palestine was a diverse and pluralistic population that included Muslim, Jewish, Christian, Druze, Baha'i, Sikh, Hindu, and Zoroastrian faiths, as well as other ethnic minorities such as Armenians.[5] The fashion of the *thobe*, however, did not reflect a religious or spiritual faith but rather the woman's regional and social affiliations, including whether she was *fellahin* (farmer), *medani* (townsperson), or *bedu* (nomad).[6] The region of Ramallah, for instance, was full of fertile farmland with olive groves, fruit orchards, and flower fields, which women captured like a painting made with thread on their *thobe*.[7] The majority of Palestinians lived in more than eight hundred villages as *fellahin*, among whom land ownership was passed through familial inheritance and agricultural traditions formed the basis of cultural heritage practices, including *tatreez*.[8] Palestinian society as a whole developed a sense of self through their care for and relationship with the land, which defined their individual and collective identities so strongly that any separation from the land was an obliteration of self.[9] During the first few years of displacement, Palestinian refugees used metaphors such as "death" and "burial" to describe their dispossession, and the older generations still mourn as they recall their exile that began more than seventy-five years ago, using the same word for pilgrimage to Mecca, *hajj*, to describe their visits to Palestine. This deep and complex embodiment and emplacement is the foundation of Palestinian identity, and it is stitched onto the *thobe* using the illustrative language of *tatreez*.[10]

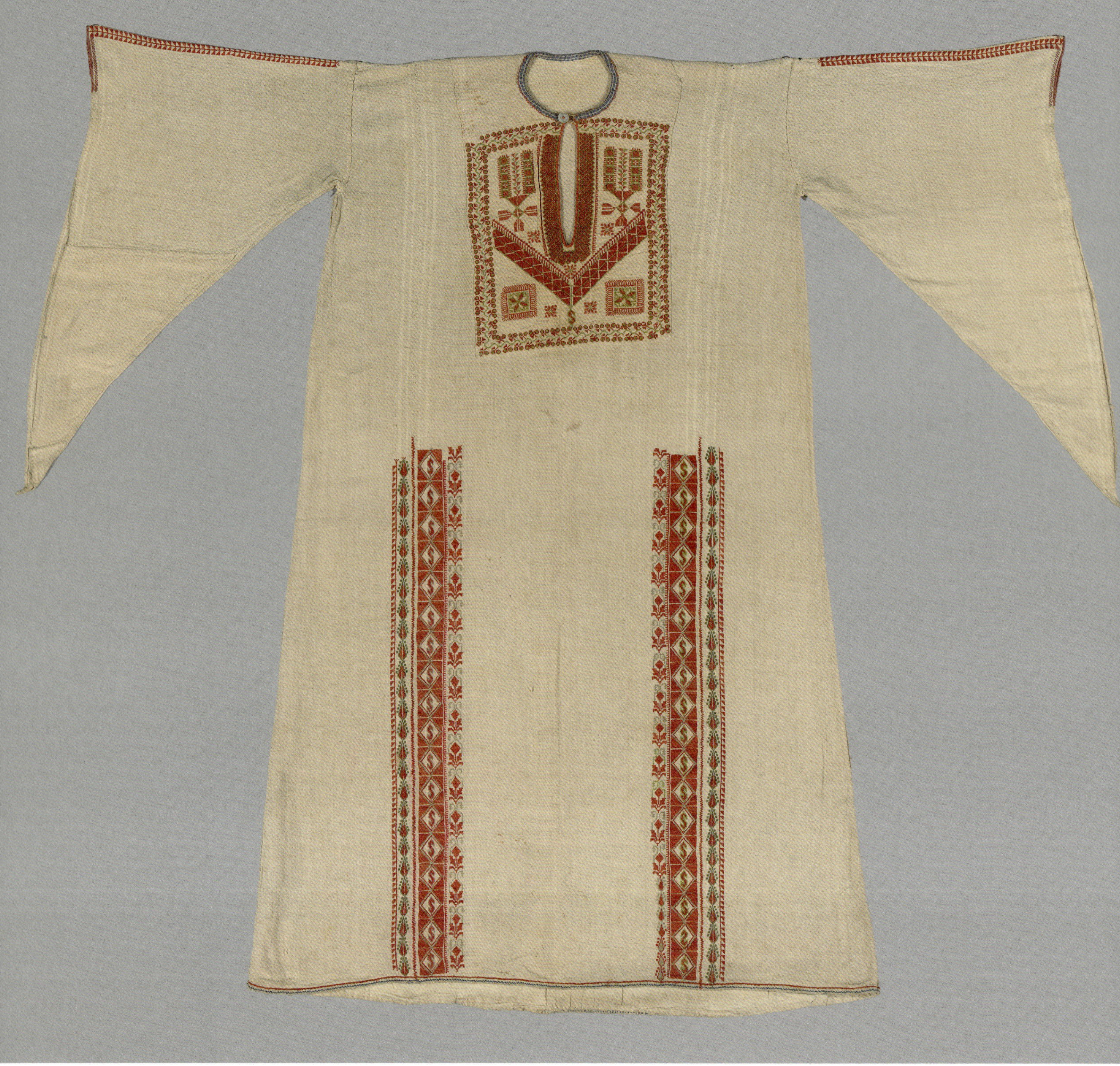

Fig. 1 Maker once known. *Thobe*, 1875–1925. Ramallah, Palestine. Cotton or linen; silk embroidery; mother-of-pearl button; 135.9 × 40.1 cm (53½ × 15¾ in.). The Art Institute of Chicago, bequest of George F. Porter, 1927.377.

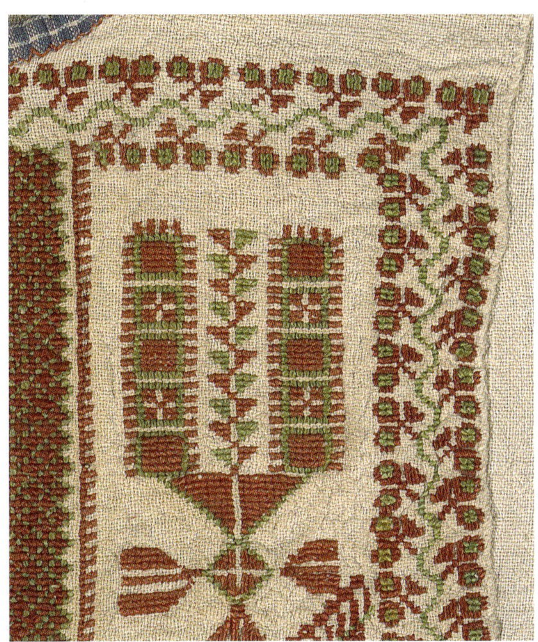

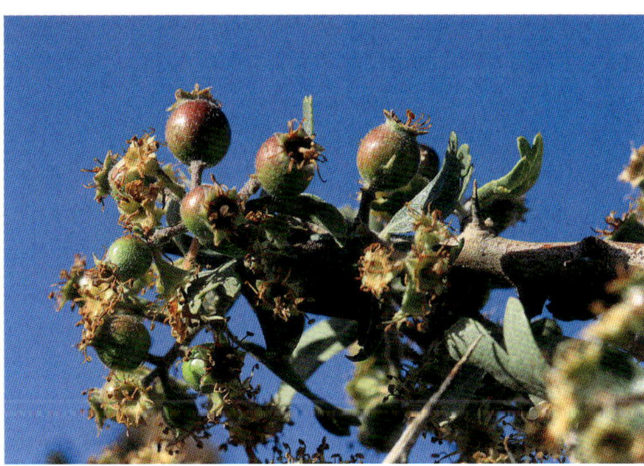

Fig. 2 **Top: detail of the chest panel of the Art Institue's *thobe* (fig. 1), which features an embroidered design inspired by the flowers on Palestine's native hawthorn tree (bottom).**

Nature served as a significant source of inspiration for *tatreez* across Palestine. The oldest patterns are primarily geometric, with abstract shapes and rectilinear forms that follow the linear, gridlike structure of the handwoven linen used for embroidery. Various *tatreez* motifs depicting the flora, fauna, and architecture of specific villages, towns, or tribes were stitched on the *thobe*, and thus it represented the wearer's regional identity. For instance, the Ramallah *qabbeh* (chest panel) always included a downward arrow composed of zigzags and amulets. A Ramallah *thobe* in the Art Institute of Chicago's collection (fig. 1) has a stitched chevron in the *qabbeh* (fig. 2, top) on locally woven linen, called *roumi.* The design meets at a downward point, with an *S* shape hanging beneath, like a pendant on a necklace; the *S* motif, referred to as *alaqa* (leech), is so significant that it is also embroidered repeatedly from the waist to the hem of the skirt, one on top of the other. During the nineteenth and early twentieth centuries, the *alaqa* was a common feature on the embroidered garments of Ramallah women.[11] Leeches were used medicinally throughout the world for thousands of years to heal an array of ailments, and, like most *tatreez*, the embroidered symbol was believed to serve apotropaic purposes, protecting the wearer from danger, disease, and evil.[12] The *qabbeh* is bordered with hawthorns native to the region (fig. 2, bottom), although the maker of this dress took creative liberties in the colors she used, the number of berries per branch, and the density of stitches.[13] The embroidered skirt panels include columns of repeated *saru* (cypress trees) and snapdragon flowers, stacked alongside the leech tiles.[14] The back bottom of the *thobe* (fig. 3, top), near the hem, shows the tall-palm motif, a quintessential feture of Ramallah dresses, that depicts the trunk of the palm tree. The tall-palm motif is found on all embroidered garments made in Ramallah during the late nineteenth and early twentieth centuries.

Other *tatreez* motifs—such as birds, flowers, and *saru*—are found across Palestine, although with unique design variations and different names from village to

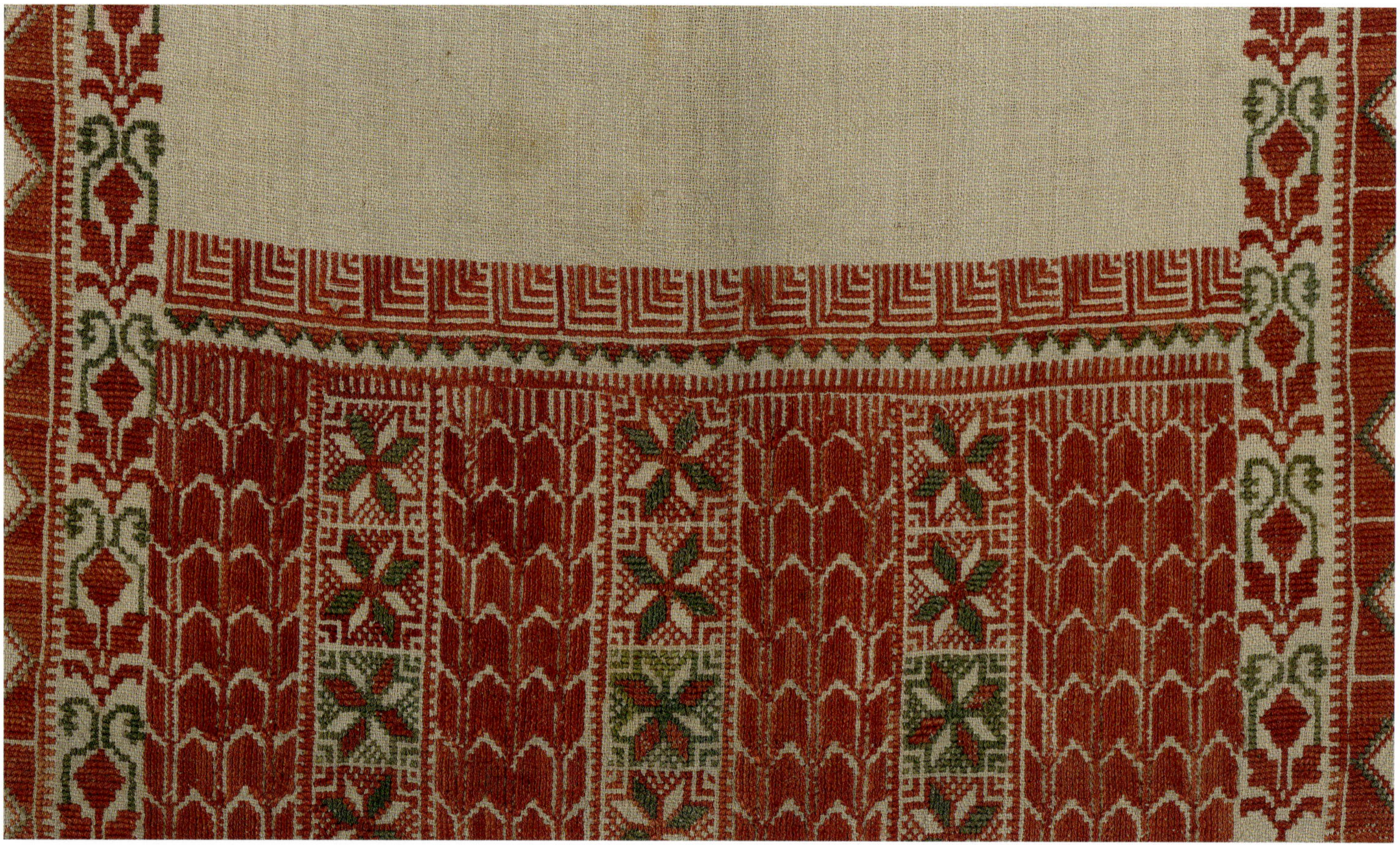

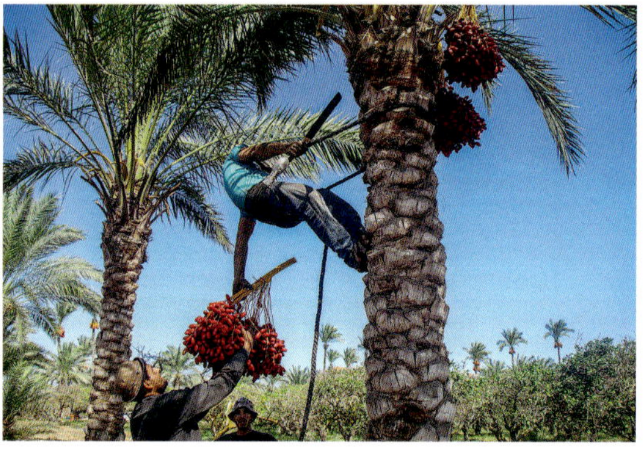

Fig. 3 **Top: The back bottom of the Art Institute's *thobe* (fig. 1), with columns, from left to center, of cypress trees, leeches, moons, snapdragon flowers, and tall palms like the one from which these Palestinian farmers harvest date palms (bottom).**

village.[15] The eight-pointed shapes enclosed in tiles underneath the downward arrow of the *qabbeh* in the *thobe* are called moons in Ramallah, although each village had a different name for the motif: crushed sugar in Bethlehem, stars in Yaffa, and roses in Gaza.[16] *Saru* were embroidered differently on the *thobe* depending on the governing styles of each village—for example, they were stitched horizontally in al-Khalil and vertically in Gaza.[17] In some villages, the *saru* were also called trees of life. This name likely reflects their important role in organizing land in Palestine: *saru* were planted as fences for farms and held the same importance to the *fellahin* across all villages, regardless of what the motif was called or which of the hundreds of variations were stitched.

The *saru* motif is just one example in which *tatreez* serves as a proxy for land; arrangements of cacti, trees, and other plants once demarcated borders, boundaries, and fences in each home and village in historic Palestine (see figs. 4–5). The motif is used the same way in garments, delineating different sections of embroidery, including in the Art Institute's example.[18] Cactus is a prickly, fruit-bearing plant and a dominant feature in the landscape of Palestine, traditionally planted to separate people's orchards and olive groves. The Arabic word for the cactus plant, *saber*, also means patience, an important virtue that mothers teach their children through embroidery. The metaphor of the cactus as a form of *saber* is cited through the Palestinian proverb *saber as-sabbar* ("the patience of the cactus"), which reminds *fellahin* that the cactus thrives because of its patience and resilience (*sumud* in Arabic); it grows in harsh terrain and yet still bears a sweet fruit beneath its thorny skin and prickly leaves.[19] Beyond the *tatreez* pattern representing the prickly pear, cactus fruit plays another important role in embroidery: before eating the fruit, the *fellahin* would brush the cochineal insect off the leaves to process, along with the kermes insect, into a vibrant red pigment, used to dye the mainly red thread embroidered in the region for centuries.[20]

In the eastern Mediterranean, *tatreez* and *thobe*-making are centuries-old regional traditions, and the Ramallah *thobe* of the nineteenth and twentieth centuries preserves one of the oldest and most famous styles: a long-sleeved, ankle-length dress, embroidered in cross-stitch on locally woven, undyed linen. A similarly constructed *thobe* dating to 1283 CE (fig. 6, far left) was found on one of eight mummified females in Qadisha Valley, Lebanon. Medieval garments in the region, including this one, incorporated red, blue, and brown silk threads, with motifs of both curvilinear and rectilinear shapes similar to the *thobe*. The everyday *thobe* of the Ramallah and Yaffa regions was still embroidered using red cross-stitch on *roumi* in the nineteenth century. While it is impossible to be certain of the origins of *tatreez* in Palestine or in the eastern Mediterranean as a whole, these aesthetic and stylistic similarities in materials, patterns, and techniques illustrate the continuity of cultural heritage, as well as the dependability of oral transmission and material culture for passing these traditions on throughout the centuries (see fig. 6).

During the mid- to late nineteenth century, a typical woman's ensemble included a *khirqa* (shawl), *wuqaya* or *smadeh* (coin-lined bonnet), and, for those married, a *jellaya* (overcoat dress).[21] The Ramallah *jellaya* in the Art Institute's collection (fig. 7) is a remarkable late-nineteenth-century

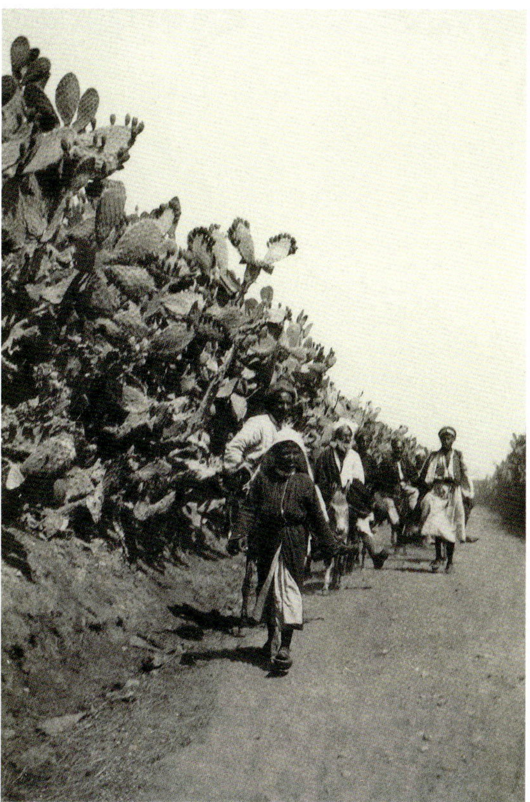

Fig. 4 **Photograph by Finnish ethnologist Hilma Gradquist of a "cactus hedge on the way to Gaza," 1925–31.**

Fig. 5 **Bullet-riddled cacti in the village of Deir Yassin after the massacre of April 9, 1948, by Irgun-Stern militia, in which nearly two-thirds of those killed were children, women, and elderly Palestinians.**

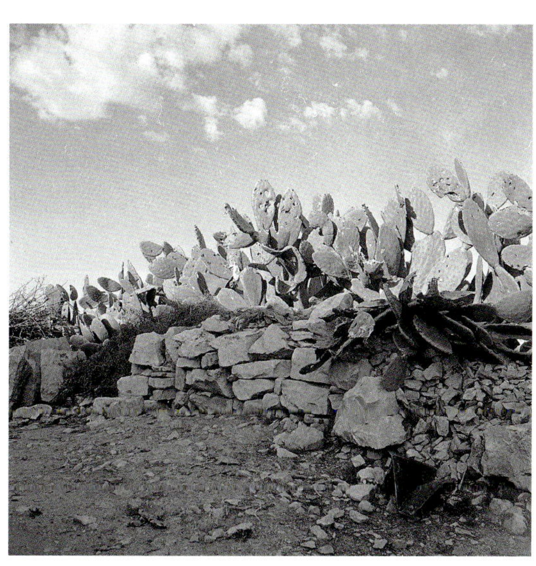

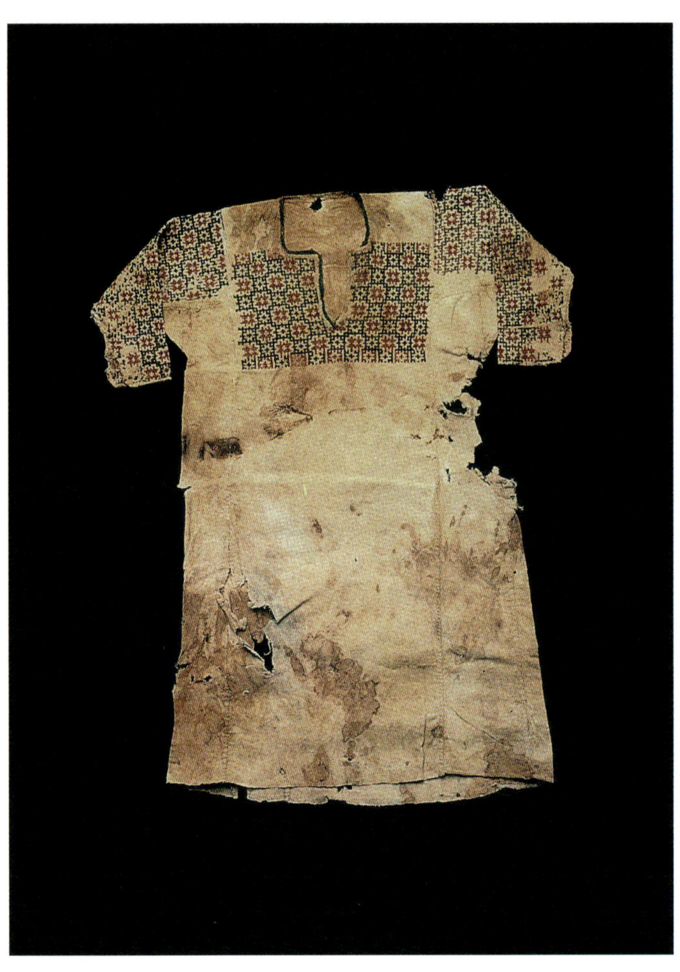 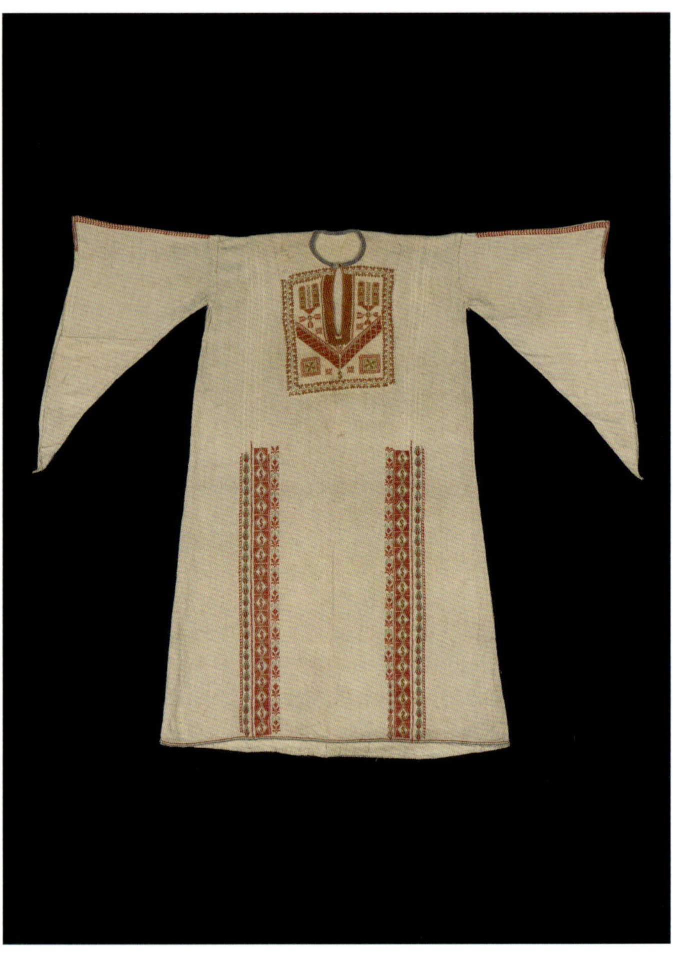

Fig. 6 **Left to right: Maker once known.**
Thobe, 1283. Qadisha Valley, Tomb of Tyre,
Lebanon. National Beirut Museum. The Art
Institute's *thobe* (fig. 1), 1875–1925. Maker
once known. *Thobe*, about 1900. Ramallah,
Palestine. Linen and silk, embroidered;
glass button; 136 × 146 cm (53 9/16 × 57 1/2 in.).
The British Museum, London, 1981.23.3.
Maker once known. *Thobe*, 1950s–1960s.
Palestinian refugee camps. 142.2 × 144.8 cm
(56 × 57 in.). Tatreez Institute Collection,
Washington, DC, 2025.6.20.

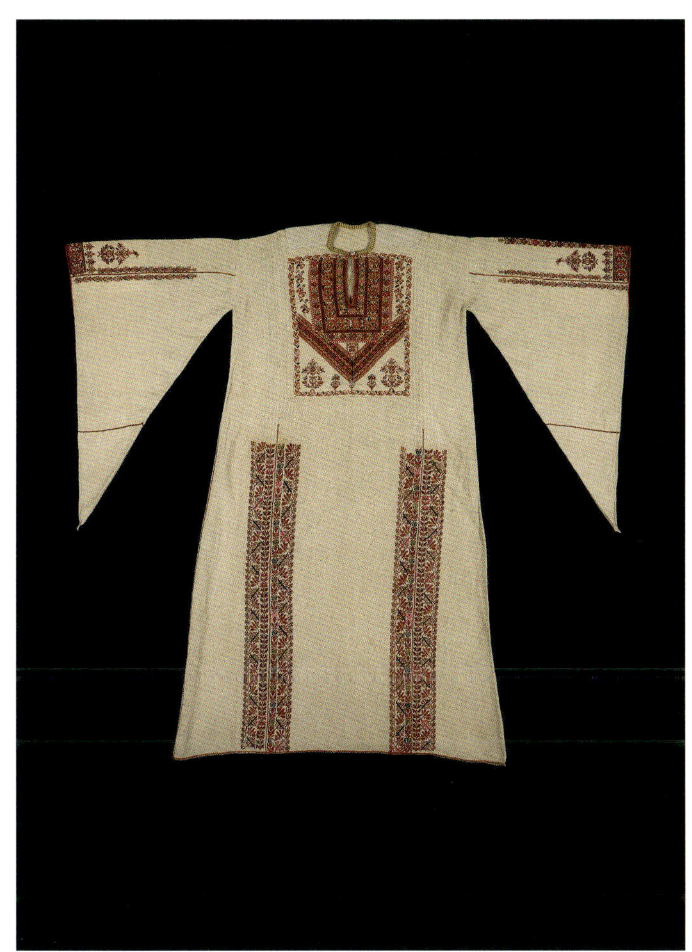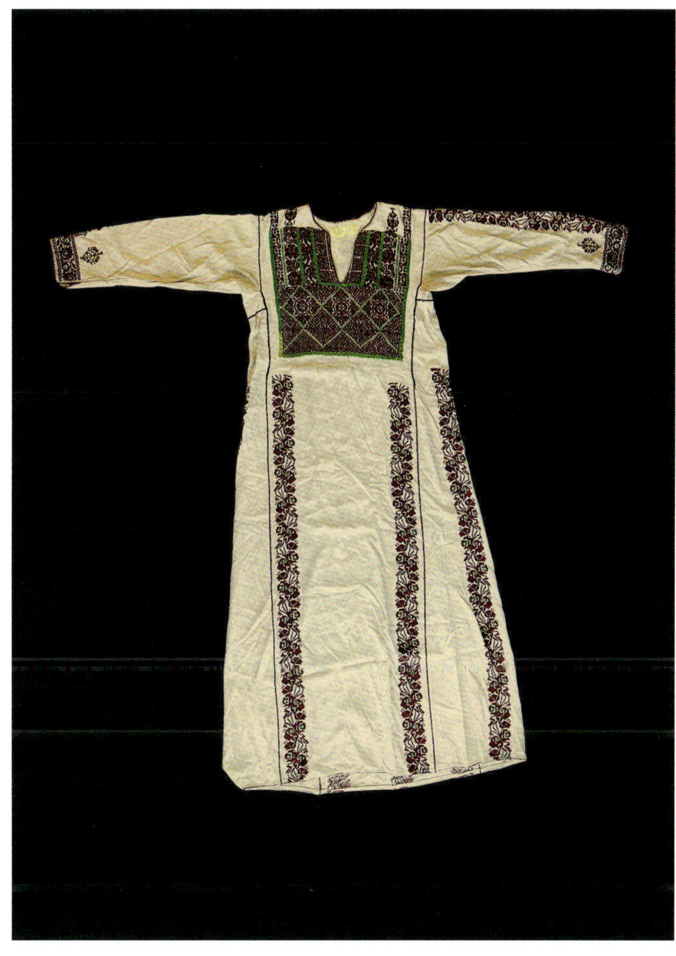

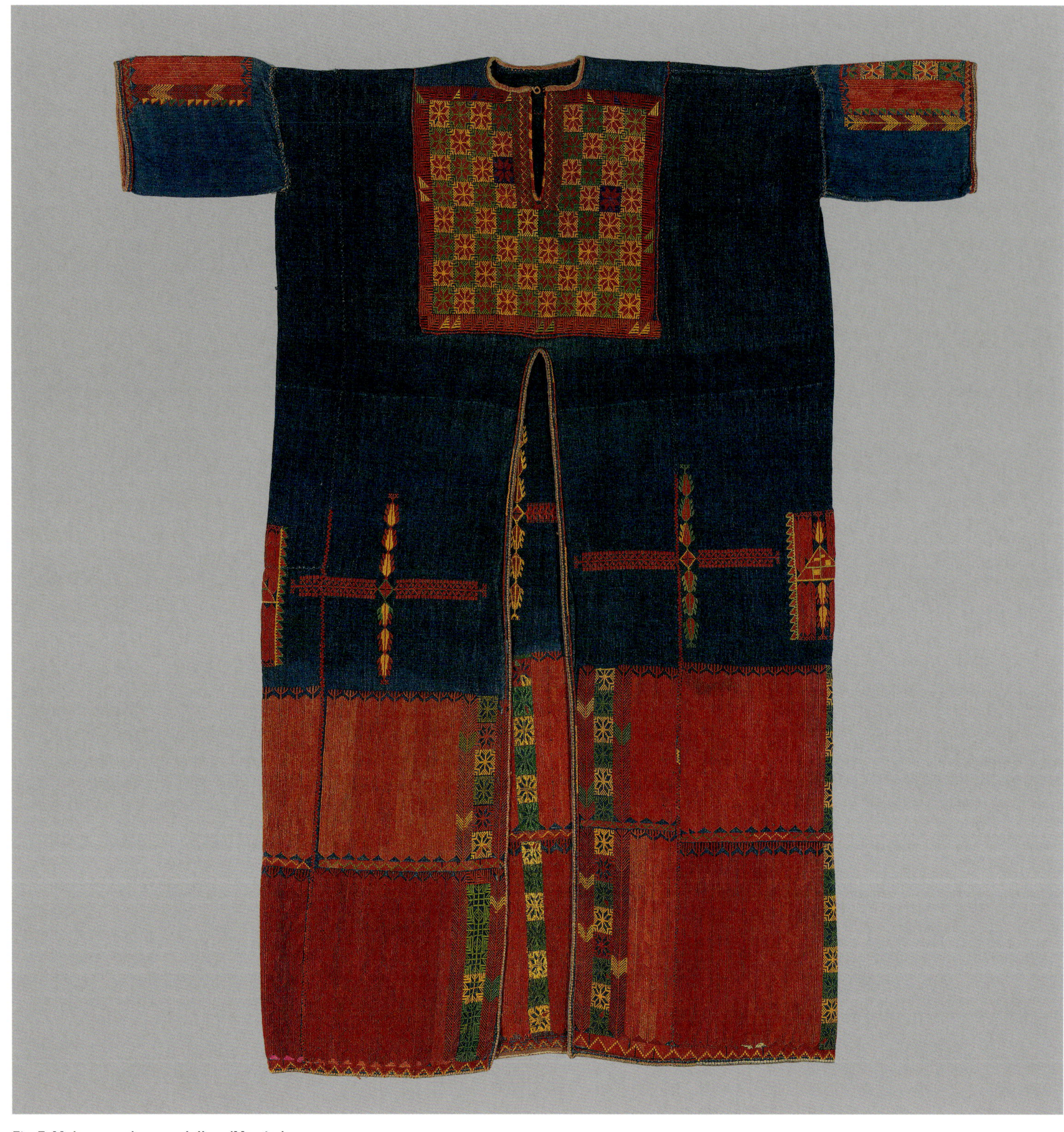

Fig. 7 Maker once known. *Jellaya* (Married Woman's Overcoat Dress), mid–late 19th century. Ramallah, Palestine. Linen, plain weave; pieced; embroidered with silk in cross-stitches (*tatreez*); 134 × 120.1 cm (52¾ × 47¼ in.). The Art Institute of Chicago, bequest of George F. Porter, 1927.378.

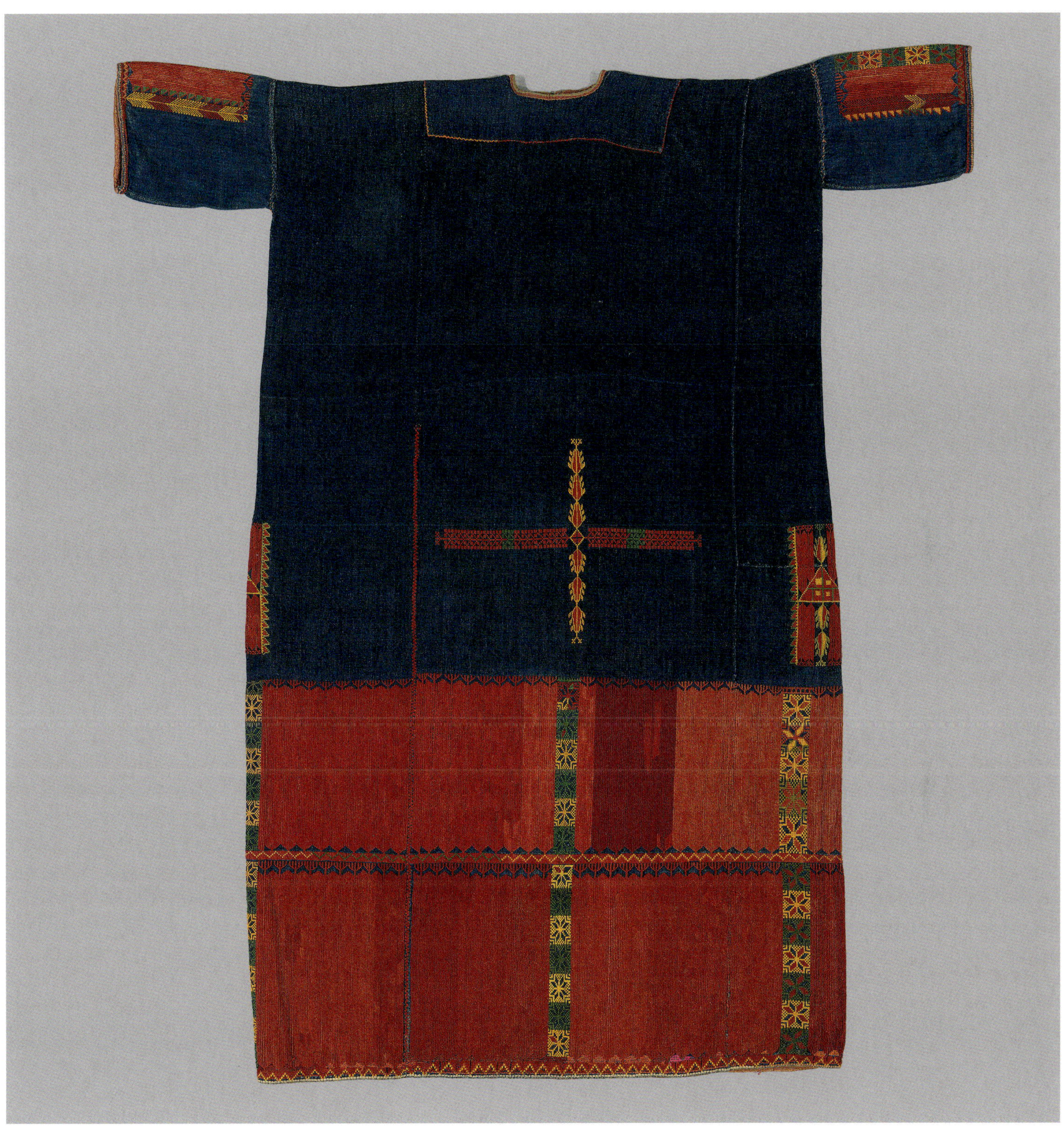

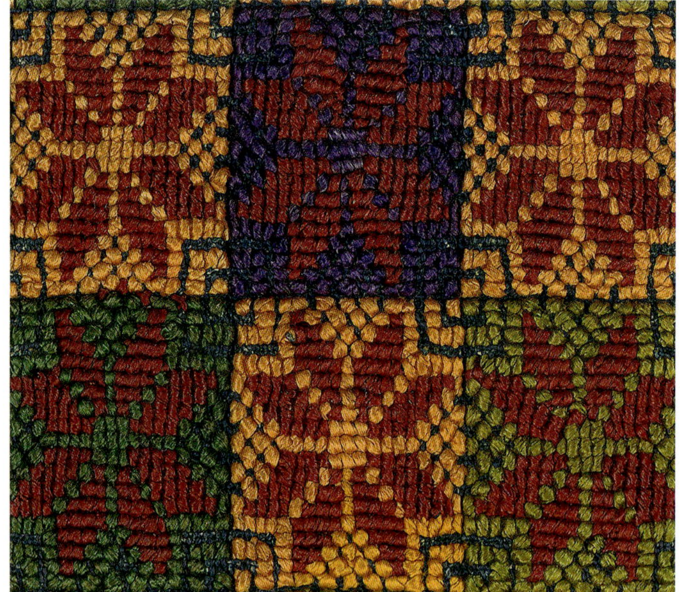

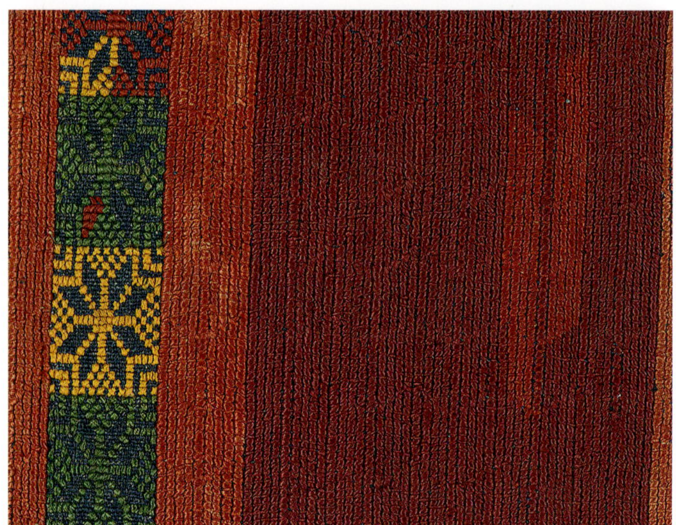

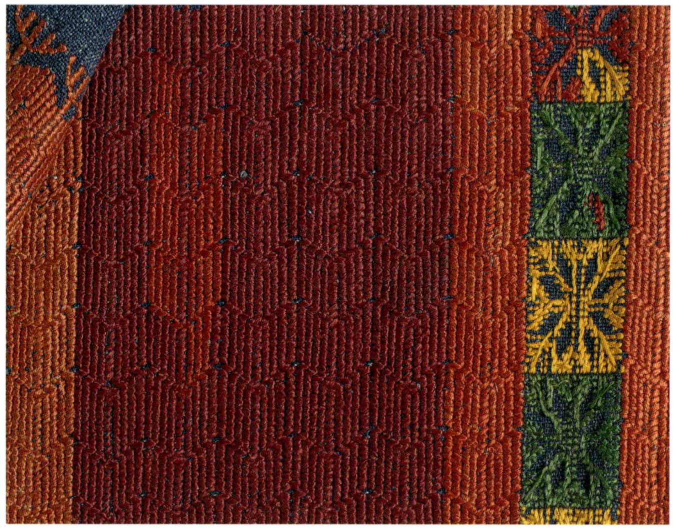

Fig. 8 Details of the Art Institute's jellaya (fig. 7), showing two different types of stitches. Top: the *qutibet fellahi* (villager's stitch or cross-stitch) in the green-and-yellow "moon" motif on the chest panel. Middle and bottom: the front and reverse of the *mushabak* (netted stitch) in the red tall-palm motif on the skirt. The variety of red shades of thread may derive either from the aging of the natural dyes or from differences inherent to thread dyed in batches. A variety of green thread colors were used in the chest panel as well.

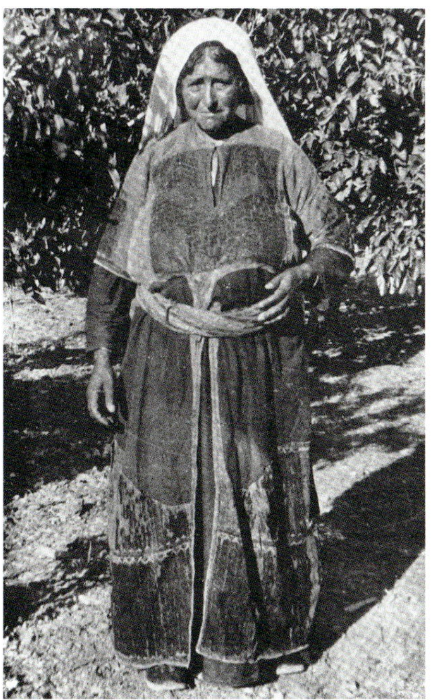

Fig. 9 **A Ramallah woman wearing a** *jellaya***,** possibly early 20th century.

Fig. 10 **William Holman Hunt (English, 1827–1910).** *The Miracle of the Sacred Fire, Church of the Holy Sepulchre* **(detail), 1892–99. Oil on canvas; 92 × 125.7 cm (36 × 49⅔ in.). Harvard Art University, Cambridge, Massachusetts, Fogg Art Museum, 1942.198. The woman at center wears a** *jellaya***, with the tall-palm motif rendered in mushbak stitch visible in the lower half of the skirt.**

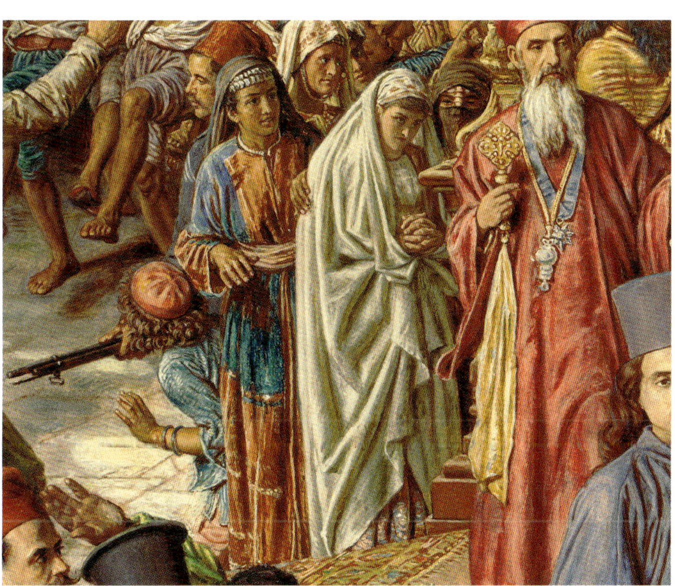

version, with two stitch types on the dark-indigo-linen garment: *qutibet fellahi* (villager's stitch or cross-stitch) and *mushabak*, or netted stitch (see fig. 8).[22] The *jellaya* is short-sleeved with a front slit from the waist to the hem, sometimes with tassels for fastening. The *jellaya* was only worn by a married woman on her wedding day and on every celebratory occasion she attended thereafter (see fig. 9). It was such a prominent part of the Ramallah woman's dress ensemble that it was depicted in Orientalist paintings by European painters. English painter William Holman Hunt's *Miracle of the Sacred Fire*, for example, features a woman wearing a *jellaya*, with the tall-palm motif densely repeated in *mushabak* stitch throughout the lower half of the skirt (fig. 10). Often, a blue bead is woven into the *mushabak* stitch in the lower back half of the *jellaya* skirt to protect the wearer from the evil eye.[23] The Art Institute's *jellaya* has no blue bead attached to the red embroidery; perhaps the maker believed she had enough luck on her own. The Ramallah *jellaya* went out of fashion at the turn of the century, transforming into a black or dark-blue *thobe* for daily wear with much less embroidery.[24] The Art Institute's *jellaya* perhaps represents the final iteration before the style disappeared.

The *thobe* of Ramallah is rich in symbolism and meaning, experiencing several stages of modification before *al-Nakba*, which means "the catastrophe" in Arabic and has been defined by the United Nations as "the mass displacement and dispossession of Palestinians during the 1948 Arab-Israeli war."[25] After the inauguration of the Friends Girls' School in Ramallah by American Quakers in 1869, embroidery began to be taught in a school setting. This new influence corresponded to a rise in European curvilinear motifs in *tatreez* patterns on the *thobe,* such as embroidered swans that were not native to Palestine and were called "ducks" by Ramallah women. Similarly, following the popularization of the white-lace dress worn by Queen Victoria at her 1840 wedding to Prince Albert, white—as opposed to dark indigo—became the preferred color for the

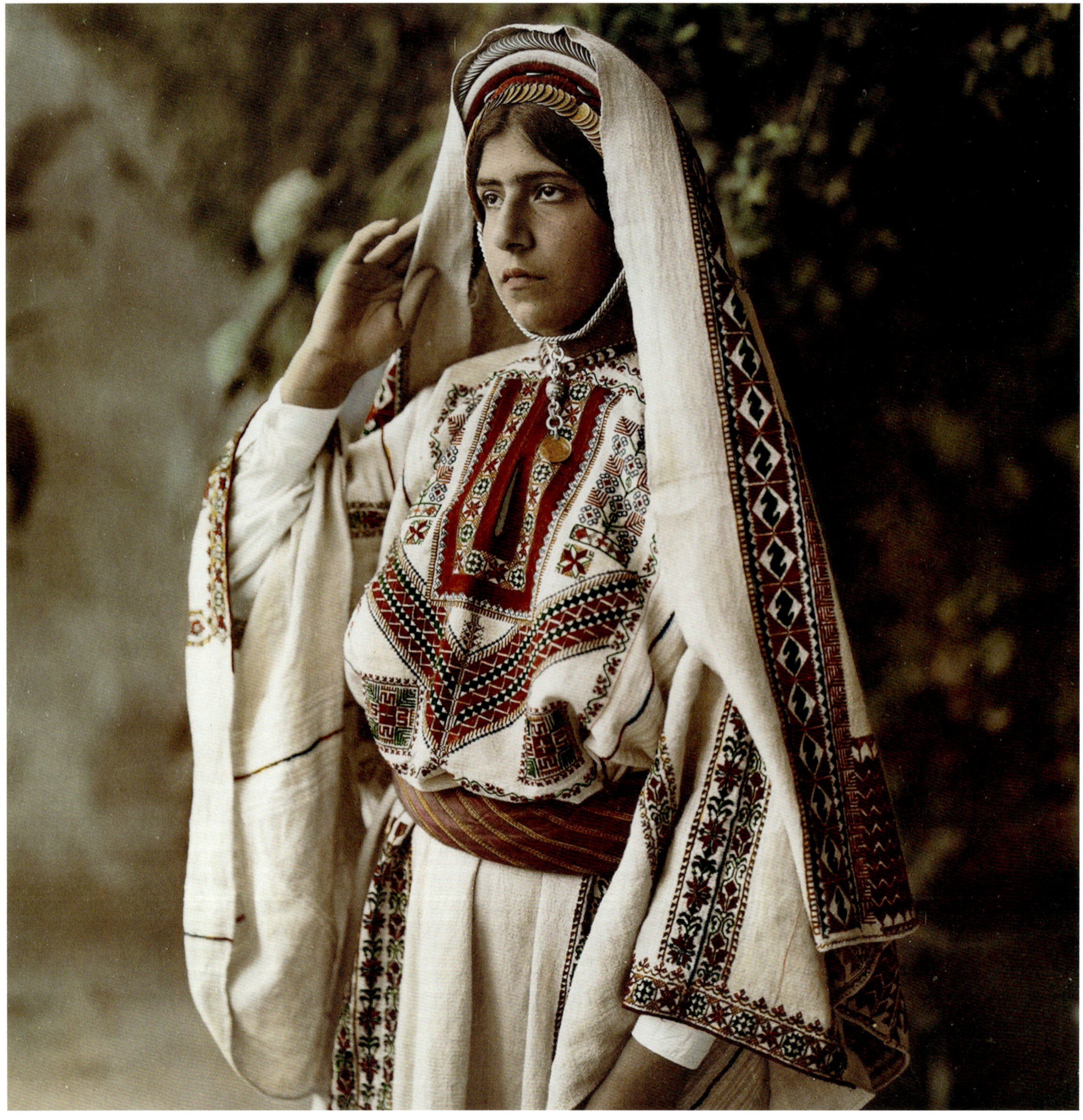

Fig. 11 **A young, unmarried Ramallah woman wearing a heavily embroidered white *thobe* and elaborate *khirqa*, identified as "The Bride, Palestine" in the March 1914 issue of *National Geographic*.**

GHNAIM

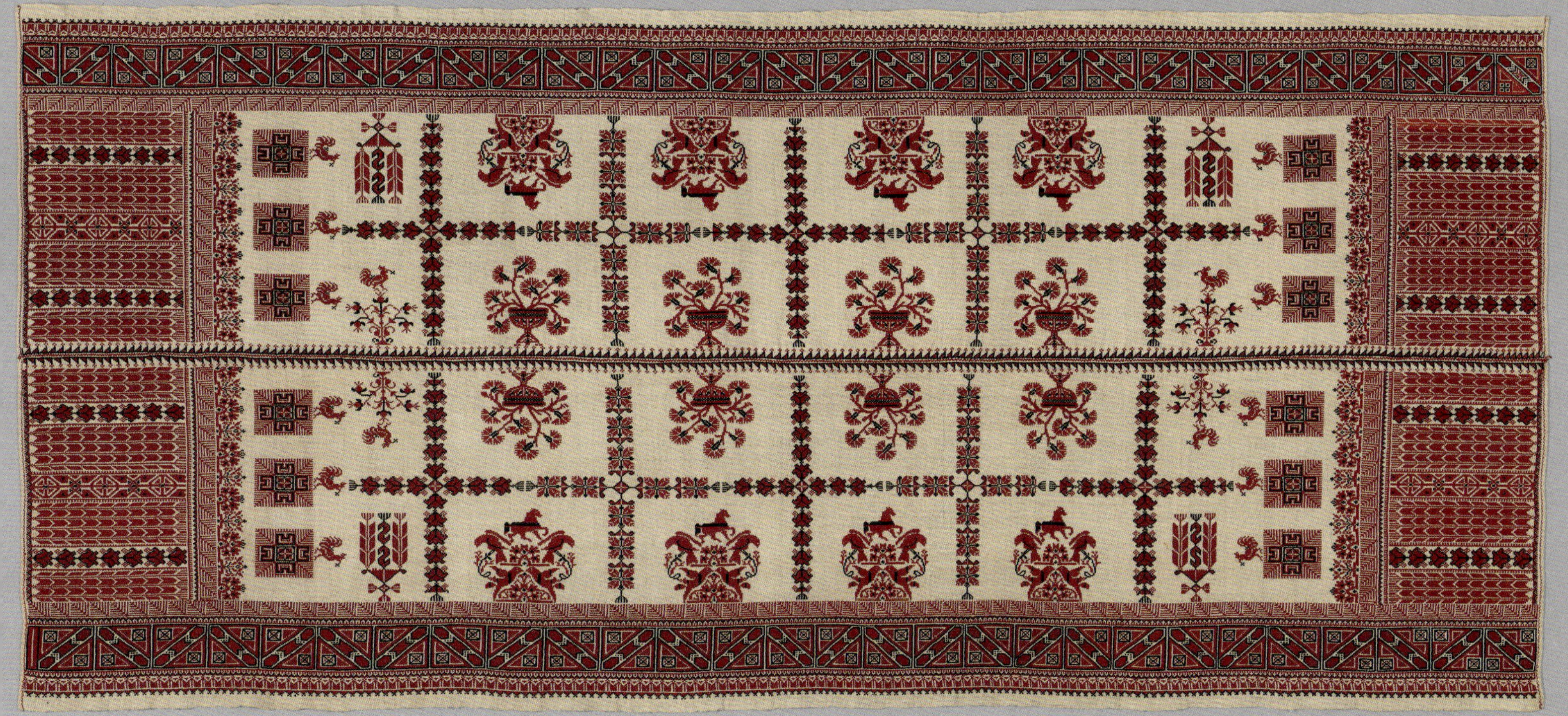

Ramallah bride. A March 1914 *National Geographic* article includes a photograph (fig. 11), captioned as "The Bride, Palestine," of a young Ramallah woman wearing a heavily embroidered white *thobe* with a similarly elaborate *khirqa*, revealing that by this time the shift to the white wedding dress was complete. By the late nineteenth century in Ramallah, the dark-indigo-style *jellaya* was embroidered much less elaborately as it transitioned from a married woman's attire to the daily wear of all women and girls.[26] While the women of Ramallah held their traditions in high esteem, they also enjoyed keeping up with world fashion trends and appreciated other cultural approaches to embroidery.

Like the white *thobe* and the bridal *jellaya*, the *khirqa* (see fig. 12) reflected the socioeconomic status of Ramallah at the time it was produced, through the chosen colors, materials, and *tatreez*. At the start of World War I, many Palestinian women independently managed the affairs of their farms and households, while their husbands immigrated to the Americas for better employment opportunities.[27] Throughout the 1910s these men sent money back to their families in Ramallah to invest in building businesses, homes, and schools. As the town flourished, the embroidery and dresses of Ramallah women began to change as well.[28] When Palestinian men returned from South America, they brought back embroidered Spanish shawls covered with floral designs that began to influence the style of the *khirqa*.[29] The natural dyes in reddish rust and burgundy tones of the mid-nineteenth century were replaced by a

Fig. 12 Maker once known. *Khirqa* (Shawl), early 20th century (before 1944). Ramallah, Palestine. Linen and silk; embroidered; 89.9 × 202.2 cm (35⅜ × 79⅝ in.). The Art Institute of Chicago, gift of Hawley L. Smith, 1964.547.

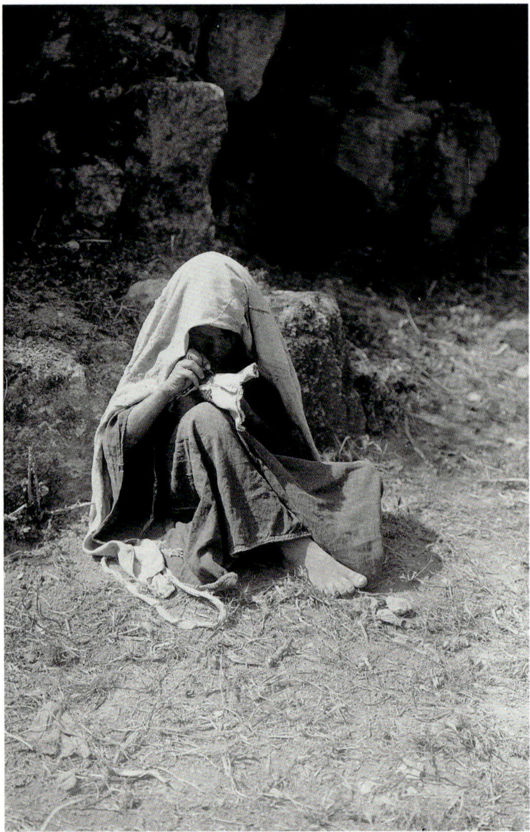

Fig. 13 **A young Palestinian woman embroidering outdoors, 1900–1920.**

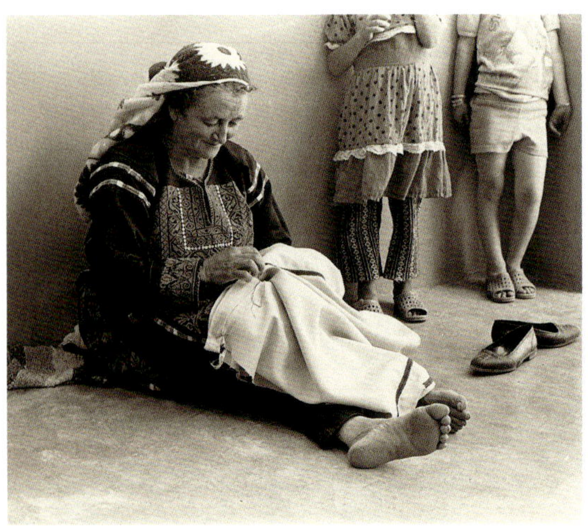

Fig. 14 **Fatima Yousef from the village of Kobar in Ramallah embroiders a Palestinian dress, 1970s.**

mixture of natural and synthetic dyes to produce brighter reds and black by the mid-twentieth century. Increasingly profuse embroidery incorporated both traditional and European designs.[30]

In the aftermath of *al-Nakba*, Palestinians found themselves living and working under utterly different political exigencies and changed material realities.[31] Women could no longer afford silk fabrics and threads, nor could they find locally woven fabrics in the refugee camps. In the 1960s a contemporary iteration of the *thobe* emerged with a simple tailored cut and narrow sleeves, similar in appearance to the Ramallah dress, with four to six vertical panels in the skirt.[32] The six-branch dress, named after the number of embroidered skirt panels, used curvilinear floral patterns to express a collective national identity that was no longer tied to a specific town, tribe, or village.[33] The beauty of the six-branch dress was that it allowed women to embroider thin panels in the skirt and widen them over time as their economic situation improved and they could afford more thread (see figs. 13–14). Due to its simple cut, widely used floral patterns, and affordability, the six-branch dress continues to be produced today and represents the new Palestinian identity, one that exists beyond borders (see fig. 15).

Time and again, Palestinian women and girls pick up the needle and thread to preserve *tatreez* in the refugee camps, under military occupation, and in exile. It is through the strength, technical mastery, and resilience of Palestinian women that this cultural heritage has survived and thrived against all odds. The resilience of the Palestinian spirit in the face of difficulty is like the fruit held by a shell of cactus thorns. Only in *saber* and *sumud* do the lessons of Palestinian elders and the stories of the land coalesce, whether to peel the prickly skin off the cactus fruit, learn the intricate art of *tatreez*, or endure the endless exile that separates the farmer from his beloved orchards. The collective memory of Palestinians and their land persists, together, in partnership like two inseparable lovers. In every successive wave of war and dispossession, the lasting presence

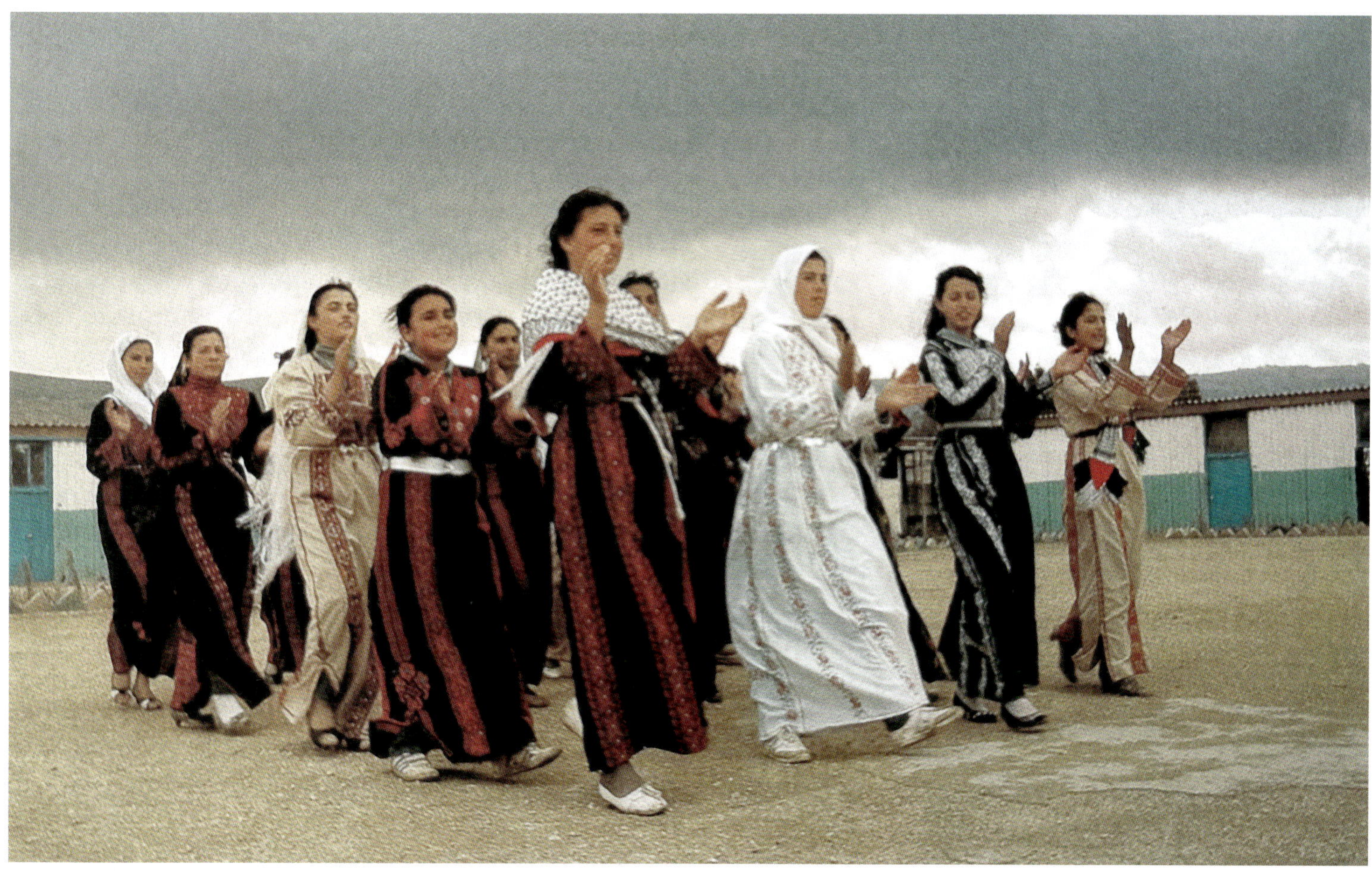

Fig. 15 **Palestinian women dancing in six-branch dresses, 1985.**

of plants and trees rooted in the soil are the *saber* and *sumud* that enable the return of elders to destroyed and depopulated villages to remember each place in relation to nature—what once was and who once lived.[34]

In North American museums, embroidered works by Palestinian women are often stripped of their makers' names and biographies. The stitches and garments, measured to each individual's head, neck, waist, and arms, now serve as silent witnesses to the lost stories of their lives. The makers, once known by their community for the garments they made and wore, are no longer known. Somewhere along the way, it was decided that their names did not need to be recorded. And yet, despite the destruction of orchards, towns, and villages, along with the deaths of those who nurtured them, Palestinian women continue to embroider the natural landscape on land's surrogate: the *thobe*.

Once again, Palestinian life, land, and *tatreez* face a renewed threat of erasure. In memory of the land that once was, Palestinian hands find a way to stitch with *saber* and *sumud* using *tatreez* patterns—old and new—with a deep and abiding hope for freedom, peace, and justice.

Appendix

A Tribute to the Palestinian Makers Once Known: A Selection of Tatreez Patterns from Ramallah

In 2021 UNESCO inscribed the art of embroidery in Palestine—encompassing practices, skills, knowledge, and rituals—on the Representative List of the Intangible Cultural Heritage of Humanity.[35] In tribute to the Palestinian women who embroidered the extraordinary pieces in the Art Institute of Chicago's collection, as well as for the survival of this intangible cultural heritage, three *tatreez* patterns found on the garments themselves have been provided for the world to stitch in memory of the women who were once known on the land where they once lived.

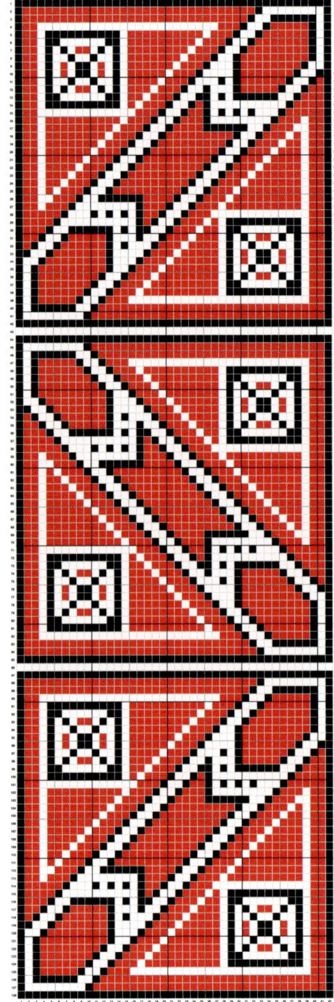

Motif name: **Zigzag Tile,**
بلاط متعرج
Garment: **Maker once known,** *Khirqa* **(fig. 12)**
Region: **Ramallah,**
Time period: **1920–40**
Location on garment: **Border**

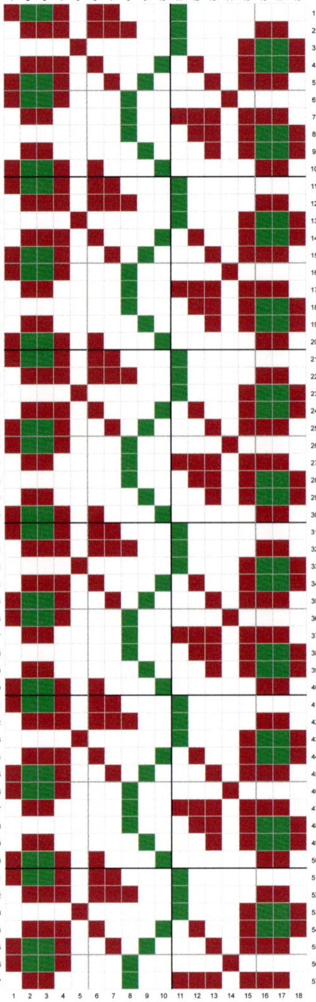

Motif name: **Hawthorn Flower,**
زهرة الزعرور
Garment: **Maker once known,** *Thobe* **(fig. 1)**
Region: **Ramallah**
Time period: **Late 19th century**
Location on garment: **Chest panel border**

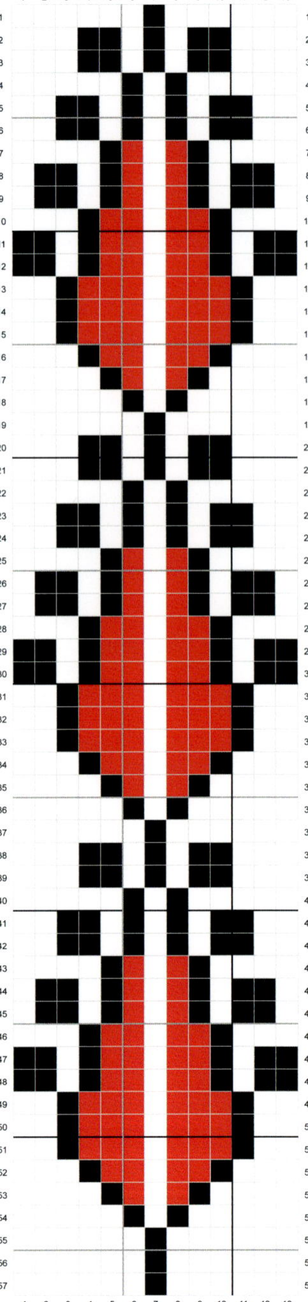

Motif name: **Cypress Tree,**
شجرة السرو؛ **Tree of Life,** شجرة الحياة
Garment: **Maker once known,** *Thobe* **(fig. 1); maker once known,** *Jellaya* **(fig. 7)**
Region: **Ramallah**
Time period: **mid-19th century**
Location on garment: **Skirt**

Notes

1   "A Lover from Palestine" ("Ashiq min Filastin") appears in Mahmoud Darwish, *Diwan: al-A'mal al-'Ula*, vol. 1 (Riad El-Rayyes Books, 2009), 92–93. Darwish was an award-winning Palestinian author and poet. His poetry often deployed the metaphor of two lovers to refer to himself, "the lover," and his "beloved" Palestine. In an earlier verse, Darwish writes "And I have vowed / To fashion from my eyelashes a kerchief / And upon it to embroider verses for your eyes." Traditionally, a bride would embroider on a kerchief and give it to her groom on their wedding day. The groom would wave it while leading the *dabke* dance during festivities. In the poem, Darwish embroiders the kerchief himself with the words "Palestinian she was and still is"—an enduring gift to his lover, Palestine.

2   The Arabic term *tatreez* is translated as embroidery. Contemporarily, *tatreez* is synonymous with Palestinian embroidery. The *thobe* is Arabic for dress. All Arabic terms appear in italics according to guidance from Gregory Younging, *Elements of Indigenous Style: A Guide for Writing By and About Indigenous Peoples* (Brush Education, 2018).

3   Widad Kamel Kawar, *Threads of Identity: Preserving Palestinian Costume and Heritage* (Rimal Books, 2011), 1.

4   "Palestine" is defined in a variety of ways. As referred to in this essay, it is geographically defined as the land west of the Jordan River and east of the Mediterranean Sea, bounded to the north by present-day Lebanon and to the south by the Sinai.

5   See J. B. Barron, *Palestine: Report and General Abstracts of the Census of 1922* (British Mandate, October, 23, 1922), content.ecf.org.il/files/00785_1922PalestineCensus English.pdf. See also Alexander Scholch, "The Demographic Development of Palestine, 1850–1882," *International Journal of Middle East Studies* 17, no. 4 (1985): 485–505.

6   Sometimes, the woman's religious identity was represented in jewelry or medallions attached to headdresses.

7   See Kawar, *Threads of Identity*, 69.

8   See Shelagh Weir, *Palestinian Costume* (Interlink Books, 1989), 16.

9   See Rosemary Sayigh, *Palestinians: From Peasants to Revolutionaries* (Zed Press, 1979), 109.

10   See Nasser Abufarha, "Land of Symbols: Cactus, Poppies, Orange, and Olive Trees in Palestine," *Identities: Global Studies in Culture and Power* 15, no. 3 (2008): 343.

11   See Margarita Skinner, *Palestinian Embroidery Motifs: A Treasury of Stitches, 1850–1950* (Rimal Books, 2007), 117.

12   See Vogelsang-Eastwood, Gillian. *Encyclopedia of Embroidery from the Arab World*. (Bloomsbury Academic, 2016), 115–124.

13   See Skinner, *Palestinian Embroidery Motifs*, 146.

14   See Skinner, *Palestinian Embroidery Motifs*, 157.

15   See Nabil Anani and Suleiman Mansour, *Guide to the Palestinian Art of Embroidery* (Inaash Al-Usra Association and Al Abliyya Publishing, 2011), 82.

16   See Widad Kamel Kawar and Tania Nasir, "The Traditional Palestinian Costume," *Journal of Palestine Studies* 10, no. 1 (1980): 125. See also Skinner, *Palestinian Embroidery Motifs*, 165–69.

17   The phrase *governing style* refers to more than just a traditional style of dress worn in Palestine—rather, it indicates a strong regional delineation of style that is governed by fashions of the given village, town, or nomadic group, including the type of fabric, placement of embroidery, thread colors, and the cut of the sleeves, neckline, and skirt.

18   See Walid Khalidi, *All That Remains: The Palestinian Villages Occupied and Depopulated by Israel in 1948* (Institute for Palestine Studies, 2001).

19   See Abufarha, *Land of Symbols*, 347.

20   See Skinner, *Palestinian Embroidery Motifs*, 155; and Weir, *Palestinian Costume*, 26.

21   See Hanan Karaman Munayyer, *Traditional Palestinian Costume: Origins and Evolution* (Olive Branch Press, 2020), 107.

22   See Tania Tamari Nasir, Omar Joseph Nasser-Khoury, and Shirabe Yamada, with Widad Kamel Kawar, *Seventeen Embroidery Techniques from Palestine: An Instruction Manual* (Sunbula, 2019), 109.

23   See Gillian Vogelsang-Eastwood, *Encyclopedia of Embroidery from the Arab World* (Bloomsbury Academic, 2016), 115–24.

24   See Jan Macdonald, "Palestinian Dress," *Palestine Exploration Quarterly* 83, no. 1 (1951): 61.

25   "About the Nakba," United Nations: The Question of Palestine, accessed April 24, 2025, un.org/unispal/about-the-nakba/. For further discussion, see Rabea Eghbariah, "Toward Nakba as a Legal Concept," *Columbia Law Review* 124, no. 4 (2024): 889, 901.

26   See Munayyer, *Traditional Palestinian Costume*, 114.

27   See Kawar and Nasir, "The Traditional Palestinian Costume," 119.

28   See Kawar, *Threads of Identity*, 69.

29   See Kawar, *Threads of Identity*, 71.

30   See Munayyer, *Traditional Palestinian Costume*, 181.

31   See Rachel Dedman, *At the Seams: A Political History of Palestinian Embroidery* (Palestinian Museum, 2016), 44.

32   See Weir, *Palestinian Costume*, 274.

33   Dedman, *At the Seams*, 44.

34   See Michel Khleifi, dir., *Ma'loul Celebrates Its Destruction*, 1985, youtube.com/watch?v=JH_kOFkzk1E.

35   See "The Art of Embroidery in Palestine, Practices, Skills, Knowledge, and Rituals," UNESCO, accessed June 12, 2025, palestinefilminstitute.org/en/maloul-celebrates-its-destruction.

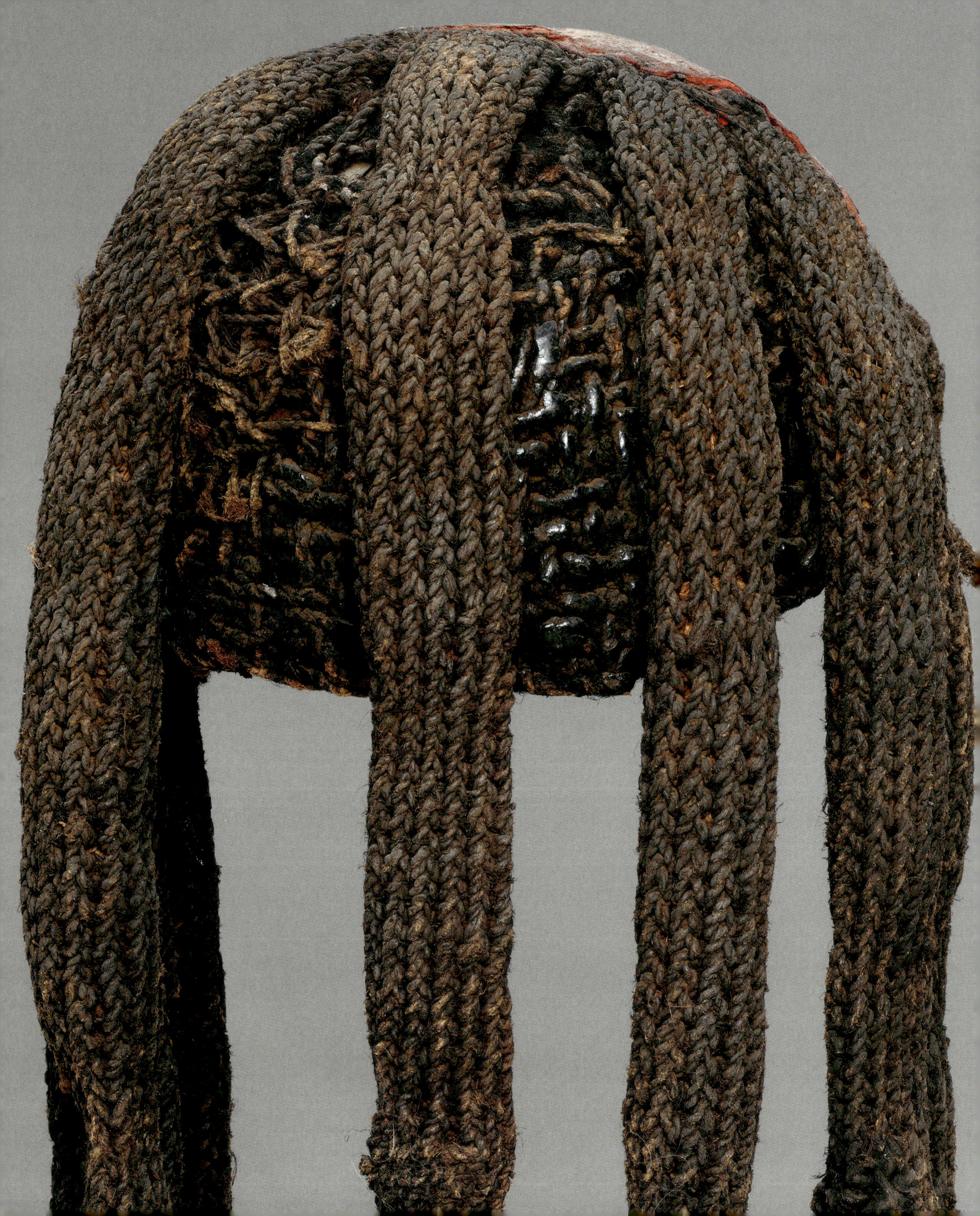

Material Inheritances, Lasting 'Til Sunday

Nneka Kai
Artist, educator, and writer

I'm going to braid my hair
Braid many colors into my hair
I'll put a long braid in my hair
And write your name there.

—Tracy K. Smith, "Duende"[1]

Sundays at my childhood home in Atlanta were spent cleaning, stewing hour-long pots of turkey wings and black-eyed peas, blasting music, and bickering with my brothers about which of us would be the first to get our hair styled for the week. Sunday in my household was a day for rest and revival. I didn't come to understand it this way until later in my life: My mother cultivated a weekly day of care in our home. Braiding, twisting, and puff-balling were reserved for Sundays because that was when we had time—my mother did not have to go to work and so could dedicate herself to these tasks with care and attention, and we could all appreciate one another and our home. My mother was building a language of interiority, an identity of self and place. The things around us—the table, the chair, the music, the hair—were all part of this restorative space-making. When it was my turn to get my hair done, I excitedly imagined what design my mother would create, running to grab the most comfortable chair, along with the comb and grease (see fig. 1). This act of care required tools and time, and she always started the task by saying, "I need your hair to last." A single mother with three young children and little time to spare, my mother committed a day for care. On those days, she not only addressed the wear and tear of the prior week but also taught us about a material inheritance that stretched across the Atlantic Ocean, connecting us to West Africa before the slave trade, where hair was a significant part of community, identity, and spirituality.

My mother knew the importance of our kinky texture and the self-actualizing potential of the process and techniques of hair styling. Since the Middle Passage, Black hair has been literally subdued, crushed, and straightened to conform to dominant Eurocentric beauty standards. This has made the wearing of natural Black textures and styles—from Angela Davis's atro to Allen Iverson's cornrows—an act of resistance and a statement of freedom. Black hair is a unique material language, a signifier of the fight for liberation, carried upon one's head. My mother was, of course, aware of these truths, and so her process of braiding and

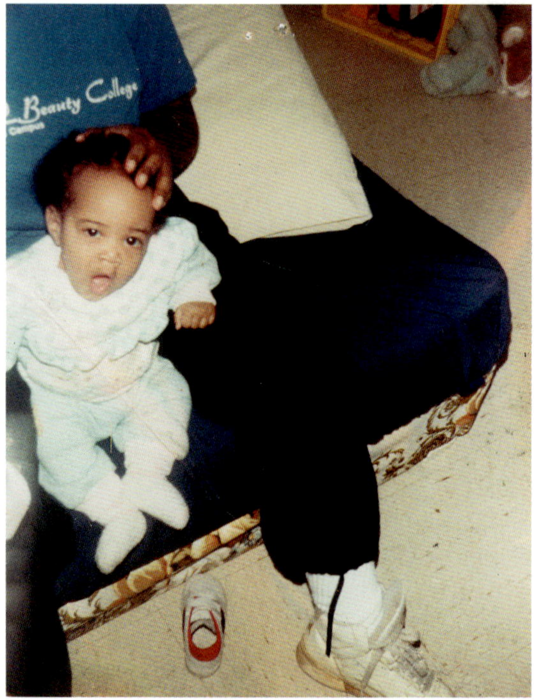

Fig. 1 **The author at two years old, getting her hair done.**

twisting our hair became a ritual. Pulling from her roots, she created a weekly practice in which she instilled a method of survival and a source of pride, inscribing into her children's hair a language that could never be fully silenced. My brothers and I thus learned this language and spoke it out loud. These childhood teachings have shaped, for instance, my research and studio practice, in which I use Black hair as a material and a methodology. In my practice, hair informs a physical and conceptual dialogue with ancestry and Black femininity and a praxis for understanding and cultivating Black life in the United States and throughout the global diaspora.

As a participant in the exhibition *On Loss and Absence: Textiles of Mourning and Survival* at the Art Institute of Chicago, I knew I wanted to foster a revival, to reimagine care and restoration rooted in my Black feminine experience, which traditional Western art historical frameworks do not encompass. I wanted to confront this absence by engaging with the Art Institute's textiles collection through a practice—braiding—that informs both my self-understanding and my understanding of textile art. I took inspiration from *Mining the Museum*, Fred Wilson's 1992–93 exhibition and artist intervention at the Maryland Historical Society in Baltimore, in which he challenged the museum's collection and its relationship to history, power, and race by, among other things, "juxtaposing silver repoussé vessels and elegant 19th-century armchairs with slave shackles and a whipping post. Texts, spotlights, recordings, and objects traditionally consigned to storage drew attention to the local histories of blacks and Native Americans, effectively unmaking the familiar museological narrative as a narrow ideological project."[2] The project was extremely influential, and yet more than thirty years later museums are still grappling with the legacy of systemic racism. The Art Institute has expanded its representation of Black artists across the collection, but there is still work to be done; this exhibition and book are part of that effort. Thus, in creating a work for this exhibition, I asked myself: How can I contribute to filling

these absences? How can I revitalize these material losses?
I wanted to reconsider how objects in the museum can be
activated and redefined through embodied experience. By
centering generational techniques of hair braiding, I hoped
to open a pathway for the material and process to tell their
own story.

     During a family gathering over a decade ago, my
nana presented us with our ancestry, giving everyone a
booklet containing a copy of a certificate from the genealogy research company African Ancestry, along with
hand-drawn family trees and maps connecting us from
Georgia to Cameroon. "We are a part of the Bamiléké tribe
in Cameroon," my nana explained. "That is where we come
from; this is your history." Her curiosity restored a missing
link in my family's legacy. I felt a sense of wholeness; a part
of my being had been restored. The afterlife of enslavement
and broken kinship has made it difficult for Black people
in the diaspora to trace their precise roots. My family and I
are lucky to now know our connection to Africa despite the
challenges of tracing Black lineage and the high cost of DNA
research. I wanted to find a way to extend the experience to
others by applying Wilson's idea of "mining" to our collective loss and the quest to re-envision and reconstitute what
remains. My grandmother's gift and my mother's skilled
hands guided me as I responded to the collection.

     The performative work of art I devised is entitled
Lasting 'Til Sunday. It situates the technique of hair braiding
as a tender ritual, a performance of kinship through the
material of hair and the process of braiding, a way to access
cultural and familial connections stripped by commerce and
colonialism. In a section of the exhibition on resistance and
survival, the Art Institute's textiles galleries act as the stage
for this revival. I set a scene similar to those Sundays when
my mother restored our home and hair, with three elements
constituting the work: a video, a chair, and a live braiding
session. The video documents my mother cornrowing my
hair in the Chicago Stock Exchange Trading Room at the Art
Institute (see fig. 2). Our voices narrate our experience of

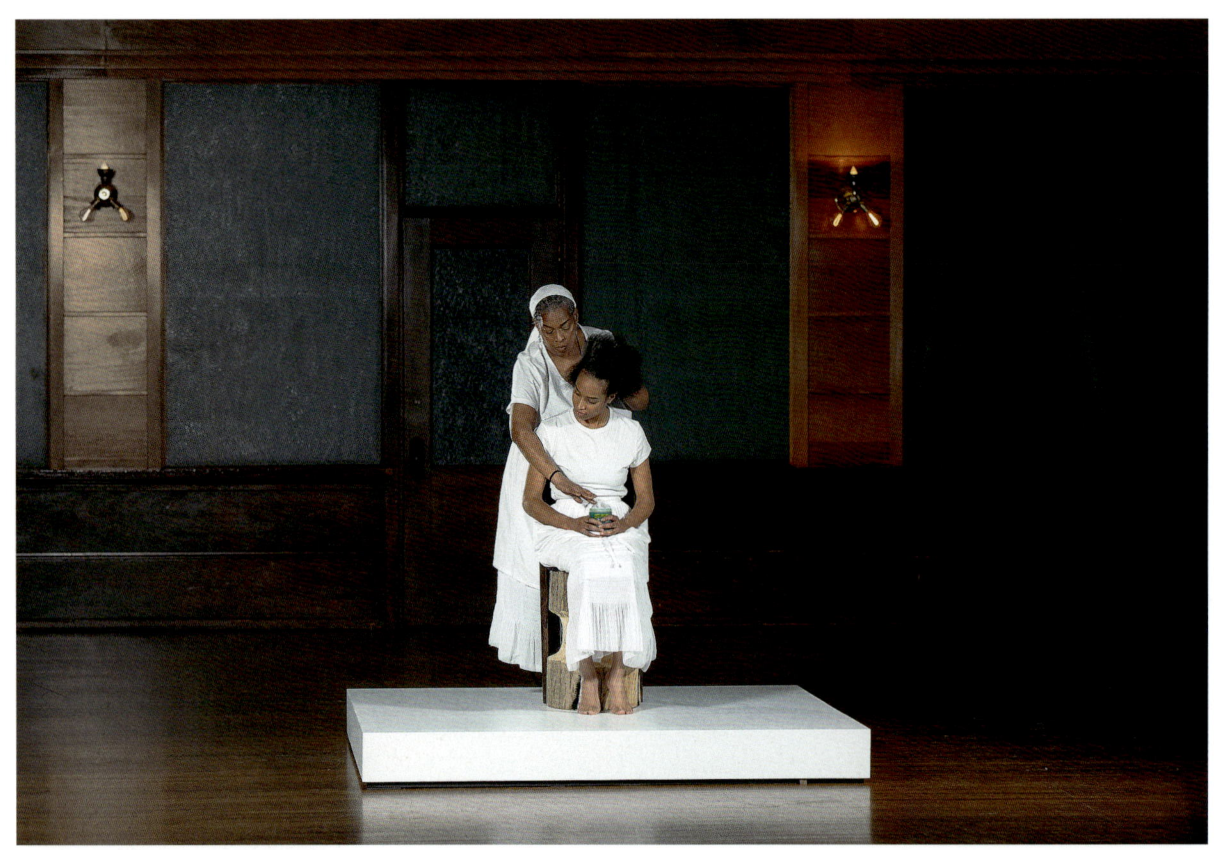

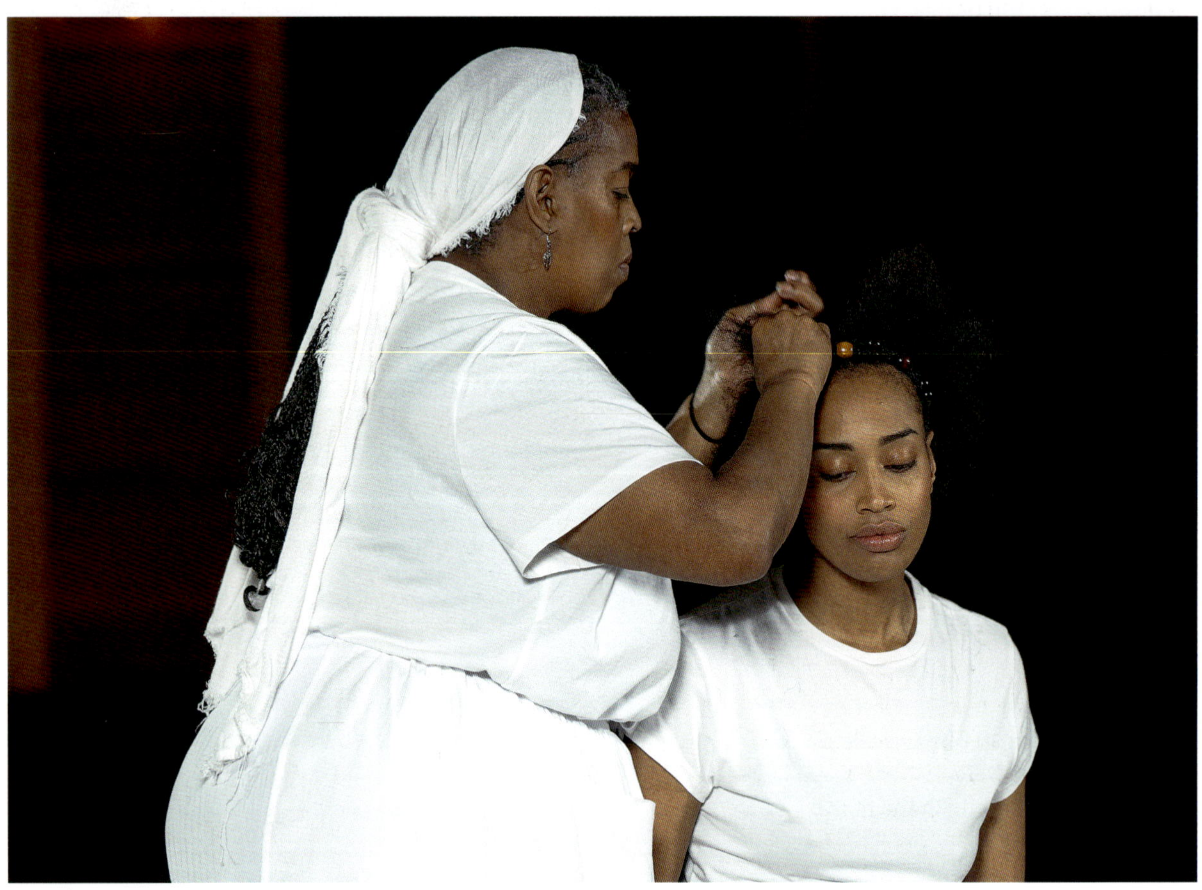

KAI

this practice. The video plays adjacent to the braiding chair,
a handcrafted chair in which I invite local community members to sit during the live braiding session. The braid begins
in the video with my mother, passed down through her
hands to my head, and extends out into the gallery space.
I mirror her act through the live braiding session, in which
I offer my hands to braid the hair of invited participants.
This live approach is necessary to capture the physical act
and ephemeral nature of braiding. A braid is a textile that
rests on the head, its lifespan even more fleeting than that
of the body carrying the style. It is impossible to convey the
meaning of Black hair without the presence of Black bodies:
It is within our bodies that we carry this material inheritance
and through embodied knowledge that we tell our story. To
braid in the gallery is to act out our love in public, like getting
your hair braided outside on the stoop. In spite of continual
discrimination and suppression, we persist in performing
our material inheritances. We braid in the open, to be seen
for who we are, to remember—and remind others—that we
are alive.

In selecting works to be displayed in the gallery
where *Lasting 'Til Sunday* would take place, I was drawn to
objects that would illustrate the continuity of braiding as
a motif in African art and expression. A twentieth-century
Bamiléké dance hat (fig. 3) in the Art Institute's Arts of
Africa collection caught my attention. Unlike the heavily
beaded and figurative Bamiléké objects I had seen in many
museums, this hat stood out for its muted colors, austere
design, and materially rich composition. I immediately
noticed the six long, cross-looped wool "braids" secured to
the dome-shaped, woven-wood basket. The braids' knitted
outer structure contains an unknown fibrous material that
gives them physical weight. Even without knowing the inner
contents, I was sure that the braids carried a metaphorical
weight as well: During the ceremonies at which the hat was
worn, the braids were the physical space in which the material and spiritual worlds met. This hat traditionally would
have been worn by a masked dancer who, during secret

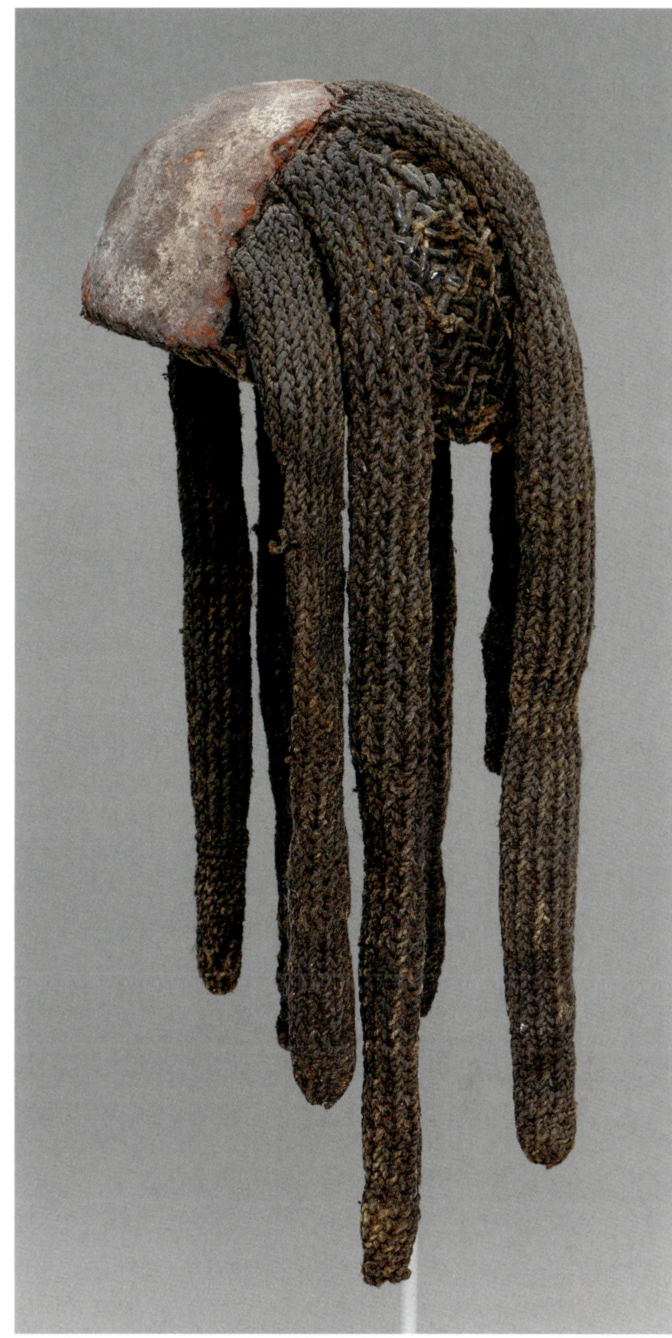

Fig. 3 Dance Hat, 20th century. Bamiléké;
Cameroon, coastal West Africa. Wool, rattan,
and human hair; 55.9 × 27.9 cm (22 × 11 in.).
The Art Institute of Chicago, gift of Donald
Young and Shirley Weese Young, 2015.309.

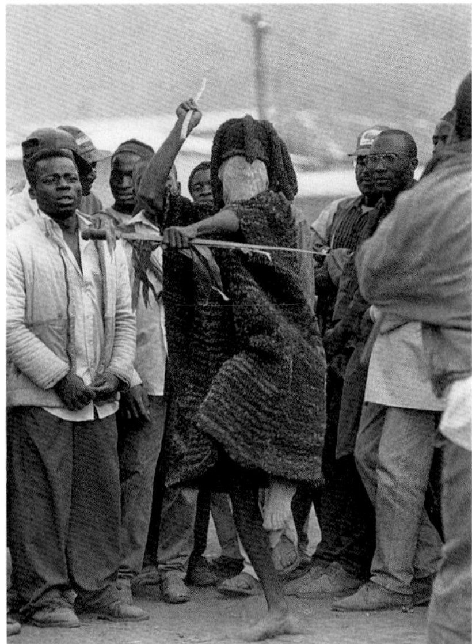

Fig. 4 **A performer wearing a dance hat similar to the one in fig. 3. The image purportedly documents a burial ceremony. The representations of braids in the performer's hat were used to invoke a spiritual being that would medicinally heal, honor, and protect those who attended the ceremony. Hair and hairstyles were valued in Cameroonian grassfield cultures not only for their aesthetics but also as performative extensions of the body that allowed the wearer to transcend the material world.**

ceremonies, would act as mediator between the worldly and otherworldly realms, using their body as a transmitter to heal attendees with medicine (see fig. 4). A cloth covering the wearer's face would have brought attention to the motion of the hat. I could envision the braids swaying rhythmically during these performances, mirroring the dancer's gestures—that is, I could sense that it was all about the braids. Further examination by Art Institute staff revealed that the hat has stiffened over time, potentially due to moisture, temperature, or lack of use. Its status illustrated for me how objects can be altered, transformed materially and conceptually, once they enter museum collections. The Bamiléké dance hat was not meant to be still and silent but rather to be activated through the wearer's performance.

As a child, I danced after my mother completed her design for my hair. My head swayed back and forth as pony beads clattered against my ears. We lose part of the story if we discount the essential presence of the body when we study the visual and cultural aesthetics of Black hair. Since the Bamiléké hat was acquired by the Art Institute in 1960, it has been separated from the dance that activated it; it is now frozen in time, unmoving behind glass. Although I have never witnessed the ceremonies it was once part of, through my material inheritance I can recall the essence of what has been lost in the museum context. This hat is a piece of my whole, enabled through my nana's discoveries to become a tangible element of my creative research, another seed for *Lasting 'Til Sunday.*

Other objects in the exhibition were similarly inspiring, representing the complex ways Black hair is tied to Black people's expression across regions and cultures and throughout time. The adinkra funerary wrapper (fig. 5) and ink stamps (fig. 6) are objects from the Asante culture, a prominent cultural group in the West African region that is now Ghana. The patterned adinkra cloth communicates belief systems and other specific messages through the handstamping of abstract motifs and symbols. Hairstyles of court attendants were often among the elements of Asante

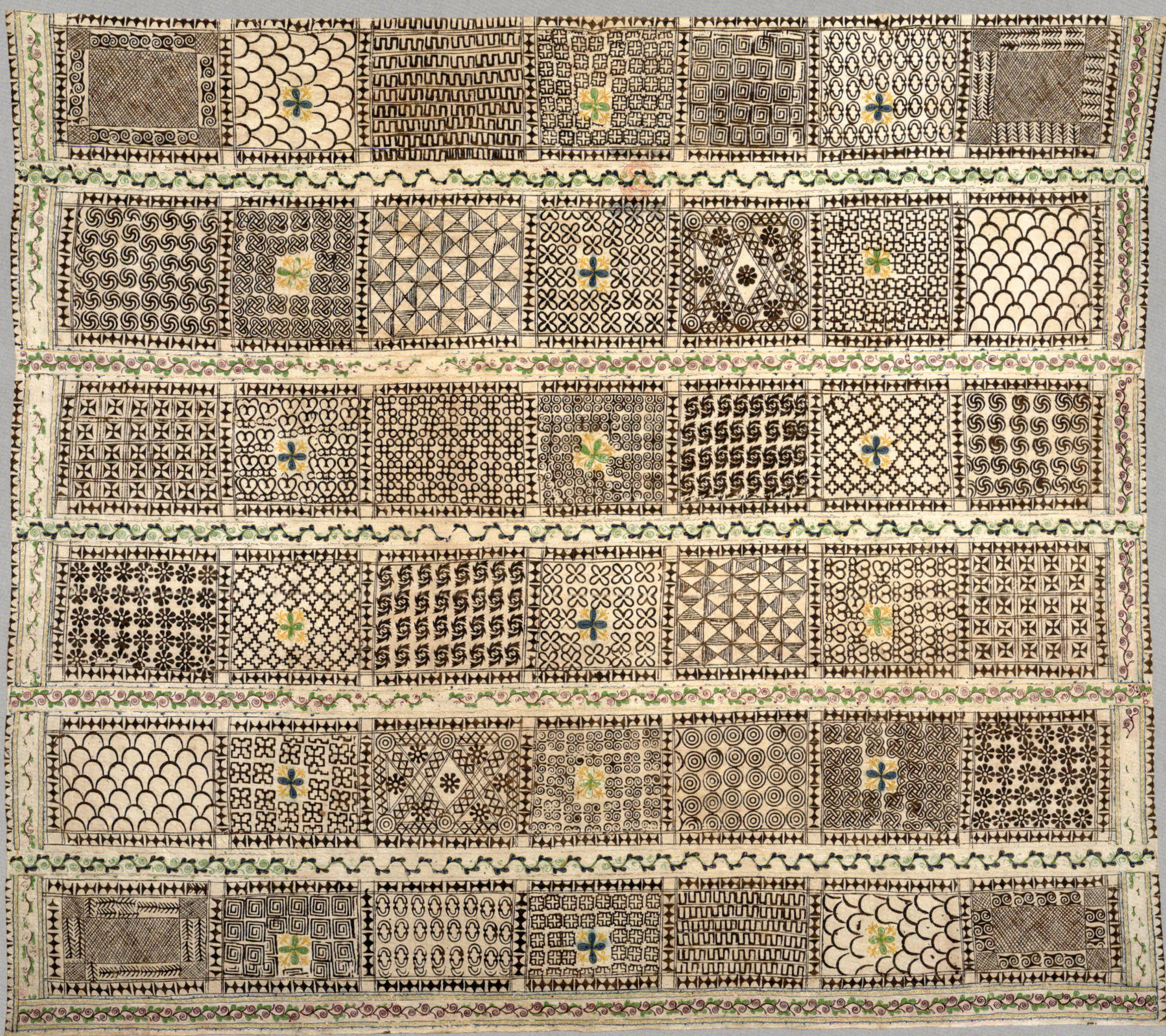

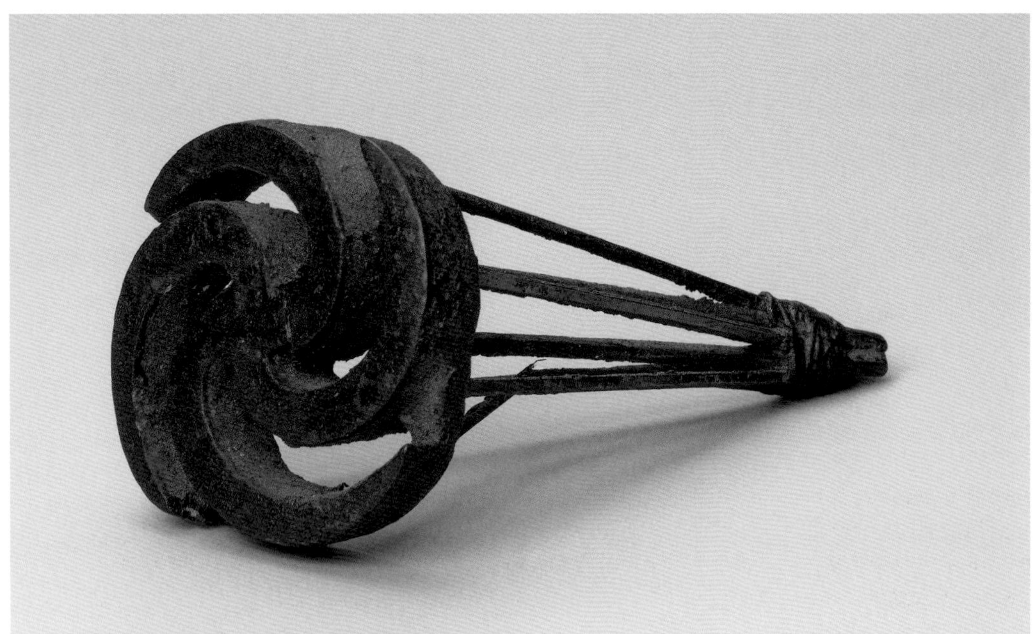

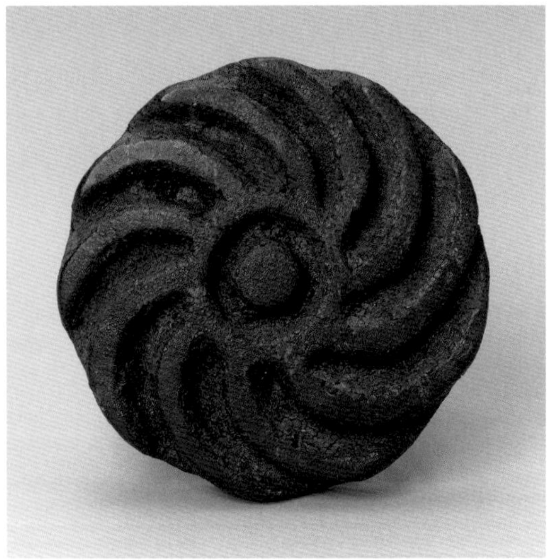

Fig. 6 "Hairstyle of Court Attendants"
Stamps for Adinkra Textile, late 19th–20th
century. Asante culture; West Africa.
Calabash, sticks, cloth, and string; top:
5.8 × 5.1 × 10.5 cm (2¼ × 2 × 4⅛ in.); bottom:
7 × 7 × 13.1 cm (2¾ × 2¾ × 5⅛ in.). The Art
Institute of Chicago, gift of Doran H. Ross,
2008.46 and 2008.52.

culture represented in the wrappers' designs. Local crafts-people carved these symbols from dried calabash gourds, which were then stamped onto the cloth with a special inky pigment. Such cloths were traditionally worn by Asante dignitaries on special occasions, specifically during periods of mourning. These cloths, which are additionally adorned with embroidery, represent one of the many ways hair is used in African culture to communicate and memorialize identity. The live braiding session activates these objects, too, since they are displayed in the same gallery: The performance interweaves past and present, opening up ways to imaginatively activate and experience objects outside their still display, centering and publicizing what is often marginalized and private.

Lasting 'Til Sunday explores fiber's fundamental role in accessing disparate memories and reclaiming narratives. It also highlights the multiplicity of Black diasporic textile traditions. Perhaps most radically, it reimagines the galleries as a space of care and healing, where objects are not simply viewed but rather activated and experienced. Objects in museums cannot speak for themselves, but those who come from these traditions can translate what Western art historical practices miss by calling upon our material inheritances to present an embodied knowledge.

Notes

1   Tracy K. Smith, "Duende," in *Duende: Poems* (Graywolf Press, 2007), 46.

2   Kerr Houston, "How Mining the Museum Changed the Art World," *BmoreArt*, May 3, 2017, bmoreart.com/2017/05/how-mining-the-museum-changed-the-art-world.

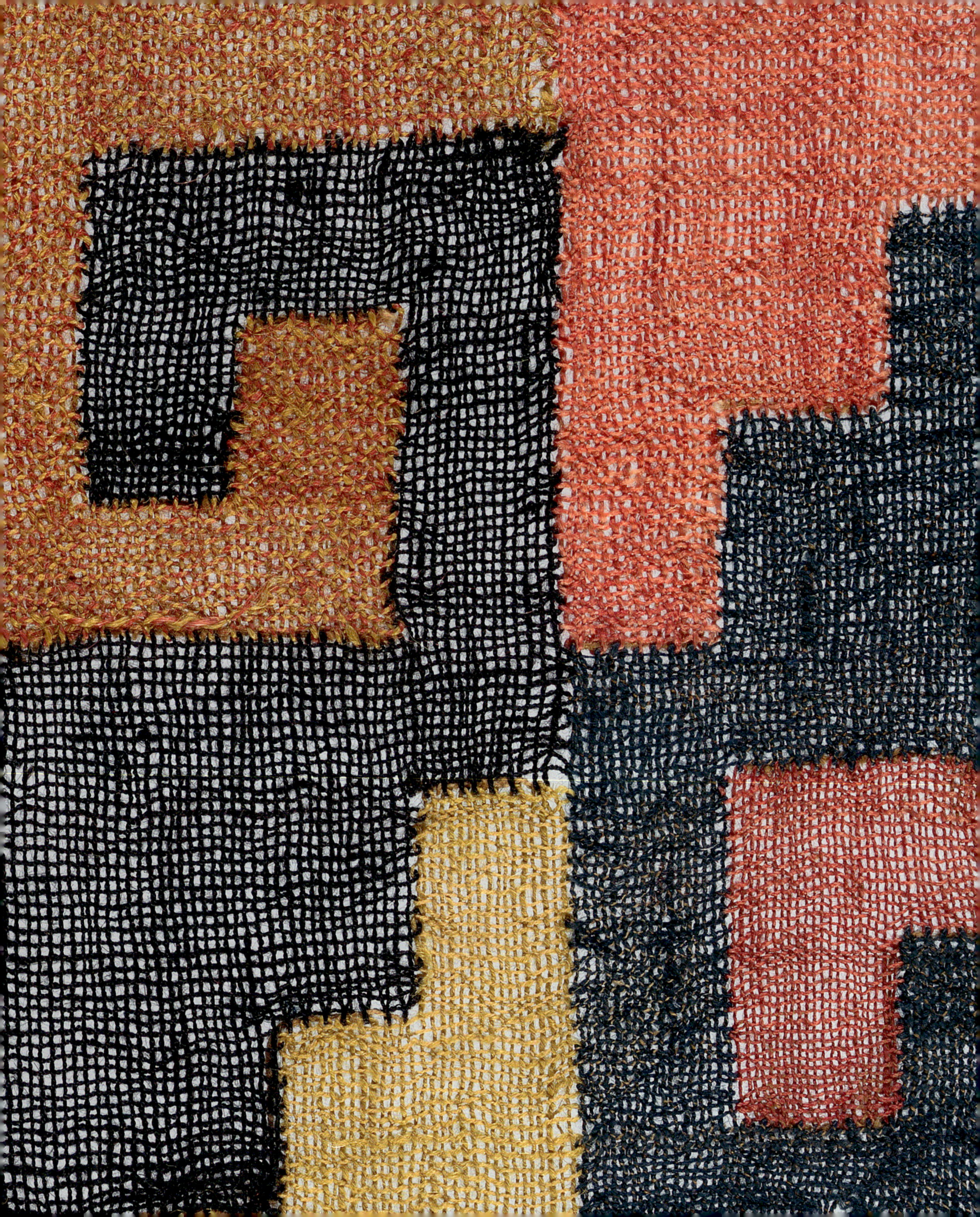

The Heartbeat of Andean Weaving

Alipio Melo
María José Murillo
Danitza Willka

Noqanchis weaving collective

El tejido Andino es el sistema de escritura y almacén de información más avanzado que [la humanidad] ha creado. Su práctica es una vía de comunicación entre el origen y el instante. Se fundamenta en una red de coordenadas cuyo centro es el ombligo de quien teje, conectado al centro de la Tierra a través del tronco de un árbol. De allí se proyecta la tradición e ingresa la información.

Andean weaving is the most advanced writing system and information-storage method that humanity has ever created. Its practice is a means of communication between its origins and the present moment. It is based on a network of coordinates, with the weaver's navel at the center, connected to the Earth's center through the trunk of a tree. From there, tradition is projected, and information is received.

—Mario Osorio Olazábal[1]

In the Andean weaver's universe, textiles have energetically and dynamically expressed emotions, knowledge, and histories for more than five thousand years, giving form to identity, language, memory, and tactile vision. Like Andean textiles, the Quechua language originates from and remains connected to Nature, reflecting our vibrant relationship with the Earth. We develop a deep bond with the animals, environments, plants, and tools that contribute to our weaving processes, cultivating these relationships through care, collaboration, and affection.

We write this essay as Noqanchis, an Andean weaving collective that the three of us—Alipio Melo, María José Murillo, and Danitza Willka—formed in 2021, having grown up in Arequipa and Pitumarca, Cusco, Peru. The word *Noqanchis* translates as "we all" from Runasimi, which itself means "the word" (*simi*) "of the people" (*runa*). The language, also known as Quechua, reflects a deep social and cultural connection: The words for "I" (*noqa*) and "we" (*noqanchis/noqayku*) have the same root, underlining the inseparable link between individual and community in the construction of Andean identity.

As a collective, we aim to weave together our worldviews and experiences as contemporary textile artists and weavers trained in different contexts: in the *ayllu* (community and family), where art is integral to life and tradition, and in the fine arts, rooted in Western modernity, in which art is seen as an end in itself and detached from Nature, culture, and daily life. We seek to integrate Andean weaving epistemologies into our collective and personal artistic practices while also addressing the neglect of this ancestral textile legacy in Peruvian art education despite its rich artistic and cultural significance. Our goal is to foster dialogues that build bridges to contemporary art ecosystems. The cultural perspectives, processes, and terminology that we share in this essay are rooted in the weaving traditions of Pitumarca—both the territory in southern Peru and a name for the textile tradition from which Alipio and Danitza originate. More than any other community in Cusco, we

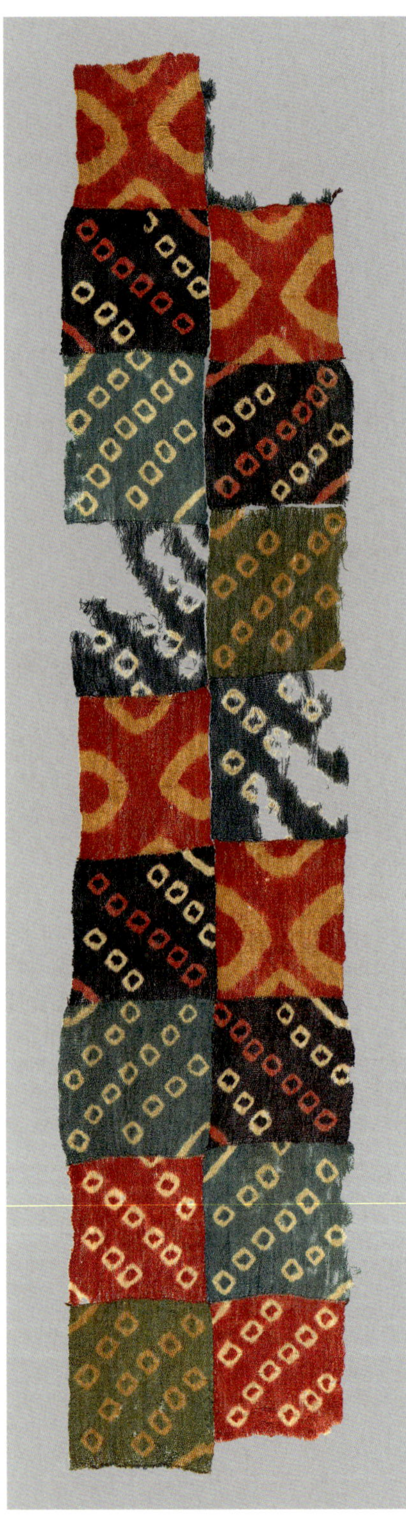

Fig. 1 *Ticlla-Watay* Fragment, 600–800. Nasca-Wari; Uyujalla Basin, Ica Valley, south coast, Peru. Wool (camelid), plain weave of discontinuous warps and wefts; *ticlla-watay* (discontinuous warp and weft, scaffold-weave, resist-dyed); 111.8 × 24.1 cm (44 × 9½ in.). The Art Institute of Chicago, purchased with funds provided by Mrs. Henry G. Barkhausen, 1956.171.

have preserved backstrap weaving traditions and revived complex techniques like *ticlla-watay* (discontinuous warp-and-weft tie-dye) and *anillado* (cross-looping) and sacred iconography like the *espiral escalonada* (stepped fret). We are also known for the exceptional quality of our *willma* (wool fibers), sourced from our own alpacas.

Ticlla-watay (see fig. 1) is an ancestral textile that integrates two important and complex pre-Hispanic techniques, the *ticlla* and the *watay.* The ticlla technique involves weaving individual sections of discontinuous warp and weft in plain weave, while watay is a resist-dyeing method by which designs are created using binding to prevent dye from penetrating certain areas. Mastery of the watay process, which requires a deep understanding of the order and layering of dyeing phases, is vital to achieving the rich range of colors and meaningful shapes or designs in this textile vocabulary. In the intricate process of ticlla-watay, individual pieces are carefully scaffold-woven on one loom, disassembled (not, crucially, cut), tie-dyed, and reassembled to create the final textile. This intricate textile language was developed by our Nasca (coastal) and Wari (mountain) ancestors, but its practice, along with many other pre-Hispanic techniques, declined due to colonial invasion.[2] Alipio describes his experience with the technique:

> To get the watay dyeing technique correct involved many attempts that included things like tying it with rubber or synthetic wool and bands. However, the dye kept seeping through the tie. So we kept trying with different materials until we got it right by using strong and thick alpaca twine. First, we managed to get two colors and then even up to three. After that I became kind of addicted. I wanted to do more and more, but my hands hurt too much after a while. Since then I have pursued a great desire to get lots of colors and designs, like coconuts,

little squares, all kinds of things. I feel proud
because it is difficult, not easy. You need
the strength to tie it well, you need to think
about what color you are going to take out
first, then what color you are going to dye
last, how many colors you are going to take
out. You must think. You can't do all that
in just a little while. It comes out with love,
with time, which you must give to the weaving. I am here for the love of weaving—for me,
no technique is too difficult, I will always be
weaving, recovering our ancestors' labor.

The espiral escalonada (see fig. 2) consists of two
parts: the staircase (space-time/Pacha, or father) and the
spiral (origin and continuity/Mama). Together, they form
a motif representing the unity of duality, a key Andean
principle. This lightweight, gauzelike textile is naturally dyed
and made from connected areas of *pampa* (plain-weave
sections) that underline the relationship of its construction
to its semiotic value. The term *pampa* refers both to plain
sections in the textile and to plainlands. Similarly, the verb
pallay in Quechua means "to pick up"; it is used to describe
harvesting grains, plants, or flowers—picking them up from
the field—and to describe the action of weaving, when you
pick out threads to form the designs. (*Pallay* is also used
as a noun meaning "design.") Exclusive to the Indigenous
region of Abya Yala (the Americas), the espiral escalonada is
a ubiquitous element in Andean and Mesoamerican textile
iconography, used to reveal the interaction of opposing yet
complementary forces (feminine/masculine, interior/exterior,
moon/sun, darkness/light). María José connects her own
cultural identity to the juxtapositions embodied in this motif:

As I move between Western weaving techniques and the ancestral Andean backstrap
loom, I have explored the complexity of my
heterogeneous and "mestiza" cultural identity,

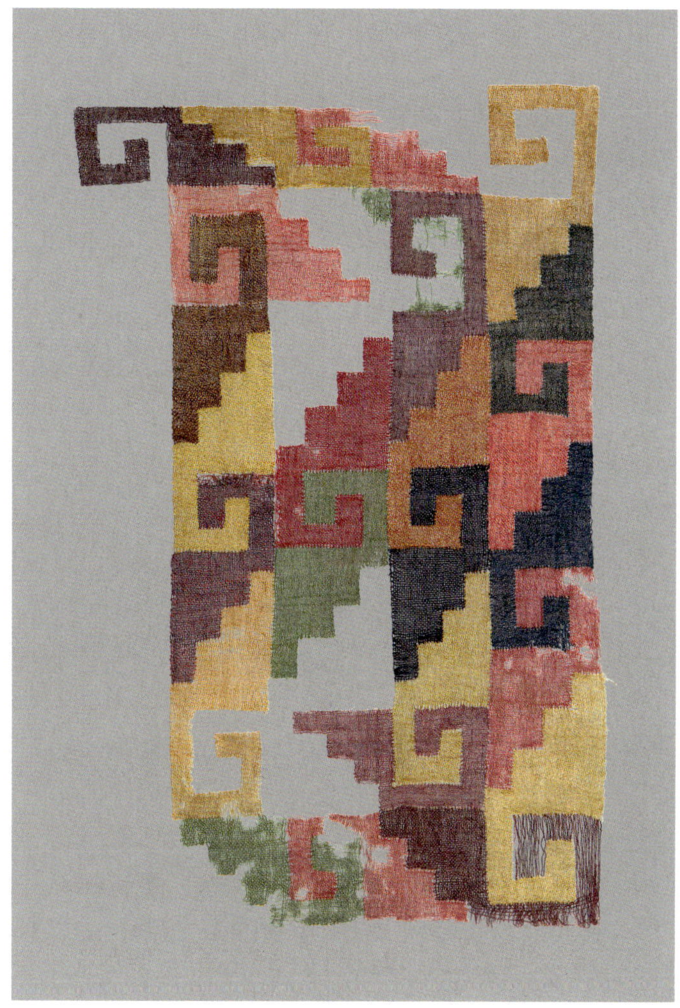

Fig. 2 *Espiral Escalonada* (Stepped-Fret)
Motif Fragment, 200–500. Nasca; south
coast, Peru. Wool (camelid) and cotton; plain
weave of discontinuous single interlocking
warp and weft, scaffold weave; 51.8 × 32.7 cm
(20 ⅜ × 12 ⅞ in.). The Art Institute of Chicago,
purchased with funds provided by Mrs.
Edwin A. Seipp, 1956.76.

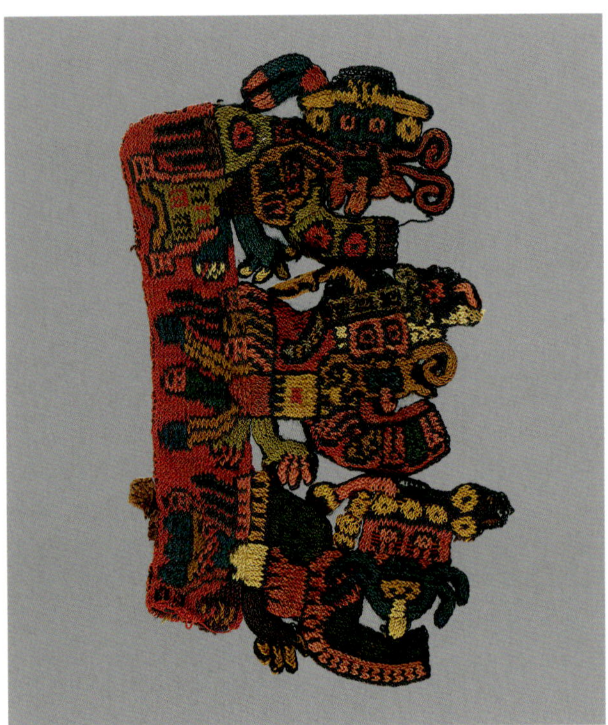

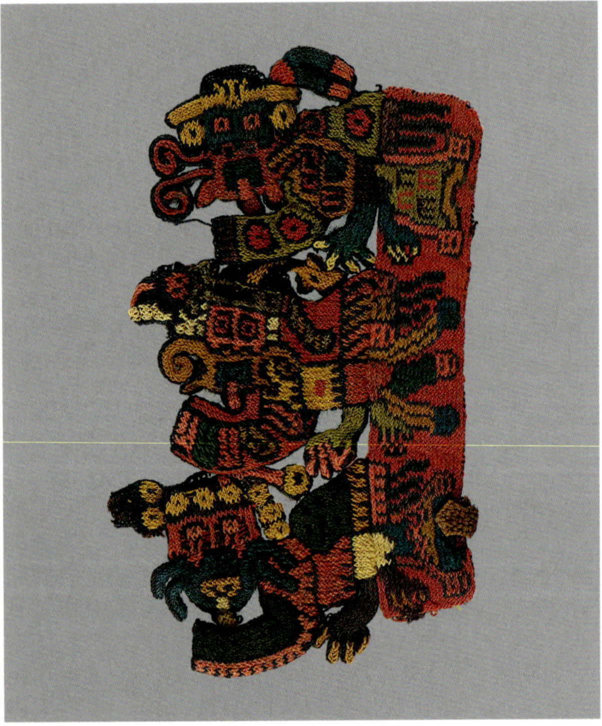

Fig. 3 *Anillado* Fragment, 100 BCE–200 CE. Nasca; possibly Coyungo, Nasca Valley, south coast, Peru. Cotton, plain weave; embroidered with wool (camelid) in *anillado* (cross-loop) stitches; extensions in button-hole stitches overworked with cross-loop stitches; 11.4 × 6.7 cm (4½ × 2⅝ in.). The Art Institute of Chicago, purchased with funds provided by Mrs. Chauncey B. Borland, 1956.405.

a product of the original trauma of colonization. Through this subjectivity, two ways of knowing and seeing the world—one with Eurocentric roots and another belonging to the pre-Hispanic Indigenous horizon—are in permanent conflict, clashing with one another. For me, weaving is the matrix in which opposites can coexist and interact without dissolving either identity, thereby birthing a *ch'ixi* (mottled) and energetic language.[3] The act of weaving becomes the vindication of an Indigenous cultural identity, as ancestral as it is contemporary, which I aim to place in dialogue with my Western heritage. This contradiction holds the potential to be transformed into a complementary creative force, one that I strive to nurture and express as a Latin American artist.

The cross-looping method anillado (see fig. 3) is an ancient, three-dimensional needlework technique developed by our Paracas ancestors over two thousand years ago and refined by the Nasca culture. Paracas artists use anillado to create two-sided figures representing concepts of life, death, time, and space through motifs related to the natural and supernatural worlds. To achieve this sophistication and subtlety in material language, they use multiple needles made from animal bone, wood, or metal to work with multiple threads at once in a variety of naturally dyed colors.[4] Danitza describes the anillado technique as a conversation with the ancestors:

For me, it is great to be able to replicate weaving techniques from our ancestors and to be able to connect with our Andean roots—to see what things they tried to tell us through the figures they created replicating nature and agriculture. This was

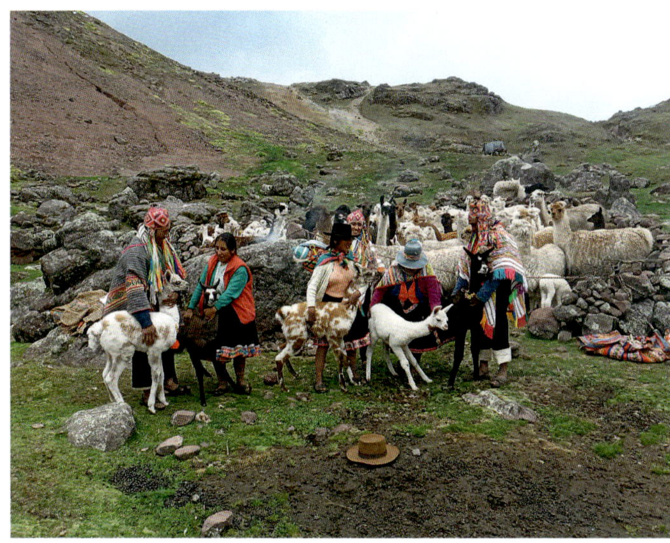

Fig. 4 **Celebrating the Paqocha Ch'uyay with the family, Pitumarca, Cusco, Peru, 2015.**

their way of transcendence. When I prepare for cross-looping, the first thing I set is the fineness; I try to make the cross-loop as fine as possible so that it matches that of our ancestors from the Nasca culture, to be just like theirs. I don't like to make it coarse. The three-dimensionality of this technique is also present in the fact that we weave with the mind, with the heart, and with the hand. I believe that this is how they wove in the past and that is how we weave today.

Our primary tool as weavers is the *awana*, our ancient backstrap loom. Its simple construction allows us to produce a wide range of textile structures, from more basic designs like the *ch'uru* (the mother of all designs, which weavers learn first) to complex, multilayered techniques. The loom consists of two wooden bars. One end is anchored to a tree, stone, or stake, while the other connects to the *baticula*, a strap tied to the weaver's waist. We use *k'allwa* (wooden slats) to adjust the weave and *ruk'i* (an alpaca or llama bone) to aid in creating designs.

I. *Awaq Paqarini* (The Birth of Andean Weaving)

The first heartbeat of weaving season in the Andes awakens to the rhythm of the Paqocha Ch'uyay celebration (see fig. 4). On this special day—always a Monday connected to carnival, in February or March—we celebrate our alpaca herds amid the phallcha, a sacred flower of the highlands. The petals of this flower fall like confetti on each *paqocha* (alpaca), as a way to wish them well and help them prosper. We prepare wine and food and spend time with our neighbors, playing music and dancing. During this important celebration we make a sacred offering called *haywakuy* to the Earth and the *Apu* (deity, protection, and sacred mountain). This offering is specially prepared for four *Apukuna* (deities): for

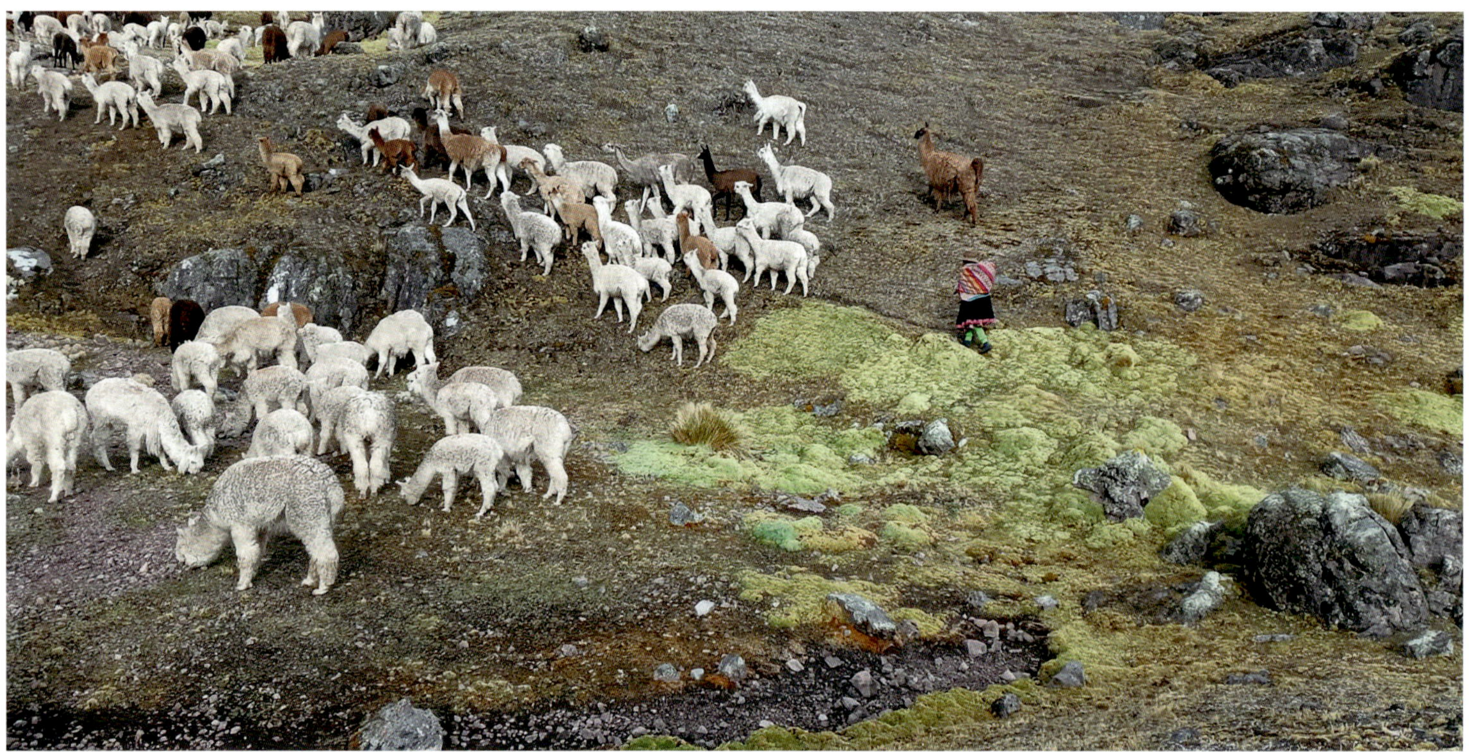

Fig. 5 **Alipio's mother, Estefa Irco, with her alpacas and llamas in Pampananta, Pitumarca, Cusco, Peru, 2017.**

Fig. 6 **Alipio with his mother, Estefa Irco, during the *willma rutuy* (fiber-harvesting season), Pitumarca, Cusco, Peru, 2017.**

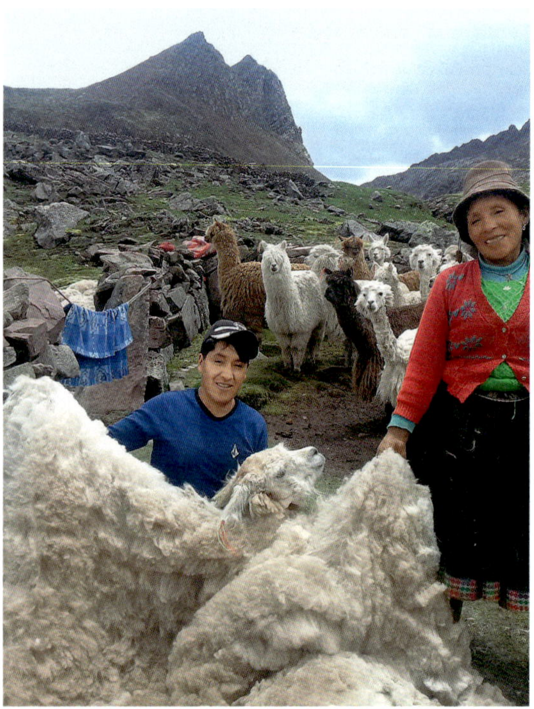

Pachamama; for the most respected, large, and well-known hills; for lightning; and for snowfall. These offerings are made with exceptional care so that they protect the alpacas well. They are prepared especially by the spiritual *yachayni-yoq* (healer), as not just anyone can do it. We assist by blowing the *koka k'intu* (coca leaf used in ceremonies), and the offering is burned at midnight, unseen by others. This is done with great respect, including removing shoes along with chullos and other hats, while asking for the alpacas to be protected from disease, drought, and lightning.

Once we secure the protection of the Apukuna, we focus on the foundation of Andean weaving: nurturing and cultivating fibers through the care of the alpacas. The heartbeat of Andean weaving starts with their pasture; we spin and weave in the fields with them to protect them from foxes and other threats. Our alpacas thrive at over five thousand meters above sea level, feeding on small grasses and herbs in *bofedales* (Andean wetlands). The best willma grows here at the foot of the snowy mountains, where it is known for being finer and softer—truly special.

Alipio tends to a herd of more than a hundred alpacas:

It's very special to be up there [in the high mountains]. I was born and raised there, so my heart, my views, and my thoughts lean toward being up there too. I love my alpacas so much; I don't want them to suffer, that's why I'm constantly with them, caring for them. My mother is always up there too,

MELO, MURILLO, AND WILLKA

spinning, and weaving. Some days are difficult if it snows or rains. I'm always thinking
of ways to shelter my alpacas so they don't
die. At night, when I'm sleeping during a
heavy rainfall, I always wake up thinking
about them: How are they doing? Is the baby
alpaquita doing well? I'm sure it is cold . . .
what can I do? I ask God for them to be strong
and resilient. When I return to my house in
Pitumarca, the first thing my mother always
asks me is "How are the alpacas doing?"

This is how we pasture in the high mountains, where, in
addition to cultivating the fiber, we nurture a relationship of
companionship and exchange: *paqochantin, llamatin, push-
kantin michiq purishan* (the weaver, alongside her alpaca
and her *pushka* [drop spindle], walk through the fields nurturing one another; see fig. 5). María José elaborates on her
experience of these relationships:

> It has been essential for me, in addition to
> the study of backstrap-loom weaving, to learn
> Runasimi. The languages—oral and textile—
> complement one another and have revealed
> to me perceptions of the world and human
> experience that are different from those of
> the Western world, coming instead from the
> pre-Hispanic, Indigenous horizon. These
> languages make me perceive how the past
> emerges and bursts into the present to speak
> to us. Runasimi is an agglutinative language
> composed of suffixes. One of the suffixes that
> has resonated with me most during my learn-
> ing process is the one for "company": *-ntin/
> nintin*. Unlike the suffix *-wan* (with), *-ntin/
> nintin* denotes a deeper form of companionship
> that involves the transmission of knowledge
> and values among Earth beings, both human

and nonhuman. Thus the weaver, together with
her alpaca and her pushka, walks through the
highlands weaving their lived relationships.

The fiber-harvesting season, or *willma rutuy* (see
fig. 6), occurs between November and December. During this
time we carefully shear our alpacas and select the best fiber
for spinning. We need ample willma for clothes like *llikllas*
(women's traditional cloths) and ponchos (men's traditional
cloths). We produce *q'aytu* (handspun thread) in the field, as
we tend to our alpacas. When we sit at home, we don't spin
much thread, but when we are out pasturing, *purispa, purispa*
(walking, walking), in the fields, we can spin quicker.

Before willma rutuy, we perform *phukukuy* (vital
breaths) to the Apukuna, wishing for good fibers, no rain,
and fair prices. We exhale from deep within, placing our
intentions into the air with a breath of life. Pachamama, our
sacred mountains, and Nature absorb it all. These beliefs are
fading; once, offerings were made with great respect, but,
as Danitza explains:

> The respect is no longer the same as before.
> We know that the feeling of weaving is get-
> ting lost in some communities and among
> some people, since they've neglected their
> traditions and environment. To me, from
> the moment of its raising and shearing, the
> weaving already has life—it is something
> that must be felt to be able to weave. You
> need to know what you are weaving, why
> you are weaving, and the feelings that come
> with that. There are different feelings for
> each textile according to its destiny.

In the fields, we spin through cold, heat, and heavy
rains, always with love and respect. We spin with the
intention of connecting with our pushka, considering the
q'aytu—how will it develop and what will it become. There

are various spinning techniques: for a lliklla, we spin finely (*ñañu q'aytu*), while for thicker fabric we spin coarser (*rakhu q'aytu*). Each family also has its unique spinning style, and each person's hand is unique—for example, yarn spun by men is rougher and stronger, while yarn spun by women is finer and softer. Each fabric serves a specific purpose and has its own distinct feel.

Made with love and respect, the q'aytu is prepared for natural dyeing, enhancing its value. The Andean process of natural dyeing adds further layers of meaning and nurturing. Despite the rise of synthetic dyes, the grandmothers and grandfathers continue to collect plants near their homes, cultivating a dialogue with Nature through its colors. The *tiñiy* (dyeing) community activity requires deep knowledge of the relationships between plants, minerals, and other natural elements to enable the fibers to take in not only the color but also the voice of each element in the dye. This process is crucial, as the native plants we use are special; they establish a connection to Pachamama, and many are capable of warding off supernatural evil. Each color holds meaning related to our intentions for the weaving.

We primarily dye using regional plants. Ch'illka leaves produce our greens and can yield four tones when combined with other herbs. Black or white varieties of *qollpa* (a type of clay containing copper sulfate) fix, enhance, and deepen colors. Macerating indigo with human urine creates our various blue shades, while our yellows come from the q'olle flower. Our browns are sourced from *qaqa sunkha*, a lichen referred to as "beards of the mountain." Our turquoise tones are from another lichen, *kinsak'uchu*. In Pitumarca we have a characteristic red, *puka ch'umpi*, in addition to intense reds achieved with cochineal. This color is derived from a rare tree that the locals refer to as *labram*. We take pieces from the trunk, which are pressed and boiled for a day and left to macerate for two days. The curious thing about this color is that it becomes more vibrant the longer it is exposed to the sun. Additionally, we obtain the colors *yana* (black), *yuraq* (white), *ch'umpi* (brown), *oqe* (gray) from the natural fibers of our alpacas.

Once we finish the arduous and rewarding work of natural dyeing, we spin the yarn with our largest pushka using different techniques: *phariy* for gentle weaving of chullos and stockings, *q'ullko* for tighter threads to withstand backstrap-loom tension. The *k'antiy* technique involves spinning fabric in the air to ply two threads into a stronger one. Based on the intention for our weaving, we tone the colors so that each *kurur* (ball of wool) can connect to form the color palette of the textile. The process of joining yarn balls is referred to as *tupachikuy*, meaning "to find or meet each other with intention and affection." The resulting fabric embodies our vision and reflects our origin, identity, and emotions. The heart of each weaver will always guide those color relationships.

II. *Pallay Rikchariynin* (The Awakening of Designs)

The *allwiy* (weave) involves a reciprocal practice in which we pair the warp and also count the threads to create our designs. Performing this process also connects us to our roots, as María José describes:

> In Runasimi, *pallay* refers to both textile design and, as a verb, the act of delicately picking up or harvesting with the fingertips. The pallay gives cloth a tangible meaning— the pallay speaks! Its counterpart, the pampa, is a plain, monochromatic fabric that, while lacking complex design, communicates from a broader perspective. In Andean tradition, textile work is profoundly intertwined with the Earth's functions.

During weaving, the relationships between numbers, shapes, and spaces come into play, allowing the thread to find its purpose. Because this is such an important stage in the formation of each fabric, we begin by blowing our koka k'intu to ask Pachamama and the Apukuna to protect the life that will be created from that organism of threads. The weaver also breathes their own life, feelings, and intentions into the weaving, as Alipio describes:

> I am ready to start warping my own weaving, and in it I will put all my experiences, my sufferings, and everything that happens in life. Through weaving, I write my stories. Depending on the purpose of the weaving—whether it's for a celebration or as *pago a la Tierra* (an offering to Mother Earth) or for a married or single person, whether you are sad or mourning someone's death or if that llik[l]la is for everyday use—that is how we will begin to prepare the warp. For a celebration or party, it may need more designs or color so it shines. If you want to use it daily, then we may create subtler designs. Depending on the kind of life the fabric will have, we prepare it differently. If it is beautifully warped and well prepared, you will be motivated to weave it.

Once the warp is prepared, we secure the *khata* (cross) that sustains the textile's life, with one group of threads supporting the khata and lifting the *illawa*, the system of threads that holds and lifts a group of warps; another group of warp threads is separated and held by the *toqoro*, a wooden stick. Khata sustains our lives too, as Danitza explains: "Khata is always present in our lives in different ways, it makes the weaving progress to completion. In our lives, we have links with different people, who little by little help us grow and train ourselves. Khata is present even in our braids. If everything in our lives was loose, it would have no meaning."

We start weaving by preparing the *polo tiyachiy*, which serves as the foundation of the textile. We assess and adjust the warp as needed, making final decisions about the pallay and pampa. Using a strong thread called *polo q'aytu*,

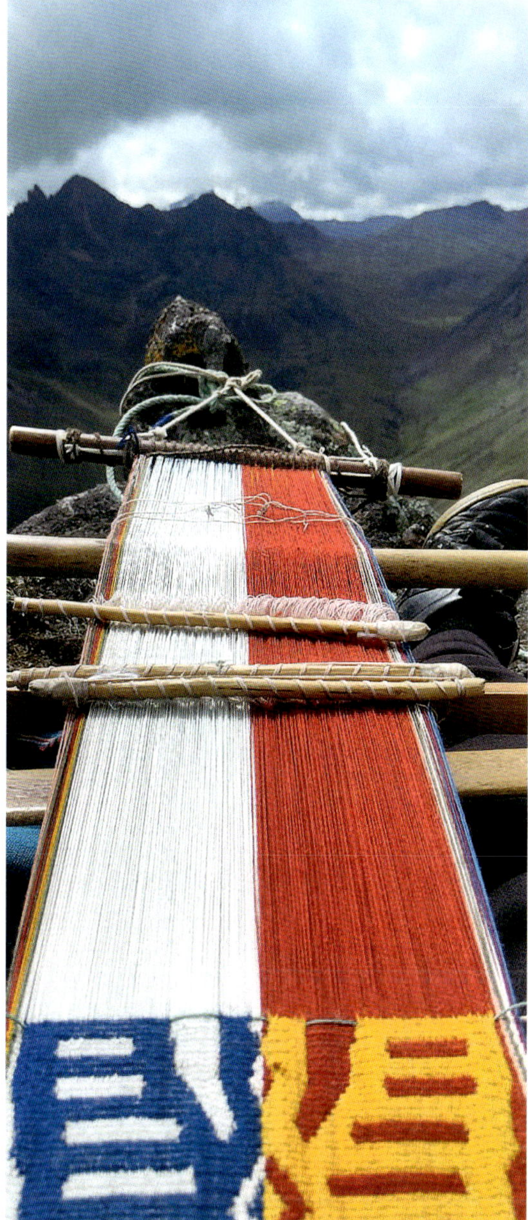

Fig. 7 **Alipio's backstrap loom, with a double-cloth weaving, Chachacumani, Pitumarca, Cusco, Peru, 2023.**

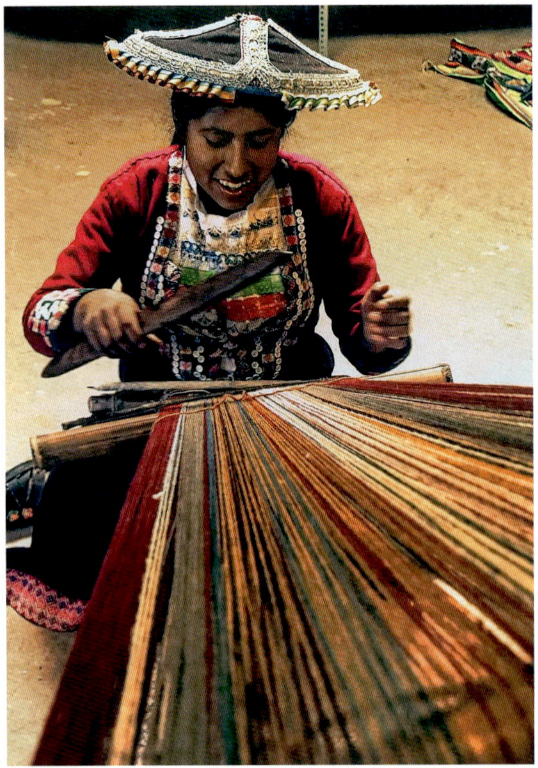

Fig. 8 **Danitza weaving on her backstrap loom, 2019.**

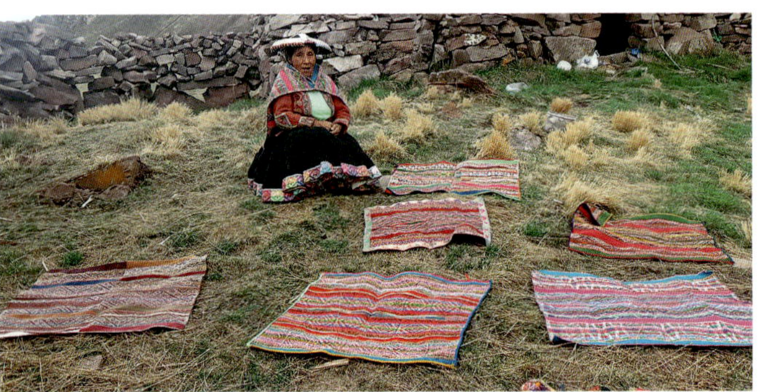

Fig. 9 **Alipio's mother, Estefa Irco, extends her llikllas with love, 2019.**

we tightly secure the warp to a wooden stick; this thread is the first weft and the basis for the loom's life. The portability of our *awana* (backstrap loom) is essential; we can easily roll it up and take it anywhere, anchoring it to the ground as an extension of our body (see fig. 7). The setting deeply influences the meaning of our work; weaving in the same place all the time would deprive us of inspiration and nourishment from the Earth. We weave in the fields, we weave on rock, we weave in the high mountains. The backstrap loom helps us preserve our cultural identity, enabling it to persist and evolve as we honor our ancestors' traditions. Through innovations, we express our current existence through this loom. Danitza weaves her own identity (see fig. 8): "The creation of the fabric with the loom is very personal. Each weaver feels differently about their cloth, like an identity. Apart from being a sacred heritage, weaving is also the blood of the family, according to the tradition you've been taught. Personally, as a textile artist, I make my own designs using my life and my presence—I capture my future and present."

III. *Awakunaq Puriniy* (Finished Weavings Are Now Walking Through Life)

Weaving on the backstrap loom concludes during the *p'itay*, in which, with lots of patience, we apply finishes with excitement and dedication. Using a *yauri* (needle), we pass *miñi* by *miñi* (weft by weft), as in the Andes we do not cut the warp threads—doing so would be like cutting the life of the cloth. Our textile, woven to completion on all four edges, is simply untied from the loom. *Awayniy ishkay uyayoq* (my weaving has two faces): the three-dimensional nature of an Andean textile arises from the connection of its four finished sides (four-selvage), which creates a vital energy, like a circulatory system, that flows through its threads from the first weft to its final destination off the loom, uninterrupted and with no cut threads—a crucial technical feature of Andean textiles.

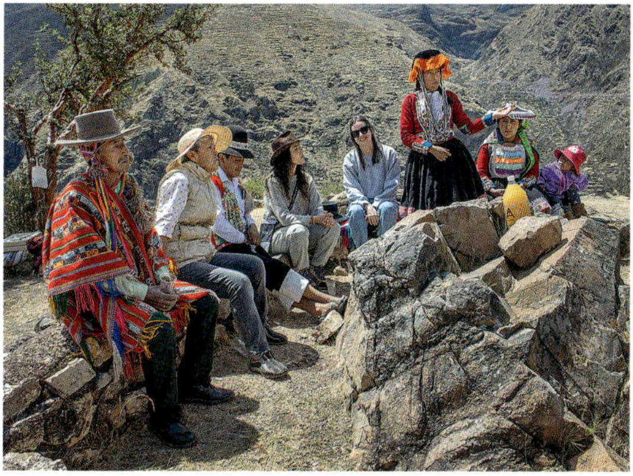

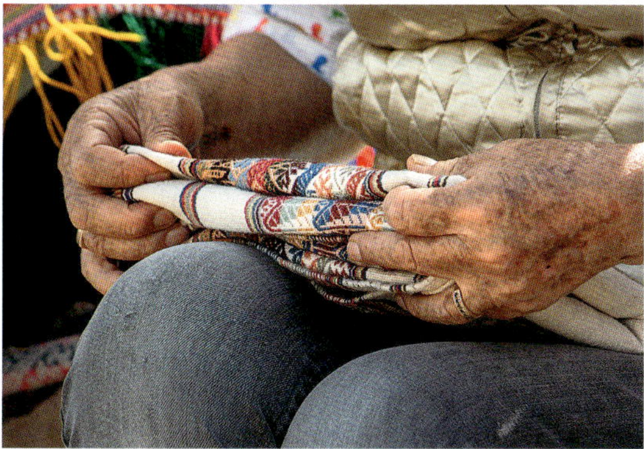

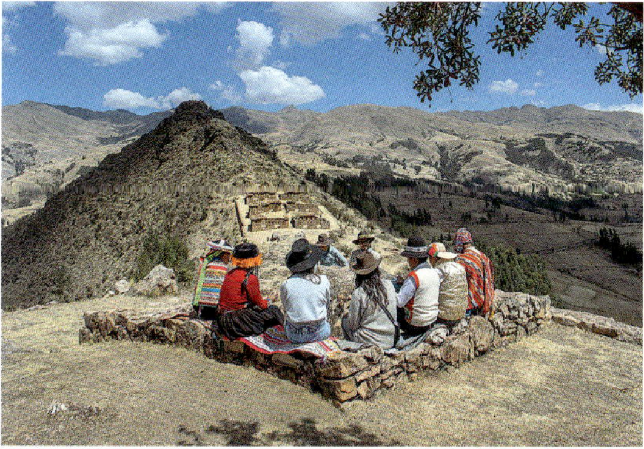

Fig. 10 Photographs from *Sí tenemos ojos/ ÑAWIYOQMI KANCHIS (We Have Eyes)*, a *rimanakuy* (reciprocal dialogue) organized by Noqanchis and led by Georgina Maldonado. Participants included Amira, Nélida Irco, Florencia Portocarrero, Martin Rixe, Verovcha, and Domingo Huillca Espinoza.

Once we finish weaving, we untie and spread the fabric out, admiring it with pride and love (see fig. 9). We finish its borders with *lloq'e* threads for protection, driving away evil and safeguarding the cloth's life. This moment signifies the cloth's birth. Our lliklla, *chuspa* (bag), *unkuña* (carrying cloth), and poncho accompany us throughout life; as well as being useful, they mediate our relationship to the community, Nature, and the sacred. In the Andes, weaving integrates cultural, natural, political, and social ecosystems into daily life.

The Revolution of the Eyes

Our project *Sí tenemos ojos/ÑAWIYOQMI KANCHIS (We Have Eyes)* (see fig. 10) sought to create a space of creation, exchange, learning, and participation between fiber artists and educators with the goal of exploring and deepening the relationship between textiles, language, and writing. Through the particularity of the geographical space of the Andes, conceived as a vital field that transcends the physical and taps into the bio-emotional, the project sought to collectivize ideas surrounding the gaze, literacy, and touch. It involved organizing a *rimanakuy*, a reciprocal dialogue, in Machu Pitumarca led by Quechua educator, interpreter, and translator Georgina Maldonado.[5] Drawing on her experience as a primary-school teacher, Maldonado facilitated discussions that bridged Runasimi and Spanish, explored the cultural significance of eyes in the Andean world, and interrogated the divide between literate and nonliterate societies. This dialogue inspired our installation for the exhibition *On Loss and Absence*, which takes the form of a *khipu* (see fig. 11). The Quechua term *khipu* means "knot" and refers to traditional Andean devices used to record information, one of the various writing systems Indigenous people used in pre-Hispanic Peru. The khipu we created honors textile and Indigenous literacies by reinterpreting the iconic eyes from Andean textiles dating from Huaca Prieta to today.

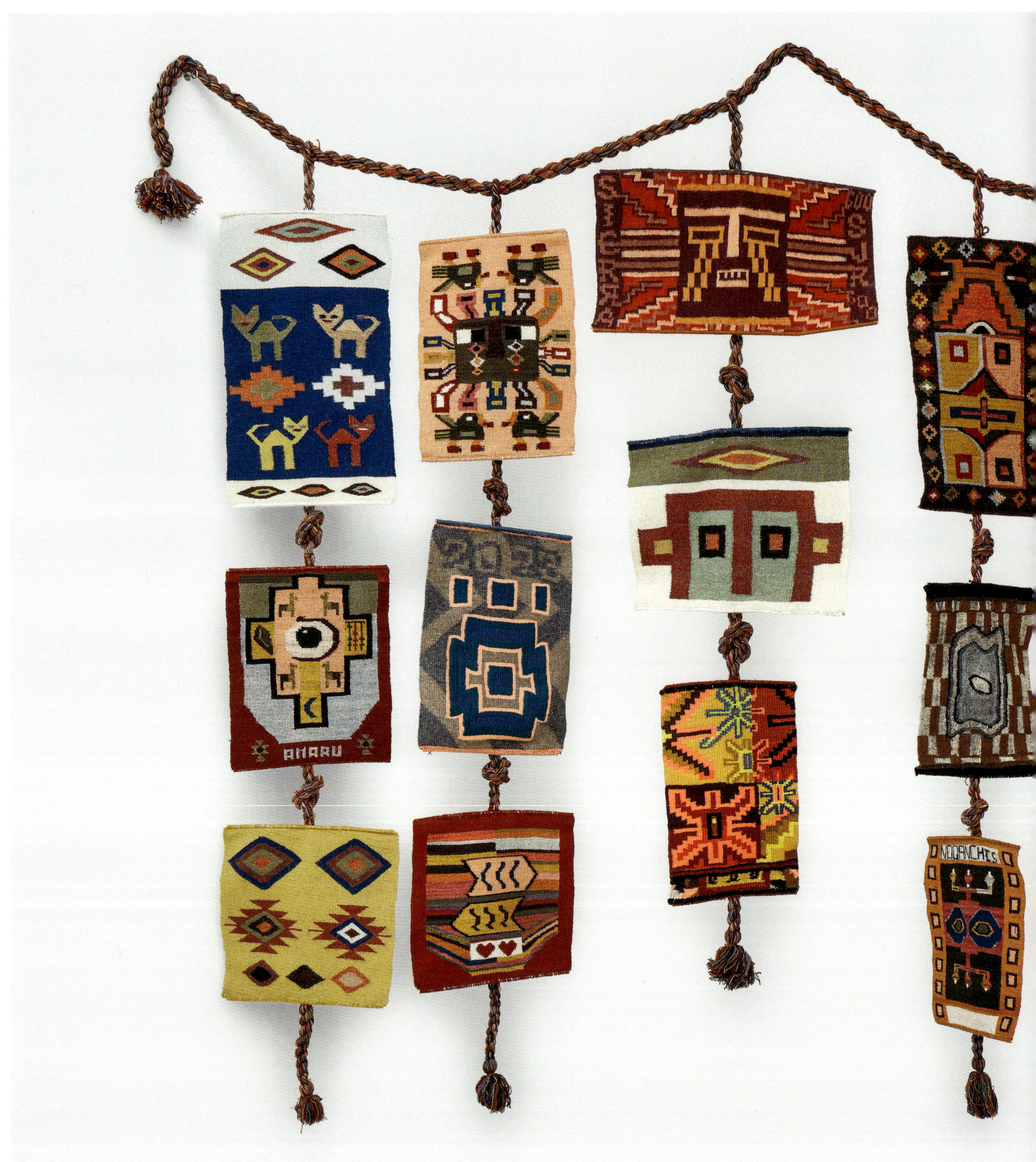

MELO, MURILLO, AND WILLKA

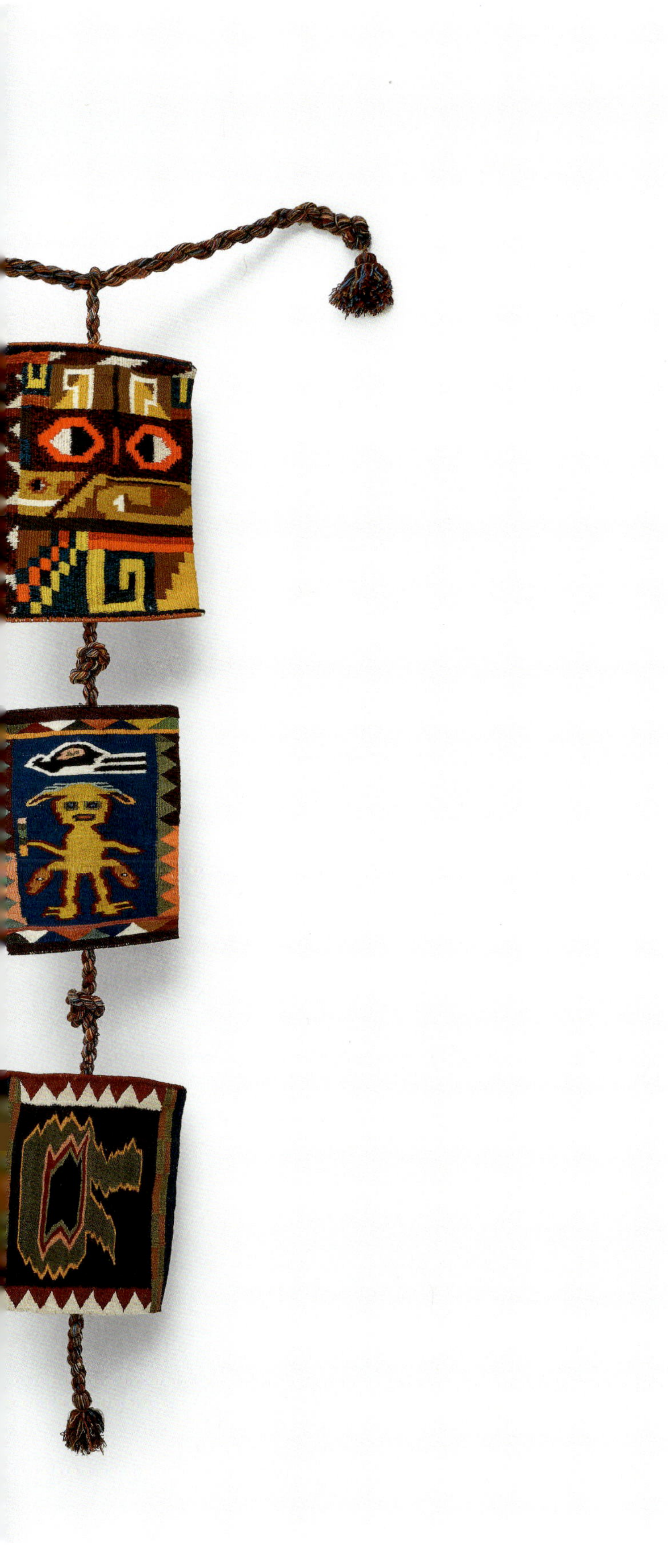

Fig. 11 Colectivo Noqanchis (Pitumarca, Cusco, Peru, founded 2021): Alipio Melo (Peruvian, born 1989), María José Murillo (Peruvian, born 1989), and Danitza Willka (Peruvian, born 2001). *Sí tenemos ojos/ ÑAWIYOQMI KANCHIS (We Have Eyes)*, 2024. Hand-dyed alpaca wool and synthetic fibers; tapestry weaves; connected with wool cord; 190 × 230 cm (75 × 91 in.). Courtesy of the artists.

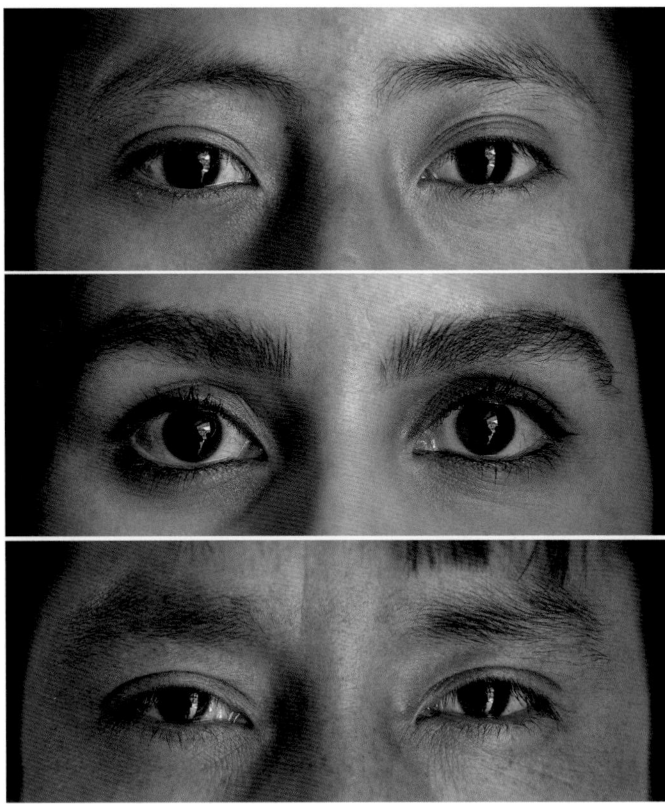

Fig. 12 **Noqanchis: Danitza Willka, María José Murillo, and Alipio Melo.**

The Runasimi spoken today is not the same as that spoken in pre-Hispanic times. That ancestral Indigenous language no longer exists. In its place we have a "mestizo" Runasimi, a product of colonial invasion that emphatically resists disconnection from its Indigenous roots and reveals deep cultural tensions and oppositions. In this language one can perceive layers of the Western world's epistemological imposition on and destruction of the Indigenous. This perennial clash and conflict between two cultural horizons is alive in the language itself—for instance, in the way knowledge is produced, validated, and disseminated through colonial hierarchies that fragment and challenge the construction of a cultural identity emancipated from its original trauma.

In Cusco Runasimi, the phrase *manan ñawiyoqchu kani*, which translates literally to "I have no eyes," is used to describe someone who cannot read or write. This expression is especially troubling, ironic, and painful in view of the outlook and vision that revolutionized the textile medium forever. From the artists of ancient Peru to contemporary Andean creators, this genealogy of "eyes" has birthed one of the most significant textile manifestations anywhere in the world, in all of time. In truth, in the Andes one sees not only through the eyes but also through the hands. It is precisely through this tactile and haptic gaze—developed over more than five thousand years of artistic tradition—that we have cultivated our unique way of seeing and understanding the world, all from the specificity of the language of weaving.

Ñawpaq-Quepa (The Past Is Ahead of Us)

In the Andean world spatiotemporal notions of past (*ñawpaq*) and future (*quepa*) are interconnected and interchangeable, with the past situated ahead of us, in front of our eyes, while the uncertain future lies behind. From this perspective, the Noqanchis collective aims to foster a creative and reciprocal dialogue with ancestral weavings in the Art Institute of Chicago's collection. Our use of ancestral motifs and techniques does not constitute an uninterrupted lineage; rather, we have carefully revitalized these traditions, together with their associated epistemologies, through concentrated effort and dedication. This dialogue moves in a spiral, allowing for continuous feedback from the past to inform the future and our contemporary textile practices.

The process of Andean weaving incorporates diverse knowledge areas including astronomy, biology, chemistry, and mathematics, with the ayllu serving as the key platform for learning. Our ancestors, the *machula*, laid the foundations of this material language, passed down through generations. For us, weaving represents a living school of relationships and knowledge and emphasizes the need to return to our origins and foster awareness of the Earth, with our hands as well as our eyes (see fig. 12).

Notes

This essay was translated from the original Spanish by Eriksen Translations.

1   Mario Osorio Olazábal, *Uasikamak: El ordenador del espacio que habita el ser* (Cartolan, 2012), 144.

2   Master weavers from the Cusco Traditional Textiles Center (CTTC) have been revitalizing the ticlla-watay technique since 2021 by integrating knowledge from the association of Pitumarca weavers, experts in the ticlla technique, with knowledge from the association of Sallac weavers, experts in the watay technique. Alipio is among the creators who have incorporated this laborious double-technique method into their repertoire; he currently coordinates the Ticlla-Watay Recovery Project promoted by the CTTC.

3   *Ch'ixi* describes a plain-weave structure that results from the *ley pallay* textile technique, which presents patterns of black and white squares without mixing the two colors.

4   In 2017, along with ten weaving organizations including the Munay Ticlla association of Pitumarca, the CTTC began a project to recover the cross-looping technique. Reintroduction workshops aimed to re-create the Paracas calendar, a textile that was repatriated from Gothenburg, Sweden, in 2014 after its location was made known through the exhibition *Paracas: A Stolen World* at the Museum of World Culture in 2008. Preserved in its entirety, this valuable and impressively large work is one of the few textiles that have been created exclusively using the cross-looping technique.

5   *Rimanakuy* is an Andean concept with the main goal of generating a space for mutual dialogue and facilitating an enriching exchange of worldviews. The Quechua suffix *-naku* indicates reciprocity of action.

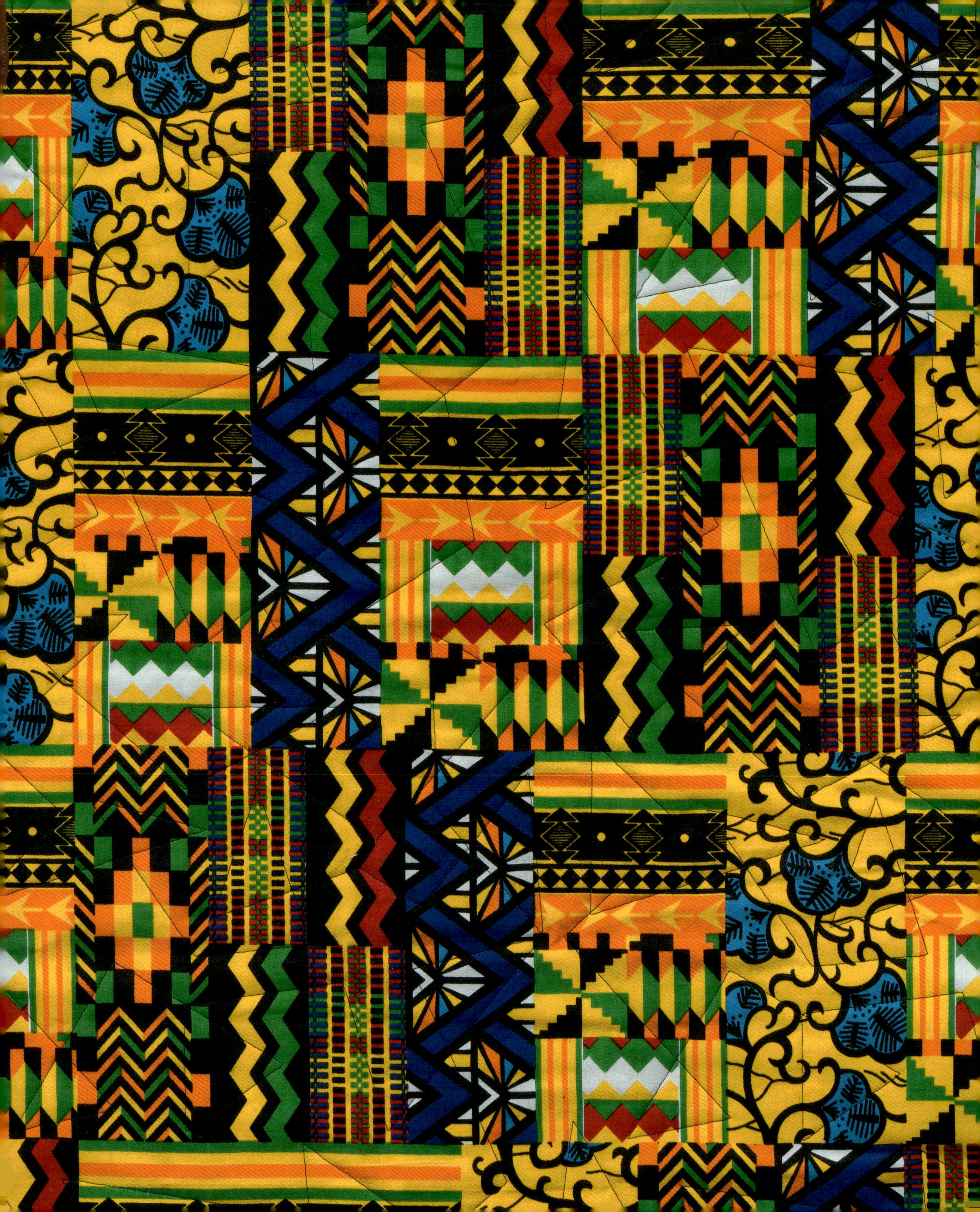

Remembrance as Resistance

The Quilts of Dorothy Burge

Sharbreon Plummer
Artist, curator, scholar, and writer

Artist, activist, and community organizer Dorothy Burge (see fig. 1) serves as a beacon to a community that is often forced into the shadows. James Baldwin once compared the role of the artist to that of a lover, stating: "If I love you, I have to make you conscious of the things you don't see."[1] Burge embodies this sentiment, using the art of quilting to make viewers more conscious of the voices and stories of people who have been silenced and erased. As a Chicago native she has seen firsthand the ways systemic racism and policing practices affect her local community as well as all the beauty that remains in spite of these challenges. Her larger-than-life quilted portraits are objects for veneration, mandates to imagine, and calls to action for anyone willing to listen. Depicting everyone from political prisoners to her own family members, her portrayals flatten hierarchies of significance to give those whose lives and stories are often deemed less important a narrative presence and physical permanence that persists even after social attention fades away. Reflecting on her practice, Burge has said, "I just keep thinking to myself, what can I do? How can I use art to speak to some of this? If we knew these stories … if our young people knew these stories, how would their lives change?"[2] Her work thus invites viewers, especially younger generations, to question who is—and is not—offered the privilege of remembrance while reminding us to strive for all to be liberated from structural oppression.

Mourning has been an unwelcome visitor in the lives of Black people in the United States for centuries. In Illinois today, Black men make up 6.6 percent of the population but represent 53.3 percent of people killed at the hands of law enforcement.[3] Black residents of Cook County, where Burge lives, are jailed at seventeen times the rate of white residents, a disparity that has increased over the past twenty years even as fewer people overall are charged with crimes.[4] The individuals behind these statistics are human beings with varied and complex lives. Many are children, parents, and caregivers of people who love and depend on them and who are therefore also deeply affected by their absence.

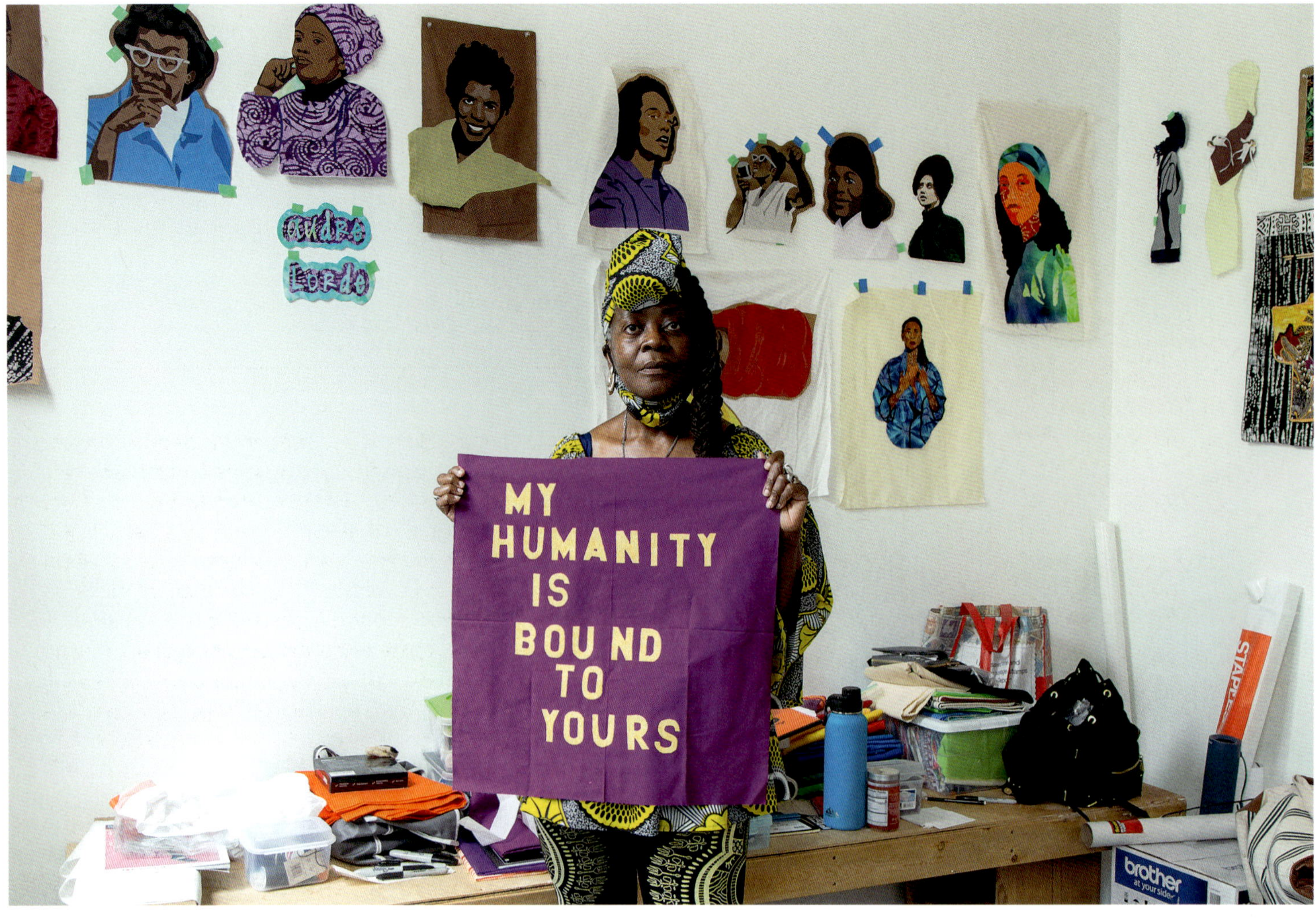

Fig. 1 **Burge in her studio at the Hyde Park Art Center, Chicago, 2022.**

Those left behind grieve not only for lives cut short but also for the dreams and possibilities that can no longer be achieved due to the stigma and limitations that accompany incarcerated people even if they are freed.

Burge's work as an artist is deeply intertwined with her lifelong commitment to activism and fighting against personal and structural injustices. From protesting the murder of Malcolm X as a student at Chicago's Lindblom High School to marching for the release of Nelson Mandela as the first Black graduate in industrial design at the University of Illinois Chicago, Burge has spent decades mobilizing for the betterment of local and global conditions for Black people across the diaspora. Her experience of Chicago's segregation and educational exclusion during the Civil Rights era fuels her desire to make historical wrongs visible and pay respect to victims through quilting as an act of veneration and memory keeping.

Veneration is defined as showing respect or reverence for a person's dignity and impact. Practices of restoring dignity are enmeshed with Black survival, as signified by movements such as #SayHerName and rituals

                                        PLUMMER

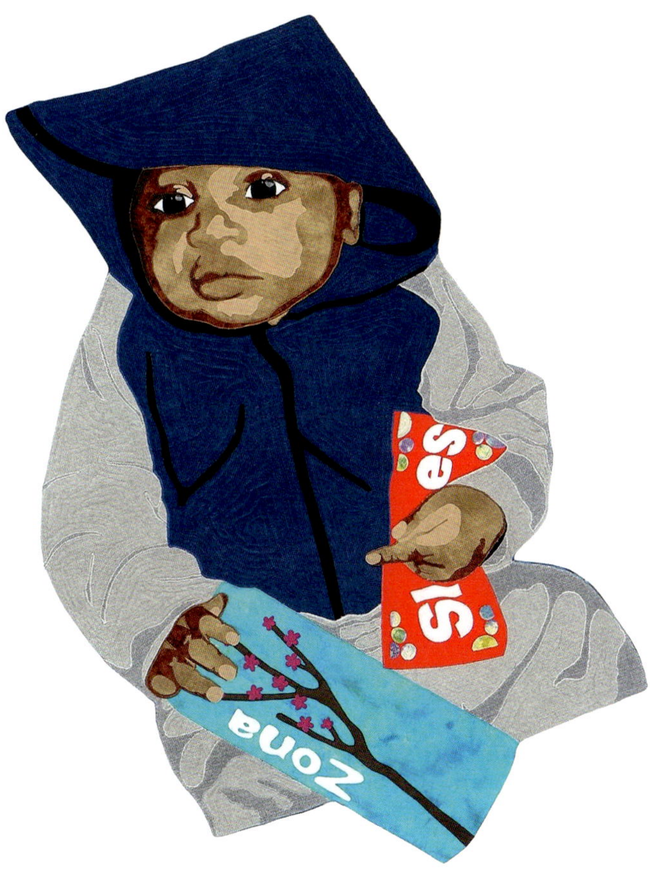

Fig. 2 Dorothy Burge (American, born 1954).
Trayvon Could Be My Son, 2012. Cotton and
corduroy fabrics and cotton batting; 127 ×
79.4 cm (50 × 31¼ in.). Smithsonian American
Art Museum, gift of Fleur S. Bresler,
2023.40.22.

such as keeping vigil at sites of harm and improvising communal altars. These acts create a home for grief and offer a glimpse of a world free from the pain of the present. Burge's quilts participate in and extend these acts, personalizing this history of remembrance by connecting it to familial and ancestral traditions: Burge's art plays on quilts' associations with comfort and status as heirlooms to treat victims of injustice and violence as extended family, honoring their lives and stories through tactile portraiture. In works such as *Trayvon Could Be My Son* (fig. 2), Burge used an image of her own great nephew as an infant clutching Skittles and a can of iced tea to signify the innocence of Trayvon Martin, who was carrying these items when he was killed in Miami in 2012.[5] The image encapsulates the pain Burge felt as a mother witnessing the murder of an innocent Black boy as well as the reality that this child could easily have been one of her own family members. Burge's depictions confront viewers with the humanity of those killed and ask them to place themselves and their loved ones in the position of the victims and their families.

Burge's homage to Martin was a critical moment in her practice—one that birthed a distinctive technique and connected her to a like-minded artistic community. A self-taught quilter whose initial forays into the medium were exploratory, Burge quickly realized that art quilts gave her the flexibility to relay important stories in complex and nontraditional ways. "When I created the Trayvon Martin quilt, it lit a fire in me. I didn't want him in a square. I wanted to hold him," she explains. Thus emerged Burge's figurative style of quilting, which releases the subject from a rectilinear frame and gives them a human shape, placing them in space and time with the viewer. This approach has another advantage, according to Burge: "When I discovered how to [make them transportable] I decided to start making most of them that way." Burge often brings her quilts out of the studio or gallery and into public spaces of mourning and outrage. She has even carried them at protests and vigils as alternatives to traditional text-based signs or photographs.

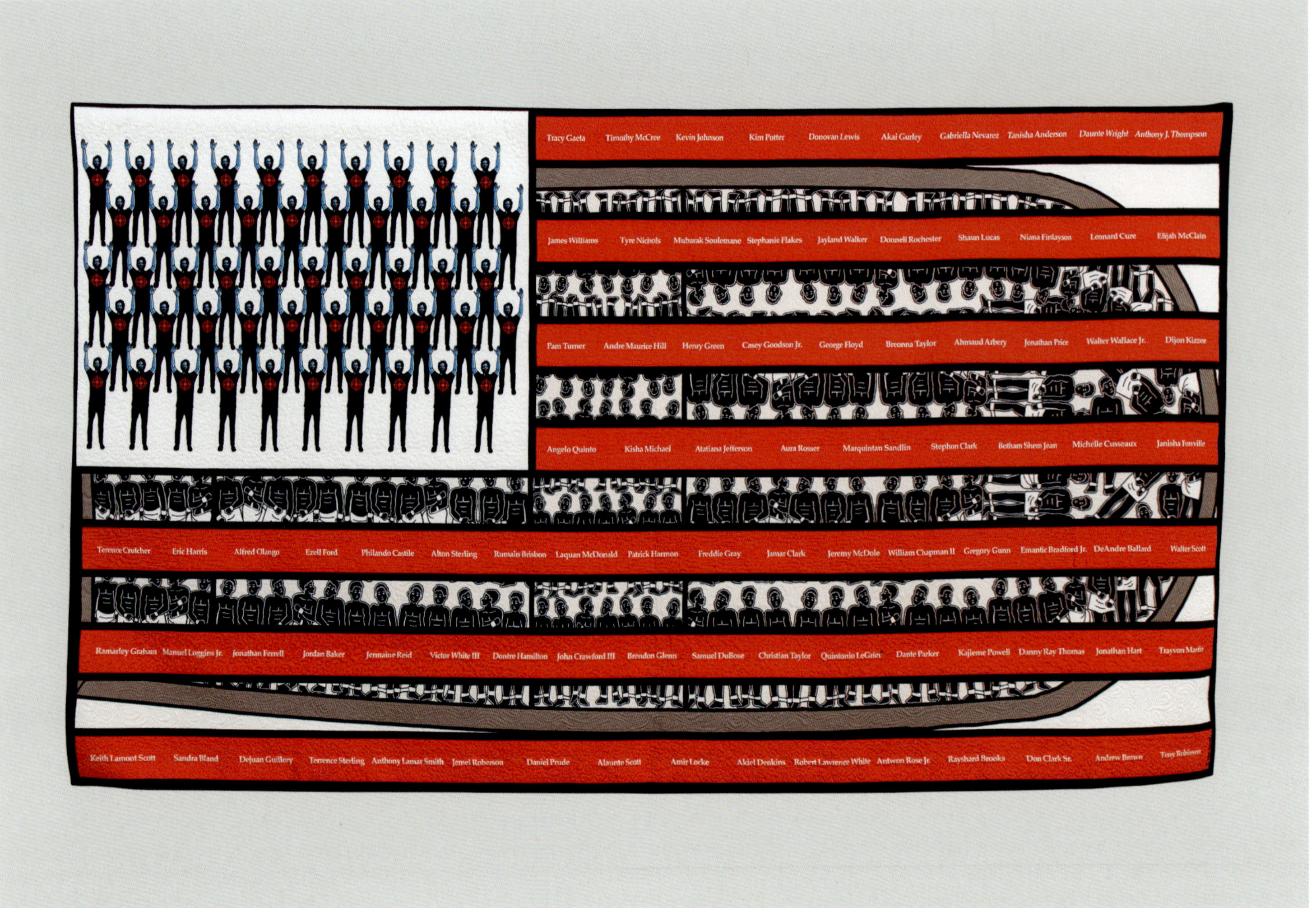

Fig. 3 Carolyn Mazloomi (American, born 1948). *Hands Up . . . Don't Shoot #2*, 2024. Polyester and cotton woven fabric, cotton thread, cotton batting, fabric paint; machine quilted; 147.4 × 259.1 cm (58 × 102 in.). The Art Institute of Chicago, Barbara E. and Richard J. Franke Endowment and Barbara Howard Estate funds, 2024.865.

While the material culture of protest can be described as bold and declarative, Burge's quilted portraits evoke comfort and softness while recalling religious iconography also aimed at inspiring reverence and remembrance. Serving as a soft altar, her quilted work unites the flawed, earthly present with divine justice and peace at moments when connection to the spiritual realm is most needed.

Trayvon Could Be My Son was also Burge's initial entry into the Women of Color Quilters' Network (WCQN), which remains an artistic home where her activism can reach beyond the streets of Chicago. Founded by Dr. Carolyn Mazloomi in 1985, the WCQN is a leading force in preserving and promoting African American quilt history while also demonstrating the rich stylistic diversity of the African American quiltmaking tradition—and the role that quilts can play in advocating for systemic change. As demonstrated by the AIDS Memorial Quilt and the more recent Quilt for Palestine, quilts have become deeply intertwined with calls for social change and efforts to visualize freedom.[6] These initiatives and the work of the WCQN are part of a long tradition: Quilts were part of the visual culture of the antislavery

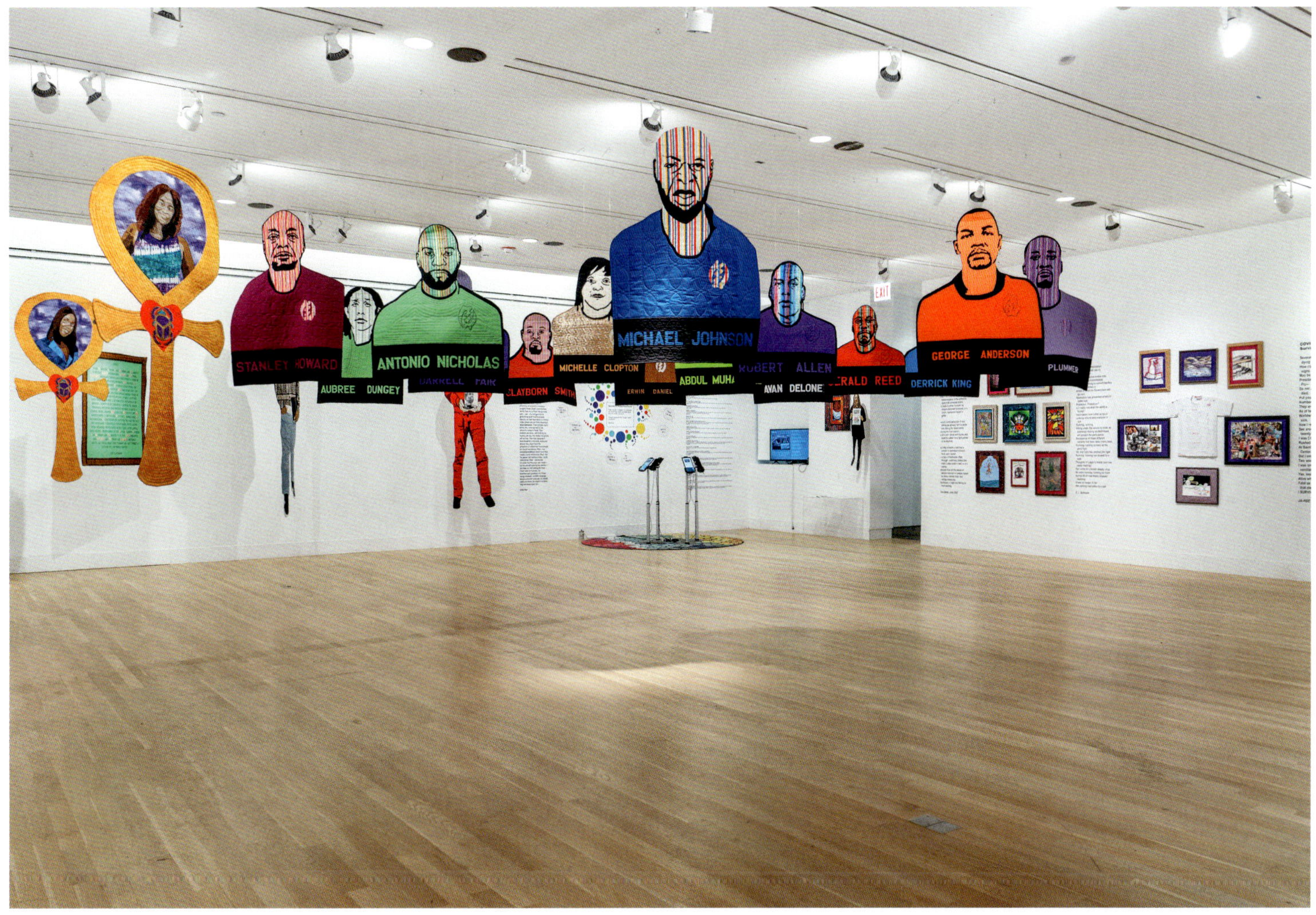

Fig. 4 Installation view of Burge's series *Won't You Help to Sing These Songs of Freedom* in the exhibition *Makes Me Wanna Holla: Art, Death and Imprisonment*, Logan Center of the Arts, University of Chicago, July 7–September 10, 2023.

movement, which, like Burge's art, centered solidarity, justice, and empathy, asking the viewer to identify with the victims.[7] Members of the WCQN regularly use the medium of quilting to address difficult topics, creating inventive designs relating to mass incarceration, the transatlantic slave trade, racism, and global human rights. Mazloomi's work as an artist (see fig. 3), activist, curator, and writer has inspired generations of artists, including Burge, to speak truth to power through their quilts.

Burge's series *Won't You Help to Sing These Songs of Freedom* (see fig. 4) seeks to bring attention to decades of injustice and suffering connected to the criminal justice system in Chicago. For nearly twenty years between 1972 and 1991, more than one hundred twenty Chicagoans—most of whom were Black men—were tortured into confessions under the direction of Chicago Police Department Commander Jon Burge (no relation to the artist).[8] Jon Burge's victims are still navigating psychological trauma and the life-altering social stigma of incarceration. Dorothy Burge is one of the original organizers of the Chicago Torture Justice Memorials (CTJM) Project,

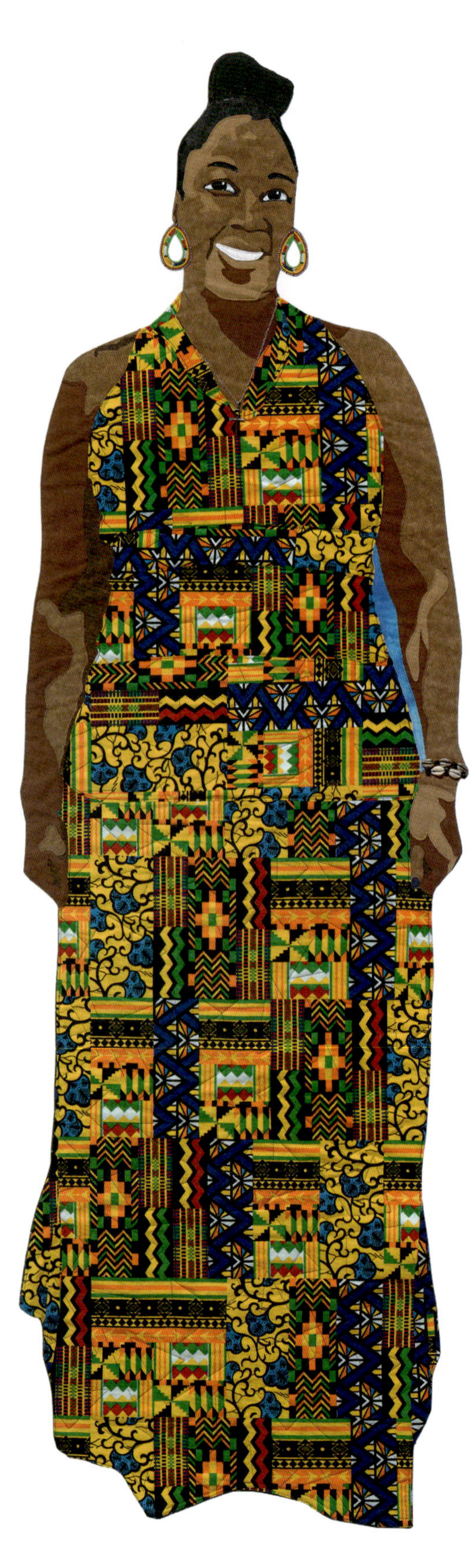
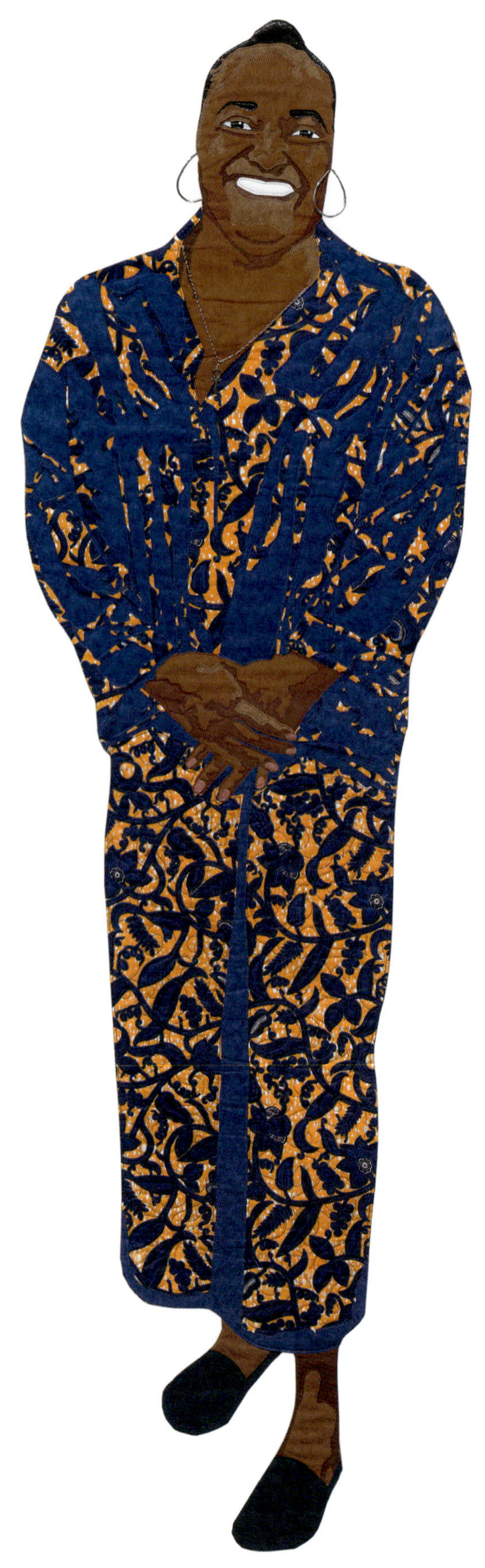

PLUMMER

created in 2010 to bring attention to Jon Burge's victims' ongoing fight for justice and accountability. CJTM worked for years to pass a reparations ordinance for survivors and their families, which was approved by the city of Chicago in 2015.[9] In addition to ensuring that the ordinance is properly instituted, the group continues to advocate for the release of the remaining victims and to provide support services for those who have been freed.[10]

Burge's artistic practice is an integral part of this activism. She spends time researching cases, listening to individuals' stories, and learning about who they are beyond their mugshot or arrest record. Her colorful portraits for *Songs of Freedom*, depicting survivors like Robert Allen, Derrick King, Gerald Reed, and Clayborn Smith, signal that their worth is not diminished by their experiences. The artworks' vibrant colors, disarming at first glance, demand attention—viewers are confronted with the human cost of this violent legacy. The portraits immortalize the men's faces and also include their names, ensuring they are not reduced to mere statistics. Through *Songs of Freedom*, Burge reminds us that structural transformation is the only path to ending the perpetual harms enacted against Black people.

Two of Burge's most recent works encourage us to turn mourning into hope. While a prison sentence can often seem to mark the end of life as one knows it, Burge created these quilts to demonstrate that renewal and rebirth are possible after incarceration. At ten feet tall, they depict formerly incarcerated torture survivors La Tanya Jenifor-Sublett (fig. 5) and Michelle Clopton (fig. 6), women who embody the hope and promise that can be restored through community care and support. Female victims of the prison industrial complex have often received less advocacy and coverage than male victims. Black feminist movement-builders like Burge have highlighted these absences, noting that Black women are the most vulnerable demographic in cases of state violence but also the most frequently ignored or erased. At twenty-six years old, Clopton was detained and brutally interrogated for over seventy-two hours by Chicago Police regarding the murder of Dora Cobb. Threatened with a death penalty for a murder that she did not commit, she and her codefendants confessed after being tortured. Out of desperation, Clopton—who was three months pregnant—pled guilty and was sentenced to sixty years in prison.[11] Jenifor-Sublett was one of the few women in Illinois to come forward as a torture survivor. At the age of nineteen, she was convicted under the "theory of accountability"—she was connected to a victim and assailant but was not present at the scene of a murder that had taken place. She was also abused by the Chicago Police Department and after a forced confession, was sentenced to forty-two years.[12]

Burge's use of scale and choice of materials in her portraits of these two women are intentional: By increasing their visibility through larger-than-life figures adorned in brightly colored, densely patterned West African fabric, she also increases the visibility of their stories, while showing them in a position of power diametrically opposed to their treatment in society and in the penal system. Jenifor-Sublett was released in 2013 after serving twenty-one years. She is now a mental health worker, organizer, and speaker, and serves as program director for the Chicago Torture Justice Center's Peer Re-Entry Program. Fueled by the injustice she faced, she now utilizes her position to support others re-enter society after incarceration, creating pathways toward healing by focusing on the release of guilt and shame. Clopton, who was released in 2023, is now an organizer and motivational speaker and plans to open a food pantry at her brother's church. "I just want to enjoy life and the rest of my time here," she shared in a recent interview. "I want to do good by others and make an impact."[13] Mainstream media often presents incarceration as the end of a life, but Burge's work presents Clopton and Jenifor-Sublett as examples that inspire new possibilities for the future of the formerly incarcerated, encouraging us to commit to using the skills we have the same way she uses her art: to fight for our collective freedom.

Notes

1   James Baldwin, "The Black Scholar Interviews James Baldwin," in *Conversations with James Baldwin*, ed. Louis H. Pratt and Fred R. Standley (University Press of Mississippi, 1989), 156.

2   Dorothy Burge, conversation with the author, August 20, 2024. All subsequent quotations from the artist are from this conversation.

3   See "Illinois Data on Police Shootings and Violence," Law Enforcement Epidemiology Project, University of Illinois Chicago School of Public Health, accessed October 24, 2024, policeepi.uic.edu /illinois-data-on-police-shootings -and-violence.

4   See Josh McGhee and Jared Ruteck, "Fewer People in Cook County Are Being Charged with Crimes. Why Are Black People Making Up a Larger Share of Defendants?," Injustice Watch, December 1, 2021, injustice watch.org/project/the-circuit/2021 /the-circuit-racial-disparities-explainer/. Experts attribute these growing racial disparities "to long-standing disinvestment and overpolicing in Black communities. They argue that local lawmakers have leaned too heavily on the criminal justice system to solve social problems, rather than addressing root causes of crime that disproportionately affect Black people, such as poverty, school inequity, a scarcity of living-wage jobs, and a lack of affordable housing."

5   "Reporting Trayvon," *Columbia Journalism Review*, April 2, 2012, cjr.org/behind_the_news/reporting _trayvon.php.

6   On the Aids Memorial Quilt, see aidsmemorial.org/quilt. On the Quilt for Palestine, see Valentina Di Liscia, "Every Artwork in the Massive Quilt for Palestine Unveiled at the Met," *Hyperallergic*, April 18, 2024, hyperallergic.com/903079 /every-artwork-in-the-massive-quilt -for-palestine-unveiled-at-the-met/.

7   See "Abolition," World Quilts: The American Story, International Quilt Museum, University of Nebraska-Lincoln, accessed October 24, 2024, worldquilts.quiltstudy.org /americanstory/engagement/abolition.

8   In 1972 Jon Burge was promoted to detective with the Chicago Police Department (CPD) and assigned to work on the city's South Side. The year of his promotion, he and his subordinates began torturing Black men to force admissions of guilt. In 1992 city attorneys finally recognized a pattern of torture and violence that led to Burge's firing in 1993. In 2010 Burge was convicted of perjury and obstruction of justice for falsely denying that he and detectives under his command had engaged in torture and abuse. He was sentenced to four and a half years in prison. The city's resolution regarding Burge's misconduct can be found at chicago.gov/content/dam /city/depts/dol/supp_info/Burge -Reparations-Information-Center /BurgeRESOLUTION.pdf; it notes the City of Chicago's plans to work directly with Chicago Torture Justice Memorials, of which artist Dorothy Burge is a founding member, on reparations efforts. See also "A Report on the Pattern and Practice of Torture and Wrongful Conviction by CPD Detectives," Chicago Alliance Against Racist and Political Repression, November 2021, caarpr.org/torture -report; "Shielded from Justice: Police Brutality and Accountability in the United States," *Human Rights Watch*, June 1998, hrw.org/legacy /reports98/police/uspo53.

9   The approved ordinance can be found at chicago.gov/content/dam /city/depts/dol/supp_info/Burge -Reparations-Information-Center /ORDINANCE.pdf. On developments since the ordinance's passing, see Logan Jaffe, "The Nation's First Reparations Package to Survivors of Police Torture Included a Public Memorial. Survivors Are Still Waiting." ProPublica Illinois Newsletter, July 3, 2020, propublica.org/article/the -nations-first-reparations-package -to-survivors-of-police-torture -included-a-public-memorial-survivors -are-still-waiting.

10   The artist is currently the internship coordinator for CTJM. For more on the organization's goals, seechicagotorture.org/about/.

11   See "Survivor Stories: Michelle Clopton," Chicago Alliance Against Racist and Political Repression, accessed October 24, 2024, caarpr .org/survivors-1/michelle-clopton.

12   To hear Clopton's and Jenifor-Sublett's stories in their own words, see Jewél Jackson, host and producer, *Change Agents: The Podcast*, "Say Her Name: Women Survivors of Chicago Police Torture," Juneteenth Productions, June 19, 2024, change agentsthepodcast.buzzsprout.com /1600336/episodes/15272068. See also Samantha Aguilar, "Chicago Torture Justice Center Works to Expand Reparations for Police Violence," *The Daily Northwestern*, February 9, 2020, dailynorthwestern .com/2020/02/09/campus/chicago -torture-justice-center-works-to -expand-reparations-for-police -violence; and interview with La Tanya Jenifor-Sublett, *Chicago Torture Justice Center Newsletter*, March 2024, issuu.com/chicagotorturejustice /docs/march_2024.

13   "Say Her Name: Women Survivors of Chicago Police Torture," at approximately 25:00.

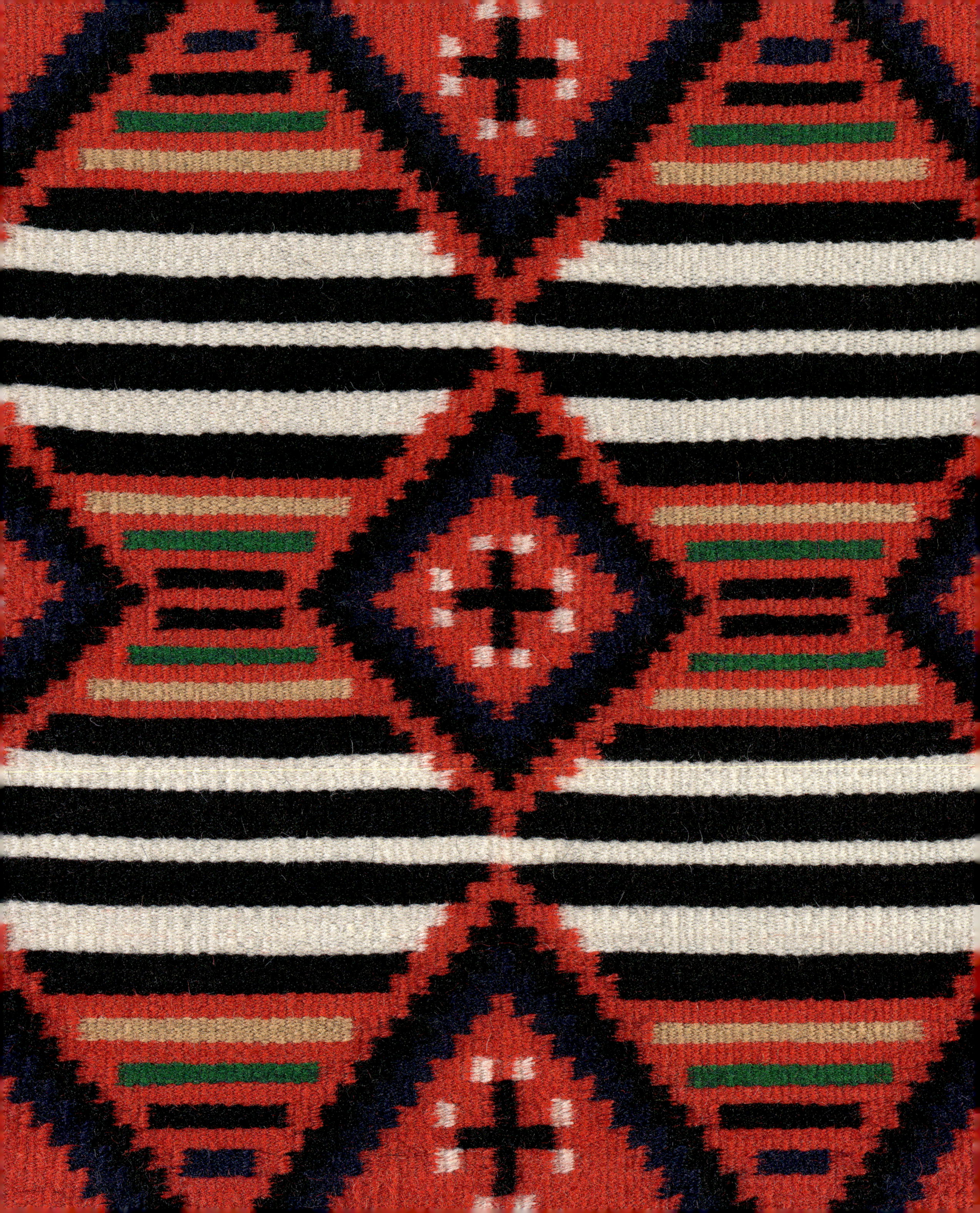

The Enduring Beauty of Diné Textiles

L y n d a   T e l l e r   P e t e
B a r b a r a   T e l l e r   O r n e l a s

Fifth-generation Diné tapestry weavers

Born to the Water's Edge Clan, Tábąąhá

Born for the Water-Flows-Together Clan, Tó'aheedlíinii

Maternal grandfather born for Red Ochre on Cheeks People, Tł'ááshchí'í

Paternal grandfather One-Walks-Around Clan, Honágháahnii

Diné (Navajo) textiles provide a livelihood for my family and community, members of the Diné Nation in Newcomb, Toadlena, and Two Grey Hills, New Mexico, where people across generations practice the art of weaving and exercise the protocols that govern and identify this tradition. Weavers serve as examples of resilience and resistance, as they push their art forward against the headwinds of colonization; marginalization; local, regional, and global commercialization; criticism; racism; and cultural fragmentation. Weavers in our family live in adherence to the Blessing Way, also known as the Beauty Way, which acknowledges that we live and weave in an interconnected world integrating ancient knowledge, cultural protocols, and traditional pathways while also adapting to the present without compromising the core tenets of *hózhó*, the Diné concept of harmony, as reflected in our lives as weavers. Harmony is everything to the Diné; we all strive to be good people, in harmony within ourselves and with our environment.

The three communities of Newcomb, Toadlena, and Two Grey Hills are tight-knit, with families living in close proximity to one another. Most of the people there are farmers, ranchers, or artisans such as basket makers, jewelers, and potters. But these communities are collectively known best for the regional Two Grey Hills weaving style, regarded as the highest form of all Diné weaving. Many famed and legendary weavers lived and wove in this area, as many do to this day.

At the Art Institute of Chicago as in so many other Western museums, the names of Diné weavers who made objects in the collection are often not known. Racist colonial ideologies have historically led white collectors and institutions to view works of Diné origin, among other Indigenous works, as products of a culture in general rather than a particular artist; the names of individual makers were often not recorded, because they were not considered important. In response to these collection practices, my sister Barbara Teller Ornelas (fig. 1) has created a series of twenty-five

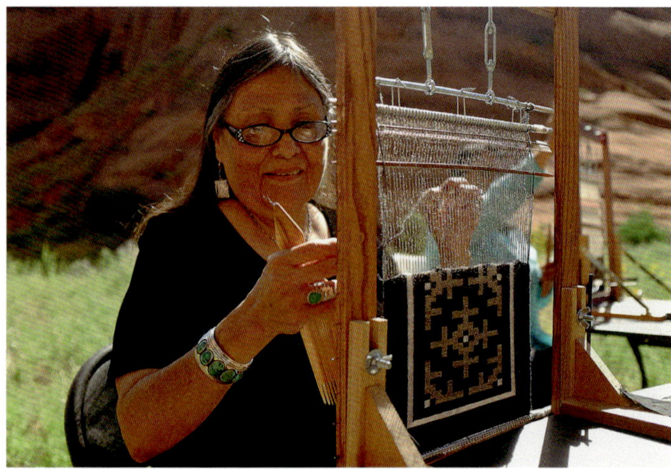

Fig. 1 Barbara Teller Ornelas weaving, 2016.

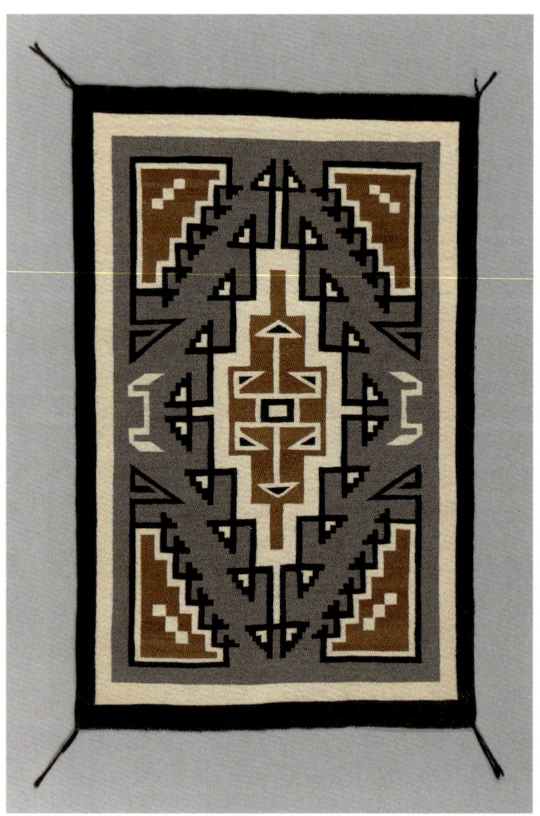

Fig. 2 Tsosie Hyden (Diné [Navajo], active mid-20th century). Rug or Wall Hanging in the "Two Grey Hills" Style, 1960s. Wool, single interlocking tapestry weave; twined selvages, heading and finish terminating in tassels; 120.7 × 78.1 cm (47½ × 30¾ in.). The Art Institute of Chicago, gift of Mr. and Mrs. Robert Karr, 1980.687.

sets of First-, Second-, and Third-Phase Chief Blankets, so named for major periods in the evolution of Diné weaving.[1] She describes her inspiration here:

Through my more than forty-five years of being a professional weaver, I have always been honored and inspired by opportunities to view weaving collections in museums. In 1999 I took my children to see a Van Gogh exhibition at the Los Angeles County Museum of Art.[2] As we were waiting in line, I noticed that the Southwest Museum directly across the street had an exhibition of Navajo (Diné) weavings.[3] Now I was anxious to get through the Van Gogh exhibition and see the Navajo textiles. But my children were so excited about the Van Gogh paintings, so we continued with our tour. I noticed that he had written letters to his brother detailing his thoughts. His life and practice were well documented.

After the tour, I took my kids to the Navajo textiles exhibition. There were First-, Second-, and Third-Phase Chief Blankets, woven in the mid- to late 1800s. As we were looking at the old weavings, questions were forming about the Diné weavers. Why were they not mentioned by name? Where did they live? Were they part of our people who went to Bosque Redondo?[4] Were they safe from the soldiers long enough to make these beautiful weavings? How were these textiles collected?

So many unanswered questions. My children were both very curious as well and anxious for me to give them some answers. So I made up a story about a young mom who wakes up early, says her prayers, and runs to get water

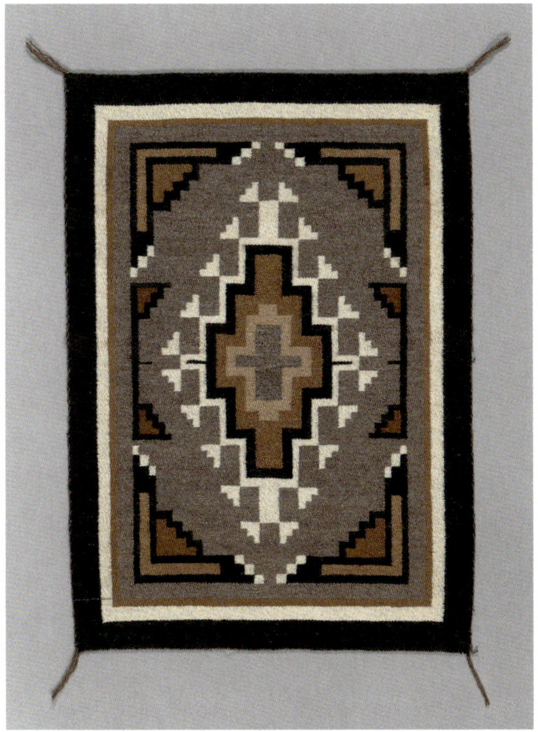

Fig. 3 Sara Begody (Diné [Navajo], active mid-20th century). Rug or Wall Hanging in the "Two Grey Hills" Style, 1960s. Wool, single interlocking tapestry weave; twined selvages, heading and finish terminating in tassels; 78.3 × 56.5 cm (30 ¾ × 22 ¼ in.). The Art Institute of Chicago, gift of Mr. and Mrs. Robert Karr, 1980.689.

from the well for the day. She makes breakfast for her kids and makes sure they are safe and happy. She says her prayers, sits in front of her loom, and arranges her weaving tools. She sings her weaving songs and starts to weave. Beating down the wool wefts with her comb, creating a rhythmic, pleasant sound, she tells her babies, "This is the heartbeat of your family." The sounds of her singing and weaving bring a lot of love and peace to her home.

As we were leaving, I asked a member of the museum staff how many weavings were in the exhibition. "Seventy-five," she said. Seventy-five silent weavers. No names attached. I thought of my great-grandmother, both my grandmothers, my mother, my sisters, and my aunts—their names are connected to their weavings. We've come a long way and it is wonderful to be a part of that change. This is where I made up my mind to make seventy-five weavings to honor those unnamed weavers. I committed to making twenty-five sets of the First-, Second-, and Third-Phase Chief Blankets—seventy-five total weavings. I've woven twenty-four sets so far and have held off weaving the last one.

Out of the thirty-one Navajo textiles in the Art Institute's collection, six are by known weavers, including several from Two Grey Hills (see figs. 2–3) along with works by legendary weavers Hosteen Klah and Daisy Taugelchee.[5] Unlike those of most Diné weavers, Klah's and Daisy's lives, work timelines, and weaving styles are relatively well documented.[6] There are published biographies of Klah and many articles about Daisy, along with numerous catalogues of exhibitions and collections featuring their work.[7]

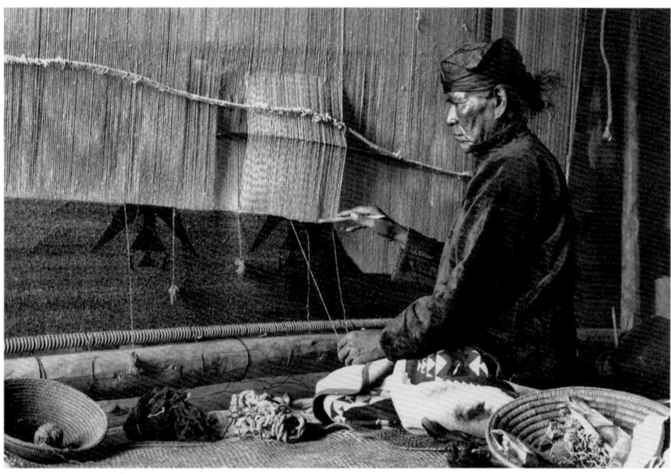

Fig. 4 **Hosteen Klah beginning a "Night Sky" weaving, 1925. Courtesy of Bancroft Library, University of California, Berkeley.**

In my research for this essay, I encountered adulation and praise along with grouchy criticisms by traders, gallery proprietors, and collectors of Indigenous art. While the things I read about Daisy and Klah were interesting, I did not get to know the real Daisy and Klah through these texts. Archaeologists, collectors, curators, ethnographers, gallerists, traders, and many more have studied and critiqued the weavers, but none have been Diné.

Hosteen Klah: Medicine Man, Weaver, Gardener, Pastoralist

Klah (fig. 4) was born at the Bosque Redondo Indian Reservation in New Mexico in late summer 1867 to Asdzą́ą́ Tsosie of the Dzilt'aadi clan and Hashké Holyé of the To'ahani clan, who were imprisoned there for nearly a year. His sister, Ahdesbah, followed a year later. After the family returned to Newcomb, Klah was raised near the Chuska Mountains, the homeland of his great-grandfather Narbona, our fiercest warrior, who died from battle injuries in 1849. While Klah learned to become a Medicine Man, Asdzą́ą́ kept her daughter close, fearing she would be kidnapped for her weaving skills by marauding bands of slavers.

Ahdesbah had two marriages and four daughters. Only the three youngest girls' names were recorded: Gladys Manuelito (Mrs. Sam), Irene Ball (Mrs. Jim), and the youngest, Daisy Gould Nabahi.[8] Gladys and Irene learned weaving from their uncle Klah and assisted him with sandpainting rugs, although some critics claim that certain works are solely theirs.[9] To these critics I say that Klah practiced *K'é'*, our system of kinship, which involves caring for family, sharing values, knowing history, preserving weaving culture, and embodying kindness and hózhó. Displays, publications, and records relating to these rugs should reflect this collaboration, with Klah credited as Gladys's and Irene's teacher and mentor, because the skills of preparation and weaving were learned and passed down within the family.

TELLER PETE AND TELLER ORNELAS

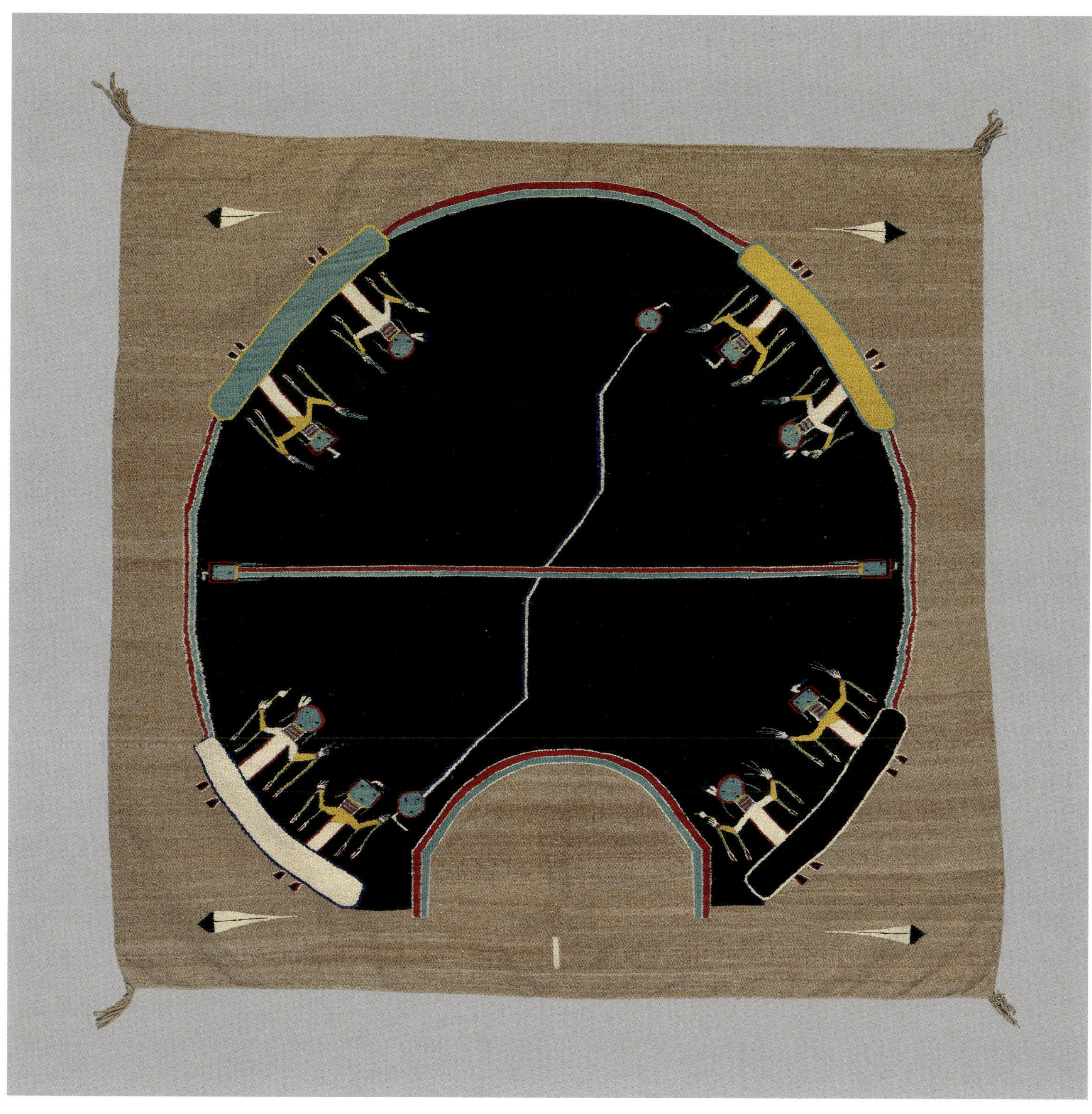

Fig. 5 Hastiin Tła (Left-Handed Man, also known as Hosteen Klah; Diné [Navajo], 1867–1937). *Rainbow People Have Arrived (Nááts'íílid Bee Yikáh)*, about 1925. Wool, dovetail and single interlocking tapestry weave; edges finished with three-strand weft twining with four knotted corner tassels; 160.8 × 172.2 cm (63 ¼ × 67 ¾ in.). The Art Institute of Chicago, Ada Turnbull Hertle Endowment, 2002.299.

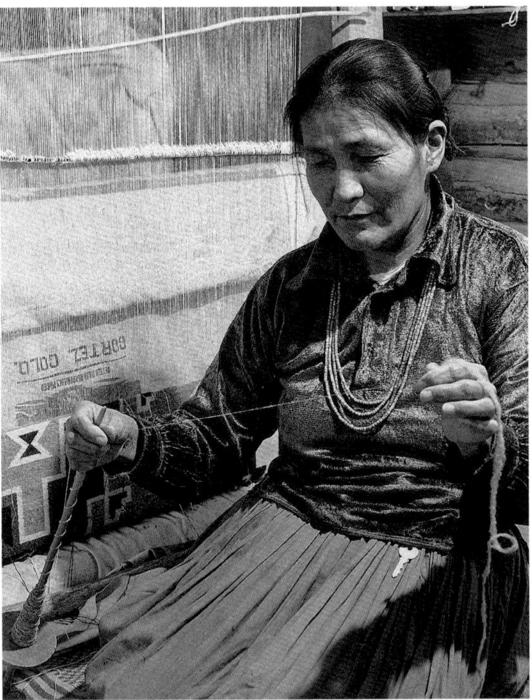

Fig. 6 **Daisy Taugelchee spinning, 1955. Courtesy of the Amon Carter Museum of American Art, Fort Worth, Texas.**

In adulthood Klah became a Medicine Man and weaver, known for his sandpainting rugs (see fig. 5), typically sixty-eight by sixty-eight inches. He mastered numerous healing ceremonies, which involved hand-painting sacred symbols with colored sands. At the end of such ceremonies, these paintings are destroyed and returned to the earth. Most of the ceremonies Klah learned involved depictions of sacred animals, items, plants, environmental phenomena, and Holy People. Learning a design often took decades. Critics in Klah's Diné community regarded it as taboo to make sacred healing designs permanent by weaving them into rugs, although the artist introduced slight variations to avoid exactly replicating sandpaintings. Also controversial was his decision to invite a non-Diné woman, anthropologist and museum founder Mary Cabot Wheelwright, to sit in on ceremonies to sketch the paintings and record the chants; this broke sacred protocol, and doing so may have weighed greatly on Klah's mind. But his eyes were on the future: Two of his apprentices died, and Klah knew that he would die before he could train another one in the numerous complex designs and chants numbering in the thousands, corresponding to different ailments. The recordings were a kind of last resort, a way to preserve the future of healing ceremonies for the people he loved. (They are now in safe storage at the Wheelwright Museum in Santa Fe.) Klah lived a long life, and, because of his Medicine ways, he was not harmed by breaking protocols in weaving the healing chants and sandpainting rugs.

Klah attended the world's fairs in Chicago in 1892 and 1934, and he traveled to the Atlantic Ocean, the Gulf of Mexico, the Pacific Ocean, and the Great Lakes.[10] He faced racial discrimination, enduring, for instance, the humiliation of "no colored allowed" policies for drinking water, eating, and lodging, but his frequent companions in these travels, married white traders Arthur J. and Franc Johnson Newcomb, never left his side. Klah collected sand from beaches, focusing on the earth beneath the water rather than water itself, as he sought landmarks tied to creation

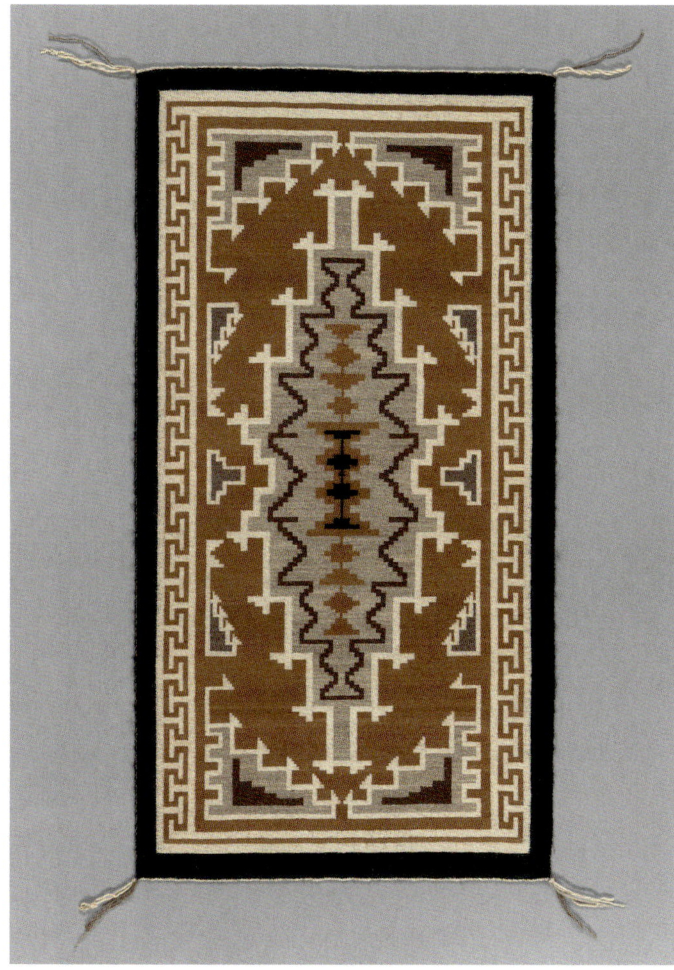

Fig. 7 Daisy Taugelchee (Diné [Navajo], 1909–1990). Rug or Wall Hanging in the "Two Grey Hills" Style, 1960s. Wool, single interlocking tapestry weave; all edges twined, twining elements form corner knotted tassels; 85.4 × 45.2 cm (33⅝ × 17¾ in.). The Art Institute of Chicago, gift of Mr. and Mrs. Robert Karr, 1980.688.

stories and Holy People. He died at the age of seventy in the 1937 flu epidemic, near Fort Wingate, New Mexico, surrounded by family and giving instructions on caring for his ceremonial items. He requested a nontraditional burial, which was honored. When Franc Newcomb wrote about his death, she did not mention the final gesture of a Diné's last rites, which she may have witnessed but could not have understood: Throughout his life, Klah shared his wealth and time, training weavers and chanters; his hands worked hard, especially his index fingers, and upon his death, a favorite ring would have been placed on one of them, signifying that his work was done.[11]

In beauty it is finished.[12]

Daisy Taugelchee, Master Weaver of the Two Grey Hills Regional Style

Daisy (fig. 6) was born in 1911 to Mrs. Yazzie. She was born for the Ma'ii Deeshgiizhnii clan, for her father, Hosteen Yazzie, Naasshashi clan, and raised by her paternal grandmother, Sage Brush Hill Woman, a highly esteemed weaver. Her sister Mildred Yazzie Natani was also a very well-known weaver, but it was Daisy whom collectors, scholars, and traders championed. Daisy went to the Toadlena Boarding School probably at age six or seven and received her English name, Daisy Marion Yazzie. She later attended the Albuquerque Indian School for four years and the Phoenix Indian School for two years. She married Chee Taugelchee in the late 1920s and had two sons, Chee Jr. and Chester, and a daughter, Janie, along with many nephews, nieces, and grandchildren.

There were interruptions in her life. In the late 1940s she exercised her matriarchal rights to end her marriage for her personal safety. Her partner after that period was Dee Cohoe, and they moved for a short time to Rico, Colorado, where Dee was employed as a uranium miner. Upon his death in 1954, Daisy moved back to Toadlena and resumed making

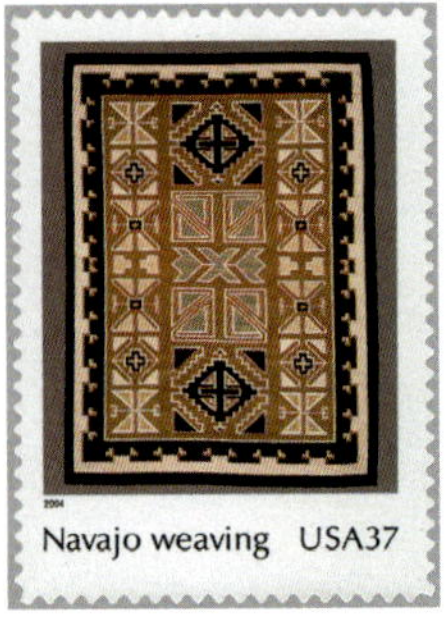

Fig. 8 **"Navajo Weaving" stamp issued in 2004 by the United States Postal Service, featuring one of Daisy Taugelchee's weavings.**

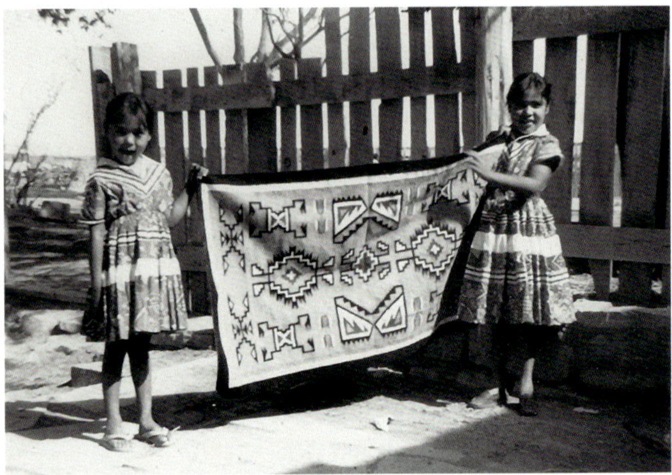

Fig. 9 **The authors photographed by their mother, Ruth Teller, at the Two Grey Hills Trading Post, where their father worked, 1964. Weavers came to the Teller home to have their works photographed before they were sold; the rug in this image is one such weaving.**

her signature large tapestries (see fig. 7). In the summer of 1963, her house was struck by lightning and burned to the ground, together with all her looms and a nearly finished tapestry. She left the community of Toadlena after many ceremonies, believing that the supernatural forces were too strong for her to remain in her homeland. She moved to the border town of Farmington, New Mexico, to live with her son Chester and her daughter-in-law Priscilla Taugelchee, whom she trained to be an exceptional weaver. Daisy never wove large tapestries after 1963.

Daisy's career peaked in the 1930s and 1940s. Having attended three government residential schools, she could negotiate her tapestry prices in English. Her works are considered tapestries rather than rugs because of her extra-fine spinning skills, through which she created yarn as fine as sewing thread that enabled her to achieve a weft count of eighty to one hundred and thirty threads per inch.[13] She was celebrated with accolades and exhibitions, including being honored with a US postage stamp (fig. 8) in 2004. Still, she faced criticism for lacking a distinct style in her early works and for inconsistency later in her career. Her reserved nature made her a challenging interview subject. When she stopped weaving large tapestries after the 1960s, some questioned her skills, often judging her through colonial perspectives.

Early in my childhood, I heard about Daisy from my father, Sam Teller, who clerked at the Two Grey Hills Trading Post (see fig. 9) from 1947 to 1982. Daisy sometimes came to the post to sell her tapestries. My older siblings recalled her visiting on days they worked there. My mother, Ruth Teller, and my maternal aunts, Margaret Yazzie and Mary Louise Gould, would ask my father endless questions about Daisy and her tapestries—who drove her, how much did she get, did she wear her best turquoise jewelry, and so on. I conjured a view of Daisy, walking into the post with purpose, a regal figure who exuded confidence, knew her worth, and was ready to negotiate, nay, command her price. With the sale of one huge tapestry she bought a truck, in which

TELLER PETE AND TELLER ORNELAS

she was driven around by relatives. Traders clamored to acquire Daisy's tapestries knowing that they could quickly resell them for a higher price. Yet some complained that her work was inconsistent; for instance, her earlier pieces did not command the highest prices because they supposedly lacked a significant or easily identifiable style. But that is how the skills of weavers develop: As is the way of our Holy Person Spider Woman, it takes time to work on your weaving and to achieve the artistry that makes sense and creates beauty.

The design styles of Daisy's students likely also contributed to the noted inconsistencies. To boost her family's earnings, Daisy sometimes put her name on works by her daughter Janie, granddaughter Katherine, and other relatives. Like Klah, she practiced K'é', with the family collaborating on flock care and wool processing and elders passing down specialized techniques. While she spun most of the wefts, she allowed her family to create their own designs. As a teacher she was compassionate and generous, leaving a lasting mark on their textiles.

Some found Daisy difficult to interview due to her stoic and uncommunicative nature and it was sometimes suggested that she should have been more graceful. Living near uranium tailings may have contributed to her Parkinson's disease. This condition can cause a lack of facial expression, an alternative explanation for her perceived demeanor. As her muscles stiffened, she adapted by weaving smaller tapestries. Daisy was a resilient, strong Diné woman, and she lived her life to her body's capacity.

When I recently spoke with my friend and colleague Ann Lane Hedlund, she asked me why Daisy would leave her edge cords long. The final stage in creating a weaving involves folding the textile into a square and cutting the tassels to the same length. This step holds cultural significance; it is akin to cutting off a newborn's umbilical cord. Instead of cutting hers to shorter lengths, Daisy left the long edge cords on her tapestries. I did not have an answer to Dr. Hedlund's question at the time, but it stayed with me.

The answer emerged as I reviewed photo albums of weavings by my mother and my sister. I noticed their evolving styles—fancier designs during happier times and subtle changes reflecting losses. We all weave in joy and in grief, and our tapestries show that. Cutting our edge cords symbolizes letting go of the past and creating a sense of home in the present. The cut pieces are buried or kept by the weaver after a tapestry is sold. Daisy left her cords long because she did not want to let go of her weavings. Throughout her tumultuous life, she longed for comfort, love, and peace and to be safe in her environment. But she also wanted freedom, freedom to weave with abandon. She left the cords long because she kept each of her masterpieces in her heart, in her soul, their true home, forever, even after her passing in 1990.

In beauty it is finished.

* * *

Throughout my research, I found that Klah and Daisy have been judged by colonial standards. Their lives were rooted in Diné traditions, and both broke certain weaving protocols as necessary.[14] They were students first and later passed on their knowledge as teachers. Their lives were shaped by tremendous losses and buoyed by their resilience, their ability to live with painful absences. They walked and wove in the Beauty Way and left for their journey on the Rainbow Trail just as they wished. Nothing more, nothing less.

In beauty it is finished.

In beauty it is finished.

Barbara, too, has followed a distinctive path in creating the seventy-five promised works—twenty-five sets of First-, Second-, and Third-Phase Chief Blankets—in honor of the unnamed weavers whose works she encountered so long ago. She describes the final set here:

> For my First Phase (fig. 10, left), I decided
> to set up the warps male style, because this

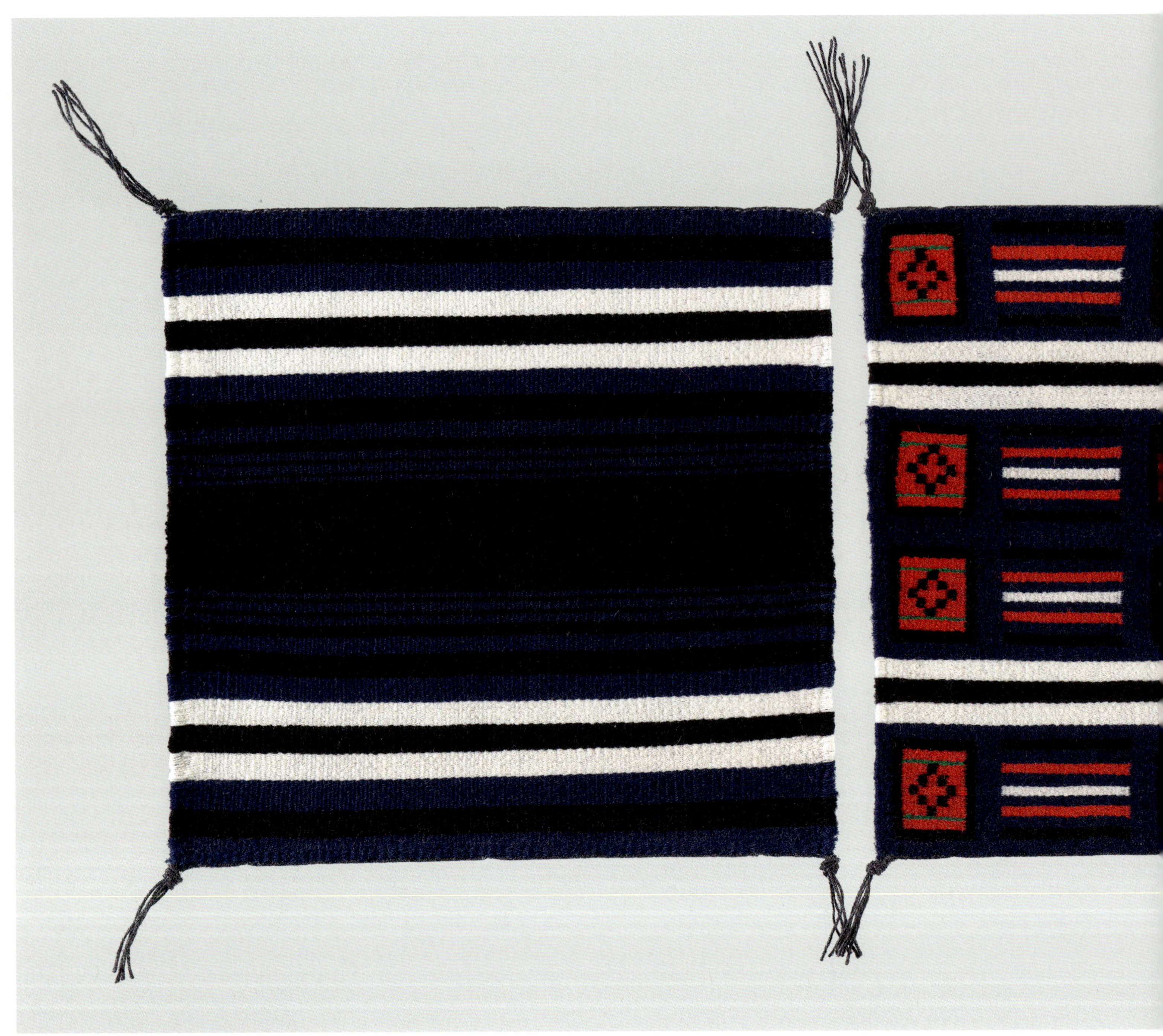

Fig. 10 Barbara Teller Ornelas (Diné [Navajo]; born to the Water's Edge Clan, Tábąąhá; born for the Water-Flows-Together Clan, Tó'aheedlíinii; maternal grandfather born for Red Ochre on Cheeks People, Tł'ááshchí'í; paternal grandfather One-Walks-Around Clan, Honágháahnii). *Contemporary Chief Set (Three Miniatures)*, 2024. Wool; dovetail tapestry weave; extended selvage cord fringe; warp: hand-carded wool and mohair; weft: commercially processed, aniline-dyed merino wool, respun by the artist; each: 24.5 × 26.1 cm (9 5/8 × 10 1/4 in.). The Art Institute of Chicago, Don F. and Jean F. Stuck Endowment Fund, 2024.866a–c.

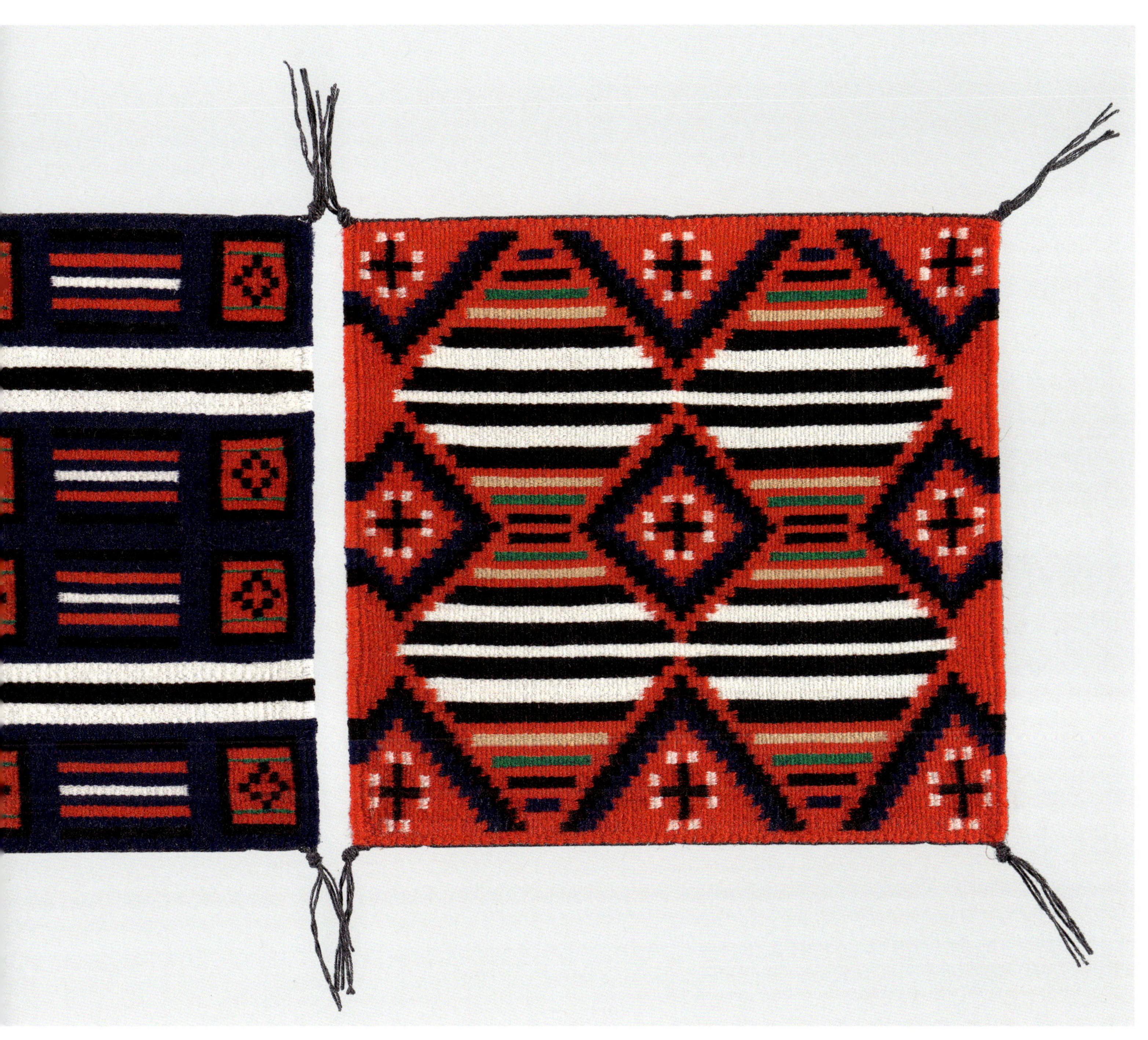

particular weaving is associated with honor-
able chiefs from other Indigenous nations.[15]
Different nations would trade with the Navajo
weavers to honor their chiefs and be looked
upon as a wealthy nation. Everything this
weaving represents is male, the style most
sought after by collectors of Navajo textiles.

I set up the warp for my Second Phase
(fig. 10, middle) female style, which is the way
most of my weavings are set up. The pattern
is very significant to me: It is the design
Navajo women wove for their dresses while
they were imprisoned at Bosque Redondo.
I added a small amount of green because it
means a small amount of peace is achievable.
I think of all the trauma they went through
and how, upon returning home, they wove
rugs to reclaim everything they had lost.

My Third Phase (fig. 10, right) is also warped
and woven in the female style. I chose this
design because it means so much to me and
to all Navajo weavers. The symbol is a Spider
Woman's Cross. My weaving starts and
ends with Her blessings. Because this is my
last set, I'm honoring Spider Woman. I want
people all over the world to know about Her
and what She represents.

These sets send a message to the world:
"We will be nameless no more!"

When asked, I have always said, "I'm saving
the last set for something special."

I wove the last set for this exhibition.

In beauty it is finished.

In beauty it is finished.

In beauty it is finished.

In beauty it is finished.

   TELLER PETE AND TELLER ORNELAS

Notes

1   Date ranges vary among textile scholars, but First Phase refers to the early classic period of Diné weaving, from 1700 to 1840. The Navajo weavings in this era were simple banded patterns created mostly from shades of undyed wool. Some makers used indigo traded from the Spanish. Common colors were black, blue, brown, gray, and white. The blankets were used for everyday functions. The large black-and-white striped styles were mainly worn by males. Those with narrow stripes in brown and blue were typically worn by females.

Second Phase refers to the classic period from 1840 to 1863, marked by improved weaving and heavy trading. Navajos spun their wool finer, sometimes unraveling and respinning commercially woven items like blankets and clothing. Most of these items were red, a color that Navajos were then just getting acquainted with and soon prized for weaving. Navajos would trade with the soldiers at Bosque Redondo for their red underwear or dye wool with cochineal and lac. Navajos started weaving simple geometric design elements into the early striped patterns. As more commercial yarns were brought to the Southwest, the weavings became more consistent.

Third Phase refers to the late classic and transitional period from 1863 to 1890, when Navajos began weaving more elaborate designs. Navajos imprisoned at Bosque Redondo were supplied with new weaving materials. This era of blankets was prized by other tribes as well, but only the chiefs were able to afford them. Many photographs emerged showing chiefs wearing these blankets, and they became known as Chief Blankets. The Chief Blanket became well known for its nine design elements, again paired with wide stripes for males and narrow stripes for females.

2   *Van Gogh's Van Goghs: Masterpieces from the Van Gogh Museum*, Los Angeles County Museum of Art, January 17–April 4, 1999.

3   *Common Threads: Pueblo and Navajo Textiles in the Southwest Museum*, Southwest Museum, Los Angeles, October 25, 1998–September 26, 1999. The museum closed permanently in September 2022.

4   Bosque Redondo was a prison camp where Navajos were incarcerated from 1863 to 1868, after the US government sanctioned the army to round them up. It was a military reservation, a temporary holding area while the government decided our future—to be sent to Oklahoma or to Florida.

5   In addition to the three weavers discussed in this essay, the named weavers with works in the Art Institute's collection are Sara Begody (1980.689), Sadie Curtis (1995.156), and Tsosie Hyden (1980.687).

6   I refer to Daisy by her first name because in the Navajo-weaving world she is a celebrity known mainly by her first name, like Cher or Madonna; when you say "Daisy," everyone knows you are talking about Daisy Taugelchee.

7   Biographical information in this essay is from Franc Johnson Newcomb, *Hosteen Klah: Navaho Medicine Man and Sand Painter* (University of Oklahoma Press, 1971); Ann Lane Hedlund, *Reflections of the Weaver's World: The Gloria F. Ross Collection of Contemporary Navajo Weaving*, exh. cat. (Denver Art Museum, 1992); and Rebecca M. Valette and Jean-Paul Valette, *Navajo Weavings with Ceremonial Themes: A Historical Overview of a Secular Art Form* (Schiffer Publishing, 2017).

8   The daughters' names were recorded in the ledger at Newcomb's trading post, which was owned by Klah's biographer, Franc Johnson Newcomb. See Newcomb, *Hosteen Klah*, 71.

9   It is not clear when or how Klah learned weaving. It often takes more than half a lifetime to learn the Medicine ways, and Klah strove to learn as many healing ceremonies as he could. Most accomplished weavers start to weave before age eight and become masters around age fifty. But Klah was no ordinary Navajo.

10   Klah demonstrated weaving and completed a rug at the 1892–93 World's Columbian Exposition in Chicago. A newspaper reported on the occasion of the second world's fair in Chicago that Klah wanted "to see what changes had been made in forty years." See Newcomb, *Hosteen Klah*, 113, 192–93.

11   The Diné Medicine folks respect the final rites of death and last wishes, and there are protocols that have to be performed. In the final act of these rites, a favorite ring is placed on the index finger of the deceased's dominant hand to signify that their work is finished in beauty. This knowledge is passed down from generation to generation.

12   From a Blessing Way chant, repeated four times.

13   On weft counts, see Lynda Teller Pete and Barbara Teller Ornelas, *How to Weave a Navajo Rug and Other Lessons from the Spider Woman* (Thrums Books, 2020). Saddle blankets and rugs for floors are woven from bulky-weight wools with eleven to twenty-nine weft counts. Rugs from functional to collectibles are from thirty to seventy-nine weft counts, made with either worsted-weight or sport-weight wools; these can be hand-carded and handspun, but most these days are commercial wools. Tapestry-weight woven rugs are made by very few weavers, and the weft counts are from eighty on up. In the Navajo weaving world, the word *tapestry* does not refer to a loom frame or a weaving technique but rather to the weight of the wool used to weave.

14   At points in our careers, Barbara and I have also broken some weaving protocols so that the younger generation can learn the art of weaving even when the conditions of their modern lives don't complement their desire to maintain tradition perfectly. For example, a Navajo weaver living in Seattle or Portland and trying to follow protocols might only finish a rug every five to ten years because tradition says you can't weave during rainstorms. A weaver with a forty-hour-a-week job and a family to care for also would struggle to finish a rug due to not being able to weave at night. Some of these protocols were made for the poor economic times in the past. We have enlisted modern Medicine folks who treat us every year to a blessing to continue our work as weavers, scholars, and authors and to live in harmony and practice K'é.

15   In our family, we weave female style, meaning we are all right-handed weavers. The male style is basically for left-handed weavers. When a rug is finished, no one can tell if it was woven female or male style; it's just a technique for using your dominant hand. Every part of the looms, warps, and tools that we use correspond to male and female usage, just as every element in our universe is addressed male or female—we have male rain, female rain, wind, rain, clouds, fog, etc. For more on male and female style, see Teller Pete and Teller Ornelas, *How to Weave a Navajo Rug*.

All the warps on the three pieces are hand-carded wool, blended with mohair for strength. All the wool is commercial wool that was unspun and respun finer. The colors are all aniline dyed. All the pieces are fourteen warps to the inch with a one hundred and twelve weft count. The first phase took six weeks to weave, the second phase took two months, and the third phase took me nearly three months.

Contributors

Jerry Bleem is an artist, teacher, writer, Franciscan friar, and Catholic priest with degrees in philosophy, theology, and art. His studio practice explores the cultural construction of meaning by gathering discarded and nonprecious materials and reshaping them through time-intensive accumulation. He is currently a professor, adjunct, in Fiber and Material Studies at the School of the Art Institute of Chicago. Bleem also writes a monthly column on the intersection of art and religion for *U.S. Catholic* magazine.

Valerie Cassel Oliver is the Sydney and Frances Lewis Family Curator of Modern and Contemporary Art at the Virginia Museum of Fine Arts, Richmond, where she organized the exhibitions *Isaac Julien: Lessons of the Hour—Frederick Douglass* (2022), *The Dirty South: Contemporary Art, Material Culture, and the Sonic Impulse* (2021), and *Howardeena Pindell: What Remains to Be Seen* (2018). She was previously senior curator at the Contemporary Arts Museum Houston and director of the visiting artist program at the School of the Art Institute of Chicago.

Gustavo Da Silva is a doctoral candidate in Cristian Koepfli's lab at the University of Notre Dame, Indiana, specializing in DNA sequencing and computational genomics. He uses cutting-edge techniques (including Nanopore and Illumina sequencing) to analyze DNA sequences and various genomes, decode genetic diversity, and improve genomic tools. He focuses on methodological development, applying these approaches to studying pathogens like malaria.

Isaac Facio is associate conservator of textiles at the Art Institute of Chicago and senior lecturer at the School of the Art Institute of Chicago. He holds master's degrees in Fiber and Material Studies (School of the Art Institute of Chicago) and Textile Science and Technology from the University of Manchester, England. He specializes in three-dimensional weaving, mechanics, and textile production. He studied at L'École des Beaux-Arts, Paris, and was artist-in-residence at Fermi National Accelerator Laboratory, Batavia, Illinois. He serves on the board of the Textile Society of America.

Wafa Ghnaim is an art and dress historian, researcher, embroiderer, and educator specializing in Palestinian fashion and adornment. She is currently a Mellon fellow at the Museum of the Palestinian People, Washington, DC, and was previously a Chester Dale Fellow at the Metropolitan Museum of Art, New York. Her first book, *Tatreez & Tea: Embroidery and Storytelling in the Palestinian Diaspora* (2016), documents embroidery patterns and oral histories passed down from her mother, a legacy she continues through the Tatreez Institute, an educational initiative and dress collection dedicated to the preservation of dressmaking traditions.

Jen Chen-su Huang is an artist and writer whose practice has been supported by the Fulbright Commission and the Textile Society of America, among others. She received her MFA in Fiber and Material Studies from the School of the Art Institute of Chicago and her BA from the University of California, Berkeley. She is currently a PhD candidate in Performance Studies at New York University's Tisch School of the Arts and teaches at Parsons School of Design in New York.

Nneka Kai is an interdisciplinary artist, educator, and writer. She holds an MFA in Fiber and Material Studies from the School of the Art Institute of Chicago and a BFA in Textiles from Georgia State University, Atlanta. Kai is a recipient of the 2023 Artadia Awards for Atlanta. Her work has been shown in solo and group exhibitions in California, Chicago, Kentucky, and New York. Kai currently teaches at Pratt Munson College of Art and Design in Utica, New York.

Cristian Koepfli is an assistant professor in Biological Sciences at the University of Notre Dame, Indiana. He obtained his doctorate in Microbiology from the Swiss Tropical and Public Health Institute in Basel, Switzerland. His research focuses on the diagnosis, epidemiology, and genomics of infectious diseases, in particular malaria parasites. He is an expert in the development of PCR assays for sensitive detection and of next-generation sequencing-based assays for parasite genotyping. He applies these methods to surveys in Ethiopia, Ghana, Kenya, and other countries, often including thousands of human blood samples.

Sarah Molina is a doctoral candidate in History of Art and Architecture at Harvard University, Cambridge, Massachusetts, where she specializes in the study of Islamic art and textiles of the early modern world. Sarah previously held Andrew W. Mellon, Samuel H. Kress, and National Science Foundation fellowships at the Art Institute of Chicago.

Noqanchis is an art collective founded in 2021 by Alipio Melo, María José Murillo, and Danitza Willka after they worked together at the Centro de Textiles Tradicionales del Cusco (CTTC) in Peru. Noqanchis connects Andean weavers with textile artists to intertwine their worldviews and experiences as contemporary creator and challenge distinctions between fine art and craft. Melo, born in Pitumarca, Cusco, began weaving at the age of seven as the only male weaver in his community; he is now one of the most accomplished weavers in the region and an expert in the care of alpacas. He is currently the president of the adult weavers group in the CTTC's Munay Ticlla association. María José Murillo was born in Arequipa, Peru. Through weaving, she embarks on a path of re-existence, reclaiming her Andean roots, long excluded from the artistic education she received in her homeland. She earned her MFA in Fiber and Material Studies at the School of the Art Institute of Chicago. Willka was born in Pitumarca and inherited her deep knowledge of weaving from her mother and grandmother. She was part of the young weavers group of the CTTC's Pitumarca association for six years.

Lucinda Pelton is a textiles conservator at the Los Angeles County Museum of Art. Previously, she was the Kress Fellow in Textiles Conservation at the Art Institute of Chicago. She earned her MA in Textile Conservation from the Fashion Institute of Technology, New York, and a BA in Art History from Hunter College, New York. She was previously an intern at several New York institutions, including the Museum at FIT, the Cathedral of St. John the Divine, and the Ukrainian Museum.

Sharbreon Plummer is an interdisciplinary artist, curator, public scholar, and writer. She recently curated *Of Salt and Spirit: Black Quilters in the American South* (Mississippi Museum of Art, 2024) and co-organized Stitch by Stitch (School of the Art Institute of Chicago, 2022), a conference about the historical relationship between quilting and social justice. She is the author of *Diasporic Threads: Black Women, Fibre, and Textiles* (Common Threads Press, 2022) and the forthcoming *Black Quilts: Memory, Method and Medicine* (Chronicle Books, 2026).

Jenni Sorkin is Professor and Chair of History of Art and Architecture at the University of California, Santa Barbara. Her books include *Live Form: Women, Ceramics and Community* (2016), *Revolution in the Making: Abstract Sculpture by Women Artists, 1947–2016* (2016), and *Art in California* (2021). She is a member of the editorial boards of

the *Journal of Modern Craft* and the University of California Press and currently serves as co-executive editor of *Panorama: The Journal of the Association of Historians of American Art*.

Lynda Teller Pete and **Barbara Teller Ornelas** are fifth-generation Diné (Navajo) weavers who have been weaving since they were young girls in Two Grey Hills, New Mexico, where their father ran the trading post and their mother demonstrated weaving for tourists. The sisters are internationally acclaimed for their fine tapestry weaving, and their work has been exhibited at galleries and museums throughout the world and featured in numerous magazines, books, and television programs, including PBS's *Craft in America* series. They teach weaving workshops and act as national and international cultural ambassadors for their art form. Together, they are the authors of *How to Weave a Navajo Rug and Other Lessons from the Spider Woman* (Thrums Books, 2020) and *Spider Woman's Children: Navajo Weavers Today* (Thrums Books, 2018).

Cybele Tom is a sculpture conservator and doctoral candidate in Art History at the University of Chicago. She holds an MA in Art History and Conservation from New York University's Institute of Fine Arts. Her research currently focuses on intermediality, practices of mimesis, and issues of materiality in the art of medieval and early modern Western Europe.

L Vinebaum is a scholar and artist working at the intersection of textiles and politics. They are an associate professor in Fiber and Material Studies at the School of the Art Institute of Chicago and contributed to publications including *A Companion to Textile Culture* (Wiley, 2020) and *The Handbook of Textile Culture* (Bloomsbury, 2017). They were previously associate editor of *Textile: Cloth and Culture* and co-vice president and academic symposium chair of the Textile Society of America.

Melinda Watt is Chair and Christa C. Mayer Thurman Curator of Textiles at the Art Institute of Chicago, where her exhibitions include *Gio Swaby: Fresh Up* (2023), *Fabricating Fashion: Textiles for Dress, 1700–1825* (2022), and *Morris & Co.: The Business of Beauty* (2021). She was previously a curator at the Metropolitan Museum of Art, New York, where she co-curated *Interwoven Globe: The Worldwide Textile Trade, 1500–1800* (2013–14) and *English Embroidery from the Metropolitan Museum of Art, 1580–1700: 'Twixt Art and Nature* (2008), among other projects.

Anne Wilson is an artist and emeritus professor in Fiber and Materials Studies at the School of the Art Institute of Chicago. Her work is in permanent collections around the world, including the Metropolitan Museum of Art, New York; the Art Institute of Chicago; the Victoria and Albert Museum, London; and the 21st Century Museum of Contemporary Art, Kanazawa, Japan. Wilson was named a 2015 United States Artists Distinguished Fellow, and she has been recognized by the Driehaus Foundation, the National Endowment for the Arts, and the Tiffany Foundation, among others.

Folayemi Wilson is an artist, designer, writer, and Associate Dean for Access and Equity and Professor of Art at Penn State College of Arts and Architecture. Her work celebrates the Black imagination as a technology of resistance and self-determination. Her writing and reviews have appeared in numerous publications, including, recently, *The Black Experience in Design: Identity, Expression, and Reflection* (Allsworth Press, 2022) and *Expansions*, a publication of the 2021 Venice Architecture Biennial. Her art is part of the collection of the National Museum of African American History and Culture in Washington, DC. An oral history of her work was featured in *Bomb Magazine* in 2023.

Index

Page numbers in italics refer
to illustrations.

A

`Abbasi, Riza, *Youth in European
Clothing* (1634), *126*
Abbasid Caliphate, 103
Abbasi-Ghnaim, Feryal, 26
aDNA (ancient DNA). *See* DNA recovery
and analysis
Africa
slave trade, 31, 49
textile traditions, 22, 31–32, 71–73,
155–56
See also Asante culture; Bamiléké
people; Kongo culture; Kuba
people; Mali; Nigeria; Yoruba
people
African Americans
activism, 34–35, 39, 178–83
ancestry research, 153
Black Lives Matter movement,
34–35, *35*, 39
hair braiding, 151–55, 156
hair texture, 45–46
mourning, 177–79
quilts, 31, 32–34, 38, 177–84
survival, 177–79, 181–84
systemic racism against, 177–78,
181–83
textile traditions, 22, 31–32, 38
violence targeted at, 16–17, 34–36,
38, 177, 179, 181–84
afterlife. *See* transition of realms
agarose gels, 58, 60, 62
AIDS, 16
AIDS Memorial Quilt, 180
Ailey, Alvin, 36
Albert, Prince, 43
Allen, Robert, 183
alpacas, 162, 165, 166–68, *166*
altar frontal (Spain or Italy), 116, *117*
ancient DNA (aDNA). *See* DNA
recovery and analysis
Andean textiles
DNA recovery, 58, *60*
as living beings, 26, 121
microstructures, 119–22
weavers, 25–26
See also alpacas; Nasca

culture; Noqanchis; Paracas
people; Peru
anillado (cross-looping), 162, 164–65,
164, 175n4
Antiquarian Society, 101
Armenian vestments, 112–13, *112–13*
Art Institute of Chicago
Chicago Stock Exchange Trading
Room, 153, *154*
textile collection history, 91–92,
96–97, 101
textile fragment displays, 91–92, *92*
Textile Study Room, 98, *98*
art quilts. *See* quilts
Asante culture (Ghana)
adinkra wrapper, 156, *157*, *158*, 159
stamps for adinkra textile, 156,
158, 159
Ayer, Edward E., 91, 105n3

B

backstrap looms, 161–62, 165, 169–71,
169, *170*. *See also* Noqanchis
bacteria, DNA recovery and analysis,
61, 62
Badisches Landesmuseum, Karlsruhe,
95
Baldwin, James, 177
Ball, Irene, 190
Bamiléké people (Cameroon)
dance hats, 155–56, *155*, *156*
descendants, 153
Begody, Sara, rug or wall hanging in the
"Two Grey Hills" style (1960s), *189*
Benin City, Nigeria, 70
biological remains, 51, 54. *See also* DNA
recovery and analysis
birds
cranes, 79, 84, *84*, 85, 86
embroidered, 79, 135, 143
symbolism, 73, 74
Black Americans. *See* African
Americans
Black Lives Matter movement
Lewis on, 34–35
speaking names of victims, 39
street mural, Washington, DC, 34,
35
boats. *See* ships
Bock, Franz, 95–96
Bosque Redondo Indian Reservation, New
Mexico, 188, 190, 198, 199n1, 199n4

Bowser, Muriel, 34, *35*
Breckenridge, Carol, 101
British Empire, 43, 96. *See also* Victoria,
Queen
British Museum, 97
Bruÿn, Maria de, darning sampler
(1808), 110, *111*
Buddhism
cosmology, 17
death of Buddha, 17, 107, *109*, 110, 113
practices, 86
view of death, 107
Bulletin of the Art Institute of Chicago,
91–92
Burge, Dorothy, 177–185, *178*
La Tanya Jenifor-Sublett (2025), 23,
182, 183–84
Michelle Clopton (2025), 23, *182*,
183–84
quilted portraits, 23, 177–84
Trayvon Could Be My Son (2012),
179, *179*, 180
*Won't You Help to Sing These
Songs of Freedom*, 181, *181*, 183
Burge, Jon, 181–83, 185n8
burial garments
child's tunics (Egypt), 25, 51, *52–53*,
55, *57*, 61
woman's overskirt (Kuba), 15–16, *15*
yoke tunic fragment (Egypt), 58, *59*
burial shrouds and wrappings
adinkra, 156, *157*, *158*, 159
Bead net funerary shroud with
Amulets (Egypt), 75–76, *76*
DNA recovery and analysis, 25, 58–62
Fragment of a funerary shroud
(Egypt), *60*, 61
funerary bundle mask (Paracas),
122, *122*
of Jesus, 107–10
Kuba cloth, 31
mediation of transition of realms,
15–16, 17
preservation, 55–56

C

canopic jars (Egypt), 58, 61, *61*
cartonnage chest panel (Egypt), 75, *76*
Cave, Nick, 16–17, 35–36, 38, 41
Soundsuit (1992), 36, *36*
Untitled (2017), 36, *37*
Untitled (2023), 38, *39*

On Loss and Absence: Textiles of Mourning and Survival was published in conjunction with an exhibition of the same title organized by the Art Institute of Chicago, September 6, 2025–March 15, 2026.

On Loss and Absence: Textiles of Mourning and Survival was made possible by the generous support of the Mellon Foundation.

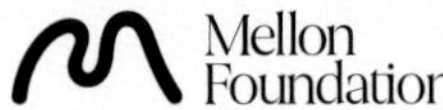

Mellon Foundation

First edition

Printed in Belgium
30 29 28 27 26 25 1 2 3 4 5

Authorized representative in the EU:
Easy Access System Europe
Mustamäe tee 50
10621 Tallinn, Estonia
gpsr.requests@easproject.com

ISBN: 978-0-300-28408-9 (hardcover)

Library of Congress Control Number:
2025941898

Published by
The Art Institute of Chicago
111 South Michigan Avenue
Chicago, IL 60603-6404
artic.edu

Distributed by
Yale University Press
302 Temple Street
P. O. Box 209040
New Haven, CT 06520-9040
yalebooks.com/art

This book was made using papers and materials certified by the Forest Stewardship Council, which ensures responsible forest management.

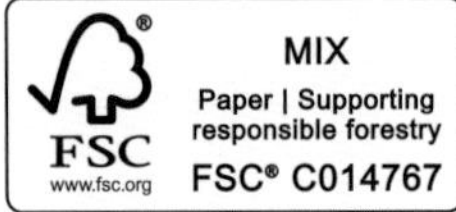

Edited by
Kit Shields
Production by
David Khan-Giordano
and Lauren Makholm
Photography research by
Noah Lopez and Kristie Kahns
Proofreading by
Juliet Clark
Indexing by
Mary Mortensen
Design and typesetting by
IN-FO.CO (Adam Michaels,
V.E. Chen)
Separations by
Professional Graphics,
Rockford, Illinois
Printing and binding by
Graphius, Ghent, Belgium

Publishing, the Art Institute
of Chicago
Katie Reilly, Associate Vice
President, Publishing
Lisa Meyerowitz, Editorial Director
Lauren Makholm, Director of
Production

Imaging, the Art Institute of Chicago
Bonnie Rosenberg, Director of Imaging
Nathan Keay, Associate Director,
Photography
Elyse M. Allen, Assistant Director
of Production

Photography Credits

The Art Institute of Chicago makes reasonable efforts to identify and contact copyright holders when necessary, but also asserts its fair use rights in the reproduction of applicable illustrations in its publications. We adhere to the standards set by the Association of Art Museum Directors' Guidelines for the Use of Copyrighted Materials and Works of Art by Art Museums. We make every reasonable attempt to ensure the accuracy of credit and caption information for each image. Any uncredited creators or rights holders are encouraged to contact the Art Institute of Chicago. The following credits apply to all images in this book for which separate acknowledgment is due.

p. 18, fig. 5: © Michael Olszewski
p. 20, fig. 8: Photo courtesy of
Karen Hampton
p. 22, fig. 10: Courtesy of the artist
p. 32, fig. 1: © Danny Lyon / Magnum
Photos. @dannylyonphotos2 /
bleakbeauty.com
p. 35, fig. 6 (top): Photo by Aurora
Samperio / NurPhoto via
Getty Images
p. 35, fig. 6 (bottom): Tasos Katopodis
/ Getty Images News Collection
via Getty Images
p. 36, fig. 7; p. 37, fig. 8; p. 39, fig. 10:
© Nick Cave. Photo by James
Prinz Photography. Courtesy of
the artist and Jack Shainman
Gallery, New York.
p. 40, fig. 11: © Carina Yepez
p. 45, fig. 3: Courtesy of the artist
p. 71, fig. 2: Royal Anthropological
Society
p. 73, fig. 4: Image courtesy of the
artist, © Yanira Collado
p. 92, fig. 1; p. 98, fig. 6: Art Institute
of Chicago Institutional Archive
p. 118, fig. 4: Courtesy of Musea
Brugge and artinflanders.be.
Photo: Hugo Maertens
p. 126, fig. 14: © The Trustees of the
British Museum
p. 135, fig. 2 (bottom): Photo: Yousef
al-Qutob, WAFA Palestinian
News and Information
p. 136, fig. 3 (bottom): ZUMA Press,
Inc. / Alamy Stock Photo
p. 137, fig. 4: The archival material of
Hilma Granqvist is the property
of Åbo Akademi University
Library and The Palestine
Exploration Fund. All rights
reserved. Copyright © Åbo
Akademi University Library and
The Palestine Exploration Fund
(the archives) and Copyright
© Society of Swedish Literature
in Finland (granqvist.sls.fi)
p. 137, fig. 5: Copyright 1948 AP.
All rights reserved.
p. 139, fig. 6 (left): © The Trustees of
the British Museum

p. 139, fig. 6 (right): Courtesy Tatreez
Institute Collection
p. 143, fig. 10: © President and
Fellows of Harvard College
p. 144, fig. 11: Library of Congress
p. 146, fig. 13: Library of Congress,
Prints & Photographs Division,
LC-DIG-matpc-05294
p. 146, fig. 14: Courtesy of the
Palestinian Museum Digital
Archive, The Emile Ashrawi
Collection. © Emile Ashrawi
p. 147, fig. 15: Shelah Weir, *Palestinian
Costume* (Interlink Books, 2008),
p. 275.
p. 152, fig. 1: Courtesy of the author
p. 156, fig. 4: Hans-Joachim Koloss,
*World-View and Society in Oku
(Cameroon)* (Dietrich Reimer
Verlag, 2000), p. 339, fig. 274.
pp. 165–74, figs. 4–12: Courtesy of
the authors
p. 178, fig. 1: Photo: Joshua Clay
Johnson
p. 181, fig. 4: Courtesy of the artists;
Logan Center Exhibitions;
the Center for the Study of
Race, Politics, and Culture;
and the Pozen Center Human
Rights Lab at the University
of Chicago. Image © Robert
Chase Heishman
p. 180, fig. 3: Image courtesy Claire
Oliver Gallery, photography
by Christopher Burke Studio
p. 188, fig. 1: Courtesy of Craft
in America. Mark Markley
photograph.
p. 190, fig. 4: Dane Coolidge
photograph collection, BANC
PIC 1905.17171:49--PIC,
The Bancroft Library, University
of California, Berkeley
p. 192, fig. 6: © 1979 Amon Carter
Museum of American Art
p. 194, fig. 8: Copyright United
States Postal Service. All
rights reserved.
p. 194, fig. 9: Photo: Ruth Shorty
Begay Teller

Jacket illustrations: (front) detail of
Quilt Block, 1875–1900 (p. 34, fig. 5);
(back) detail of Vestment for a First-
Degree Taoist Priest, Qing dynasty
(1644–1911), 18th century (p. 80, fig. 1).